ISRAELI–EGYPTIAN RELATIONS 1980–2000

CASS SERIES: ISRAELI HISTORY, POLITICS AND SOCIETY
Series Editor: Efraim Karsh
ISSN: 1368-4795

This series provides a multidisciplinary examination of all aspects of Israeli history, politics and society, and serves as a means of communication between the various communities interested in Israel: academics, policy-makers, practitioners, journalists and the informed public.

ISRAELI–EGYPTIAN RELATIONS

1980–2000

EPHRAIM DOWEK

Foreword by Yitshak Shamir

FRANK CASS
LONDON • PORTLAND, OR

First Published in 2001 in Great Britain by
FRANK CASS & CO. LTD
Crown House
47 Chase Side
Southgate
London N14 5BP

and in the United States of America by
FRANK CASS
c/o ISBS, 5804 N. E. Hassalo Street
Portland, Oregon, 97213-3644

British Library Cataloguing in Publication Data:

Dowek, Ephraim
  Israeli–Egyptian relations, 1980–2000.
  – (Cass studies in Israeli history, politics and society; 13)
  1. Egypt – Foreign relations – Israel 2. Egypt – Foreign
  relations – 1952– 3. Israel – Foreign relations – Egypt
  I. Title
  327.5'694'062

ISBN 0 7146 5162 1

Library of Congress Cataloguing-in-Publication Data:

A catalog record of this book is available from the Library of Congress

Typeset in 10½/12pt Baskerville by Cambridge Photosetting Services
Printed in Great Britain by
MPG Books Ltd, Bodmin, Cornwall

This book is dedicated to the Israeli diplomats and their families who have served or are serving in Egypt despite the daily difficulties and the ever-present dangers to their personal safety, in recognition of their outstanding contribution to the building of peace with our great Arab neighbor.

Contents

Illustrations

Foreword

Ephraim Dowek's book *Israeli–Egyptian Relations* comes at the right time. It brings to the reader an accurate and detailed description of the numerous and unceasing efforts to build, consolidate and preserve peace between Egypt and Israel.

Israelis certainly remember the euphoria that, some 20 years ago, overtook almost everyone in Israel when President Anwar Al Sadat landed at Ben Gurion Airport and appeared on the staircase of the plane. We all thought that it was the end of wars and that an era of peace and peaceful coexistence had arrived. Here, we can read the whole story, a story that is still far from having reached its conclusion. The struggle for peace continues and the victory of real, genuine peace is yet to come.

Ephraim Dowek is highly qualified to present to the public all the stages, the ups and downs, the victories and the setbacks of this exhilarating saga. He was born and educated in Egypt, he has a thorough knowledge of the country and its people and is well versed in all aspects of Egyptian reality and outward behavior as well as in the hidden sides of Egyptian policies. He served in Egypt for five years as an Israeli diplomat, first as minister plenipotentiary and later as ambassador. In the book he relates, in a most vivid manner, all that occurred during this period. In spite of the difficulties and obstacles he encountered, he fulfilled his duties with dedication and skillfulness. He made the utmost effort to succeed in the mission entrusted to him, that of promoting co-operation and understanding between the two peoples and the two governments. His approach is absolutely realistic; he shows no inclination to distort the facts he has personally witnessed. In his writing, one can feel that, despite his strong belief in peace and his ambition to show that this goal is attainable and that obstacles can be removed, he is very careful – as a person trained to report truthfully – not to deviate from accuracy and rationality.

His depiction of the work of Israel's dedicated representatives in Egypt is not heartening. All the fields of their many activities are thoroughly reviewed including relations with the authorities, economic ties, tourism, cultural co-operation, the struggle for normalization and social life. Everything is there; no field has been neglected and, to our great sorrow, one cannot perceive any spectacular success or real breakthrough in any of these fields.

The reason for this sad situation does not lie only in objective difficulties. The heavy hand of Egyptian bureaucracy is clearly felt. It openly interferes everywhere, scatters artificial obstacles and prevents normal relations from developing. It takes strong preventive action whenever it feels that things might move in the right direction. Not even a beginning of genuine understanding and co-operation has developed through the years. The Israeli diplomats speak with sad irony about the 'daily ration of venom they have to swallow' when reading Egyptian newspapers and magazines. From the first day, the Egyptian intelligentsia banned any interaction with Israel and the ban is strictly implemented under the vigilant eye of the various professional associations. Moreover, any attempt to develop friendly relations with other Arab countries is swiftly and openly countered. This attitude is unacceptable and frustrating. Even foreign diplomats are reluctant to maintain social or professional relations with their Israeli colleagues, fearing that this might impair their relations with the local population and government officials.

The author, who after a few years in Egypt was appointed our first ambassador to India, describes his transfer as if he had moved from darkness to bright light. India established relations with Israel only a few years ago, after almost 45 years of estrangement and enmity. There, from the first moment, he found open doors and open arms. Relations developed very quickly in every field of activity. The Indian officials would report to Ambassador Dowek the repeated Egyptian approaches aimed at forestalling increased interaction between India and Israel and ask him ironically if he was certain that Egypt and Israel did indeed maintain a relationship of peace ...

The author explains however, that despite these endless sad stories, we ought to prefer even this kind of peace to a total absence of relations or, worse than that, to hostile confrontation. The main reason is that, as long as there are formal relations between the two countries, guns remain silent and there is no war. Perhaps this explains the motto that President Sadat constantly repeated: 'No more wars' – as if he wanted to comfort us by promising that some day we would witness the end of all wars. In the author's opinion, the Egyptians have arrived at the conclusion that in order to establish an amicable relationship with the west, and especially with the United States of America, they are compelled – for their own sake – to maintain with Israel relations of peace, even if this peace is *cold*.

It seems that our Egyptian neighbors are piling so many obstacles on the road to normal relations in order that, God forbid, Israel should not benefit, even marginally, from the relations between the two countries, relations that are necessary for their own interests. By doing so, they are atoning for the alleged sin of having made peace with the Israeli enemy.

Reading this book and pondering on the large number of puzzling and unpleasant facts it relates, Israelis will begin to understand the reasons for the many difficulties which burden the relationship with our Palestinian neighbors within the country itself and the never-ending peace negotiations with them.

Having finished perusing *Israeli–Egyptian Relations*, one cannot refrain from sending cordial greetings to the representatives of Israel in Egypt and expressing admiration at the wonderful work they are doing in an extremely difficult situation. Let us hope that some day their efforts will bear fruit and genuine peace will, despite everything, be achieved.

Yitshak Shamir
Former Prime Minister of Israel

Preface and Acknowledgments

I am not a writer or an historian. I do not pretend to know in the small-est detail the intricacies of the peace process or the complexities of mid-eastern politics – be it the 'old middle east' or the 'new middle east' as some nowadays qualify the region, implying that it has undergone a drastic change. However, in view of the various positions I have been entrusted with, I have been privileged to be in a prime observation out-post for the last 17 years. I have taken an active part in the shaping of policies and in the development of events in my immediate surroundings or at a distance. In a sense, I have been a small screw in the mighty machine of peace, but it was a screw that was installed in the inner bowels of the machine and contributed to its smooth functioning and, sometimes, even more than that.

I have closely known all the key figures that were – and many still are – involved in the peace process. I have had hundreds of official and unofficial conversations with top personalities on both sides and I have participated in a score of negotiations at all levels and on all topics. I have drafted numerous reports and read thoroughly confidential reports from many sources. I have scrutinized situations as they developed and analyzed their implications and I have actively participated in many tactical as well as strategic evaluations. In many cases, I have taken personal initiatives and sometimes I have prevented steps which, in my opinion, were counter-productive. I have swallowed, day after day, the bitter venom dripped by the Egyptian media and I have dissected with magnifying glasses Egyptian leadership speeches and statements as well as editorials and articles in the press that reflected their opinions and way of thinking. I have criss-crossed the country and have had lengthy conversations with the common people and with Egyptian intellectuals. To sum up, I have accumulated over the years considerable experience and have collected first-hand information which, I believe, will be of interest to the reader.

The fact that I was born and educated in Egypt, speak and read Arabic, know Egypt's history, ancient and modern, appreciate its culture and am aware of the mentality and intrinsic qualities of its people – all this gives a special dimension to my ability to evaluate events and hidden intentions ... Having served in Cairo twice, as minister plenipotentiary in the early

1980s and as ambassador in the early 1990s – without having severed ties with Egypt in between – adds to my findings an important factor of time continuity that enables me to verify any conclusions and assumptions I make.

For a long time, I hesitated on the didactic approach I should adopt in writing this book and pondered what would be the best way to bring to the reader, without becoming tedious and repetitive, the multitude of events I witnessed or was part of. From the outset, I did not intend to write an autobiography in which I would relate what happened in a chronological order. I also had no intention to write a book of history that required lengthy research work, backed by hundreds of quotations from official documents and press reports. In addition, I did not want to repeat stories that had been widely publicized and, most of all, I did not want to create a false 'rose-tinted' picture of the situation. I was determined to write with the utmost honesty and objectivity, and bring to the reader not only 'la petite histoire de l'histoire' (the small stories that are behind the making of history) but also a comprehensive analysis of the relationship between Israel and its great neighbor. I have particularly striven to give an insight into the short- and long-term motivation and goals of both sides from an angle different from the usual stereotypes *marketed* to the general public since the signing of the Camp David accords.

I finally decided on a simple approach, which I hope will be interesting for the reader and allow him or her to acquire a comprehensive overview of Egyptian–Israeli relations – topic after topic. I have dealt with the whole period from 1980 to the present day as if it were a single continuum and I have presented each topic as a single entity – going from one period to the other within the same chapter. I have also decided to rely almost exclusively on my memory and, to the best of my understanding, I have not deviated from the objective truth. I have not made things sound more beautiful or more ugly than they were in reality. I have not added anything and I have not withheld anything. I have not concealed facts and I have not fabricated stories. It is possible that in some minor details my memory has failed me but I certainly had no intention to mislead and, if slight errors have slipped in, they do not impair the general picture presented to the reader.

The book covers a period of almost 20 years and revolves around events, people and topics that are intimately interwoven. Each chapter is dedicated to a specific aspect of the relationship between the two countries – one facet of many – that stands on its own feet. At first, the reader might get the impression that there is no direct link between the various chapters but, very quickly, he or she will grasp that this is not the case and that all the chapters add up to a single picture – complete and clear.

The book's main purpose is to shed light on Egypt's thinking and the guidelines of its policies and actions with regard to Israel and the peace process. I have however also tried to provide, briefly, complementary information for readers who do not regularly follow press reports from the middle east or who have, over the years, lost touch with certain aspects of the political problems of the area. I have done so in brackets within the text itself and not in footnotes as is customary.

In general, I have mentioned the names and titles of the persons cited in relation to specific events. However I have refrained from doing this whenever it seemed to me that I might endanger or embarrass them. I have also refrained from touching upon topics or events that it is not yet time to publicize. In any case, I could not cover everything. I had to make difficult choices and limit myself to the essential. I believe, nevertheless, that the reader will find plenty of material that will allow him or her to grasp the full picture and form his/her own opinion as to the past and, perhaps, as to the future.

As already mentioned, I have avoided quoting the exact wording of documents or interviewing persons related to the many events described in the book. However, directly or indirectly, my thinking and my opinions have been influenced by the persons with whom I have worked or with whom, over the years, I have had lengthy discussions with the aim of better understanding Egypt's goals and policies. Unconsciously, throughout the book, I have reflected their views as a 'human sponge' that gathers every drop of water with which it comes into contact.

I am indebted to all of these individuals. They have contributed in many ways, though they are certainly unaware of it, to the crystallization of this book – structure and content alike. I will cite here only a few of them: Ambassadors Moshe Sasson and Eli Ben-Elissar, Generals (res.) Abrasha Tamir and Dov Sion, the writer Yitshak Bar Moshe, the journalist Semadar Peri, Foreign Affairs Egyptian Department Head Ela Afek, and, collectively, all the colleagues with whom I have worked and to whom I am dedicating this book.

Special thanks are due to Rami Tal, an eminent journalist and good friend, who took upon himself the editing of the Hebrew version of the book and helped make it more concise and readable. I do hope we will have other opportunities to work together in the future.

I would also like to express my deepest appreciation to the former Prime Minister of Israel, Yitshak Shamir, for taking the time from his heavy schedule to read the manuscript and write an enlightening introduction.

I cannot conclude without expressing heartfelt thanks to my wife Sarah, not only for the patience she has shown during the long months I have dedicated to writing this book but also for accompanying me in the most difficult postings and contributing, to a great extent, to the success of my missions.

May 2000

1 · *Calling Card*

I was born in Cairo in 1930. When I left the country at the beginning of 1949, a little while after I turned 18, I never thought that I would ever come back, not even for a short visit. In the British passport I was carrying at the time, the Egyptian security services had stamped a seal that said in large Arabic letters *Horug Bidun Awda* (or, in plain English, Exit without Return). Thirty-two years later, in June 1980, I landed at Cairo Airport not as a refugee or as a returning resident but as the minister plenipotentiary (no. 2 in the embassy) of Israel to Egypt. No doubt the authorities knew exactly who I was and what my background was. However, no one asked for my old passport or hinted at the fact that I had been banned from ever returning to the country where I was born, spent all my childhood, received most of my education and for which I still had deep feelings.

My first mission lasted a little more than three years (1980–83), during which I had the opportunity to follow from the very first the throes of the birth of relations between Egypt and Israel and to participate actively in their shaping. Seven years later, towards the end of 1990, I returned once again to Egypt, this time as the fourth ambassador of Israel to that country. My stay lasted only two years but these were years of strife and feverish activity, on the eve of the Madrid conference and the change of governments in Israel, during which relations between the two countries went through a very delicate phase. Between these two periods, I visited Egypt several times in various capacities. Indeed, I am a living confirmation of the old Egyptian saying 'One who drinks water from the Nile will return and drink from it again'. Each time I thought that this would be the last time, I found myself coming back and drinking again from the Nile (to be quite honest, like all other foreign residents, I drank mineral water imported from France ...). I should also add that, since my first return in 1980, I have maintained throughout the years a living contact with Egyptian diplomats and friends. I even served for long periods in various diplomatic postings alongside some of them, and followed closely their attitude towards the peace process and their personal behavior towards Israelis.

I do not want to tire the reader with too many details. My autobiography covers 69 years, of which more than 50 were dedicated to public service in various positions and fields. I will limit myself to those elements which, in my view, shed light on the background that shaped my inner being. As I previously mentioned, I was born in Cairo. I have, however, never been an Egyptian citizen and I never aspired to become one though I had, and still have, very warm feelings for the country of my birth and a tremendous admiration for the qualities of the Egyptian people. I was one of the many hundreds of thousands of residents who had no nationality or held a foreign one, residing permanently between the two world wars in Egypt with the passive acceptance of the Egyptian authorities of the time and under the protection of the British crown. None of them could obtain Egyptian citizenship no matter how much they wanted to – not even if they and their families were born in Egypt and had lived in the country for several generations. Egyptian nationality laws are very strict and make it almost impossible for residents not of Egyptian stock to claim citizenship of the country.

I was born into a family whose roots spread over several countries in the middle east and Europe and has held British citizenship for many generations. For long years, my great-grandfather, and after him my grandfather, occupied the position of honorary consul of Great Britain in Iskenderun province (originally part of Syria, and Turkish since 1938). This position, though honorary, carried much power and influence owing to the capitulation treaties signed by the Ottoman Empire and the European powers. At the end of the First World War, my father, who was born in Aleppo (Syria), and his two brothers established themselves in Egypt. They also maintained offices in other countries of the middle east and Europe and circulated from one country to the other in accordance with the needs of their business. I am the only one who was born in Egypt; one of my two brothers was born in Italy, the second in Great Britain. At home we spoke several languages but French was predominant, as was the custom among the Jewish community and the Egyptian intelligentsia of the time. I studied in Christian schools preparing for the French matriculation but, because of a law passed in 1945, which made admission to university conditional on a thorough knowledge of the Arabic language, I was compelled to shift gradually to Arabic and successfully passed the Egyptian baccalaureate. I even studied sciences for one academic year before I left Egypt and emigrated to Israel in early 1949, one year only after the establishment of the State of Israel.

Until after my *Barmitzvah*, I was far from active Judaism and even farther from Zionism. My family was not too religious and kept only the main traditions of the faith. Like many youngsters, I was attracted at a very young age to leftist Jewish groups who advocated that the Jewish intelligentsia should integrate into the local population and participate in Egypt's struggle to free itself from the colonial yoke and improve the lot of the common people. For family reasons, I had to transfer to Alexandria for several months and live with my maternal grandparents. There, the atmosphere was totally different and very soon a friend convinced me to join the Maccabi club, a scout organization that was in reality a militant Zionist youth movement called *Hehalutz Hatzair* (Young Pioneer). At the age of 15, I found myself, almost without realizing it, transformed into a militant Zionist.

Upon my return to Cairo, I joined a *gariin* (a group of youngsters intending to create a kibbutz) and began thinking seriously about emigrating to Israel at the end of my studies. Like all Zionist youth movements, *Hehalutz* educated its members to turn upside down the social pyramid of the Jewish people, relinquish the traditional Jewish professions and join agricultural collective settlements in Israel. Clearly, my parents were not too happy with the mutation in my political thinking and goals and they prevented me from abandoning my studies. I continued, however, to be a militant in the movement and very soon it became the focal point of my life.

In May 1948, with the declaration of the State of Israel and the war that followed, many Jewish youngsters and most movement leaders were arrested and sent to internment camps. The burden of continuing Zionist activities and reorganizing the movement clandestinely fell upon the shoulders of the younger generation. I was catapulted to a position of leadership together with a few other youngsters of my age. We took in hand what was left of the movement, recruited new members, organized a system of small cells and continued educational and paramilitary activities. Very quickly, Egyptian security forces spotted me and I had to leave Egypt in a rush to avoid arrest. I was entrusted by the movement with the task of arousing public opinion in Israel to the sad situation of the Jewish internees in Egypt and preparing the field for a quick rescue of Egyptian Jewry. In April 1949, I arrived in Israel on a ship carrying several thousand survivors of German extermination camps – just in time to take part in the festivities of Israel's first independence anniversary.

In Israel, I followed the usual track pursued by most youngsters educated in the pioneering movements: agricultural and ideological training in one of the old kibbutzim, creation of a new kibbutz, military service, transfer to a development town, continuation of university studies. Finally, like everyone else, I was attracted by the whirlpool of utilitarian ideas that overran the country in the early 1960s and brought about a drastic change in its social values and the sanctification of one's career and wellbeing.

To be more specific, I passed my agricultural training in Ein Harod, a kibbutz that was plagued by the intense political strife that prevailed at the time in Israel. Within a few months my group – friends since kindergarten – split because of sharp ideological divergences (which, in retrospect, appear to be somewhat ridiculous). In 1951, I was among the founding members of Kibbutz Kfar Aza on the Gaza Strip and, at an early age, I had to cope with many economic and organizational tasks that prepared me for future challenges. In the army, I was in the first class of the *Nahal* (a unit that replaced the *Palmach*). Mota Gur, the future chief of staff and a young captain at the time, was my direct commanding officer. At the age of 20, I married Sarah, a member of my group in the movement, and we soon had two children, Shmuel and Ada. Twenty years later, we were blessed with another daughter, Tali.

I left the kibbutz in 1953 for family reasons and established myself in a development town called Beit Shaan. There, I was elected secretary of the workers' council and, two years later, I was elected for two consecutive terms to head the municipal council, becoming at the age of 25 the youngest mayor in Israel. I played a significant part in building the town and in the absorption of thousands of new immigrants – including David Levy who, many years later, was to become a salient political figure in Israel, and as the then foreign minister was to appoint me ambassador to Egypt in 1990.

In 1963, at the request of Golda Meir, who believed that Israel should be represented in the newly independent African countries by diplomats who had wide experience of development and not only traditional diplomatic skills, I joined the ministry of foreign affairs. I was appointed ambassador to Chad at the age of 33. Since then, I have held many challenging positions including minister plenipotentiary and ambassador to Egypt, permanent representative to the UN in Geneva, deputy permanent representative to the UN in New York with personal rank of ambassador, and head of the international co-operation department. My last posting, just before retiring, was as the first Israeli ambassador to India after 45 years of animosity.

Concurrently, I returned to the student bench at the age of 40 and completed with distinction my BA and MA in international relations at the Hebrew University of Jerusalem. I also had a short political *intermezzo*. In 1978, I was elected, on the list of the legendary Teddy Kollek, deputy-mayor of Jerusalem for town planning and urban development. Two years later, I was called back to the ministry of foreign affairs and asked by Yitshak Shamir (then foreign affairs minister) to join the staff of our embassy in Cairo as minister plenipotentiary. In spite of my deep love for Jerusalem and my direct responsibility for the development of the city, I could not resist the temptation. Egypt was at the center of national attention and had become the focus of most of the diplomatic activity. How could I, a refugee from Egypt who had dreamt all his life of establishing peace with the country in which he was born, refuse to make his modest contribution to this wonderful saga? I felt as if I had been preparing myself for this task all my life and had acquired the tools and qualities necessary to cope with it. I resigned from the Jerusalem municipality, returned to the foreign ministry and within a few weeks I was back in Cairo.

2 · *Breaking Away and Points of Contact*

When I left Egypt in a hurry in 1949 and emigrated to Israel, I was determined to put behind me for ever the chapter of my life in that country. I decided to cut myself off from the past. I threw away all the fancy suits I had brought with me and purchased, with the very few pounds I had in my pocket, khaki trousers, biblical sandals and a wide belt, which almost everyone in the country wore. I wanted to become a pioneer, a peasant who dedicates his life to tilling our ancestral land. More than anything else, I wanted to look like the tough unpolished *sabras* (youngsters born in Israel) in my outward appearance, behavior, way of speaking and even my way of thinking. At the time, they embodied for me everything I dreamt of being. I boiled with wrath when people called me *ole hadash* (new immigrant) and even more when they described me, with a touch of contempt, as 'oriental Jew' or 'Egyptian'.

Over the years, I learned to accept the facts of life and to disregard the way people looked at me. I realized that how I looked upon myself and what I felt in my inner being were more important. Very early on, I saw myself as *ish hayeshuv* (a person with his two feet anchored in the country) and, in time, people began to consider me as such and to treat me as an equal among equals. I should add that I was not an exception. All the members of my group in the kibbutz, who like me had emigrated from Egypt after years of education and preparation in the *Hehalutz* movement, underwent the same process. To assert our identity as Israelis, we made a point of speaking among ourselves only in Hebrew, but sometimes habit was stronger than determination and we found ourselves speaking French mixed with a few Arabic words.

We did not miss Egypt and we had no nostalgia for the country of our birth. The only memories we often spoke about were almost exclusively centered on the good food we ate at home and, specially, on detailed descriptions of the large succulent ice creams covered with lots of whipped cream we used to eat at Groppi (a Swiss pastry shop). One should recall that these were the difficult days of restrictions and rationing in Israel, days when food was scarce throughout the country and especially in a young kibbutz. The nostalgia for Groppi's ice creams was so intense that, 32 years later when I returned to Cairo, after I had eaten my fill of ice creams of all kinds and flavors almost all over the world, one of the first things I did was to run to Groppi and order a double portion of *Marquise aux marrons* (a mixture of ice cream and chestnuts) that was the specialty of the house. Great as my nostalgia had been, my disappointment was much greater …

When I left the kibbutz, leaving behind my friends of many years, one more thread with my past was severed. I found myself in a totally different neighborhood and threw myself entirely into the running and developing of my small city, Bet Shaan. Egypt for me became even more remote. I followed, as did everyone else in Israel, the upheavals in that country and President Nasser's rise and fall. However, I felt totally disconnected from those events. Only in 1956, after the Sinai operation, did I return to an Egyptian atmosphere. Hundreds of refugees from Egypt established themselves in Bet Shaan, wretched and destitute, after being uprooted from their homes and expelled overnight from the country. Naturally, when they learned that the mayor was born in Egypt, they saw in me an anchor of salvation that might help them morally and materially. They came to me seeking advice, orientation, comfort, help, and sometimes only words of encouragement. Most of them spoke mainly Arabic. I had to speak with them and even to deliver speeches in that language, which had become rusty in my mouth. It helped refresh my memory and Arabic became once again an active language for me. Many years later, it made my work in Egypt easier. At the time, however, I did not dream that I would join the diplomatic service – and even less that peace would one day prevail between the two countries and that I would have the privilege of representing Israel in my country of birth.

At the beginning of 1960, the late Ehud Avriel (a senior politician and diplomat) came to visit Bet Shaan. At the time he headed the Mapai (Labor Party) immigration committee of which I was a member. After the official discussions, we sat in my house over a cup of coffee. Out of the blue, he asked me what I intended to do after I finished my term of office as mayor. I did not take his question seriously (at the time, I had just been re-elected for a second term of office of four years). I answered, without giving it much thought, that at some point in the future, I would like to work in the ministry of foreign affairs because I had mastered many languages and, being born in Egypt, I might contribute to bringing about peace with that country. Ehud did not react. We continued chatting casually and we did not touch on the subject again. Years went by. I completely forgot about this conversation. My second term was prolonged for two more years and concurrently I was given a favorable place on the party's list to the Knesset (parliament). I dedicated myself to city and party affairs and did not give the slightest thought to our conversation.

It seems that Ehud Avriel, unlike me, did not forget what I had told him. In the meantime, he had been appointed deputy director-general for Africa. He recommended me, without even telling me, to Golda Meir (who was at the time minister of foreign affairs) for the position of ambassador to Chad. My knowledge of Arabic and French, as well as my experience in management and development, pleased Golda and, by the end of 1963, I found myself in Chad, swimming in the deep and unknown waters of diplomacy.

I dealt with Black Africa for almost ten years continuously. My only contact with Egypt was indirect and came many years later. In 1971, in my capacity as deputy director of the African department, I analyzed minutely a speech delivered by President Sadat at a meeting of African heads of state. In his speech, Sadat called on the African states (many of which had at the time very close relations with Israel) to help Egypt retrieve its land and compel Israel to accept a just peace. Indeed, this was the first time that an Arab leader had raised officially the possibility of peace with Israel (though with conditions which seemed, at the time, completely unrealistic). I forecasted that Sadat's appeal would have a strong impact on the African leaders because it sounded genuine and sincere. I assessed that it would bring about increased pressure on Israel and a worsening of its position in Black Africa with all that entailed in terms of negative votes in the international organizations. Only a few months later, the OAU (Organization of African Unity) endorsed Sadat's appeal and established a high-level committee to study the situation and find ways to promote peace. It was composed of three presidents who were considered the most friendly to Israel: Leopold Senghor from Senegal, Mobutu Sese Seko from Zaire and Ahmed Ahidjo from Cameroon. The committee visited Israel and held intensive talks with the Israeli leadership. They volunteered to mediate between Egypt and Israel with a view to finding a peaceful solution. Israel refused politely but firmly. Finally, the committee reached very strong anti-Israeli conclusions, which paved the way to the severance of diplomatic relations with Israel by almost all African countries on the eve and in the course of the Yom Kippur War (October 1973).

I was among the casualties, happily not of the war but of the severance of relations. A few weeks before the war, I had been appointed ambassador to Zaire and made all the necessary arrangements. Plane tickets were issued to me, my luggage was dispatched and I was to leave immediately after Yom Kippur (my wife had insisted on being with the family during the festival). On Thursday 4 October, I received a phone call from a childhood friend who had extensive business links in Zaire. It was the late Meir Meyohas, one of the founders of the *Hehalutz* movement in Egypt and one of the Jewish activists arrested in Egypt in a spy case known as the 'scandal' (*Haperasha*). He told me that a friend in Zaire had informed him that President Mobutu was going to announce the next day in the UN General Assembly that he was severing relations with Israel: between friends and brothers, he had to choose his brothers (i.e. the Arabs). I immediately phoned the ministry and was told that the information was totally unfounded because only a few days earlier President Mobutu had enthusiastically approved my appointment and had publicly pledged eternal friendship with Israel. My information was correct. Only a few hours later, I received a phone call from the ministry confirming that Zaire had severed relations with Israel.

I had no time to lament. Two days later, Egypt attacked Israel on Yom Kippur – a Saturday. On Wednesday, I was already in New York representing Israel in the Third Committee of the UN General Assembly (Decolonization and Human Rights) and lobbying the third-world countries. It was not an easy task! The war was at its peak; every day more countries were announcing that they were severing diplomatic relations with Israel which they condemned as the aggressor. Diplomats, even those of most friendly countries, were apprehensive at being seen in the company of Israeli diplomats. My colleagues in the delegation and I walked through the corridors, ostracized by almost everyone as if we were lepers.

Egypt was represented in the Third Committee by a senior diplomat, Ambassador Teymur, who a few years later became head of the UN protocol department and maintained excellent relations with me during my last posting in New York (1989–90). At the time we did not exchange a single world and he led the Arab attacks on Israel very efficiently. He presented a draft resolution depicting Israel as a Nazi country that had a special alliance with apartheid South Africa and was responsible for the Sharpeville massacre (a small township near Johannesburg where police fired on black demonstrators, killing and wounding many). Clearly, Israel had nothing to do with the incident and the draft resolution was but a blatant exercise in slander. Nevertheless, more than half the committee's members sponsored the draft resolution and an overwhelming majority passed it.

As usual, the resolution was brought before the General Assembly for final approval. In his presentation speech, Teymur attacked Israel, harshly calling it, among other pearls of vocabulary, a Nazi state thirsty for children's blood. I decided to ask for the right of reply and put the ball back into the Egyptian court. I dug into the archives and found an article written by President Sadat in the early 1940s which praised Hitler and Nazism. I prepared a very strong speech focusing on Sadat's stands and brought it for approval to Ambassador Yossef Tekoa (at the time, permanent representative to the UN). He complimented me on the speech but requested me to replace quotations from Sadat's article with quotations from a lesser Egyptian authority saying: 'Ephraim, we must be careful not to stain Sadat's reputation by stigmatizing him as a supporter of Nazism and an admirer of Hitler. Who knows: perhaps one day, we will have to negotiate peace with him and how then would we be able to explain that we are sitting with a Nazi?'

I must confess that, at the time, I thought Tekoa's remark far-fetched and a little hypocritical. Only a few years later, when the peace negotiations with Egypt began, could I appreciate how far-sighted and how right Tekoa had been. As a matter of course, I complied with his request, went back to the archives and found another quotation that met my purpose.

It was from a book by the great Egyptian writer and journalist Anis Mansur (later a strong supporter of peace and a close personal friend) which read:

> The Germans have killed one million Jews, the Germans have killed two million Jews, the Germans have killed three million Jews, the Germans have killed four million Jews, the Germans have killed five million Jews, the Germans have killed six million Jews – what a pity that the Germans have not killed all the Jews!

As could be expected, neither my speech nor the quotation from Anis Mansur had any impact on the pattern of voting and a crushing majority passed the resolution in the General Assembly. Incidentally, this resolution was a forerunner of a new Arab strategy of depicting Israel as a racist state and comparing the plight of the Palestinians with the struggle of black Africans against apartheid. In less than three years, Arab efforts were crowned with success and the UN General Assembly passed a resolution defining Zionism as a form of racism. It took 20 long years and a complete change in the world political setup to have the UN annul this shameful resolution.

At the time, I had the opportunity to see at close hand the then Egyptian foreign minister, Mohamed Zayat. I even witnessed him burst into tears (literally) at a meeting of the Security Council where he appealed to the international community to intervene immediately and prevent the wiping out of the Egyptian Third Army (which was surrounded by Israeli troops). For some reason, I had the impression that Zayat was short and fat. Many years later, when I met him several times in Cairo, I realized that, though he was indeed very fat, he was also very tall. Maybe the events of the period made him look smaller, at least in my eyes! To his credit, I have to say that, though he had strongly opposed the peace process and resigned from office because of Sadat's initiative, he was very forthcoming each time we met incidentally and had no inhibitions about speaking to me in public.

For curiosity's sake, I include one unrelated anecdote: at one of the Security Council meetings, I brought to Ambassador Tekoa instructions from the then foreign minister, Abba Eban, not to attack the Soviet Union because negotiations were under way behind the scenes. Tekoa was already in the middle of a vehement anti-Soviet diatribe. I scribbled a few words on a piece of paper and passed it to him. He stopped speaking, read my note attentively and then resumed his attack on the Soviet Union. He even shifted to Russian so that they could hear him directly and not through the simultaneous translation. When he finished, he turned to me and said: 'This is the only language the Russians understand!' (He did not mean the Russian language!)

At the end of the General Assembly session, I returned home and was immediately drafted into the reserves. I spent three months preparing a booklet on the organization and structure of Egyptian institutions show-ing the interaction between them and the internal hierarchy. This research work necessitated the intensive reading of Egyptian publications and brought me back, in the most practical way, to an Egyptian atmosphere and the Arabic language.

One month later, I found myself in Rio de Janeiro, where I had been appointed consul general. I stayed there almost five years and again I had no direct involvement with Egypt to the exclusion of reading ministry reports and following events in the press. In November 1977, a few days after President Sadat stated in the Egyptian parliament that he was ready to go to Israel for the sake of peace, I was invited to address senior navy officers. After my lecture, one of the officers asked me how serious Sadat was about peace and if he would really come to Israel. My answer was very blunt: 'It is sheer propaganda. Sadat will come to Jerusalem only when hair grows on the palm of my hand!' One week later, Sadat *did* land in Israel and the memorable event was broadcast live all over the world. The same day, I received a phone call. On the line was the officer who had asked the question about Sadat's visit. He inquired ironically if I had gone to my barber to shave the hair that had grown on the palm of my hand. I grum-bled a few words of apology and decided, deep down, that I would never again make a prediction that could be proven wrong within a few days.

When I returned to Israel in 1978, I was appointed secretary-general of the World Organization of Jews from Arab Countries (WOJAC). It dealt with the registration of claims on personal and communal property left behind in the claimants' countries of origin. In this capacity, I renewed contacts with all the existing associations of Jews that had emigrated from Egypt and even tried to persuade them to unite in order to improve the prospects of their claims. This proved to be an even greater 'Mission Impossible' than securing compensation for their abandoned properties. At least, it gave me the opportunity to study the problem in all its facets and tackle it in a learned manner, when two years later I was sent to Egypt as the first minister plenipotentiary.

I stayed only a few months in WOJAC. I resigned when Teddy Kollek asked me to run on his list for the municipal council. I was elected and, a few weeks later, I became deputy mayor. I was convinced that I was putting behind me diplomacy and that, from now on, all my activity would be dedicated to Jerusalem. I must confess that I envied my colleagues in the ministry who where going to and fro between Israel and Egypt and were involved in the peace negotiations. Deep in my heart, I felt a little frustrated that peace with Egypt had taken off and that I, an experienced diplomat born in Egypt who knew fluent Arabic and understood the Egyptian mentality, had no part in the historic events. But my work for Jerusalem, under the inspiring and dynamic guidance of Teddy Kollek, overtook me completely and Egypt again became remote from my thoughts.

3 · Returning to Egypt

For almost two years I dedicated myself to building Jerusalem, a task that I found most exhilarating and gratifying. Working with Teddy Kollek was an unforgettable experience. He inspired his team with his spirit and enthusiasm and extracted from us the best we had. No one, however much he tried, could follow Teddy's pace of work – he was indefatigable. Every day from six in the morning to midnight, he tackled each and every aspect of Jerusalem's administration and dealt with the smallest details. He toured the city, planned new activities, gave direct instructions and made sure they were carried out, dictated tens of letters, gave interviews to local and foreign journalists, received an unceasing chain of guests and presided over numerous working meetings. Teddy dealt personally with all financial aspects and was a formidable one-man machine for raising funds from private and public donors for his many development projects. To sum up, he never stopped and never rested. He demanded the maximum from his team but much more from himself. Jerusalem, and only Jerusalem, was the center of his life and I am sure that when he went to sleep for very short hours, he also dreamt about Jerusalem. Teddy's energy was contagious and I, like everyone else near him, found myself working round the clock and plunging up to the neck into Jerusalem's problems and, to my deep regret, also into a series of small conflicts of a personal nature that plague the average politician. About Egypt, peace or diplomacy, I did not even think ...

Among other tasks, I was responsible for relations with Jerusalem's Arab citizens. The fact that I spoke Arabic pleased them and made our contacts easier. I began speaking in the Palestinian dialect and later, when I arrived in Egypt, it took me a few months to get rid of it and return to the Egyptian dialect. Like all other Israelis, I followed events in the press and together with them I was elated when my friend, Dr Yossi Hadas (later director-general of the ministry of foreign affairs), raised the Israeli flag on the temporary building of our embassy in the heart of Cairo. I was profoundly moved when Dr Eliahu Ben-Elissar (whom I did not know at the time) presented his credentials to President Sadat as the first ambassador of a Jewish State to Egypt in 2,000 years.

Suddenly, the impossible had become possible ... I could visit the country of my birth whenever I wished. I had no special nostalgic feelings but I was tremendously curious to see again the places where I had spent my childhood, and visit the house in which I had grown up. I wanted to return to the schools where I had studied, meet Egyptian friends from my past, go to all the tourist resorts I remembered vaguely and to others to which I had never been ... Most of all, I was curious to get to know the new Egypt and compare it with the Egypt I remembered and cherished. The Egyptian authorities made it difficult to receive visas but I was in no hurry – I had waited 32 years and I could easily wait a few more months.

In early 1980, the foreign ministry notified me that my leave of absence was coming to an end and that there was no possibility to extend it again. I was given the choice of resigning or rejoining the ministry. I knew that there was no point in trying to change the course of events and I communicated verbally to the deputy director-general for administration, Ambassador Mordechai Drori, that I intended to resign at the end of my leave and continue as deputy mayor of Jerusalem. Drori asked me to come and see him before I took any concrete steps. When we met, he tried to convince me to return to the ministry and accept the position of minister plenipotentiary in our recently opened embassy in Cairo. He stressed that he had been requested by the new minister (Yitshak Shamir) to offer me the job and that Ambassador Ben-Elissar had already agreed to my appointment. I replied that the offer was very flattering but that I had to refuse because I did not want to sever myself from my tasks in Jerusalem.

I thought that this conversation had settled the matter but a few days later I was summoned to a meeting with the director-general, Yossi Chehanover. He went straight to the point, insisted that I accept the appointment and explained how important the posting in Cairo was at this juncture. To increase the pressure, he took me for a short conversation with the foreign minister. Shamir repeated all the arguments on the importance of the position and added that he needed someone with my background to complete Ambassador Ben-Elissar's team and work hand in hand with him. (Ben-Elissar was a political appointee and not a career diplomat.) Only later did I fully understand what Shamir was hinting at: the position had been offered to Yossi Hadas, at the time deputy director-general for Egypt and one of the officials involved from the outset in the peace process with Egypt. He had agreed conditionally but the chemistry between him and Ben-Elissar did not work and the two did not see eye-to-eye on the day-to-day functioning of the embassy and the division of labor between them.

I could not flatly refuse a direct request from the minister and I asked Shamir to give me a few days to think the matter over. The proposal, I cannot deny, was enticing and flattering. I had been frustrated not to have taken part in the first stage of peace with Egypt, but now here was I, being called upon to join the process in an important position on the front line. The proposal came directly from No. 2 in the Likud Party despite the fact that my political identity as a Labor member was written on my forehead. It was obvious that it was motivated by purely professional considerations and I confess that it was a pat on the ego for me. In the next few days, I consulted with my family and close friends but I found it very difficult to reach a decision and I postponed, for as long as I could, 'catching the bull by the horns'. Finally, it was fate that decided for me. While all this was happening, I clashed forcefully with the town engineer, Amnon Niv, about our mutual responsibilities. He questioned my authority and wanted to impose his point of view. We brought our disagreement before Teddy Kollek and to my surprise, and great disappointment, Teddy decided against my stand. I could not accept his decision, which would have given predominance to a municipal functionary over an elected officer and made me into a rubber stamp. On the spur of the moment, I wrote a letter of resignation and sent it to Teddy. I also informed the foreign ministry that I accepted the appointment in Cairo.

Teddy tried to convince me to reconsider my resignation and even, if need be, to change portfolios to avoid further clashes. I was too hurt to accept a compromise solution (which the average politician would have accepted). I insisted on my immediate resignation. It is possible that by doing so I disappointed Teddy, who was my political mentor, but I felt that I could not compromise my principles. We parted as good friends and, at the farewell party, he gave me a personal gift – a shield bearing a medieval map of the world showing Jerusalem at the center of the three continents known at the time (Europe, Asia and Africa). He had engraved a touching dedication: 'My dear Ephraim, in Cairo too you will feel that Jerusalem is the center of the world'. Many years later, after my appointment as ambassador to Egypt, I replied to his cable of congratulations: 'My dear Teddy, Jerusalem has been, is and will always be the Center of the World for me, whether I am in Cairo or in any other place'.

I went back to the foreign service and prepared intensively for my new functions. I went through the files thoroughly and met, at an accelerated pace, with most officials dealing with Egypt and the peace process. One week later, I flew without the family to Egypt for a short acquaintance (or should I say re-acquaintance?) trip and for the transfer of responsibilities from Hadas to me.

It is not easy to describe the intensity of my feelings or the thoughts that went through my head at a record speed during the short flight from Ben-Gurion Airport to Cairo. I felt as if I were the first man landing on the moon … I did not know what I would find, how I would be received, what were the security dangers in Cairo, how I would integrate with the team of colleagues that had arrived a few weeks before me. I wondered how the Egyptians would look upon a high-ranking Israeli diplomat who was born in their country and whether my school friends would speak to me or rather see me as a Zionist enemy. I asked myself if I would recognize Cairo and the places where I used to hang out in my youth: my house, my neighborhood, my school, the streets, the shops, the cinemas, the people and everything I had known so well. How strange – I was about to land in the country where

13

I was born and had lived for 18 years of my life yet paradoxically I did not know that country or, to be more accurate, I had ceased to know it.

After 70 minutes that seemed to me an eternity, we landed at Cairo airport. It was late at night. Though it was relatively cool, I felt waves of heat going through my body as if I had reached internal boiling point. Shuddering (literally), I managed to climb down, with difficulty, the plane's staircase to the ground. Most of the embassy's staff was waiting for me. I took a deep breath, forced myself to calm down, put a smile on my lips and tried as much as I could to appear to be a cool-headed, poker-faced diplomat. I went towards my colleagues with my arm outstretched for a handshake. They received me as an old friend with extraordinary warmth – hugging me and repeating time and again 'Welcome on board'. I could immediately feel that they were accepting me as part of the Israeli family in Cairo. From every side, I heard words of greetings not only in Hebrew but also in Arabic – the Hebrew *Barukh haba* (welcome) of my colleagues mixed with the Arabic *Ahlan wa Sahlan* (welcome) of the Egyptian officials and security guards. I was again, at least outwardly, cool and restrained. I acted in the most natural manner as if I were in the habit of visiting the capital of the Arab world every second day of the week, and that there was no relevance to the fact that it was the city in which I was born 50 years earlier.

I was taken to the VIP lounge for a moment and offered an Egyptian coffee, so sweet that it was difficult to sip (tastes do change!). I gave my diplomatic passport to the Egyptian protocol officer and was rushed out of the airport without having to wait for the usual formalities. I entered the embassy's car, together with my Egyptian bodyguards and, escorted by several police cars and colleagues from the embassy in their private cars, we drove at top speed through the empty streets to the Sheraton-Gizeh where I was to stay. All the way (almost half of Cairo) I tried to catch the slightest glimpse of something I knew, something familiar, but in vain. When we reached Midan Al Tahrir (Liberation Square), the biggest square in Cairo, I could not restrain myself and simply pass through it. I ordered the driver to stop the car and got out surrounded by worried bodyguards who did not understand what was happening and what was the need to take a stroll at that hour of the night. I had lived for many years in a seven-floor building on that square and recalled it as one of the most beautiful squares in the world. I had walked through it and the streets around it thousands of times. I knew every single shop, every building, every corner, and every statue … I hoped that here I would find something I recognized, something that would remind me of my youth … I walked and walked, looked up and down, crossed the streets, stopped at shops and returned at least ten times to the building where I had lived. Nothing – I didn't recognize anything, I remembered nothing. Even the square looked to me totally different from the recollection I had. A fly bridge for pedestrians, painted in light blue, covered almost the whole square and made it appear small and insignificant. I did not say a single word, returned to the car and we drove on. Only on Gizeh Bridge did I recognize the four bronze lions guarding the bridge and the statue of Saad Zaghloul, the legendary leader of the struggle against British colonial rule in the early 1920s. Only then was I convinced that I was back in the Egypt of my youth.

That night, despite my weariness, I could not sleep. I lay in bed with my eyes open, literally seeing scenes of my youth, remembering the smallest details. From time to time, I went out onto the balcony, watched the lights shining everywhere and admired the Nile flowing with majesty at the footsteps of my hotel. My head was bursting with thoughts and feelings that I could not and did not want to restrain. I promised myself I would plough the city and search for my roots, which must be scattered in a thousand and one places. Only after sunrise did I finally succeed in taking a short nap. I awoke, tired and aching all over but full of feverish energy. I took a quick shower, dressed and drove to the embassy for my first day of work as minister plenipotentiary in Egypt.

I stayed two weeks in Cairo. I had long conversations with Ben-Elissar and with Hadas (with each one separately, for obvious reasons). I also spoke privately, with each member of staff and had a few meetings in the Egyptian ministry of foreign affairs. I accompanied to Alexandria a delegation that was received by President Sadat at the Ras Eltin Palace (at the time, Israeli delegations were arriving almost every second day) and I had the honor to meet him, face to face for the first time. I also managed to find an apartment in a location of my liking (a great disappointment awaited me in relation to it). I even had the time for a strong fit of diarrhoea, which – so my colleagues told me – was a sign that I was now fully integrated.

I flew back home to fetch my family, satisfied with what I had achieved in my short stay. I felt hopeful as to the future though I already realized that Cairo would not be an easy posting and that serving there would necessitate much strength, both physical and mental. In Israel, I concluded my affairs with the municipality of Jerusalem and went through the formalities of my rejoining the foreign service. I met various persons dealing with Egypt, received last-minute instructions, prepared my personal luggage, bought a few gifts and flew back to Cairo – this time with my wife Sarah, our small daughter Tali and the family dog Lucky. All was done within one week at a stepped-up pace – Hadas had already left and returned to the position of deputy director-general for Egypt and, paradoxically, he did not want the position of minister plenipotentiary in Cairo to remain vacant for more than a few days.

Sarah, who was also born in Cairo and had left as a child, was very upset during the flight and did not cease asking me questions and expressing her apprehension as to the future. I tried, as best I could, to calm her and to answer her questions though I was far from having all the answers. Ambassador Ben-Elissar and Nizza, his wife, received us with great warmth on the tarmac. We gave our passports to the Egyptian protocol officer, boarded the cars and drove in a long convoy to the Sheraton-Gizeh where we were to stay until we could move into the apartment I had rented.

It was early July, at the peak of the Ramadan (the Muslim one-month fast). In spite of the late hour, it was very hot and stuffy as usual in that season. The streets were illuminated with garlands of lights of different colors and Arab music was shrieking from every corner. We drove slowly through the crowds until we reached the city center where literally hundreds of thousands of men, women and children of all ages were blocking the traffic, standing in the streets or seated on the sidewalks or in temporary restaurants that had popped up overnight everywhere. They ate, drank, laughed and shouted without restraint. They seemed indifferent to the scores of cars trying slowly but stubbornly to move ahead. Drivers did not take their hand off the car horns, bringing the noise and turmoil to an infernal crescendo. Joy and happiness were everywhere; no one seemed to mind time, heat or overcrowding.

For Sarah who, despite my warnings, expected to find the Cairo of her childhood, it was a tremendous shock. She looked around and identified nothing she saw. Suddenly, she found herself in a totally strange environment, far from everything she knew, completely surrounded by a dense and noisy crowd – all of them Arabs. She felt as though she had landed in an inimical world where she was totally helpless. Her frustration, and maybe fear, increased with every moment. For a few days, she refused to go out of the hotel. It was a kind of safe haven for her where she felt secure and protected. All my diplomatic skills did not convince her to pop her head out. Even promises to take her to Groppi and treat her to 'a good ice cream' like the ones she liked so much 'in her youth', did not help. This kind of shock was not new to the Israeli community in Cairo; they called it the 'Cairo Syndrome'. Practically every newcomer went through it, with greater or lesser intensity, depending on his personal background and mental preparation to cope with the unexpected challenges of serving in Egypt. Happily, with the help of Nizza Ben-Elissar, Sarah overcame the crisis in a few days. She realized that the Cairo she had known had gone for ever and she adapted herself to the new environment. She went everywhere on her own and did not hesitate to visit even the most populous neighborhoods.

Almost ten years later, with my appointment as ambassador, Sarah and I were again on our way to Cairo on the El Al night flight. Tali was not with us; she was serving in the army like all youngsters of her age. Lucky was also not with us – the poor thing had died during our first stay from eating a dose of rat poison that the municipality of Cairo had scattered all over the city to cope with an outbreak of rats. Both of us were totally relaxed; we did not feel any curiosity or stress. We knew exactly what to expect. Our first stay had been an excellent vaccine against nostalgia for the Egypt of our youth. We also knew 'the rules of the game' as they had been set by the Egyptians from the outset – what Israeli diplomats were allowed to do and what they were forbidden to do in terms of social contacts with the local population and embassy activities in the various fields of life. We also had no fear for our personal security and wellbeing; we knew that the man-in-the-street would receive us with open arms and that the Egyptian authorities would go out of their way to make sure that no harm befell us.

The circumstances of my appointment had also been much less dramatic than the previous time – at least for me. I did not have to make crucial decisions as to my future; I was totally reintegrated in the diplomatic service and a natural candidate for the post. I expected to be approached and I waited patiently without taking any initiative. Any step on my part would have been counterproductive and, in any case, I was not too eager to return to Egypt though I realized the importance of the position and believed I could help improve relations between the two countries. At the time I had been in New York for only one year. I liked my work at the UN and enjoyed every minute of my stay in this hectic city.

First, I was approached in an indirect manner. The deputy director-general for administration of the time, Ambassador Yitshak Shelef, phoned me in New York and inquired if I intended to present my candidature for Cairo. I answered that I had no intention to do so. He asked what would be my reaction if I were appointed to the post. Once again, I repeated that I would not put forward my candidature but I hinted that if I was officially appointed it would be very difficult for me to refuse. Two or three days later, I was awoken at five in the morning by a phone call. The minister, David Levy, was personally on the line and informed me that I had just been appointed ambassador to Cairo. He expressed the hope that I would accept the position. I gave a positive reply on the spot (I had earlier consulted with Sarah and knew that she agreed to the posting). I thanked the minister for the appointment and for his friendship. My hand was trembling when I placed the phone back on the stand. I was overtaken by emotion, not because of the important appointment and not even because fate was bringing me back to the country of my birth as the full-fledged ambassador of Israel. I had already experienced those feelings when I had been appointed to Egypt the first time. There was nothing new in the situation from this point of view. What moved me deeply was that, by an irony of fate, I was being appointed to the most important posting of my career by David Levy, the young immigrant I had had the privilege, as mayor of Beit Shaan, of helping in his first steps in Israel in the mid-1950s. Who could then have dreamt, in his wildest dreams, that David would one day become the foreign minister of Israel and that I would join the diplomatic service and be appointed by him, towards the end of my career, ambassador to Egypt.

The media received my appointment very positively and this was a source of encouragement for me. Before I left New York, I visited the late Lubavitcher Rebbe, Rabbi Schneerson, the prestigious head of the Habad movement, and received his blessing. He also handed me two one-dollar banknotes (not only one, as he usually did) and said: 'I give you one dollar for the wellbeing of your family and the second one for the success of your important national mission'.

I was planning to remain in Israel for only a few days, but in the end I had to stay, to my great satisfaction, for more than five weeks. The Egyptian authorities had decided to avail themselves of the change of ambassadors to send a message of dissatisfaction regarding the political situation in the region. They delayed giving the *Agrément* to my appointment (an automatic diplomatic step that would normally take 10–15 days). In the ministry, there was considerable concern and many colleagues believed that the Egyptians were intending to downgrade diplomatic relations between the two countries without giving us official notification. I, personally knowing their *modus operandi*, had no apprehension whatsoever and I enjoyed tremendously the extension of my stay at home. I used the time to prepare myself thoroughly. I met with my predecessor, Professor Shimon Shamir, for an extensive briefing, read and reread the files, had long discussions with officials dealing with Egyptian matters, and met political personalities – among them President Herzog, Prime Minister Shamir, many ministers and the main opposition leaders. I also took time to enjoy at leisure my family and friends. Finally, the Egyptian *Agrément* arrived and, the very next day, Sarah and I left for Cairo on the El Al flight.

As usual, we landed at Cairo airport at a late hour of the night. The staff of the embassy and their families received us; the Egyptian chief of protocol and many other high officials, journalists and quite a few bodyguards – Egyptians and Israelis – were also there. We knew most people from our previous stay. We hugged, shook hands and exchanged greetings, boarded the cars on the tarmac and drove in a long convoy straight to the ambassador's residence in Maadi. On the way, we looked around, curious to know if there were marked changes in the landscape. We immediately noticed that the main roads were much wider and seemed much cleaner than in the past. We were also very surprised by the substantial diminution in honking by car drivers (in our previous stay, they never took their hands off the horn). We were too tired to take a ride through the city and we knew we had plenty of time to do so in the days and months ahead.

The next day, I went very early to the embassy. I called a meeting of the staff and received an extensive briefing on the internal situation, the ups and downs in the relations between the two countries and the prospects for the future. On the very same day, I was received by the chief of protocol and I presented, as customary, a copy of my credentials to the minister of foreign affairs, Ismat Abd el Meguid. We had a *tour d'horizon* on the problems of the hour and I requested him to step up the presentation of my credentials to President Mubarak as a gesture of good will. I stressed that the long delay in providing the Egyptian *Agrément* had given the impression that relations between the two countries were going through a difficult period (indeed, the situation was quite tense). I reminded him that Ben-Elissar had presented his credentials only one day after his arrival and that Moshe Sasson had done so after less than one week. I refrained from telling him that at the time, as chargé d'affaires a.i., I had to use heavy pressure to encourage the Egyptians to grant special treatment to Moshe. The minister replied that relations between the two countries were excellent and that there was no reason to single out Israel when many ambassadors (among them ambassadors from Arab countries) had arrived before me and were still waiting patiently. He added that since I had given him the copy of my credentials, I could already function as a fully-fledged ambassador to the exclusion of taking part in events in which the president participated. It was pointless to pursue the matter further; it was clear that Egypt found no useful purpose in making a gesture towards Israel (indeed, relations were at their lowest).

Five to six weeks went by before the date of the presentation of credentials was set. I made use of the time to pay courtesy calls on my diplomatic colleagues, to renew old relations and to try to establish new ones in the Egyptian political and governmental establishment. I also devoted some time to reviewing the internal functioning of the embassy and to defining, together with the staff, the goals and means of our future activities. Our main task, as I saw it, was to enable the embassy to function as quickly as possible as normally as all other Israeli diplomatic representations in the world, despite the limitations imposed by the local authorities. I also wanted to put behind me the resignation of my predecessor, Ambassador Shamir, and reduce the tension between the two countries. I celebrated my 60th birthday in a moving party organized, without my knowledge, by my colleagues in the embassy and Sarah, my wife.

To the credit of the Egyptians, I have to acknowledge that, in spite of the resumption of relations with most Arab countries, they did not try to conceal the presence of an Israeli ambassador in Cairo. I was included in the first bunch of ambassadors who were to present their credentials to President Mubarak and who had piled up in the last four months. In total we were eight, including five from Arab countries: Tunisia, Algeria, Qatar, Yemen and Oman. Representatives from the protocol department of the presidency came early in the morning to fetch us (each one separately) in black limousines and took us to the presidential palace in Heliopolis, escorted by six policemen mounted on motorbikes sounding their sirens along the way. There, we were taken to a small lounge and the chief of protocol introduced us to each other. To be on the safe side, the protocol people had brought us much earlier than necessary and we had to wait for two long hours before the beginning of the presentation of credentials (each ambassador was to have a separate ceremony). We sat together and chatted informally. The Arab ambassadors except the Yemenite spoke to me and behaved quite naturally, totally disregarding my being from Israel. I was elated and I began 'building castles in Spain ...' – seeing myself opening lines of communications with other Arab countries through a friendly and permanent dialogue with the Arab ambassadors in Cairo. My optimism was totally unfounded. This was the only time during my stay in Cairo that I had the opportunity to speak with Arab ambassadors or shake their hands. The days of the Messiah had not yet come!! No big loss, but I have to admit that it was somewhat disappointing and frustrating.

The presentation of credentials runs like a chain production in a factory. A short ceremony, national anthems, a low bow to the president, handing over the letters of credence, handshakes and exchange of a few words with him and the Egyptian officials. Within five–six minutes (altogether) the now fully accredited ambassador exits by a side door and the next ambassador is brought in for the next ceremony. There are no speeches, no long conversations, no exchange of compliments, and no toasts (even with a glass of orange juice as befits a Muslim country). Only a very few ambassadors have the great honor of being invited by the president to sit with him for a short chat.

I was the third in the queue, between the ambassadors of Qatar and Tunisia. The chief of protocol escorted me to a small yard full of Israeli flags that had replaced the Qatar flags. I strode with confidence to the podium. I stood in front of the guard of honor. A short, crisp order was heard. The presidential guard presented arms and a military band began playing the *Hatikva*, the Israeli national anthem. I suddenly felt a weakness in my legs and tears came to my eyes. I could not control myself – how could I? As much as I wanted to curb any outward expression of my feelings, this was not for me one more ceremony like the many I had attended in my long career. Here I was, I the refugee who had fled Egypt 40 years earlier, receiving the salute of the presidential guard and preparing to present my credentials as ambassador of Israel to the president of Egypt, the biggest and strongest Arab country – the country in which I was born! How could I be passive when I was hearing the *Hatikva* echoing from every side in the very heart of Cairo, in the presidential palace itself? How could I not shiver with emotion, when Egyptian soldiers saluted the ambassador of Israel – the symbol of its sovereignty – instead of aiming at him and shooting him? How could I not be overwhelmed by this modest ceremony that encompassed for me peace itself!

The music stopped. I would have stood on the podium for a much longer time, immersed in my thoughts, paralyzed by the intensity of my feelings, were it not for the chief of protocol. He took me gently by the arm and led me to the ceremonial lounge where the president and the Egyptian officials were waiting. I followed him almost automatically, still under the effect of the storm of feelings I had just undergone. I went through the motions as if I were somewhere else. I even delivered a short speech in Arabic (special permission had previously been given to me). My voice reflected a small trembling, resulting from the internal turmoil I was going through, and a few words were not quite clear. After I had shaken hands with President Mubarak, he asked me with a smile if I had forgotten the Arabic that my Egyptian teachers had worked so hard to teach me in my youth. He then took me gently by the hand, led me to a corner in the hall and invited me to stay for a short exchange of views. Boutros Boutros Ghali, the minister of state for foreign affairs and one of the key figures in the peace process, joined us. The conversation lasted about 20 minutes (which was a long time under the circumstances and the chief of protocol showed signs of despair!); we spoke in Arabic in a friendly and quite outspoken manner. I had regained control over myself and I could calmly deliver the messages I had intended to convey (I will return to this first conversation with the president in the chapter 'Presidents and Prime Ministers').

After the ceremony, I was escorted back to the embassy where we toasted the State of Israel and the success of my mission. On that day, the presentation of credentials by eight ambassadors headed all news broadcasts. To my surprise, the three television channels described the eight ceremonies in the order in which they had taken place. I was even shown seated with the Arab ambassadors, chatting in a friendly manner. I was delighted and I began believing that I had lost touch with Egypt since my last stay, and that a major change had taken place in the broadcasting policy relating to Israel. Very quickly, I was proven wrong (or maybe right). Already, in the evening broadcasts, the script was rewritten: I was not shown conversing with the Arab ambassadors and I was transferred to the end of the line as if I had been the last ambassador to present his credentials in a ceremony totally disconnected from the other ceremonies. The next day, the same thing happened in the written press.

Two months after my return to Cairo, I was back to the old routine, and to the atmosphere I knew so well from my previous stay. Nothing had changed! Shortly after my arrival, the chairman of the Egyptian parliament was assassinated by Muslim fundamentalists and the press unleashed an orchestrated campaign against Israel accusing the Mossad – against facts and logic – of being behind the murder. I found it very difficult to accustom myself again to swallowing, every day, the bitter anti-Israeli venom dripped in the Egyptian press in ever-increasing doses.

In my first periodical report to the ministry, I wrote that returning to Cairo after a relatively long absence, I could easily notice impressive urban improvements in the city. I stressed, however, that I could not perceive even a slight change of policy or behavior towards Israel and Israeli diplomats living in Egypt. I added that it seemed to me that, since I had left Cairo, time had stopped at the same place and that everything had frozen exactly as it was before my departure. I felt like someone who had stepped out of his room for a few minutes, returned to the room, taken his pen up again and continued to write exactly from the place where he had stopped writing (seven years earlier). He did not need to refresh his memory or change anything in what he had previously written.

In later chapters, I will describe in great detail the life of the Israeli diplomats in Egypt and the interaction between the two countries and analyze the relationship between them – present and future – as I see it. I would like first, however, because of my special background, to dedicate a few paragraphs to some aspects of a personal nature. When I returned to Egypt in 1980, after an absence of 32 years, I looked out for the Egypt of my youth. I had left at the age of 18, not as a child. I had taken with me vivid memories and strong impressions and perceptions. I was aware that major changes had taken place but I thought that the main features that I had known so well were still there and that I would easily find them under Egypt's new packaging. I searched and searched and I did not find!! I went everywhere in Cairo, Damanhour, Ismailia, Suez and many other cities I knew fairly well. I drove by car, I traveled by train, I walked and walked through the streets. To the exclusion of the old centers of the cities (and even there things had changed drastically), everything was absolutely new to me as if I were visiting an alien country where I had never set foot before.

Looking back, I now realize that this was not as surprising as it appeared to me at the time. When I left Egypt, the total population was around 18 million. In Cairo, there were less than two million people of whom more than half-a-million were foreigners of all nationalities: British, French, Italians, Greeks, Austrians, Swiss, Jews, etc, etc. Alexandria had at the most one million souls of whom more than 25 per cent were foreigners. The atmosphere was cosmopolitan, almost all signs in the streets were written in foreign languages, cinemas showed mostly foreign films which they did not even bother to translate into Arabic (only two cinemas, outside the popular quarters, showed Egyptian films from time to time). Cities were immersed in green vegetation – trees on the sidewalks, private gardens and public parks – clean, well maintained and a pleasure to the eye. Department stores, mainly foreign-owned, were of an international standard – full of merchandise of the best quality, displayed in the most attractive manner. In the center, the streets were shining clean – swept and washed twice a day. Public transport was well organized and one could easily reach, comfortably seated, any place in town by bus or tram. Food, especially vegetables and locally grown fruit, were plentiful and of the highest quality. In the center resided almost exclusively foreigners and upper-class westernized Egyptians who studied in French or British schools, spoke foreign languages among themselves and were impregnated with western culture and values. In this respect, I recall that at school we were often asked to elaborate on the topic: 'Egypt, though geographically on the African continent and culturally an Arabic-speaking country, is nevertheless an integral part of Europe'. Indeed, King Faruk's Egypt looked upon itself as being European in its social norms, way of life, outlook on development and science and, most of all, in its aspirations.

When I returned to Egypt, after more than a quarter of a century, the situation was drastically different and the total population had reached 60 million. In Cairo there lived more than 12 million souls and in Alexandria more than 5 million. The foreign population hardly reached 5,000 in the whole of Egypt – mainly diplomats and technical assistants who were beginning to pour into the country in the wake of Sadat's new economic policy of *Infitach* (openness to the western world and economic development based on private initiative and foreign capital). After almost 30 years of Nasserism and almost total isolation from western influence, Egypt wanted to be, first and foremost, an Arab and Muslim country and to a lesser extent an African country. She refused to be identified in any way with Europe and rejected absolutely western values or a western orientation. All resident foreigners had been forcefully expelled from the country or had left of their own volition to find more clement skies. Their properties and businesses, as well as those of the Egyptian upper class, had been nationalized and entrusted to the management of inexperienced army officers who did not always go about things in an honest way. Thousands of new mosques had emerged throughout the country and from all sides rang the calls of the muezzins inviting believers to prayer. New quarters had popped up like mushrooms but they could not cope with the ever-increasing inflow of population from the rural areas. Overcrowding was literally suffocating. Where there used to live four or five souls, now lived 25–30 in terrible conditions. One could feel neglect and decline everywhere. The old, beautiful houses of European style were practically crumbling. The new ones were well below normal urban standards. Two million people resided permanently in old cemeteries in indescribable conditions. Health services were practically non-existent, at least by western standards. Furthermore, the infrastructure had not been developed over the years despite the gigantic increase in population: 12 million people were serviced by an infrastructure designed for three or four million at most! Electricity, water, sewage, phones, roads and such like were badly lacking and nothing was being done to remedy the situation. Sewage flooded the streets, even the most central ones. Phones worked only when they felt like it. The department stores of the past had been totally neglected and, in general, shops were almost empty of merchandise, whether locally produced or imported. Black painted placards covered almost every inch of most buildings, making the whole city resemble an immense *souk* (oriental market). Most parks and gardens of my youth had been replaced by tall private or public buildings. The few that remained were neglected and covered with litter. A thick layer of yellow dust covered the trees on the sidewalks, giving the city a surrealistic look.

Public transport was totally inadequate: buses and trams – old, rusty and covered with layers of mud that had not been removed for years – were packed with three times more commuters than the licensed number. Many more clung desperately to any available space outside the vehicles, like bunches of human grapes. The bombastic agrarian reform, initiated by Nasser in the late 1950s, had totally failed and there was a great shortage of fruit, vegetables, dairy products, groceries, meat and such like. The few items that could be found on the market were either of very low quality or sold at prices well beyond the financial means of the average Egyptian. An Egyptian friend summed up the situation for me in one gloomy sentence: the village has invaded the city and all Egypt has become one immense village. Anyone who knows what villages in Egypt are about can easily grasp what metamorphosis the country had undergone.

To me – who had known the Egypt of the 1930s–40s – it was a most painful experience. I found myself trying to convince colleagues and tourists from Israel and other countries that Egypt had known better times. It was not an easy task, things being what they were! People listened politely, smiled ironically and discarded my remarks with a nod of the head. Many times, they were more blunt and reacted by saying: 'What you are depicting is totally impossible; things cannot have changed so dramatically in one generation. The memories of your childhood must have gone through a process of idealization. You are looking at the past with your heart and not with your eyes!' After a few months, I ceased to argue or describe the Egypt of my youth. I felt that I was becoming too apologetic to no good purpose. The present was an every-day reality that could not be refuted or concealed! Nevertheless, I was not daydreaming, idealizing or lying: the Cairo of my youth, my Cairo, was a marvelous city where it was good to live! However, despite all the changes Egypt had undergone, two basic things have remained absolutely unchanged. The first is the breathtaking natural beauty of Egypt – her deserts, shores, lakes, ancient monuments and the majestic Nile that crosses the country in all its length, bringing to it life and fertility. The second is the Egyptian people – simple, kind, good-humored, peace-loving, hospitable, hard-working and content with very little … These are Egypt's two most precious treasures that no one can ever take from it.

When I came back to Egypt in 1990, I knew exactly what to expect. I knew that the Egypt of the 1940s had gone for ever. I did not try to make comparisons with the past. I looked for changes that might have occurred since I had left seven years earlier and I tried to assess the results of a decade of implementation of the new economic policy, the *Infitach*. It had been initiated by Sadat at the end of the 1970s and had been carried out assiduously by Mubarak since he had replaced him in the early 1980s. Indeed, from the first moment, I could perceive a tremendous improvement in every field of life (and this is not an exaggeration!). One could feel the feverish pace of development everywhere. The whole city had become a gigantic building yard, beautifully designed skyscrapers had been erected all over, new modern hotels had been built, and thousands of high-standard apartment buildings had emerged in the old quarters and in new ones. Furthermore, the necessary infrastructure had been provided for and the old infrastructure had been repaired, old roads had been widened beyond recognition and new ones had been opened. New bridges had been thrown over the Nile, sewage and water problems had been solved, electricity supply was plentiful (and cheap), even the phone lines worked like a Swiss watch. Traffic flowed almost normally and public transportation had improved dramatically, buses and trams were shining clean (most of them new) and were much less crowded, private cars had increased by the thousands and, most surprisingly, their horns had become almost completely silent. Many old houses had been renewed, luxurious cinemas had opened, a magnificent opera house was bringing first-class performances from all over the world, and a most impressive congress center was humming with unceasing cultural activities. Department stores and shops were bursting with good quality (and expensive) merchandise, agriculture and industry had made a great leap forward, foreign investment and aid were flowing in. Many prospective investors were waiting for the authorities' approval of various industrial projects; the beginnings of privatization and structural reforms were underway ...

I know that all this seems too good to be true. Indeed, it is a true picture of what had happened in Egypt in these last years and is still continuing. It does not mean that everything is now ideal but it is, most certainly, a very good start on the long road that Egypt has to go. Poverty is far from having been eradicated, the rich have become richer and the poor poorer, salaries are still very low, inflation is increasing. The demographic explosion is not yet controlled, overcrowding is as suffocating as ever, rural areas are still very much behind and the gap with the urban population is widening. The standard of learning has not improved as much as it should, the yoke of bureaucracy is as heavy as it was in the past, the privatization process is very slow and the eradication of graft is even slower. Most disturbing is the spread of Muslim fundamentalism that collects a heavy price in lives and dangerously impairs the internal stability which is essential for the expansion of economic and social development. In sum and without wishing to sound patronizing, Egypt is on the right path. It will not return to the Egypt of the 1940s, but why should Egypt aspire to be a part of Europe? Perhaps it is better that it has overcome its European complex and has abandoned the wishful thinking of its former elite? Why should Egypt adopt foreign concepts that have no roots in the inner being of its people? Egypt has come back to itself – it has liberated itself from the yoke of colonialism and has taken its rightful place in its own world, the Arab world. Egypt also has an African, Muslim and mid-eastern vocation. I know for certain that Egypt has taken the path of peace, democracy and accelerated development. If it perseveres in this path, and it certainly will, it may reach summits that will outshine its glorious past as one of the cradles of human civilization. It is my fervent prayer that Egypt attains in the nearest future all its goals and fulfills all the aspirations of its people. *Inshallah* (with God's help!).

4 · *Settling Down*

The first team of Israeli diplomats arrived in Cairo in early March 1980. Beyond the first contacts with the Egyptian authorities and the difficulty in adapting to a totally unfamiliar environment – which was understandably perceived as inimical and dangerous – arose the urgent need to find proper housing for the staff, the ambassador and the chancery.

This task, apparently easy, proved to be almost a Mission Impossible. There were few openings in the quarters defined as suitable for foreigners and safe for Israelis. Furthermore, landlords were reluctant to rent flats to Israelis and often even refused to speak to them. Egyptians did not yet know how to cope with the phenomenon called embassy of Israel which had 'popped up' overnight in town. It was not clear how the authorities would look upon too much eagerness to help the Israeli newcomers find a roof. Many landlords also feared (rightly as it turned out) that renting flats to Israelis might bring about, among other plagues, threats from extremist groups, a social boycott, assassination attempts, demonstrations, round-the-clock police surveillance, discomfort to other tenants, and closure of streets. More than anything else, they were apprehensive about being compelled by the *Mukhabarat* (Egyptian security services) to keep an eye on their Israeli tenants and report regularly about their activities. To deal with the *Mukhabarat* is the last thing that the common Egyptian wants! The only comforting fact was that only very few landlords were motivated by ideological considerations.

We offered to pay rents well above the market price, but even this was unsuccessful. Understandably, disappointment and frustration were increasingly felt among us. Living with one's family month after month, in one or two narrow rooms in second-rate hotels, was not easy to cope with! Time went by and housing problems seemed to become the focal point of all our diplomatic and social activity. Suddenly, *salvation* (at least partial) came through the very same factor that had helped create the difficulties: the Egyptian authorities. The time limit scheduled in the peace agreement for the opening of embassies and the exchange of ambassadors was approaching. They decided to reverse course and help solve the lodging problem, at least for the chancery and the ambassador.

Within a few days, two buildings were found: a small villa in the popular quarter of Dokki for the chancery (ironically neighboring an orphanage for Palestinian children) and a furnished flat for the ambassador on the Nile in the beautiful residential area of Gizeh, near the Sheraton Hotel. Neither accommodation met the norms set by our foreign ministry for chanceries and ambassadors' residences and were far from satisfying our minimal requirements. We nevertheless had to agree to both offers. We even swallowed with a smile the very high rents exacted from us.

Owing to the lack of time, the chancery immediately moved into the villa without making indispensable changes and repairs. As for the flat, this proved to be impossible to live in. Just in front of it, heavy equipment was digging 24 hours a day the foundations of an extension for the Sheraton Hotel and the noise was unbearable. Clearly, Ben-Elissar refused to move in and preferred to remain in the tiny suite that he had at the Sheraton. Two women secretaries 'volunteered' to move into the flat but within a few weeks they broke down and begged, literally in tears, to go back to their small hotel room. The apartment remained vacant for almost two years, up to the end of the contract (later, it was rented by the Israeli Academic Center).

In June 1980, when I arrived in Cairo, I found the chancery functioning in very poor conditions: overcrowding, renovation works, plywood partitions denying minimal privacy, corridors packed with surplus equipment and unused furniture, unceasing confusion and general tumult. The atmosphere was tense and one had the impression that it could be cut with a knife … Only the ambassador and the minister (myself) had separate small rooms of their own; the rest of the staff was packed three or four to a room. Israeli security officers were swarming all over the compound. Outside, all around the villa, scores of Egyptian security guards of all kinds and denominations were keeping a watchful eye, preventing access to the chancery almost hermetically. The surrealistic atmosphere and the very difficult physical conditions did not break the Israeli team's spirit and did not diminish their sense of fulfilling a sacred mission.

All the staff, with the exclusion of the two secretaries who had 'inherited' the ambassador's flat, still lived in hotels. The ambassador and the minister were at the Sheraton, the senior staff at the Concord (a three-star hotel) and the rest in a small hotel at a walking distance from the chancery. At the end of a hectic day's work, their only occupation, and maybe their only entertainment, was to go house-hunting with the help of local real estate agents and the embassy's Egyptian drivers. The 'game' was less than scarce and they always returned empty-handed.

I was also among the 'hunters'. I wanted to find a suitable residence as quickly as possible and spare my family the difficulties of living for a long period in a hotel. I was candid enough to think that, being born in Cairo and speaking fluent Egyptian Arabic, it would be easier for me. I decided to concentrate on the quarter of Zamalek that I remembered from my youth as the most select residential area. Every evening after work, I literally went from house to house asking the janitors if there was an apartment for rent in their building, enticing them with the promise of a juicy gratification. I found many beautiful houses and I even concluded verbal agreements with some of the landlords but when I returned the next day to sign the lease and receive the key, I was stunned to hear that they had decided to back out of the deal. Each one gave a different excuse, which was clearly untrue. Only a very few revealed, in utmost secrecy, that the *Mukhabarat* men had come to them immediately after I had left and given them 'friendly advice' not to finalize the deal. Only later did I find out that the Egyptian authorities wanted to compel all the Israelis to concentrate in the Maadi area (a new neighborhood far from the city center and the more select quarters where most of the foreign diplomats lived).

Nevertheless, after a week of strenuous efforts, I succeeded not only in finding but also actually renting in Zamalek what seemed to be a beautiful and luxurious apartment with a magnificent view of the Nile. By luck – which proved later to be a lack of luck – a British company that had rented the apartment agreed to sublet it to me with the approval of the Egyptian landlord who even allowed me to install four air-conditioning units. The lease was signed with the British company and I paid a full year's advance rent. My swift success enhanced my colleagues' esteem for my hunter capacities and Ambassador Ben-Elissar requested me – now that I was 'settled' – to take upon myself the task of finding suitable buildings for the chancery and the ambassador's residence. Very pleased with myself, I willingly agreed to do so and indeed during the first months of my stay in Cairo, I dedicated much time to this task.

When my wife Sarah and my daughter Tali arrived, my most praised success turned out to be one of the most unpleasant incidents in my career. I had not checked the water and electricity supply to the flat; I did not imagine that problems of this kind could exist in a such a select neighborhood, especially when the apartment was on the first floor of a luxurious building. But facts were facts: most of the day the taps were completely dry and electricity was not sufficient to cope with the four air-conditioning units that I had installed. The landlord had allowed me to install them but he did not warn me that they would not function for lack of power! I had to rescind the lease – we could not logically live, in the very hot climate of Egypt, in a house that lacked these two elementary commodities. I was afraid that I would forfeit the money I had paid in advance since it was well known that Egyptian landlords would not easily be induced to return money already in their pocket, especially when they were not legally compelled to do so. Happily, I was not dealing with the Egyptian landlord but with the British company and it agreed, without haggling, to return all the advance rent. My only loss was a few hundred dollars that I had spent on repainting the apartment and installing the air-conditioning units.

I moved with the family and my dog, Lucky, to the Club Med. The Sheraton and all other five-star hotels refused to receive us with a dog – dogs are impure according to Muslim tradition. The club was located in the center of Cairo on the premises of a palace that had previously belonged to Prince Mohamed Ali, King Faruk's uncle. It functioned in wooden barracks erected in one of the most beautiful gardens I have ever seen. Many of the Israeli diplomats followed my example and moved to the club. A score of Egyptian bodyguards came with us. They followed us everywhere and could not refrain from looking with wide eyes at the women guests sun-tanning in bikinis at the swimming pool. Many guests complained and, after a few days, the club's manager requested us to vacate our rooms and move to another hotel (in other words, we were expelled). Understandably, we were panic-stricken; the club had become for us a real home and a safe haven. We asked our embassy in Paris to speak to Gilbert Trigano, the owner of the Mediterranean Club, and explain our situation. He immediately gave instructions to keep us for as long as we wished. On our side, we requested the security authorities to reduce the number of bodyguards and station them less conspicuously. The arrangement worked out and we stayed in the club until we found suitable housing.

Having vacated my beautiful apartment in Zamalek, I was compelled to go back, together with the other Israeli diplomats, to my favorite sport: house-hunting! Gradually, we realized that 'Big Brother' would not allow us to settle outside Maadi and we decided at a staff meeting that we had no choice but to comply. From then on, we limited our searches for suitable housing exclusively to that neighborhood. There was no point in continuing to swim against the current. We remained, however, determined not to give in on the chancery and the ambassador's residence and we continued looking for suitable buildings in the more select and central areas. It was no great surprise that, within a few weeks, all staff members found accommodation in Maadi to their satisfaction. Suddenly, Israelis had become welcome tenants though they still had to pay much higher rents than the usual market prices. Misgivings and false excuses vanished. Landlords in Maadi had received the authorities' green light!

As for me, I still yearned to live in Zamalek. I hoped that now that all the Israeli diplomats had settled in Maadi, the Egyptian authorities would allow one exception. I decided to give it a last shot. I found a very nice apartment, signed a binding contract and even went with the landlord to choose the furniture. The landlord was enthusiastic and bestowed on my wife and me many gestures of sympathy, stressing repeatedly that he had excellent memories of his Jewish friends who had left Egypt during the Nasser regime. Two days before the date set for receiving the apartment, he sent a messenger to inform me that he was 'compelled to rescind our contract for reasons beyond his power'. Once again, it was obvious that the long hand of the security services had crudely interfered and signaled that it was impossible to do anything against their will. This time I got the message loud and clear!

I began looking for an apartment in Maadi. My family and I had been living in a cramped wooden barrack at the Club Med for more than three months by now, and I was beginning to lose patience. Finally, I found a suitable flat on the Nile, at the entrance of Maadi, with the help of one of my relatives who was visiting Cairo and had an old friend in the real estate business. The landlord dragged his feet in furnishing the flat and we had to move into an almost bare apartment. All the pressure I exerted and all my diplomatic skills did not persuade the landlord to hurry up in buying the furniture. He simply did not want to part with the money I had given him in advance and repeated endlessly that 'in Egypt things move slowly and one needs a lot of patience to accomplish anything'. After two whole months, I refused to pay the rent and I compelled the landlord to accompany me on a purchase *blitzkrieg*. In one day, I managed to buy all the furniture, carpets, electrical appliances and the household needs, proving beyond the slightest doubt that even in Egypt things could be done quickly and efficiently. One needed only good will, determination and, naturally, money!

House-hunting was not finished for me. I had to look for suitable accommodation for the chancery and the ambassador's residence in the center of Cairo. I did not spare either time or effort. Day after day, in spite of my tight schedule, I went to visit buildings, villas and apartments. The same phenomenon repeated itself: a verbal agreement with the land-lord after bitter haggling about the rent and the next day cancellation of the deal on a blatant pretext. In one case, I found a beautiful villa for the ambassador and I signed an agreement with the owner, a wealthy busi-nessman married to a German woman. A few days later, he came to me and complained that heavy pressures were being put on him to cancel the agreement. After months of house-hunting, it did not surprise me. I was stunned, however, when the gentleman added that if I doubled the already exorbitant rent and agreed to pay him – outside Egypt – ten years' rent in advance (more than three million dollars), he would take the risk of turning a blind eye to the pressures exerted on him. If the worst came to the worst, he was ready to move to Germany until the authorities calmed down. I gave him a piece of my mind in not too diplomatic a language. I was disgusted at his attempt to take advantage of the situation and extort shamelessly huge sums from the embassy (though there is no doubt that the pressures exerted on him were very real).

In another case, I found a five-floor building for the chancery. The owner received me with open arms. He went so far as to say that well before peace, Angel Gabriel had come to him in his dreams and told him that peace with Israel would soon be signed and that it would be his duty to rent the whole of his building to the embassy of Israel. Naturally, beyond the nice words and Angel Gabriel's instructions, he exacted the highest possible price. As for us, we knew that we could not rely on angels or landlords and that in Egypt Big Brother had much more leverage than angels. We acted quickly: we signed a fully-fledged contract, paid a seven-digit deposit, received the keys and even took formal possession. We stationed a few security men in the building round the clock. We thought that we had finally made it and organized an impromptu small party to celebrate the memorable event.

Two days later, the landlord came to the embassy wearing a mourner's face. He handed over to me the very same check he had received from the embassy and said that he was compelled to cancel the deal because he 'will be needing the whole building (20 apartments!!) for his daughter, who is compelled to transfer with her family from Alexandria to Cairo'. He begged me, practically with tears in his eyes, not to insist and not to sue him for breach of contract. He was clearly frightened to death. I consulted Ben-Elissar and we decided to rescind the contract and pull our people out. There was no point in creating, at this early stage, a major diplomatic incident with the Egyptian authorities and being dragged into a fight we had no chance of winning – we left fighting windmills to Sancho Pancho and Don Quixote!

I continued combing the center of Cairo. As always, the solution came unexpectedly. A man called Farag Damian came to the chancery and asked to see me urgently. I received him despite the reluctance of the security guards. He told me that he owned in Maadi 'the villa of our dreams' where he was living all by himself. He praised in lavish terms the location, the furniture, the garden (a real paradise!), the surroundings, the neighbors, the rooms, the kitchen, the flowers and what not ... He expressed his readiness for the sake of peace to rent the house to the Israeli embassy at a modest price (which proved to be exorbitant) to serve as a residence for the ambassador. Finally, after I questioned him repeatedly, he revealed that he had been called to the security services and practically ordered to vacate the house and rent it to the Israelis. He added with evident self-importance: 'As a good citizen and a genuine supporter of peace, I cannot refuse to comply'. He was, with great sorrow, ready to move out of his 'Garden of Eden' but naturally he wanted an enormous sum. I drove with him to the villa and indeed I was very much impressed. It was far from the owner's exuberant description but it was really fit to be an ambassador's residence despite its location in Maadi. I brought Nizza and Eliahu Ben-Elissar to see it and they gave me the green light to close the deal. After a few days of haggling, we signed a fully-fledged contract, this time with the tacit blessing of the Egyptian authorities. Finally, after more than six months at the Sheraton, the Ben-Elissars moved into what would become the official residence of the Israeli ambassador in Cairo.

The story of the villa is most interesting in itself. During King Faruk's period, it belonged to one of the richest pashas (a nobility title used throughout the former Ottoman Empire) in Egypt. He kept it for his Jewish mistress. After the toppling of the king, Nasser nationalized all the properties of the former elite. The villa was allocated for a symbolic few pounds to a Qatari emir who had been of service to Nasser in his inter-Arab feuds. Later, he fell into disgrace and was expelled from Egypt. He left the villa to the care of his previously mentioned business manager, one Farag Damian. However, fearing that the government might confiscate the villa, the emir transferred it officially to Damian's name in a fictitious transaction. Many years later, when the emir returned to Egypt, Damian refused to give him the villa back, claiming that he had bought it with his modest savings.

Law suit followed law suit (the last was in 1990, when I was residing in the villa which I had rented for Ben-Elissar ten years earlier). Damian won in all instances and the villa remained definitively his. However, it seems that there is some truth in the saying 'dishonesty does not pay'. Damian enjoyed neither the villa nor the money he made out of it. He was single, sick and an absolute miser. He lived as a pauper; all the rent he earned (and we are speaking of a lot of money) he deposited in a savings account at Bank Al-Eetemad in London – an Arab bank which gave somewhat higher interest. The bank went bankrupt in the wake of a corruption and embezzlement case and Damian lost everything – capital and interest. Three years later, he died in the sordid apartment he was living in and his only sister and the Coptic Church inherited all his properties and wealth.

As for the chancery, I was on the verge of losing hope. We could not reasonably go to Maadi and all other possibilities seemed to be hermetically closed. We thought that we would stay forever in the small villa in Dokki. Having nothing to lose, I decided to try my luck and check the possibilities in a 20-floor building still under construction located on one of the main squares in Cairo, right in front of Cairo University. It seemed so unattainable that, though I used to pass near it almost every day, I never dared ask before if there were vacant apartments. The contractor was on the roof and I had to climb 20 floors using stairs and wooden scaffolds. I arrived tired and breathing heavily but the effort was worthwhile. The contractor was the owner of the top two floors and he expressed interest in selling them to the embassy for an enormous sum, which he quoted on the spot without hesitation. He added that there might be some legal problems and other difficulties (i.e. the authorities' permission) but he believed he could solve them easily. I went to fetch Ben-Elissar and we both made the climb and discussed the matter at length with the contractor. The location was ideal; the two floors were more than sufficient for our needs and the contractor seemed very serious. I was given the green light to pursue the matter. A delegation from the foreign affairs and finance ministries was also impressed and approved the purchase and the price. Within a few days we worked out with the contractor a lease–purchase contract and applied formally to the Egyptian government, through the foreign ministry, to approve the sale (in Egypt no foreigner is allowed to buy real estate without prior government authorization).

We kept our fingers crossed and waited for the reaction of the Egyptian authorities. The contractor had not exaggerated his capacity to solve legal problems and remove bureaucratic and other difficulties. Indeed, three weeks later we received the formal authorization to purchase the two upper floors. On the same day, we took possession and posted our security people round the clock. The repairs and adaptation works were entrusted to our department of real estate in the ministry. Ouri Khalfon, the head of the department, brought with him from Israel workers in all the needed crafts and within two months they concluded the work and furnished the chancery from top to bottom. In a single night, we moved into our new premises lock, stock and barrel, in a well-orchestrated operation. A few months later, the contractor registered, as promised, both floors in the name of the State of Israel.

House-hunting had finally come to its happy end and we could be proud of the results. All the staff members were now settled in comfortable homes, the embassy functioned in a beautiful and well-located chancery and we had an ambassadors' residence that was an honor to the State of Israel. It had not been an easy task by any means. Determination and patience paid off! Unfortunately, Ambassador Ben-Elissar and his wife Nizza, who both spearheaded the whole housing operation, did not enjoy their new accommodation for long. In early 1981, they both left Egypt, Ben-Elissar having decided to go into politics and run for parliament on the Likud list.

When I returned to Cairo as ambassador in 1990, there were no more housing problems. Peace was stable; the embassy of Israel and the Israeli diplomats had become an integral part of the Egyptian landscape. Plenty of houses could easily be found or passed from hand to hand provided they were located in Maadi (indeed, almost throughout the last 20 years, only two Israeli diplomats were allowed to live outside that neighborhood, closer to the center of town). Rents remained well above the market price but at least the diplomats were spared the humiliations and frustrations endured by the first team.

5 · Security

Well before the establishment of embassies and the exchange of ambassadors, the Egyptian authorities had laid down very strict procedures as to the treatment and protection of Israeli delegations visiting Egypt. These procedures had three clear-cut goals:

- Protection *per se:* foiling demonstrations and terrorist attacks against the Israelis by extremist groups opposed to the peace process;
- Sending a three-pronged message: to the Israelis that they were not yet welcome in Egypt; to the Egyptian people, who tended to receive the Israelis with open arms, that Israelis should still be ostracized; and to the Arabs at large that, despite the establishment of peace, Egypt had limited interaction with Israel and was not fraternizing with it;
- Counter-espionage: strict supervision of Israeli movements and contacts in Egypt and gathering of information on negotiation tactics, goals, feelings and any other matter that might be of the slightest interest.

These procedures, and the goals they were meant to attain, did not change after the establishment of the embassies. I believe they are in force to this very day. I can personally vouch for the fact that this certainly was the case up to the end of 1992 when I was transferred from Egypt to India. At first, security measures were meant to apply to Israeli delegations visiting Egypt but, with the establishment of the diplomatic representations in Cairo and Alexandria (1980), they were also implemented, and made even more stringent, in relation to the Israeli permanent staff in Egypt. The security authorities – all departments and kinds of police units, military and civilian intelligence, censorship and many other relevant agencies – were empowered to take any action necessary to achieve the above-mentioned goals. They carried out their instructions with extreme zeal and did not hesitate to take any steps they deemed fit. They did not make the slightest attempt to conceal their surveillance activities, or render them any less conspicuous or abusive. They literally established a blockade on the chancery, the ambassador's residence and diplomats' houses and openly shadowed all their movements. Altogether, 700–1,200 (depending on the political situation) personnel of all categories, uniformed and plain-clothed, were involved in this major operation and I do not include in these numbers those whose task was to keep a discreet eye on the Israelis.

All surrounding streets were strictly controlled. In the very lobby of the chancery building, an interrogation room was established where people who wished to pay a call on the embassy were registered, interrogated at length and repeatedly thoroughly searched. They were treated in a rough, not to say tough, manner. Documents were scrutinized again and again and photocopied even if they were of a private nature. Most of the visitors were 'advised' to renounce, in their best interest, meeting the Israelis. Those who insisted were invited for further interrogation at *Muhabarat* headquarters. Only a few were allowed to proceed to the embassy but were asked to report to the interrogation room upon their return. Visiting the chancery and Israeli private homes was a traumatic experience for anyone and most particularly for Egyptian citizens. There were days when not a single person was allowed in. We would then understand that something 'unusual' was happening and our security officer would rush down to try and convince the person in charge downstairs to 'losen the knot'.

We did not hesitate to complain, time and again, to the ministry of foreign affairs and directly to the security authorities about this treatment, that stood in absolute contradiction to international norms and to security measures applied to other diplomatic missions in Egypt. We did not hesitate to point out that it was obvious that all these so-called security measures were not intended to protect us but were meant to prevent us from maintaining normal relations with the local population, make our work more difficult and render us a burden on our neighbors. After the first few complaints, we realized that we were speaking to deaf ears and that there would be no positive results, but we stubbornly went through the motions over and over again. Indeed, despite our perseverance, things continued as they were and no effort was made to introduce even cosmetic changes to meet our repeated requests.

In my second period in Egypt as ambassador, I repeatedly brought the matter before the ministers of the interior and of foreign affairs – mostly for their nuisance value and not in the hope of achieving anything. I was aware that I would always receive the same stereotypical reply accompanied by sarcastic smiles: 'You are our guests in Egypt and we have to make sure that no harm is done to you. We are determined to take all the security measures we think necessary even if they are unpleasant and make life more difficult for you and for our own citizens'. Indeed, they wanted to protect us but even more to protect themselves from us! From time to time, we were compelled to present formal complaints about blatant infringements of courtesy towards our diplomatic staff that went well beyond our, already very wide, margin of forbearance. We never received an apology and most times we did not even receive replies at all, written or verbal.

The embassy mail, even letters from Cairo itself, reached us with a delay of about four–six weeks. At first, we thought that the Egyptian post might be inefficient, but after a few weeks we decided to check the matter thoroughly. We sent to selected addresses letters in ordinary envelopes which bore no embassy identification whatsoever. All the letters without exception reached their destination within 48 hours – an efficiency the Israeli post could well envy. We raised the matter with the foreign ministry but we used very moderate language, fearing to arouse a controversy that might reflect negatively on normalization negotiations. We were still at the beginning of the road and had high expectations.

Upon my return to Cairo in 1990, I saw immediately that there had been no improvement in this field. The mail continued to arrive with a considerable delay. Though I was, at that stage, far from being naïve and knew that complaints, however strong they might be, would not bring about any change, I decided to raise the matter at every opportunity. In any case, we had nothing to lose and we knew exactly the rigid limits of normalization that the Egyptian authorities had defined. At each meeting with ministers or high officials, I took pleasure in dwelling on the delay in delivering our mail and the embarrassment it was creating for the embassy. I always brought with me some 10–20 envelopes to show that there was a great discrepancy between the date which appeared on the post seal and the arrival date stamped on the letters by our Egyptian staff.

In my conversations with the interior minister, Abd-el-Halim Moussa (I used to meet him every four to six weeks), I would complain about the slowness of the Egyptian postal services (though I knew perfectly well that they were not at fault). I would add that the great delays in delivering our mail could not be explained even by the most rigorous censorship process, which should normally take no more than a few hours. I suggested jokingly that the only 'logical' explanation seemed to be that the censorship staff believed that our letters might be booby-trapped and therefore kept them in quarantine for a long period. I even put forward repeatedly the 'constructive' proposal that censorship of embassy mail be entrusted to the security officers stationed in the chancery building and I promised to formally allow them to open and photocopy all the letters. In order to make their work swifter and more efficient, I even volunteered to put at their disposal a photocopier of the latest model. The minister would laugh loudly and gently deny that the embassy mail was censored. He would nevertheless summon to his office the head of the *Mabakhes* (the civilian secret services). He would inform him of my complaint, repeat my jokes and ask him to check with the postal authorities what could be done to speed up the mail delivery to the embassy of Israel, 'which has such a nice ambassador who is an *Ibn Balad* [born in the country]'. After this amicable conversation, there would be a slight improvement in the mail delivery but after a few weeks the situation would revert to what it had been – just in time for me to raise the matter again in my next meeting with the minister. I never found out if the reason for these inexplicable mail delays, even after the minister's repeated interventions, was poor equipment or a wanton policy of making life hard on us.

During my second stay in Cairo, another mail problem emerged around the dispatch of the monthly embassy bulletin, which was first distributed in mid-1988. It was a purely cultural bulletin. Aware of Egyptian sensitivity, we took great care not to include political items or items that could be perceived as such. The preparation of the bulletin was a one-man show, or rather a one-couple show. The writer Yitshak Bar-Moshe and his wife Norma were responsible for choice of articles and pictures, writing, translation, typing, editing, page setting and such like. They were doing an excellent job (when they left Cairo, I convinced them to continue editing the bulletin from Jerusalem and they are doing so to this very day). I was very impressed with the quality of the bulletin and even more by the fact that it existed at all. I insisted on increasing the distribution from 300 to 1,500 copies (a drop in the ocean considering that Egypt has a population of more than 60 million souls). The information department allocated the necessary budget and took the initiative to improve the printing and the paper quality, turning it into a publication of the highest standard.

Having learnt the lesson of the embassy mail, I requested Bar-Moshe to check discretely if the bulletin reached its destination. It appeared that many of the addressees did not receive it or received it sporadically – a clear indication that the long hand of Big Brother was interfering in the distribution process. I thought, naïvely, that I could 'outsmart' the security services and I instructed Bar-Moshe to send the bulletin by hand delivery in both Cairo and Alexandria. The first issue distributed by our own staff took the Egyptians by surprise and it reached all the addressees. From the next issue on, measures were taken to counter our initiative. The authorities obtained the new distribution lists from our Egyptian staff and instructed them on how to regulate the distribution. In accordance with the whim of the moment and the political situation, they decided how many bulletins would really be distributed in a specific month and whom they would reach or not reach. The remainder was, presumably, confiscated or disposed of. To be more accurate, we caught them, red-handed, disposing of the bulletins only in Alexandria. One of our security men spotted a local employee throwing away a substantial number of copies. The man confessed that he was acting on instructions. Indeed, he had been ordered to burn them far from the consulate but he did not do so because it was 'a cumbersome and time-consuming operation'. In Cairo, the local staff was more sophisticated. Most of them had worked many years with us and had learned how to 'walk between the rain drops without getting wet' and please their two bosses – the security services and the embassy – without risking their jobs or being thrown into jail. We never caught them getting rid of bulletins but we knew, from phone inquiries we regularly made, that in Cairo too not all the bulletins reached their destination.

In general terms, 1,000 people must have received the bulletin sporadically, which meant that many more read it. This in itself was a matter of great satisfaction for us, considering the limitations put on the normalization process by the Egyptian authorities. Whatever our mailing problems, the fact remained that they had allowed us to open a window, however small, to the Egyptian intelligentsia. From the Egyptian point of view, the bulletin did not represent a substantial danger. It did not jeopardize their policy of isolating the Israelis from the population at large – the situation remained under control, as it was in all other facets of the normalization process. It seems that by allowing the distribution of the bulletin, the authorities wanted to give us a safety valve to release a little steam (as they used to do in other fields of interaction between the two countries) so that the pressure did not become unbearable. In any case, distribution of the bulletin was, and still is, strictly regulated and the authorities can bring it to a standstill whenever they wish.

For obvious reasons, I will not detail the entire range of means of surveillance used by the Egyptian security services to shadow the Israeli diplomats in their slightest moves, keep track of their contacts with the local population, and discover what they say and even what they think. Suffice it to say that these means were diversified and that the Egyptians did not give a damn about the written or unwritten norms of diplomatic protocol. We knew perfectly well what was going on and we learnt to live with it! In any case, we had nothing to hide. Paradoxically, we even used some of the means of surveillance to our advantage and conveyed signals to the Egyptians that were too blunt to be conveyed by regular diplomatic channels. Many times, we teased our Egyptian colleagues and joked with them about the generous and diversified means of security they dedicated to 'our protection'. They did not deny the facts and did not show any embarrassment; they would simply say with an ironical smile: 'We are only doing our duty. You are our guest and we have to do whatever it takes to make you secure and comfortable'.

To avoid creating the wrong impression that all the Egyptians were interested in was to shadow us (not to use a cruder word), I have to say that they were also most keen to prevent any harm from befalling us. They took every step necessary (and much beyond that) to give us watertight protection. They were aware of the very real dangers that confronted us, which stemmed partly from the wild incitement in the press against Israel and the Jews in general – incitement condoned and often instigated by the government itself. They made sure that things did not get out of control. To our great sorrow, all the massive security measures put in place by the Egyptians did not prevent the spilling of Israeli blood. Throughout the years, we had many casualties.

In the early 1980s, there were only two attempts on the lives of Israeli diplomats. They both failed owing to the alertness of the targeted victims themselves and not of the Egyptian bodyguards whose task was to protect them. We lived all the time in fear of terrorist attacks. No week went by without letters or phone calls, cursing and threatening us with death 'if you continue to desecrate the soil of Egypt by your presence'. Ambassadors were the favorite target and most letters were addressed to them personally. Insults, the crudest of words and anti-Jewish verses of the Koran were poured on us. Security measures being what they were, it was obvious that the authorities were aware of the content of these letters and phone calls but our security officer made sure of formally informing his Egyptian counterparts and requesting additional protection. In addition, he called on the staff (who did not seem to be particularly worried) to show increased alertness and follow strictly the established safety rules. Some of our cars were wantonly damaged: tires were pierced, windows broken, painting damaged. Threats against the Israelis were also daubed on walls in different neighborhoods of the city and were not removed by the authorities despite our repeated requests. It was not an easy situation but, on the whole, the topic of our personal safety did not bother us more than necessary and no major dramatic incident occurred.

This changed in the mid-1980s. Terrorist attacks on the staff and Israeli tourists (I will deal later with this aspect) increased substantially and brought a heavy toll in casualties. Albert Atrakchi, one of our diplomats, was murdered while he was driving to the chancery. Most of his fellow passengers were wounded. A second murder occurred a few months later. The wife of one of our diplomats, Eti Tal-Or, was killed when terrorists attacked her car in the parking lot of the International Trade Fair. Three more Israelis were seriously wounded. Both of these attacks involved the son of the former president of Egypt, Gamal Abd-el-Nasser, who led a small leftist militant organization. He succeeded in fleeing (or more probably he was smuggled out of the country) and found refuge in Yugoslavia. A few years later, he came back and stood trial together with two accomplices (I was then back in Egypt and I followed the trial closely). Nasser Junior was found not guilty 'for lack of evidence', his two accomplices received light sentences and the court expressed its 'understanding for their motives'.

During my second tenure in Cairo, letters and phone calls were still very frequent but, happily, no major incident occurred. (I should stress that in the wake of the two murders and other terrorist attacks, we had tightened our own security measures.) There was however an attempt by fundamentalist students to fire rockets at the chancery, although they were arrested in time by the Egyptian security services (at least, this is what we were told).

A somewhat amusing incident occurred to two of our security guards. They were on their way to the American College in Maadi, walking slowly on the sidewalk. A group of youngsters began insulting them and, following an exchange of crude words, attacked them. The Israelis defended themselves and in the process broke the nose of one of the attackers. An outraged crowd gathered and threatened the guards with heavy sticks. They ran home, followed by the roaring crowd, and asked for the intervention of the policemen on duty. The policemen flatly refused to intervene and left the Israelis to their fate (which could have been quite unpleasant) and watched the confrontation complacently. The crowd, encouraged by this passive attitude, attacked the two Israelis. One of the Israelis pulled out his gun (duly licensed by the Egyptian authorities) and threatened the attackers. The latter froze on the spot and apologized profusely. The two sides parted as good friends, shaking hands and exchanging visiting cards. The very next day the two Israelis were sent back to Israel: their chiefs considered that, despite the circumstances, they had not shown enough self-restraint. In any case, even if the two guards' behavior had been judged irreproachable, they would have been sent back home to protect them from possible retaliation on the part of the Egyptian youngsters.

One more so-called security problem, which was prevalent both in the 1980s and the 1990s, related to visiting Israeli delegations and personalities. For obvious reasons, we wanted to put them in a centrally located hotel, as close as possible to the embassy. The Egyptians, on the other hand, strove to put them far from the center (mainly, at the Al-Salam Hotel near the airport or the Oberoy Mena-House near the pyramids). They invoked security considerations but in reality they did not want the Israelis' presence to be too conspicuous. Being the hosts (and paying the hotel bills), their standpoint usually prevailed. Only in rare cases, when we threatened to cancel a visit that was important to the Egyptians, did they yield to our pressures.

The hotel in which the Israeli delegations were eventually lodged was literally turned into an impregnable fortress. All around the compound (and we are speaking of thousands of meters), policemen in uniform armed with rifles or machine guns were posted every ten meters, 24 hours a day. The lobby, the restaurant, the courtyard, the swimming pool (and who knows where else) swarmed with uniformed and plain-clothed agents of each and every security agency in the country. The Israelis were not allowed to leave the hotel unaccompanied; their every movement was reported through walky-talkies to headquarters. In time, the authorities became more lenient on this topic and, in the 1990s, Israeli guests could move almost freely. They were still 'shadowed' conspicuously or discreetly mainly for their own protection but also for the sake of surveillance. As for the heavy security in the hotel premises, nothing changed. To the credit of the Egyptians, I have to say that their hospitality was more than lavish and this somewhat compensated for the heavy atmosphere caused by the massive security measures (Egyptian and Israeli).

Contrary to official delegations, Israeli tourists could reside wherever they wished and go everywhere to the exclusion of army installations and side roads (which were, and still are, out-of-bounds to foreigners of all nationalities). The surveillance of Israeli tourists did not go beyond the routine security measures taken in respect of all tourists visiting Egypt. Only once, in my second stay, was the embassy requested to intervene and convince an Israeli rabbi to move out (for his own safety) from a popular neighborhood where riots, provoked by extremist Muslim fundamentalists, had recently taken place. Unfortunately, tourists did however suffer from terrorist attacks that levied a heavy toll. In Ras Burka (a beach resort in Sinai), a soldier went amok (as the Egyptians alleged) and opened fire from very close range on a group of Israeli families, killing seven people and wounding many more. Two buses were also attacked – one near Cairo by Palestinian terrorists and the second by a policeman (also gone amok according to the Egyptians) who crossed the border and ambushed the bus. Many Israelis paid with their lives and many more were wounded.

Revolting and painful as these cases were, one should not blame the Egyptian authorities for them. They certainly do not instigate these crimes and, on the contrary, do everything possible to prevent them. Egyptian citizens and many tourists of other nationalities fall victim to such attacks perpetrated by extremist Muslim fundamentalist groups. What provokes revulsion and distress is the unconditional support of the Egyptian Bar Association for these criminals and their abject actions. The Egyptian press too, instead of condemning such despicable acts of violence, slanders Israel and Israelis in the wake of each attack and depicts the assassins of innocent civilian tourists as heroes, calling for their immediate release. No less painful and revolting is the contempt with which the Egyptian authorities have in the past treated the victims and the government of Israel. They have stubbornly refused to provide us with official information on the course of the investigations and later of the trials (in spite of repeated requests that were made even to President Mubarak). Also, they have flatly refused to provide an authorized copy of the judgments and referred us to the courts, knowing perfectly well that our request would be rejected in view of the ban declared by the Bar Association on any kind of relations with Israel.

To be fair, I have to say that (excluding the above-mentioned incidents), in my two turns of office in Egypt, I do not recall a single complaint from Israeli tourists about acts of violence that were politically motivated. This is true, even in periods of bilateral tension between the two countries and events of significant magnitude such as the Peace for Galilee operation, the bombing of the Iraqi atomic installations, and five long years of the Palestinian *Intifada*. Incitement in the Egyptian press (opposition and government alike) against Israel, depicting it as the very personification of Satan, did not reflect negatively on the friendly behavior of the large majority of the population towards the Israeli tourists. Even the wild accusations in the press that Israeli tourists were wantonly perverting Egyptian youngsters and contaminating them with venereal diseases did not bring about acts of violence against our tourists. The press also accused all Israeli tourists of being spies and sabotaging the Egyptian economy but all these verbal abuses were never translated into physical abuses by the population and this is entirely to the credit of the Egyptian people – a peace-loving, hard-working, good-humored people. However, not everything was ideal and Israeli tourists in Egypt encountered problems of a totally different nature on which I will dwell in due course.

To conclude this short insight on security-related topics, I have to add that there is also an Israeli facet to them. True, the safety of the Israeli diplomats and installations in Egypt is first and foremost the responsibility of the Egyptian government. However, in matters of life and death, Israel relies only on itself and takes independently all possible measures to reduce to a minimum the dangers inherent in residing in Egypt, the heart of the Arab motherland. Israel also takes into consideration the fact that Egypt is a pole of attraction for millions of Arab tourists from all over the region and that thousands of Palestinians, some of them active members of terrorist organizations, live permanently in the country. It also does not forget the many unfriendly (to use a mild word) diplomatic missions existing in Cairo as well as the ever-increasing Muslim fundamentalism with its millions of members and its very active terrorist groups with their proven operational record.

Security-wise, there is a fundamental difference between incidental tourists, who come for a short stay and leave the country before they become a target, and resident diplomats, who live permanently in the country. The diplomats are a walking symbol of the State of Israel: they come and go everywhere, drive easily identifiable cars, reside in permanent and known addresses and conspicuously fulfill their many tasks. Clearly, they and their families are much more vulnerable: indeed, they live in constant danger and do not know what awaits them at the next street corner or red light. Providing them with an adequate protective umbrella required, and still requires, a creative mind, skill and considerable means – it is not an easy task to forestall numerous unknown dangers that might pop up at any moment and in any place. I cannot go into detail but I am proud to say, with profound gratitude, that the relevant Israeli authorities have spared no effort in this field and have not only given a feeling of security to the staff in Egypt but have also provided them with real security. Naturally, dangers are still there: they cannot be totally eliminated – this is true everywhere in the world and this is certainly true in a country like Egypt.

I do not know of a mission more exacting than being a security guard in the Israeli embassy in Cairo. In opposition to what many might think, it is a very complex job, which encompasses a most diversified range of tasks that run non-stop around the clock – 24 hours a day, 365 days a year.

For these security guards, there are no holidays, no festivals, no week-ends, no rest and no sick leave and it seems as if they are made of steel and not flesh like the rest of us. Even when they reach breaking point, they still accept with a smile any additional task that might be required and fulfill it to the best of their ability. They never complain and never try to evade their responsibilities.

I could go into numerous interesting and spicy stories about security-related matters but I have to refrain from doing so. In this very sensitive area, where the safety and wellbeing, and maybe even the lives, of our people abroad are at stake, one ought to live by the popular saying 'Speech is silver, silence is gold'.

6 · *Ambassadors and Staff*

S ince the signing of the peace treaty with Egypt, from 1980 to 1999, six Israeli ambassadors have served in Egypt. The privilege of being the first goes to Dr Eliahu Ben-Elissar, who stayed in Egypt for only one year. He had previously been closely linked with the peace process in his capacity as director-general of the prime minister's office. His contribution to shaping relations between the two countries, in a very delicate and decisive period, was most significant.

The fact that he had been very close to Prime Minister Menahem Begin contributed to strengthening the embassy's position and helped open doors at the highest level, both in Israel and Egypt. President Sadat knew that when he was speaking to Ben-Elissar he was speaking almost directly to Menahem Begin. I worked with him, hand in hand, in the exhilarating and decisive first days after the opening of the embassy in Cairo. I always enjoyed his trust and friendship, a real friendship that continues to this very day. He gave me enough rope to fulfil the many tasks that he left in my hands and we always consulted and worked in full harmony.

Every morning, I used to come with the Egyptian newspapers and go through them together with him (Ben-Elissar did not read Arabic). I pointed to various topics, internal and external, that seemed to me important and especially to what was written about Israel, Jews and so forth. We drank together the daily dose of poison distilled 'so generously' by the Egyptian press. The fact that we shared the potion did not make its taste less bitter or less nauseating. Many times, there were personal attacks against Ben-Elissar that can only be described as despicable (not to use stronger words!). In the eyes of the Egyptian newspapers, he personified Israel's condescension and the 'long arm' they alleged it was using against the Arabs. They would sneer at him, nicknaming him Herzl (the founder of political Zionism) because of the shape of his beard. In Egyptian terms, there could be no greater insult. Once, after we had become closer, I asked him why he did not shave his beard and pull the carpet from under the feet of his Egyptian critics. He was not offended by my weird, not to say offensive, suggestion because he knew that I was speaking from the heart and had genuine respect and friendship for him. He answered: 'Is it conceivable that I should change my personality in order to please slanderers who stoop to such meanness? Tomorrow, they will want me to shave my hair too. Let them continue to call me Herzl; there is no bigger honor for me. Let us show pride and stand with our head upright.'

I felt ashamed and did not react. Today, now that I have behind me much experience of dipomatic life in Egypt, I am less naïve: I realize that even if Ben-Elissar had shaved all the hair off the whole of his body, the lousy attacks against him would have continued. These attacks were an outward symptom and not the reason for the disease! It is deeply-rooted and stems from the very outlook of Egyptians on Israel and the Israelis. Incidentally, the Israeli public obtained the impression that only Eliahou and Nizza Ben-Elissar were ostracized by Egyptian society and mocked by the Egyptian press. It is not so – all Israeli ambassadors after Ben-Elissar have been 'honored', without exception, by a substantial portion of slander and insults. All have been equally ostracized, and together with them – from day one – the entire embassy diplomatic staff. The Egyptian security services made sure that there has been no breach in the social boycott (see next chapter) on Israeli diplomats ever since the days of Ben-Elissar.

Ben-Elissar worked in very difficult conditions: the first steps in Cairo, suspicion from every side, crowded offices, the heavy security apparatus preventing minimal intimacy, residence in two small hotel rooms. Precisely at the end of his stay, one could feel that Egyptian society was beginning to open towards him and to appreciate him. I tried to convince him not to cut short his mission when it was reaching its peak but he was determined to plunge into Israeli politics despite his awareness of the inherent dangers and difficulties involved. Later he returned to diplomatic life as ambassador to the United States and then France (where he recently died in tragic circumstances). In these two countries, considered the most important diplomatic postings in our foreign service, Ben-Elissar dealt again, though indirectly and less intensively, with matters related to Israeli–Egyptian relations. I know that, in spite of all the difficulties he encountered during his short stay in Egypt and the insults he had to swallow, he was a great believer in peace and kept a special place for Egypt in his heart. I have no doubt that, as the first ambassador of a Jewish state in 2,000 years, he considered his mission to Egypt to be the most significant in his long and fulfilling career.

After Ben-Elissar left, I was chargé d'affaires a.i. for a few months (meaning that I took the helm until the arrival of the next ambassador). I did not put forward my candidacy for the post of ambassador because I considered myself not senior enough for such a position. However, I made it clear that if someone less experienced than I were appointed to the post, I would pack my bags and return back home immediately. There was no need for me to carry out my threat: the appointment went to Moshe Sasson, whom I, like many others in the foreign service, considered a diplomat of the highest stature. I had never previously worked with him, but from the first moment the chemistry between us functioned perfectly and we worked together in harmony and understanding. Though my approach and my assessments of situations were less optimistic and somewhat more radical than Moshe's, he never prevented me from bringing my views to the knowledge of the decision-makers in Jerusalem. For my part, I always respected his standpoint and acted in accordance with his instructions (which were not always to my liking). As ambassador to Egypt, directly responsible for the development of good relations between the two countries, Moshe saw his duty as smoothing edges and attaining the right balance between the positive and the negative so that the situation did not spin out of control. He used to say that there would always be plenty of people who would pour oil on the fire and advocate taking extreme stands. He saw himself as being personally responsible for the fragile peace that had just been established and did his utmost to preserve and strengthen it.

Moshe arrived in Cairo very moved and full of good will. Despite his very wide knowledge and experience of mid-eastern affairs, he did not realize the limitations imposed upon us in Egypt and the very strained atmosphere, deliberately created, in which the embassy operated. He brought with him many expectations, most of which proved to be unattainable (though not because he was not able enough or did not do his utmost to try and make them become a reality). At our first staff meeting, he informed us that the ministry had agreed to send to Cairo an expert in the Arabic language (Yitshak Nuriel) to help him draft his speeches, letters and communications; he explained that, though he knew good Arabic, he wanted them to be absolutely perfect. He was very surprised, and somewhat mistrustful, when we told him that there would be very few opportunities for him to use the skills of the Arabic expert and that he was not going to be invited to address local audiences or allowed to be interviewed in the media. To make the situation in Cairo more tangible for him, we stressed that the embassy could not even publish a small ad in the local press.

Moshe very quickly grasped the rules of the game as defined by the Egyptian authorities but he never ceased trying to bypass them. He taught us to persevere in our efforts even when the results were far from satisfactory. He never went to a meeting without preparing thoroughly what he would be saying to the journalists though he knew very well (after the first few occasions) that the media would not be allowed to publish his statements; at best, only a short press release, drafted by the relevant authorities, would be published and this would have not even a remote bearing on what had actually occurred in the meeting. As a matter of fact, this was the case not only with Moshe; all Israeli ambassadors experienced the same situation.

During Moshe Sasson's tenure, the embassy and he, on the personal level, underwent a series of crises of all kinds. Anyone else would have broken under the burden. Not Moshe! He never became embittered. He was popular with everyone he met: he charmed them with his wit, his stories and his profound knowledge of the Holy Koran and Arab proverbs. He developed a genuine friendship with top Egyptian leaders such as Mustafa Khalil, the former prime minister, and Kamal Hassan Ali, the foreign minister (later prime minister). Clearly, both sides tried to serve the interests of their respective countries but this did not prevent them from getting close to each other and establishing a frank and comprehensive dialogue.

I inherited from Moshe these close relations with both personalities but, when I returned to Egypt in 1990, their political influence had dwindled and they were no longer in public office – both had been appointed to leading positions in two important Arab banks. This did not prevent them from always receiving Israeli delegations and diplomats with open arms. They helped me many times to solve delicate problems and conveyed messages to President Mubarak until I succeeded in establishing more direct links through the head of his cabinet for intelligence matters, Dr Mustapha Al Fiki. I inherited from Moshe many more relationships, since he always made me participate in all his meetings and allowed me to develop relations of my own at all levels.

At the first staff meeting I have already mentioned, Moshe (still full of expectations) stated that he personally intended to stay in Egypt for five years and that he expected all of us to do the same. We thought that he was joking and we all burst into laughter. Knowing the difficult situation that prevailed in Cairo, none of us was ready to take such a commitment upon himself. We were dedicated to our mission and to peace no less than Moshe but we had gone through a very difficult year and could not envisage four more years of harassment and frustration. We did not believe that Moshe himself would be able to live up to his statement. We were wrong; not only did he stay for five years, but he served in Cairo seven long years, breaking all records of longevity in a single posting.

In the long run, Moshe obtained from us what he had wanted. Many of his staff served in Cairo for five years and more, though not in one stretch. All ambassadors to Cairo came from among the diplomats who had worked with him and all of them fulfilled the five-year quota he had established. Shimon Shamir, who replaced Moshe, had been the head of the Israeli Academic Center; David Sultan and I served with him as minister plenipotentiary; and Zvi Mazel, the present ambassador, was at the time political counselor. He too has reached the quota established by Moshe. None of us, including Moshe Sasson, can compete with Mohamed Bassiuni, the Egyptian ambassador to Israel, who has been in the country for 19 years in one stretch. However, this is not a fair comparison since – let us admit in all frankness – the material and moral conditions prevailing in Tel Aviv are by far better than those prevailing in Cairo.

Professor Shimon Shamir, who became the third ambassador, had joined the diplomats residing in Cairo almost one year after the establishment

47

of the embassy. He volunteered to head the Israeli Academic Center. Formally, he was not attached to the embassy in order to allow him greater freedom of action and to stress the center's academic independence. He had a regular Israeli passport and a regular Egyptian labor visa (which I worked strenuously to obtain for him) and did not enjoy diplomatic immunity and privileges. The idea of establishing academic centers in both Cairo and Tel Aviv to foster relations between the universities of both countries was first raised during the official visit of President Navon to Egypt and was approved by President Sadat himself. The Egyptian foreign ministry was not, to say the least, over-enthusiastic about the idea and dragged its feet for many months. Finally, with the help of Boutros Ghali (who was at the time minister of state for foreign relations), we concluded the agreement's details in a stepped-up negotiation conducted by me as chargé d'affaires. We had to accept a series of drastic limitations on the center's activities but our main goal was to increase our presence in Egypt and open even a small window to the local intelligentsia. We hoped that, with time, the momentum of peace and the dynamic of interaction would prevail on all restrictions.

Shimon Shamir was the right man in the right place. He enjoyed an excellent academic reputation, knew Egypt well, spoke fluent Arabic and possessed administrative capacities and tenacity of purpose. Within a few weeks, he created from scratch a well-organized center that became a pole of attraction to Egyptian students. This was not what the authorities had in mind. They took stringent steps to block his activities but he was not discouraged and continued to work with all his energy. In one case, he decided to meet the students' insistent requests and open a few Hebrew courses. He published details on the center's advertisement board (like all of us, he had no access to any other advertising facilities). A few days later, I was urgently summoned to the ministry of foreign affairs and told in no uncertain terms that the center was not allowed to indulge in teaching Hebrew since it was an academic and not a cultural center. Shamir would be expelled from Egypt within 24 hours unless he cancelled the courses and removed the advertisement from the center's board. We had no choice but to yield to the Egyptian ultimatum. Shimon 'swallowed the bitter pill' reluctantly and continued to look for new fields of activity. The very existence of the academic center, even in its very limited scope, was a thorn in the flesh of the Egyptian press and from time to time it initiated campaigns of slander, depicting it as 'a hotbed of spying and subversive activities' and calling for its immediate closure. The center was a constant feature regardless of who headed it. (When I returned to Egypt in 1990, the center and its director, Professor Yossi Ginat, were still a 'punch bag' for the press though its activities had not substantially increased and the straightjacket imposed by the authorities was far from having been loosened).

In spite of everything, Shimon Shamir managed to breathe life into the center and crystallized around himself a small group of Egyptian scholars who supported the peace process. His house was open to all. He, and his charming wife Daniella, were excellent hosts and were liked by all Israelis in Cairo. After some two years, Shimon Shamir left Egypt and resumed his academic functions in Israel.

He was 'called back to the flag' in 1988, when Moshe Sasson ended his tenure, and was appointed by Shimon Peres (at the time minister of foreign affairs) as ambassador to Egypt. He did not stay long; in 1990 he resigned the position with the formation of a narrow-based Likud government. He did not heed the insistent requests of the foreign minister (David Levy) to continue in his functions up to the end of his contract, claiming that he could not represent a government whose stands in relation to the peace process did not concur with his own. My appointment as the fourth Israeli ambassador to Egypt came against this background. The transfer of office was thorough and friendly – Shimon gave me a comprehensive written review on the functioning of the embassy and on the relations between the two countries and tutored me extensively on various topics in a series of meetings.

The widely publicized circumstances of Shimon's resignation and the motives he expressed made my first steps as ambassador to Egypt more difficult. The Egyptians saw him as a genuine hero – an idealist who did not hesitate to resign his high position in order to defend what he believed in. I, on the other hand, appeared to be an opportunist who had forsaken his principles in return for promotion. My task was not easy: I had not only to restore my personal standing but also to convince the government and people of Egypt that the new government in Israel was determined to move forward with the peace process no less than the previous one. I also had to convince the Egyptian leaders to resume the dialogue with the new Israeli government and – first and foremost – to overcome their distrust of Prime Minister Itschak Shamir and his commitment to peace. At first, I met stubborn opposition and my interlocutors frequently brought forward Shimon Shamir's resignation to vindicate their position that it was useless to deal with the new government. It took me many weeks of strenuous efforts to change the situation and convince the Egyptians to resume the dialogue with Israel.

During the visit to Cairo of a delegation of the Center for Peace in the Middle East (which I had helped organize down to the smallest details), I was asked to lecture about Israeli–Egyptian relations. After my exposé came questions and answers. One delegation member bluntly asked me how it was possible that I, who, as everyone knew, shared Shimon Shamir's political convictions, could represent the new government. I answered that there was a basic difference between Shimon and me:

> Shimon was a political appointee of the previous government and as such it was his legitimate right to resign if he reached the conclusion that he could no longer validly represent Israel. I, on the

other hand, was a career diplomat whose duty was to represent any government in place and do his best to promote its policy lines exactly as a lawyer had to defend his clients to the best of his ability.

I stressed that it was Shimon's right to resign even if it was evident that his step would have a negative impact on relations with Egypt. I, as a career diplomat, did not have this privilege and I concluded: 'One should not spit into the well from which one drinks.' It was clear from the context that what I meant was that career diplomats like me should not criticize the government they represented or publicly voice opinions against its policies.'

A few days later, two regional weeklies in Israel came out with bombastic titles on their front pages: 'Dowek – Shimon Shamir spat in the well from which he was drinking'. As a matter of course, the national press followed suit. I immediately wired the ministry explaining what had happened and requested to convey the text of my telegram to Shimon Shamir. I thought that things had been straightened out. However, it was not so. Shimon and his wife came to Cairo for the tenth anniversary of the Academic Center. We exchanged a few words but I could feel that they were both very cold. They also did not attend a dinner that my wife and I hosted in honor of all the former directors of the Academic Center. It was clear that the incident was not closed for Shimon Shamir and that he still had a grudge against me though my hands were clean. When we met again two years later, on the occasion of a dinner given by the director of the Egyptian department, Zvi Gabai, in honor of my replacement to Cairo, David Sultan, he turned his back on me. We never met again. For my part, I have only friendship and admiration for Shimon and his wife.

Incidentally, history repeated itself for Shimon Shamir. At the end of 1995, the Rabin–Peres government appointed him the first Israeli ambassador to Jordan. A few months later, he found himself in the same circumstances as he had experienced in Egypt: political upheaval, elections and, in their wake, a new government that was not to his liking. David Levy again assumed the position of foreign minister and requested Shimon to continue the excellent job he was doing in Jordan. This time, the request did not go unheeded – Shimon did not slam the door in the face of the new government and continued in his functions until the last day of his contract. It seems that the lesson of Egypt had been learned and digested.

After Shimon Shamir, I became the fourth Israeli ambassador to Cairo. My experiences in Egypt are reflected in this book and so it is unnecessary to elaborate further here. David Sultan (presently ambassador to Canada) replaced me. During my tenure, he was deputy director-general for mid-eastern affairs and kept in daily contact with me. He was well aware of the ups and downs in our relations with Egypt and had a deep insight into the Egyptians' mentality and policies. Like me he was born in Egypt and spoke fluent Arabic (he studied it at the Hebrew University having immigrated to Israel at a very young age). Indeed, he replaced me twice in Cairo: at the end of 1983 as minister plenipotentiary and at the end of 1992 as ambassador. He was lucky to serve in one of the best periods – a period marked by intensive contacts and openness in the wake of the change of government in Israel. Nevertheless, he also experienced many difficulties and had very unpleasant experiences. Among other 'jewels', the Egyptian media accused him of having killed with his own hands Egyptian prisoners in the Six-Day War of 1967. This accusation and other slanders against him brought a wave of threats on his life that compelled him to request the ministry to shorten his stay in Egypt. At the urge of the foreign minister, Shimon Peres, he remained in Egypt up to the conclusion of the normal course of his tenure and continued to do his utmost to improve relations between the two countries.

Zvi Mazel began his tenure as the sixth ambassador to Egypt at the end of 1996, with the election of the Netanyahu government. Indeed, he volunteered for the post, relinquishing an appointment as ambassador to Belgium. He is one of the Cairo veterans, having served as political counselor in the first Israeli team in Cairo. He knows perfectly well Egyptian issues, what can be expected and what is the margin of maneuver allowed by the Egyptian authorities. At first, his tenure was even more difficult than that of his predecessors. There was a further deterioration (if it is possible!!) in relations that were between the two countries and he had to make use of all his skills and patience 'to keep his head above water'. With the election of Ehud Barak and the return of the Labor Party to power in Israel, things now seem to be improving (though I doubt if we can expect a dramatic breakthrough). I wish him and his successors, from the bottom of my heart, the greatest success. I am convinced that all the people of Israel join me in these wishes: their success is indeed our success – the success of peace.

I will now turn to the Egyptian ambassadors in Israel. Substitution among them has been very small and indeed, until now, there have been only two. The first ambassador was Saad Mortada, a career diplomat who came to Tel Aviv in a straight line from Morocco; I met him in the early 1980s before I went to Cairo as minister plenipotentiary. In accordance with diplomatic protocol, I asked to pay a courtesy call on my counterpart, Mohamed Bassiuni (the present ambassador), and be introduced on that occasion to the ambassador. When such a request is made, the custom is to receive the visiting diplomat in the ambassador's office and hold a threesome meeting. I was surprised, when I arrived at the Egyptian embassy, to be taken first to Bassiuni's room for a meeting of about 15 minutes and afterwards to the ambassador's room for a long one-on-one session. From both conversations, I concluded that the personal relationship between the two men was very strained. It was clear that Mortada wanted to humiliate Bassiuni and hint to me – and through me to the ministry of foreign affairs – that Bassiuni's position in the embassy was marginal despite his official title. Mortada was very friendly and open, especially after he learnt that I was Egyptian-born and spoke fluent Arabic. He devoted most of our conversation to Bassiuni. He complained that, instead of appointing an experienced professional diplomat as his number two, the ministry had sent him an intelligence colonel, who had been for many years military attaché in Damascus and was married to a Syrian lady. He stressed that, in a country as sensitive as Israel, he needed someone who could do real diplomatic work and help him to rapidly foster relations between the two countries. Mortada also expressed his doubts about Bassiuni's commitment to peace and accused him of seeking to undermine his position in both Israel and Egypt and of trying to push him out and take control of the embassy.

I remained absolutely silent and did my utmost not to show any reaction on my face. I certainly did not disclose that, in my short meeting with Bassiuni, he had been at pains to tell me that, though Mortada was bearing the title of ambassador, he himself was the one really in charge of the embassy. He had explained in great secrecy that he was the personal envoy of vice-president Hosni Mubarak (at the time directly responsible for all intelligence agencies) and reported directly to him or to his chief of cabinet, Osama Elbaz. Bassiuni also expressed his readiness to help me overcome any difficulty I might experience in Cairo and advised me, 'as a friend', that if I wanted things to move 'quickly and in the right direction', I should raise such matters with him and not with Mortada.

I was not surprised when, at the end of our meeting, Mortada also volunteered to help me overcome difficulties in Cairo and requested me to disregard diplomatic protocol and keep in close contact with him, and not Bassiuni. Naturally, I accepted his generous offer, as I had previously done with Bassiuni, and thanked him profusely. To be frank, I never took advantage of either offer. Very soon after my arrival in Cairo, I grasped that the problems that confronted us were well beyond the scope of the two diplomats' influence. All our difficulties and the stalemate in the normalization process were, beyond any doubt, the result of an overall strategic decision taken at the highest level and whose implementation was supervised at the highest level. Neither Mortada nor Bassiuni could help.

After this first meeting, I met Ambassador Mortada many times, mostly in Egypt, on the occasion of joint committee meetings and VIP visits. I was very impressed with his personal charm, wide culture, openness, sensitivity and absolute commitment to peace. He once told me how President Sadat had come to appoint him the first Egyptian ambassador to Israel: in 1977 he had personally dealt, in his function as ambassador to Morocco, with the technical arrangements of the Dayan–Al Tohami meeting, which paved the way for Sadat's historic visit to Jerusalem. In view of the highly confidential nature of these contacts, he reported directly to the president's office and it seems that Sadat was impressed with his efficiency and his genuine enthusiasm for peace. In due time, he was urgently summoned to Cairo and offered the post. He accepted promptly though he was aware that many of his colleagues in the ministry of foreign affairs had declined 'the honor'. He did so gladly because he supported Sadat's peace initiative with all his heart and wanted to bring his own contribution to the process.

A few days later, he was again summoned to Sadat. This time, he received the 'fatherly advice' to marry again as soon as possible so that he would be able to meet his social obligations in Israel in the best possible manner. Mortada, who had lost his wife a few months earlier and was very attached to her, was still in shock and was not thinking of remarrying. However, he had to comply (in Egypt, a president's advice is tantamount to an order). With the help of his family, he found a suitable match – a very rich lady of excellent family and popular among the Egyptian jet set. Two months later, before his new wife had even set foot in Israel, he was compelled to divorce in the wake of an unpleasant scandal that had become a favorite theme of gossip in Cairo. He took up his post by himself and, within a few weeks, he became the most popular ambassador in Tel Aviv.

Unfortunately, his mission was cut short. After the massacre of Sabra and Shatila, perpetrated by the Lebanese Christian militias in September 1982, he was summoned to Cairo 'for consultations'. First, he expected to return to Tel Aviv within a few weeks but the consultations (which never took place) dragged on. After a few months, on reaching the official age limit, he was compelled to retire. For a long time, Egyptian society, and even his own colleagues in the ministry of foreign affairs, ostracized him. It seems that he had been too dedicated to his mission and thus perceived as a collaborator with the enemy. Ambassador Sasson and I continued to see him regularly and did our best to cheer him up. He finally left Egypt for the United States, where he had previously received a scholarship.

Despite unceasing Israeli pressure, the Egyptian authorities did not send back their ambassador to Tel Aviv. Very soon, they reached the conclusion that they could freeze the situation for as long as they wished without risking an American backlash (the only thing which might have deterred them). Israel herself had a very small margin of maneuver: it could not afford to call back its ambassador or take drastic measures that might jeopardize the entire peace process. Indeed, the United States had indicated beforehand (maybe inadvertently) that it would condone the recalling of the Egyptian ambassador to Israel for a short while. Immediately after the Sabra and Shatila massacre, Kamal Hassan Ali summoned the American ambassador, Alfred Atherton, and informed him that the Egyptian government was 'considering the possibility of recalling for consultations its ambassador to Israel with a view to calming outraged public opinion'. Atherton's only reaction was: 'It is the least you can do!' That was the green light the Egyptians were waiting for and the very next day Mortada was instructed to return immediately to Cairo for consultations. At first, the Egyptians claimed that it would take a few weeks for public opinion to calm down, but time passed and the ambassador remained in Cairo.

Israel increased its pressure and, later, the United States also tried to convince Egypt that it was high time to send back its ambassador. On every occasion, including in meetings with President Ronald Reagan, the matter was raised and President Mubarak would solemnly pledge that 'in the nearest future, the Egyptian ambassador will take up again his posting in Tel Aviv'. Alas, these promises were never kept and, each time the matter was raised, new promises were made and so on and so forth. There were no serious reactions, either on the part of the US or of Israel. Indeed, what could Israel have done after it had completed the withdrawal from the whole of Sinai? Recall its ambassador for consultations thus relinquishing the main outward symbol of peace? Cut diplomatic relations with Egypt? Freeze the scarce trade between the two countries or the non-existing cultural relations? Threaten a military attack? All these measures would have been totally counterproductive and would have dealt a deadly blow to peace when it was still so frail! The US was also reluctant to 'use muscle'; it had much wider interests in the region and believed that the crisis could be overcome in time without major confrontation.

The Egyptians got the message loud and clear. They made the issue one more haggling card in their diplomatic arsenal for achieving their goals of the moment. First, they put as a precondition for the ambassador's return the ceasing of the fighting in Lebanon. When the guns fell silent, they demanded free and secure passage for Arafat and his men from Beirut. When this too was achieved, they demanded the total and unconditional withdrawal of Israel from Lebanon. Finally, when this goal was also attained (to the exclusion of a small security zone), they linked the ambassador's return to the settlement of the conflict over the small Taba enclave in Sinai.

It took six whole years for the consultations between the government of Egypt and its ambassador to Israel to come to an end. Only after Israel's withdrawal from Taba, as a result of arbitration between the two countries, was Mohamed Bassiuni promoted to the rank of fully-fledged ambassador. During the whole period, he had been acting as chargé d'affaires a.i. He is still Egypt's ambassador and he has been in Israel altogether 20 years (indeed, from day one), of which 18 years as chief of mission. Today, in retrospect, I have no doubt that, as Mohamed Bassiuni told me at our first meeting, he was the real boss even when officially Mortada was the ambassador.

Bassiuni is, without doubt, one of the most successful ambassadors I have met in my long career. He is a real 'phenomenon of nature' that cannot be explained rationally: a person of a rather simple and sympathetic appearance, with a limited knowledge of English and Hebrew (after

19 years!!!) who has managed to become one of the most popular personalities in Israel (Israelis included!). He is invited to each and every event – official or private, people crowd around him and are eager to be invited to one of his parties. He and his wife, Nagwa, are lavish hosts and receive all their guests with open arms and a shining smile. He has gone through seven Israeli governments without losing any of his influence. Each time a political upheaval in Israel takes place, he maneuvers swiftly and skillfully and always falls on his feet. All doors are open for him and his door is open for everyone. He can, within minutes, arrange for himself an audience with the president, the prime minister, the foreign or defense ministers, the chief justice, the chief of staff, the Knesset's president or indeed with any minister, army officer, high official, politician or private person that he wishes to meet. In my two periods in Egypt we used to joke that, after a meeting of one of the Knesset committees Bassiuni received, within a few hours, a comprehensive report on the proceedings from every side: from coalition and opposition members, journalists and even from the secretaries who wrote the minutes ... Believe me, we were not far from the truth!

Over the years, he has become one of the *khevra* ('one of us'). Many Israeli politicians of the highest stature do not hesitate to consult him on very delicate matters. They heed his advice and even decide with him on moves that have very wide implications. Others, from all strata of Israeli society, come to him with all kinds of suggestions for fostering co-operation between the two countries and for joint activities. He receives everyone, listens to every word, does not discourage any proposal and incites his interlocutors to persevere though he knows – better than anyone else – what are his government's policies and what are the limitations imposed on normalization. He promises – without a blink – his fullest support and pledges to send an urgent report to his ministry together with his warm recommendation. Needless to say that no report and no recommendation are ever sent. Indeed (as Bassiuni knows so well), even if they *had* been sent, they would not have brought about the slightest change in the normalization policy as the Egyptian authorities at the highest level have determined it. Naturally, as things do not move and the Israelis return to see him, Bassiuni hints (and often explains explicitly), that the Israeli embassy in Cairo is not active enough or does not know how to go about the matter. I used, especially during my second tenure, to send the ball back into his court. I wrote to the Israelis, sending a copy to Bassiuni, warmly supporting their suggestions, and bringing to their knowledge that the Egyptian ministry of foreign affairs had not yet received Bassiuni's report or recommendations. I also requested them to send me a copy of Bassiuni's report so that I could pursue the matter further and bring it to a positive conclusion ... I do not know if my letters embarrassed Bassiuni or convinced his Israeli interlocutors that the Israeli embassy in Cairo was not at fault. What I know for certain is that the matter under discussion would never be raised again.

Over the years, Bassiuni has managed to establish fairly close links with most prominent people in Israel including high-ranking army officers, government officials, intellectuals, journalists, industrialists and top politicians from all sides of the political rainbow. He neglects no one and maintains cordial relations with the extreme right and the extreme left including the orthodox religious parties and the Arab parties, large or small. There is no one who understands better than he the complexities of Israeli internal politics and the yearnings and weaknesses of the average Israeli politician – in this field he is a fully-fledged professor and he makes the most of it. To a great extent, he is the 'father' of the Egyptian carrot-and-stick policy especially when it comes to invitations and visits to Egypt (see chapter 11).

No wonder that we Israeli diplomats in Egypt looked, with much frustration and envy, on Bassiuni's privileged position in Israel and the very wide margin of action he was allowed (and still is) as compared with our own gloomy situation in Cairo. We were all fond of him as a person and maintained good personal relations with him but how could we turn a blind eye to the total asymmetry between the treatment we received and that given to him? We could not publish even a small ad in the Egyptian media while Bassiuni starred every second day on Israeli television screens, radio and newspapers! More than once, we demanded at the political and administrative levels that steps be taken to ensure fair reciprocity of treatment. In other words, we demanded corrective steps in the manner in which Bassiuni was treated in Israel to make it more consistent with the treatment we received in Cairo. But it was to no avail – we were told that, in an open and democratic society such as ours, it was neither feasible nor desirable to do so. Some of our interlocutors even added that Bassiuni might be offended and that it would make them feel uncomfortable 'because he is such a nice person'. People continue to flock around him and flock to his parties. In one case, when he insisted on donating medicines to the health services in the Gaza strip, the Israeli defense forces took him in an army helicopter from one dispensary to another with the intention of convincing him that there was no shortage of medicines. Clearly, Bassiuni was not convinced – it was preposterous to think that he would admit that the dispensaries were well provided for, when the donation was meant to serve Egypt's propaganda needs. Bassiuni would not have admitted that there was water in the ocean if it stood in contradiction to his government's instructions!

Incidentally, Bassiuni's position in Egypt is much less comfortable than his position in Israel. The permanent staff in the ministry of foreign affairs consider him an outsider and are jealous of his direct links with the presidency. For his part, he retaliates by not sending copies of his reports to the ministry. There were many cases when high officials directly in charge of a specific matter were not aware of Bassiuni's initiatives and requested me to postpone a discussion 'until the report from the embassy in Tel Aviv arrives by diplomatic pouch'. During foreign minister David Levy's official visit to Egypt, we were surprised to note that in events organized by the Egyptian foreign ministry, Bassiuni was not seated in accordance with the rules of diplomatic protocol and was relegated to the back seats. In events we organized, we always made sure we bestowed on him all due honors and seated him on Levy's left side as required by protocol (the Egyptian foreign minister being seated on Levy's right).

In conclusion, Bassiuni is an asset to Egypt of the highest order. I do not see, as long as he continues 'to deliver the goods' in such an excellent manner, why Egypt should renounce his services in the foreseeable future and it will probably keep him in Israel for many more years. One should also not forget that, if he is replaced, his successor would have to present his credentials in Jerusalem with all the implications this step carries. For obvious reasons, Egypt prefers to postpone as long as possible dealing with the matter. It is regrettable that towards the end of 1998, a sad and rather obscure scandal befell Bassiuni: an Israeli belly dancer accused him of attempting to rape her. The Israeli authorities closed the case for lack of serious grounds but she continued to seek damages. I am convinced that Bassiuni will overcome this incident and that he will continue to be, as he has always been, popular with the Israeli public and close to the Israeli top brass. I by no means rejoice at his plight – on the contrary, I feel genuinely and deeply sorry for him. However, when he shouted at Israeli journalists that 'I cannot bear the situation here any more. Everyone in Israel hates me. I am the target of constant attacks', I could not refrain from thinking about the plight of our diplomats in Cairo and the daily insults and difficulties that they are compelled to swallow with a smile. Throughout Bassiuni's tenure in Israel, he has received from everyone the most privileged treatment possible. If only the Israeli ambassadors in Cairo had received a hundredth part of such 'terrible' treatment, they would have been more than gratified! In any case, as I am writing these pages, the Egyptian government has extended Bassiuni's tenure by one more year and I am sure he will continue to do an excellent job.

It is important to point out that Ambassador Mortada (Bassiuni's predecessor) was totally wrong when, at our first meeting, he raised doubts about Bassiuni's commitment to peace. There is no doubt in my mind that Bassiuni is absolutely committed to peace and works, to the best of his ability, to widen its scope. True, as one should expect from any diplomat, he implements his government's policies to the last detail even when these policies are controversial and contradict plain common sense and reality. He does so with tenacity, making the most of each and every opportunity open to him. I take my hat off to him, though I know that his success is mostly due to the shortsightedness and eagerness to please of his Israeli interlocutors and sometimes to their misplaced trust. In the history books on Israeli–Egyptian relations in this very delicate period,

Bassiuni will certainly have a very prominent place even though he did not have the privilege of being the first Egyptian ambassador to Israel. He has, indeed, contributed to shaping these relations for almost 20 years without interruption – from day one to this very day. There is no one else on either side of the fence who can pride himself with such a record (to the exclusion maybe of Osama Elbaz, President Mubarak's political adviser).

I cannot conclude this chapter without dedicating some lines to the diplomatic staff, in both embassies, whose contribution to promoting peace between the two countries has been so important. Ambassadors are like generals – as skilful as they may be, they cannot conduct wars without soldiers and certainly not win wars without dedicated soldiers. The first team of Israeli diplomats in Egypt was composed exclusively of volunteers who had taken upon themselves the difficult task of building peace with Egypt in spite of the dangers to their personal safety of serving in a hostile environment. The political officers came, as a matter of course, from the ministry of foreign affairs. They all mastered Arabic fairly well and had a wide knowledge of the mid-eastern intricacies. In the euphoria prevailing in those first days of peace, the Israeli embassy in Cairo was planned to be one of the biggest in the world.

Very quickly, it became clear that obstacles and difficulties were scattered at each step and that it was practically impossible to develop diplomatic, social, cultural or commercial activities (and indeed any kind of activity) in an orderly manner as in an embassy functioning under normal conditions. To our sorrow, until this very day, the Israeli embassy in Cairo is still not a normal embassy and is experiencing the same problems it has met from day one. The first team underwent many major crises but no one broke down. On the contrary, Israeli diplomats went out of their way to prevent needless confrontations. Life was particularly difficult for male diplomats' spouses who, in the conditions prevailing in Cairo, were deprived of any form of social or cultural activities and had literally nothing to do in the very long hours during which their husbands were going about their diplomatic tasks. Shulamit Shamir, Yitshak Shamir's wife, intervened on their behalf and convinced the ministry to employ all of them (to the exclusion of the ambassador's and the minister's wives) for four hours every day – over and above the regular staff allocated to the embassy.

When I returned to Cairo in 1990, things were not too different but in the meantime the euphoria and great expectations of the first days had given place to the harsh realities of life. The parameters of the embassy activities – in light of the restrictions imposed by the Egyptian authorities – had become clear beyond any doubt and, consequently, the diplomatic and local staff had been substantially reduced. The feeling of pioneering that characterized the first team had faded away and it had become difficult to find 'volunteers' for vacant posts. Very few diplomats were willing to accept a posting that involved intensive work (which bore practically no fruit), social ostracism, daily insults and security dangers of the highest order. Many posts remained unfilled for long periods. When minister plenipotentiary Eli Shaked concluded his stay, this most important position remained vacant for almost six months. Finally, a volunteer recruited from outside the ministry – former Knesset member Yaakov Gil who arrived in Cairo after I had left for India – replaced him.

Altogether, the number of political officers had been reduced to two – a political counselor (Dorith Shavit) and a second secretary (Yaakov Brosh). I was compelled to entrust part of the diplomatic tasks to administrative and consular officers in addition to their regular tasks. For Dorith Shavit, a woman diplomat in a Muslim country, it was not easy to fill such an important position but she overcame all the difficulties and indeed became my right hand, especially after the departure of Eli Shaked. As compared with the political section, the number of consular officers had increased in view of the growing difficulties encountered by Israeli tourists visiting Egypt. Most of the staff wives were still working in the embassy but they were now included in the regular staff following a reduction in the number of secretaries and other administrative officers from Israel.

During my two periods in Egypt (and, I assume, in between and after my departure from Egypt), the whole Israeli team was like one big family. They cared for each other, helped one another, solved together the problems of daily life and maintained close social relations after working hours in addition to the cultural and social activities organized by the embassy, the staff cultural committee and the Academic Center. They even published a bulletin named *Chattering on the Nile*, which was a ray of light for the staff and their families. There is no doubt that the difficult conditions prevailing in Egypt brought us together and helped alleviate clashes of a personal nature. To this very day, we have a deep friendship for each other and meet periodically to remember the old days. The title Egypt Veteran has become some kind of 'title of nobility' that all who served in that country, for short or long periods, are proud to bear.

For our colleagues who served in the consulate general in Alexandria, the situation was even worse than it was in Cairo. They were only two: a diplomatic officer and an administrative officer with their small families. They experienced all the difficulties we encountered in Cairo but they had no 'compensation' in the form of self-organized social and cultural activities. They also missed the intensive movement of delegations and VIP visits that we had in Cairo, which brought us opportunities to meet for working purposes with our Egyptian counterparts and participate in social functions. Furthermore, they had very little to do as a result of the limitations imposed on their activities by the Egyptian authorities.

When I came back to Egypt in 1990 in the capacity of ambassador, I thought I would be able to bring about at least an incremental change in the activities of our consulate in Alexandria. With the help of the then consul-general, I prepared a comprehensive plan of action that covered a diversity of fields and which, so I hoped, would allow us to finally breathe life into our consulate. It was to no avail! We met with the impervious wall of Egyptian obstructions and limitations. More than once, I considered recommending the closure of the consulate in view of the impossibility to fulfill minimal consular or diplomatic tasks. I refrained from doing so because lowering our flag in Alexandria would have meant that 'harassment pays' and that the Egyptian authorities had got what they had been striving for. Nevertheless, in my concluding report before leaving Cairo, I included a suggestion to that effect and recommended opening instead a consulate in Sharm el Sheikh in view of the ever-increasing consular incidents in Sinai. Indeed, in accordance with the peace treaty, Israel was entitled to do so even without closing its consulate in Alexandria but it seemed to me that there was no point in continuing 'to waste money' on a representation that was not allowed minimal activities by the local authorities.

We also had a large number of Egyptian functionaries in various administrative capacities: e.g. Arabic secretaries, drivers, trade and tourism officers, maintenance and cleaning staff. It had not been an easy task to recruit them because, at the outset, in spite of the heavy unemployment, Egyptians were reluctant to work in the Israeli embassy for fear of being branded 'traitors', boycotted socially or harassed by the authorities. Paradoxically, we finally recruited them with the help of the Egyptian security services, which in any case compelled local staff to report daily on what 'their eyes saw and their ears heard'. We had nothing to conceal and everyone was welcome to see and hear what we were doing and saying.

Most of the local staff that were recruited in the first days still work in the embassy and continue to serve faithfully their two masters – the Egyptian security services and the embassy of Israel (in that order!). When I returned to Egypt in 1990, I found most of them in the same positions they had been occupying since the early 1980s and they received me with open arms. To give but one example, my driver (I fired the previous one when I caught him stealing repeatedly and brazenly), Sherif, was a retired non-commissioned officer in the Egyptian army. His brother, an officer in the security service, was one of my personal bodyguards and introduced him to me. I found him most reliable and helpful and he became an integral part of my family. I encouraged him to continue his law studies and, when I left Cairo, I convinced Ambassador Moshe Sasson to hire him as the embassy's legal adviser, responsible for administrative contacts with the Egyptian authorities. He continues in that job to the present day and many Israelis who got involved, or 'were made to get involved' with the law, owe him their release from the not too comfortable Egyptian prisons.

As a matter of course, I know very little about the diplomatic or administrative Egyptian personnel in Israel. They treated me with the utmost courtesy and kindness each time I met any of them. Their number is much bigger than ours in Cairo, their activities go absolutely unhindered and they are free to do whatever it takes to fulfill their mission. There was a time when the Egyptian consular staff worked round the clock issuing visas to the heavy flow of Israeli tourists to Egypt but at this juncture their number has substantially dwindled. They were, however, spared the need to crisscross the country to deal with problems of individual tourists or rescue them from the hands of the authorities, as their Israeli colleagues in Cairo had to do day after day.

Indeed, in addition to Ambassadors Mortada and Bassiuni, I came to know closely only one Egyptian junior diplomat from the staff in Tel Aviv. I met him in Cairo before he was assigned to Israel. He was working in the Israel department in the foreign ministry as third secretary. He spoke fluent Hebrew and, contrary to his colleagues, he did not hesitate to maintain open and constant friendly relations with the Israeli diplomats in Cairo. After a few months, he was appointed to Tel Aviv and we lost contact with him. We did not 'fall off our chairs' when we learned that he had been compelled to leave Israel in a hurry after he proved to be an intelligence officer. A young British woman diplomat, Rona Ritchie, had fallen in love with him and given him ultra-confidential documents. She was repatriated to Great Britain and brought to trial. Our young Egyptian friend vanished into thin air and never tried to contact us again. We could now understand better his unusually friendly behavior (though we had our doubts even earlier) but we were not unduly concerned since, in any case, we knew that everything we did and said was reported on a daily basis to the security authorities.

7 · Social Life

I have already written that, for the first Israeli team, landing in Cairo was similar to the landing of the first man on the moon – a hostile and totally unknown world. True, before us, many Israeli delegations had come but they were kept far from the city center in almost total isolation and were taken in luxurious limousines to meetings, guided shopping and traditional tourist sites. Their contacts with the local population were limited to formal meetings with their official hosts, who, generally speaking, received them with warmth and lavish hospitality. Only very few succeeded in rubbing shoulders with the man-in-the-street or meeting the Egyptian intelligentsia. If they ever managed to do so, it was mostly by chance and for a few minutes. They took back home positive, though superficial, impressions. For them, the most salient experience was their visit to Cairo, the capital of the Arab world. The day-to-day life did not interest them – it was totally irrelevant; their stay never exceeded a few days and was devoted to their specific mission, during which they were pampered by their Egyptian hosts.

For the permanent Israeli team, the situation was totally different. They came to Cairo for a long period, brought with them their families, with the aim of building from scratch a meaningful relationship between the two countries and developing a substantial network of official and personal contacts. They considered themselves pioneers in the fullest sense of the word and were morally ready to endure difficulties and forgo personal sacrifices. However, beyond and above the euphoria of the moment and the sense of duty that animated them, they were ordinary men. The daily problems of life were important to them and to their families; they could not close their eyes to their environment and to the prevailing conditions. To them, everything was important: the atmosphere around them, relations with the local society (or, more exactly, non-existing relations), the standard of schooling, lodging, entertainment possibilities, cultural life, television programs, the supply of food and water, the purchase of cars and their maintenance, personal security, freedom of movement, and such like. Such topics, and many more, that in any other country would have been considered prosaic, were problems of major magnitude in Egypt or were made so by the authorities.

As for the general population, they were soon convinced by their own eyes that Israelis had no tails and were not devils in disguise, as Arab official propaganda had brainwashed them to believe over the years. They received us with warmth and enthusiasm mingled with curiosity and dismay. In the first months, people stopped us in the street and poured on us the most effusive compliments. They spoke about peace in the most superlative terms and expressed genuine grief for the lost decades of warring and warmongering. Shop owners compelled us to sit for long minutes and drink with them Turkish coffee or soft drinks. They wanted to know everything about Israel and Israelis, asked question after question, drank in every word we said and let us leave only with difficulty.

In relation to my Egyptian background, there were funny reactions. People did not realize that I knew fluent Arabic, indeed Egyptian Arabic, and they were literally stunned when, after a few minutes of conversation in English, I began speaking like one of them. They poured compliments on me and mocked the Palestinians and other Arabs who could never rid themselves of their foreign accent, even after residing long years in Egypt. I could not resist pulling their leg a little and I bragged that I had studied Arabic for only a few months. They would marvel at my accomplishment and say: 'We always knew that Jews are intelligent, skillful and diligent.' As a matter of course, after a few moments, I disclosed that I was born in Egypt and that I had studied in Cairo up to the age of 18. I never encountered a negative reaction. On the contrary, my interlocutors became more friendly, embraced me and poured on me numerous *Ahlan wa Sahlan* (welcome) and many typical Egyptian blessings and greetings that cannot be translated into any other language. They would point at me and say with pride: 'He is an *Ibn Balad* (son of the land)! He is one of us.' Many of them would recall with nostalgia King Farouk's era when 'streets where shining clean, the country was full of goods from all over the world and work was plentiful'. They also remembered that hundreds of thousands of foreigners, many of them Jews, had lived in Egypt and made the wheels of the Egyptian economy turn. They wondered why all the Jews had left and what prevented them from returning now that 'peace between us prevails for ever'. I had to use all my diplomatic skills to explain, without offending them, that the vast majority of Jews had not left the country of their free will but had been expelled overnight, totally destitute, leaving all their worldly possessions behind. I was always surprised when, at the end of such conversations, they would agree with me and say: 'What fools [meaning the authorities]! They did not know that the Jews are the salt of the earth and bring progress and prosperity wherever they live. You have left and you have taken with you all the good that was in Egypt.' (They did not mean that the Jews had robbed Egypt of its wealth but that they themselves were a source of wealth for Egypt.)

In my first three years in Egypt (1980–83), the warm feelings of the Egyptian people towards the Israelis did not change despite many difficult crises and the unceasing virulent attacks of the press against Israel, Israelis and Jews. When I returned in 1990, almost ten years later, I found the same positive feelings in the Egyptian people, though the curiosity and enthusiasm of the early days had, to a great extent, faded away. Even in between these two periods, when I visited Egypt in different capacities and could more easily mingle with the crowd, I was greatly impressed by the genuine support of the masses (in opposition to the intellectuals) for peace and by their positive attitude towards Israelis and Jews. It is my deep conviction that this is a stable feature very much linked to the national character of the Egyptian people. Only a dramatic deterioration in relations between the two countries and a reversal to military confrontation could bring about a change for the worse.

For the first Israeli team, the friendly attitude and warmth of the Egyptian people were a source of strength and comfort in the face of the daily strains and stresses – real or artificially created – they encountered at every step. Whenever the atmosphere became tense and problems seemed insolvable, the first team had an infallible recipe to ease the burden of frustration, to muster new forces and to restore their confidence in the peace process. They simply went out into the streets of Cairo and dived into the human sea of the Egyptian crowds in order to feel, straight at the source, the warmth and honesty emanating from the people. In my first period, I would do this constantly. It was easy for me to get rid of my Egyptian bodyguards and go out, by myself or with my wife, and melt into the crowd. Later, as ambassador, it was impossible for me to go out unaccompanied. My Israeli bodyguards, glued to me as if they were parts of my own body, always made sure that my Egyptian bodyguards (and they were plenty and, to their credit, most efficient and trustworthy) also accompanied me in every move I made. No incognito strolls in the streets of Cairo for the ambassador of Israel!

Nevertheless, I did not desist from going out. I would often walk into the streets of Cairo but I was deprived of direct contact with the people, even in the most populous areas. Bodyguards, Egyptians and Israelis, surrounded me from every side, their weapons pointed straight at passers-by. I do not envy anyone who tried to get near me or inadvertently blocked my passage. In the best case, the bodyguards would push him out of my way or, even, lift and remove him from my vicinity. In some cases, if the passer-by protested or showed signs of displeasure, he would receive, as a bonus, one or two slaps. All my requests to treat people more gently and not to aim weapons at them were to no avail. My wife, Sarah, could not swallow this behavior and refused to accompany me in my strolls or outings. It took much convincing, and all my diplomatic skill, to induce her to come with me to shop or simply breathe air.

Riding with me in the official car was also not a very pleasant experience. Behind us tagged along numerous security cars and the whole caravan drove at high speed, never stopping at a red light or in a traffic jam. Sometimes, we drove in very narrow streets against the traffic, compelled cars to stop or climb on the sidewalks, created huge traffic jams and even caused accidents. I could not hear the many insults thrown at us because of the double-glazing but I certainly could see the obscene gestures made at us! Once, when my patience was exhausted, I compelled my Israeli driver to stop the car and went out to apologize to people whose way we had just blocked near our chancery against all traffic rules and minimal courtesy. Startled security men flocked behind me with their weapons aimed at the Egyptian car. A lady, clearly of the upper class, shouted: 'From the moment your chancery moved into this street, our lives became unbearable. Why do you have to drive against the traffic? Even the American ambassador does not allow himself to do so! I have heard you on the BBC and I know that you are doing your utmost to foster peace, but your arrogant behavior – as if you were in a conquered territory – makes the Egyptian people hate you!!' I was confused, I knew she was right but what could I do beyond apologizing and explaining that we had no control over the security measures taken by the Egyptian authorities.

After this incident, I met urgently with the chief of the security service and officially requested him to instruct his men to make security arrangements more palatable for the general population. I specifically demanded that they respect traffic regulations in order to avoid needless incidents and clashes that threw a negative light upon us. He was not too disturbed by the incidents that I had brought to his knowledge and he tried to calm me down with gentle words. However, he did not budge an inch and made it clear that these were the security norms in Egypt and, when it came to the ambassador of Israel, he was not ready to take any superfluous risk by introducing changes of any sort in the security arrangements for courtesy or popularity considerations. I desisted from any further steps and learned to disregard what happened around me.

In flagrant opposition to the behavior of the man-in-the-street, the attitude of the intelligentsia and government officials (including in the foreign ministry!) towards the Israelis was totally different. They were restrained, not to say ice cold. They concealed their hostility with difficulty though they tried hard to show outward correctness and poured nice words and oriental compliments on us. One could feel immediately that they were not sincere. Where were the warmth, the hospitality and the smiles of the common people? It seems that intellectuals did not need any prompting from the authorities to ostracize the Israelis. They followed their ideological leanings. On the other hand, officials were under clear-cut instructions (which are probably enforced up to this very day) not to befriend Israeli diplomats, not to respond to their invitations and not to meet them, even for business purposes and in their own offices, without clearance from their superiors. Sometimes, when we were too insistent, they would accept one of our invitations but, in most cases, they would not show up and would not bother to apologize. Their seats could not be removed in time and they remained around the table, conspicuously vacant, a living insult to the host and the other guests. In time, we came to know what were the limitations of our contacts with government officials and we invited them very seldom to social events that were not directly linked to the visit of a delegation or a VIP invited by the Egyptian government. In the receptions we offered on Independence Day and other festive opportunities, very few officials showed up. Those who came had to receive the green light from their superiors in accordance with well-established criteria and their number clearly reflected the ups and downs of the relations between the two countries and the signal the authorities wished to convey at that point in time. In spite of our frustration, in order not to burn our bridges we did not cease completely to invite government officials to social events. We ceased, however, to give too much importance to their not showing up and we organized buffet events instead of seated events to camouflage last-minute desertions.

Even personal friends (from my childhood in Egypt) had to implement the limitations imposed by the authorities on contacts with Israeli diplomats. Two of my comrades from kindergarten learned from the press about my arrival in Cairo and contacted me on their own initiative. Both had important positions: one was minister plenipotentiary in the foreign ministry; the second was deputy director-general in the ministry of trade. I would invite them from time to time (separately) for lunch in a restaurant and we would recall our youth. We never touched upon politics, internal or external. Suddenly, they both ceased to contact me and, when I took the initiative, only one accepted to meet me in our usual restaurant. He informed me in the utmost secrecy that he had been instructed to discontinue all contacts with me and had no alternative other than to abide by these instructions. Almost ten years later, when I returned to Egypt, they both refused to see me though they had already retired and held no official position. Thus, my last links with my youth were severed forever.

Let me add that Mohamed Bassiuni, who has been in Israel for so many years, has set foot in the Israeli ambassador's residence only once and that was on the occasion of the official visit of the foreign minister, David Levy, in 1991. He never turned down an invitation but he never came and he did not bother to pay even a courtesy call on the Israeli ambassador though he came to Cairo quite often. It seems that fraternizing with Israelis in Tel Aviv and fraternizing with them in Cairo are two different things! The Egyptian diplomats working in the Israel department, whose official duty was to be in constant contact with the Israeli diplomats, never responded to an invitation that was not directly linked to official business such as social events organized in honor of visiting delegations.

We could at least meet them in the ministry whenever we wished. Their colleagues in the other departments refused to see us or delayed answering our requests for a meeting for a long time. We had to apply time and again and request the Israel department to intervene on our behalf. When finally they granted us an audience for a few minutes, they would limit the conversation to small talk or engage in a long monologue justifying Egypt's positions on topics of the hour, repeating stereotyped arguments and clichés we had heard hundreds of times. We never succeeded in establishing a meaningful dialogue or exchanging information as is usual among diplomats with our Egyptian colleagues, even if they dealt with matters that had absolutely no bearing on the middle east.

When the political counselor Zvi Mazel (presently Ambassador to Egypt) succeeded in holding a few working sessions with the deputy director of the African department, we were all stunned and he became our 'Hero of the Day'. But, very soon, the man was transferred abroad and his replacement severed all contacts with Mazel and the Israeli embassy. We did not lose faith and did not despair. We continued trying to establish meaningful contacts despite the unpleasantness and the frustration. It was our mission; we did not come to Cairo to sit idle or visit the pyramids. When doors were slammed in our faces, we tried to come in through the windows but, to our great sorrow, the windows too were hermetically sealed!!

It is difficult to explain or to condone such behavior on the part of Egyptian diplomats whose duties were not directly linked to the middle east. Let us say that they acted under instructions or out of fear of getting into trouble, ideological considerations or even out of sheer impoliteness. But, to this very day, I cannot understand the coarse behavior and the social boycott of the handful of Egyptian diplomats who, in the early 1980s, dealt almost exclusively with the peace process and Israeli affairs. Together with us, they had laid the foundations of relations between the two countries and had done their utmost to foster a comprehensive peace in the region. We met almost every day for long hours, had hundreds of official meetings and private conversations, discussed scores of professional matters, searched jointly for solutions on each and every problem and consulted informally on how to surmount the difficulties of the hour. We exchanged information about our families and matters of a private character and even went so far as to give each other personal advice. It seemed to me that beyond the haggling, the controversies, the divergence of interests and the limitations imposed upon them by their superiors, we had become close and developed a genuine friendship and liking for each other. But, alas, I was wrong, it was but a house of cards that fell apart on the first occasion – the wall of hostility and estrangement between us had never been removed!

During my tenure as permanent representative to the UN in Geneva (1983–86) – between my two Egyptian periods – I was on kissing terms, literally, with the Egyptian ambassador, Saad Farargy, who had been Boutros Ghali's chief of cabinet during my first stay in Cairo. In spite of his good offices, I never succeeded in meeting Egyptian colleagues (or friends, as I considered them) with whom I had worked closely for three whole years when they came repeatedly to Geneva for long periods. There was always a good excuse not to see me! Even when I returned to Egypt in 1990, though most of them had already retired from the service (in Egypt, government officials retire at the age of 60) none of them phoned to greet me or agreed to see me or responded to my invitations to social events. For them, I was a non-entity! Farargy himself, who had been appointed adviser for economic affairs in the presidency, never responded to my repeated invitations and hardly shook my hand when we met incidentally at a social gathering.

Even more shocking, at least for me, was that even the first ambassador to Israel, Saad Mortada – the Pioneer of Peace – who had maintained open relations with me after his mission to Israel was cut short, totally ignored my return to Cairo. I never succeeded in meeting or speaking with him during my stay. I presume that he had succeeded, with time, in restoring his social standing and feared being again ostracized by Egyptian society if he renewed his links with Israeli diplomats.

When I was transferred to India (1992), I paid a courtesy call on the Egyptian ambassador to that country, Adel al Gazar. I was surprised to find out that he was an old friend, from the first days of peace, when he had served as deputy-director of the Israel department in the ministry of foreign affairs. In Delhi, social life is very hectic and we used to meet practically every day. In one-to-one meetings, when no one saw us, he was warm and cordial. At social events (and there were one or two every day), he totally ignored me and passed by me without even nodding as if I were thin air. Only once in three years did he openly come to me at one of the many diplomatic receptions with a great smile on his face not minding being seen by other Arab diplomats fraternizing with the Zionist Enemy. There was a good reason for such odd behavior: he was eager to ask for my help in a delicate security problem related to a projected visit of President Mubarak to India and possible threats on his life. I checked the matter thoroughly and the next day I phoned him and gave him the information that he had requested. He thanked me profusely but after that he went back to ignoring me whenever we met in public. Incidentally, during all the years we served together in India, he did not invite me once to a social event in his residence though he responded many times to my invitations (to the exclusion of the Independence Day receptions). He invited me only once to Egypt's National Day (23 July) in the embassy premises. For obvious reasons, I did not want to act in the same undiplomatic manner as he did. I went, on purpose very late, only to make a point of my presence and, by coincidence, I arrived just as the embassy staff was taking a picture to commemorate the event. The Indian photographer, hearing me speak Arabic, thought I was one of the Egyptian diplomats and literally pushed me into the ambassador's arms for the staff picture. It was a great honor for me but I never received the picture and it is more than probable that after I left the Egyptian staff took another picture to replace the one that I had spoiled with my presence.

Other Egyptian diplomats and personalities who served in India or came on a visit to the country, and whom I knew very well, followed the ambassador's lead and did not maintain any relationship with me to the exclusion of a hurried handshake in an incidental encounter. Let me illustrate with one typical example the Egyptians' unbecoming behavior. A few weeks before my departure from India (November 1995), both the ambassadors of Egypt and Jordan were replaced. I knew both their replacements. The new Egyptian ambassador had served in the early 1990s as counselor in Boutros Ghali's cabinet and we had met frequently in Cairo. The Jordanian ambassador, on the other hand, had served as permanent representative to the UN in Geneva and our chairs were practically glued to one another (because of the seating system in alphabetical order), but we never exchanged a single word or even a nod of the head. On the contrary, at the time (before the peace with Jordan) I used to attack Jordan and embarrass the ambassador. The Egyptian ambassador had arrived earlier and had already presented her credentials but she did not pay me a courtesy visit, as is the diplomatic custom. She also joined the other Arab ambassadors in boycotting the farewell party offered by the dean of the diplomatic corps, the ambassador of Senegal (which at the time did not maintain diplomatic relations with Israel). The Jordanian ambassador not only refused to join the Arab boycott but also requested special permission from the dean to attend the reception in my honor before he had presented his credentials (in accordance with diplomatic protocol, he was not allowed to attend official functions). He embraced me publicly and reminded me of our days in the UN. Later, he asked to take the floor and delivered a short speech full of compliments for Israel and me personally. He later also paid me a courtesy call. The behavior of the two ambassadors shows in the clearest manner the opposite attitudes of their two countries towards the external symbols of peace and their different approach to peace and normalization. It can only be explained by the different standing instructions received by the two ambassadors from their respective governments: one to treat Israeli diplomats as all other diplomats and show them friendship and the other to ignore Israeli diplomats and manifest open hostility towards them on every occasion.

But there are exceptions that warm the heart. Fuad Abu Hadab, the right hand of the Egyptian deputy prime minister, Yussuf Wali, came to India on a short mission. Wali, who had heard about his trip, requested him to take a small gift for me. He accepted gladly and was stunned when he realized that Wali's small gift was two crates of oranges of 30 kilos each. Fuad had to carry them across the Indian Ocean and over half of India until he reached New Delhi and got rid of them, coming personally to my residence to deliver the two crates. For many weeks, I served my guests tasty Egyptian oranges for dessert. To my sorrow, such cases are very rare and as the saying goes, 'it is the exception that proves the rule'.

The unbecoming attitude of government officials towards Israeli diplomats in Egypt was not restricted to foreign ministry officials. The same phenomenon repeated itself in our dealings with all other ministries and public institutions. It was very difficult to be received by these functionaries even when we had important topics to tackle with them that were directly in the framework of their responsibilities. Only a few agreed to see us, after much insistence and after they had duly received the green light from the Israel department in the foreign ministry and the relevant security agencies. Mostly, these meetings were very short and our interlocutors would tell us, gently but firmly, that in all that related to Israel their hands were tied. They refused to go into the substance of the topics we raised and told us bluntly that we had to convey our requests, questions or commentaries through the ministry of foreign affairs, which was the only ministry authorized to deal with Israel-related matters.

The Egyptian political establishment also showed us little cordiality and sympathy. Ministers tried to avoid receiving Israeli diplomats and did not reply to our requests to meet them. We persisted and repeatedly phoned their cabinet. Finally, a few agreed to meet us, after having received due permission from the relevant authorities (read the security services). Most meetings did not go beyond mere courtesy calls and were no less frustrating than being ignored. Meeting the foreign minister (Kamal Hassan Ali and later Ismat Abdel Meguid or Amr Mussa) and the eternal minister of state for foreign affairs (Boutros Ghali) was relatively easy. They were directly in charge of Israeli affairs and had no misgivings in receiving the ambassador of Israel or other Israeli personalities.

When I came to Cairo as ambassador in 1990, I insisted on paying courtesy visits on all ministers in the Egyptian government. To me, it was more a question of principle than a functional need (in any case, matters pertaining to Israel had to be treated through the foreign ministry, exactly as in the early days). It was still difficult to make appointments but persistence paid more than in the past. Most ministers (many of whom I knew personally from my previous stay in Egypt) finally agreed to see me. They received me quite cordially and even engaged in meaningful conversations. Only the minister of education, a well-known doctor whom I had met at a few social events, stubbornly refused to receive me. I did not desist because, in this case, I really did have important matters to discuss with him. Finally, I had no alternative than to request Dr Mustapha Al Fiki, the president's adviser for intelligence, to intervene and arrange a meeting for me. On the spot, he phoned the minister and suddenly all obstacles vanished. The very next day, the minister received me and I complained about the difficulties I had encountered in setting up the meeting, pointing out that I was the ambassador of a friendly country that had been maintaining peaceful relations with Egypt for more than a decade! The minister did not try to evade the topic. On the contrary, he said with the utmost frankness: 'I have nothing against you personally or against Israel. I would have received you a long time ago but I was specifically denied authorization. You are experienced enough to know that, in what pertains to Israel, all strings are in the hands of the security services.'

I knew that he was right and that it would be useless to try and tackle with him issues which were normally under his jurisdiction, but I raised, for nuisance value, a few matters relating to the Israeli Academic Center in Cairo. The minister listened patiently and promised to look into the matter (probably meaning that he would convey what I had said to the security services and to the foreign ministry). Naturally, no problem found its solution either in my meeting with the minister or subsequently. As he had told me with unprecedented frankness, his hands were tied when it came to Israel. That was the case with all other ministries, government institutions and even private persons – they were, and probably still are, under strict instructions not to deal with matters related to Israel.

But to be quite accurate, I did not leave the education minister completely empty-handed – I succeeded in solving one small matter that had no direct bearing on embassy affairs or Israel. I requested him to use his influence on behalf of one of our Egyptian secretaries who had not succeeded in registering her five-year-old daughter in a good school in her neighborhood. The minister was glad that he could be forthcoming at least in this matter and gave me a small note for the school principal in his own handwriting. When I called to his attention that he had forgotten to sign the note, I was stunned to hear him say: 'It is not a slip on my part. Many people ask me to intervene in matters of this nature and it is very difficult for me to refuse. I give them notes duly signed by me but I have instructed school principals to honor only notes that are unsigned like the one I gave you.' Indeed, the unsigned note brought results and the small girl was admitted without difficulty. When I was already in India, I received a very touching letter of thanks from the mother.

In my first days in Cairo, I succeeded in establishing a reasonable working relationship with the chair persons of most committees in both upper and lower houses of parliament. They received me very warmly and expressed great interest in visiting Israel and learning from its experience in the fields under their responsibility. I began extending invitations on all sides, thinking that I had finally found a way to bypass the hostile officialdom. How wrong I was! Indeed, it appeared that there had been an oversight in the tight siege established by the authorities. As soon as the first reports of my conversations began streaming into the security services and to the foreign ministry together with formal requests to receive permission to visit Israel, I was urgently summoned to the director of the Israel department. He requested that in future my appointments with members of parliament be made through the protocol department only. He also gave me advice 'as a friend' not to waste valuable time on committee chairpersons because they had no weight and to limit myself to meeting the chairman of the foreign affairs committee, Dr Mohamed Abdellah. Very quickly, I realized that both the request and the advice had teeth: all my attempts to arrange meetings, directly or through the protocol department, with parliamentarians remained fruitless. Only Mohamed Abdellah agreed to receive me, even at very short notice (he had the green light and could afford to be forthcoming). As the reader must already have understood, not a single member of parliament received permission to visit Israel.

One more door was slammed in our face. However, we were already accustomed to it and our only reaction was to look for other fields of activity where we could establish normal relations. This was not as easy as we had thought. We found that all professional associations and trade unions – lawyers, doctors, academic staff, students, journalists and workers including street sweepers – had passed official resolutions rejecting peace with Israel and forbidding relations with Israelis. These were resolutions that also had teeth: any member that did not abide by them strictly was expelled from the association and ostracized by his colleagues in the profession. Paradoxically, at that time, the various government ministers stood, by law, at the head of the various professional associations, each one in his own field. In other words, Egypt found a subtle way 'to have its cake and eat it'. On one hand, the Egyptian government, as a collective body, apparently fulfilled its obligations under the peace treaty by officially abrogating all the restrictions of the Arab boycott and exchanging ambassadors; on the other hand, each minister individually adopted in the professional association over which he presided a resolution rejecting peace and perpetuating the Arab boycott in everyday life ostracizing Israel and banning contacts with Israelis. Clearly, we could not turn a blind eye to such an outrageous situation and we raised the matter at each opportunity and at all levels of the Egyptian hierarchy. Each time, we received the same stereotypical answer.

> Egypt is a democratic country. The government cannot interfere in the internal affairs of professional associations and trade unions. These are independent and sovereign bodies that do whatever they see fit, free from external influence or interference. The resolutions that have been passed against Israel reflect the profound revulsion of all strata of the Egyptian people at the trampling of Palestinian human rights by Israel and the continuation of the illegal occupation of Palestinian territory.

It is interesting to point out that members of professional associations who visited Israel or maintained open relations with Israelis on behalf of the government or with its tacit blessing were never called to order by their associations and were not punished or expelled. Clearly, the professional associations were not acting on their own initiative. They were under clear-cut instructions from the relevant authorities. Once again, we swallowed the bitter pill and continued to look for alternative fields of action as if nothing had happened. We knew we were debasing ourselves in the Egyptians' eyes and, more so, in our own eyes – it is not easy to be spat at and say that it is raining but this is exactly what we did, and indeed had to do. We were in Egypt to develop friendly relations with its people and government and we could not allow ourselves to be discouraged by obstacles and difficulties. It was our duty to persevere and try to find even a small window through which we could penetrate the Egyptian armor.

After strenuous haggling with the Egyptian authorities, we opened the Israeli Academic Center in Cairo as a bridge to the Egyptian academic setup. But here also, doors remained closed. Universities were and remain the most difficult nut to crack. Indeed no contacts were ever allowed, to the exclusion of a very few exceptional cases. I am ashamed to admit that I personally, with all my Egyptian background, managed to set foot in an Egyptian university only twice. In my first period (1980–83), I decided, with the ambassador's blessing, to try and stampede the universities. I instructed my secretary to make appointments for me with all university rectors both in Cairo and Alexandria. All of them received my request for a meeting but not a single one replied, positively or negatively. They simply ignored our repeated phone calls.

To my great surprise, after a few weeks I received a phone call from the rector of the Ein Shams University (the second largest university in Cairo). He invited me to visit the campus officially the very next day. He sounded anxious to receive a positive answer and, naturally, I did not play hard to get. I came full of expectations and good will, hoping to foster inter-university co-operation. I was received with all due honors and taken everywhere in the campus, meeting with students and academic staff. At a formal meeting with the university board, I put forward several proposals for possible interaction with our universities. The rector not only enthusiastically agreed to all my proposals but also added several suggestions of his own. I hurried back to the embassy and reported in detail to the ambassador and to a staff meeting specially convened for the occasion. Naturally, I also dispatched a long cable to Jerusalem stressing the unique opportunity and requesting adequate funding for the future co-operation program with the Ein Shams University. We were determined to move ahead with maximum speed, but disappointment and frustration were much quicker. Only a few days later, we read in the newspapers that the rector had been removed from office. It appeared that he was involved in a multi-million embezzlement scandal. He was so desperate that he believed that befriending diplomats – even Israeli diplomats – and securing foreign assistance for the university would restore his lost honor and forestall any criminal action against him. My visit must have been the last nail in his coffin. In any case, no co-operation stemmed from my memorable visit to an Egyptian university (in chapter 14, I will deal with the semblance of co-operation between Egyptian and Israeli universities established with US help).

My second visit came almost ten years later and was even more frustrating. In one of my many heart-to-heart conversations with Yussuf Wali, the deputy prime minister and minister of agriculture, I complained that we were given no access to Egyptian universities and were prevented from meeting with students to explain the Israeli standpoint. Wali, in a typical reaction, invited me on the spot to attend the next day the inauguration of an agricultural exhibition organized by his ministry at Cairo University. He urged me to come despite the boycott so that 'everyone knows that the highest authorities in Egypt have no reservation about maintaining friendly relations with Israel and properly receiving its representatives in Egypt'. I could not turn down Wali's invitation though I was experienced enough to know that the boycott policy was dictated by the authorities themselves and would continue to be strictly enforced notwithstanding Wali's gesture. I confess that I was also prompted to accept the invitation by my curiosity to see the campus I had frequented in my youth.

Despite security instructions, I told my driver to fly the Israeli flag on my car so that everyone knew that the Israeli ambassador was being received at Cairo University. Indeed, I was the only ambassador invited to the event and Wali personally received me at the entrance with several of his aides and the university top brass. He embraced me warmly and kissed me on both cheeks. His escort received me with vigorous handshakes and many *Ahlan wa Sahlan* (welcome). I joined the minister's retinue and went everywhere with him as if I were an integral part of his retinue. It was clear that my presence was embarrassing the Egyptians (to the exclusion of Wali himself), especially after the prime minister and many ministers, including the minister of defense, had arrived and joined the official retinue. After a short while, I felt uncomfortable. I did not want to force my presence on the Egyptians and little by little, I remained behind and continued to visit the exhibition on my own (naturally surrounded by my Israeli and Egyptian bodyguards) and melted into the mass of visitors. Two students walked a few steps before me and spoke in loud voices. One of them said that he had heard that the Israeli ambassador had dared desecrate the university campus and was presently at the agricultural exhibition. He added that if by chance he came to meet him, he would tear out, with his own hands, a very delicate and private part of the ambassador's body. His colleague burst into laughter and said that he too would cut his ears and nose and throw him out of the campus. I caught up with the two students and addressed them as calmly as I could in Egyptian Arabic: 'I understand that you are eager to meet the Israeli ambassador. Here he is just in front of you!' At first, they thought that I was pulling their leg but when I added in the juiciest slang a piece of my mind about what they had just said and their sacred campus, they were stunned. I never in my life saw two persons more shocked than our two students (especially after they saw my bodyguards brandishing their weapons). They swore on everything that was dear to them that they had only been joking and had not meant what they had said. They walked with me to up my car, asked numerous questions about Israel and parted with handshakes and effusive Egyptian words of flattery.

As expected, my second visit to an Egyptian university was not a success and did not bring about a breakthrough in our relations with Cairo University. I continued to search for ways to reach the students in their own fortress and I requested on numerous occassions to be allowed to speak to the students face to face. I received polite but negative answers. Universities were (and still are) out of bounds for Israelis: diplomats, academicians or private persons.

The only Egyptians who were interested (and still are) in maintaining normal relations with the Israelis were the businessmen and industrialists. They hoped that they would be able to establish commercial relations (imports and exports) and to promote joint ventures in various fields with the help of Israeli technology and investment. In the first days (up to mid-1981), scores of Egyptian businessmen literally besieged our chancery, thirsty to hear about business opportunities and co-operation projects between the two countries. They also brought forward their own proposals and were keen to move ahead as quickly as possible. Most of them accepted our social invitations with manifest pleasure and reciprocated by inviting us to their houses without inhibitions. But this honeymoon was short-lived. At first, the authorities made it clear to the business community that they had no intention of encouraging trade or other relations with Israel and they did not look favorably on such a flirtation with the Israelis (I will develop this topic in chapter 13). When persuasion failed to diminish the businessmen's enthusiasm, the authorities began taking restrictive steps and did not hesitate, whenever necessary, to use police pressure or other means of dissuasion. The majority of businessmen preferred not to invite trouble and abandoned us, discouraged by the meager results and the severe measures taken by the authorities. Only a few continued to maintain with us social and/or commercial relations, and sometimes both. Many of them were taken in the middle of the night to the premises of the security services, held in small cells, interrogated for long hours and told that the situation was not yet ripe for developing a normal relationship with Israel. Finally, they were released and sent back to their families, but not before being warned categorically to discontinue their relations with Israel and the Israelis if they wanted 'to avoid trouble'. Paradoxically, some of these businessmen were requested to maintain their relations with the Israeli diplomats and even intensify them. The only condition was that they were to report periodically on what we were doing, saying and thinking. In other words, they were to choose between severing ties with the Israeli diplomats or spying on us. To entice them to make the right choice, they were promised to be allowed to do business with Israel.

Indeed, businessmen were not the only ones to be given such a choice. Any person who was in contact with us was as a matter of routine summoned to the security services, threatened and made to choose between ceasing to see us or agreeing to spy on us (I may be using a non-diplomatic word but this is the accurate one!). Many preferred to sever relations with us and told us the reason frankly. A few submitted to the dictate, continued to see us and reported regularly to the authorities.

In spite of all the difficulties, a small group of so-called friends consolidated around us: businessmen, lawyers, journalists, writers, judges, professors, retired officers, politicians, functionaries, agriculturists, women leaders and so forth. We realized that some were friends on 'special commission', others were conditional or temporary friends, but a few certainly became, and remained throughout the years, genuine friends. All of them were very pleasant persons, and of the highest intellectual level. We enjoyed being in their company and exchanged opinions on many issues with them. It was a sort of safety valve that helped us to overcome the feeling of isolation and hostility and ease somewhat the strains and stresses we had to endure. Ironically, there is no doubt that beyond their utilitarian reasons, the Egyptian authorities allowed this small group of people to gather around us for exactly the same reasons that we had for continuing to meet them, though we knew that they were reporting to the security services after each conversation. It seemed that the authorities did after all want to let us have a minimum of social life to ease the pressure but they did take stringent measures to prevent too many Egyptians flocking around us or maintaining relationships with us that were not controlled. Their goal was to convey a two-pronged message: to the Israelis that the Egyptian people did not yet accept them, and to the Egyptians that Israelis were still to be ostracized.

To the credit of our friends, genuine or not, one has to say that they persevered in their contacts with us for many years and, when I returned to Cairo, I resumed my relations with them from the point at which I had left on my departure seven years earlier. Some of our friends paid a heavy price for maintaining relations with the Israeli enemy in the form of social ostracism and attacks in the press. Muslim extremists murdered one of them, Mohamed Foda, a brilliant liberal intellectual. True, there were more profound reasons for his assassination, but there is no doubt his relations with us, and his articles in support of peace and normalization must have had a negative impact.

An interesting case, though not a typical one, is that of Amal Choukri, a painter of the Coptic faith, who glued herself to the Israeli team almost from day one. She claimed not to be afraid of the pressures exerted by the authorities to cut her relations with us and pretended to have stubbornly refused to report to the security services on her contacts with us.

She would respond to all our invitations and invite us regularly to social events in her house. She succeeded in organizing an exhibition of her paintings together with those of Ruth Levine (a renowned Israeli painter) in one of the most select hotels in Cairo, the Meridien. Naturally, the embassy covered all expenses but the very fact that the authorities had allowed such an event to take place was cheering though somewhat strange (in view of their longstanding policy of isolating us). Amal Choukri even managed to receive the green light from the security services to visit Israel, together with her husband, at the invitation of the government of Israel. As for me, I went only once to her receptions. I was suspicious of her pro-Israeli enthusiasm and I did not like her too much as a person. Nevertheless, as I have explained, there was no point in severing our links with her. One more report to the Egyptian security services or one report less did not change the situation. She really went out of her way to please and entertain the Israeli team in Cairo and, frankly speaking, we could not afford to be too selective about our friends.

Amal Choukri's alleged friendship and her open contacts with the Israelis lasted many years until an opposition newspaper published a series of articles branding her as a traitor who fraternized shamelessly with the Zionist enemy out of personal interests. She was threatened with a social and economic boycott if she did not sever her relations with the Israelis. She panicked and published three interviews in the same newspaper admitting that she had security services blessing and that her contacts were aimed at keeping a close eye on the Israelis' plans and inner thoughts. She added many spicy stories, slandering her alleged Israeli friends in the most loathsome manner. As a matter of course, ties with her were totally severed. In my second turn of office in Egypt (1990–92), I met Amal Choukri many times at social events but I totally ignored her though she tried very hard to re-establish contact with me. Not even social isolation could bring me to socialize with her or shake her hand.

Since the opening of the Israeli diplomatic representations in the early 1980s, the Egyptian authorities had relentlessly pursued a policy aimed at reducing to a minimum our contacts with the Egyptian people. Ten years later when I returned to Egypt, nothing had changed – on the contrary, the measures taken by the authorities to implement this policy had become harsher, more conspicuous and more offensive. Let me give only two examples to illustrate what I mean.

In the early 1980s, a handful of young Egyptian intellectuals in Alexandria crystallized around Yitshak Oron, the minister-counselor for cultural relations. They were true idealists who believed in peace and strove to bring together intellectuals and youngsters of both countries. They kept in permanent contact with the consulate-general and met from time to time in private houses. I was astonished, when I came back to Egypt in 1990, to find that the group had managed to continue its activities though the authorities had repeatedly harassed many of them. They came to Cairo especially to renew their contacts with me and asked for my permission to found an Association of Israeli–Egyptian Friendship. It was clear to me that the authorities would never allow such an association to be established – since this would be in flagrant opposition to their policy of isolation and social ostracism. Fearing that they would be made to pay a heavy price for their brazen impudence, I tried in vain to dissuade them. They refused to heed the voice of caution, stressing that after ten years of peace, there should be no objection to such a natural step. They sent letter after letter to the authorities, requesting permission to found the association. The reaction was not long in coming; some of them were arrested and thrown into jail. When they were released, they spoke no more about Israeli–Egyptian friendship. On the contrary, they severed their ties with us and published in the press statements and slanderous stories in the style of Amal Choukri. The group disintegrated and only a very few continued to be in touch with us – who knows at what price and under what conditions?

One of our friends (one of the very few we could define as a genuine friend) gave a reception for his daughter's wedding at the Navy Officers' Club. Naturally, he invited all the Israelis and came personally to deliver the invitations. Since he did not meet me, he phoned later and spoke to me personally to make sure that my wife and I would attend the happy event. On the very same day, he was summoned to the security services, scolded and ordered without ceremony to cancel immediately the invitation to the ambassador of Israel. They did not know that the rest of the staff had also been invited. A few hours before the event, he phoned me and begged me not to come adding, with the utmost frankness, that my coming might jeopardize his future. I accepted his apologies, calmed him down and naturally cancelled my plans to attend the wedding (I did however send a small gift). The other Israelis did not know what had occurred and they all went to the wedding (occasions of that kind being very rare). Those who arrived first were not requested to identify themselves and entered the premises with the crowd of guests. The late-comers were stopped by soldiers in uniform and their invitations checked. They were told that Israelis were not allowed to enter military compounds. They insisted, pointing out that they had been duly invited and mentioning that their colleagues were already seated inside. The soldiers were not convinced, denied them access and ejected them from the club. A few moments later, a group of armed soldiers presented themselves at the Israelis' tables and asked them to leave the club immediately as it was strictly out of bounds for Israelis. There was no point in trying to discuss or resist expulsion (as their diplomatic immunity allowed them to do). They left, deeply hurt by the stinging public affront. The next day, I protested officially to the foreign ministry about such behavior which contravened the rules of elementary politeness, let alone diplomatic protocol. In comparison, I emphasized the excellent treatment and warm hospitality bestowed on the Egyptian diplomats in Israel. The cynical answer I received was more offensive than the insult itself: 'The wedding was a private event. The Egyptian government cannot interfere in the family's considerations as to the list of guests and dictate whom they should welcome or not.'

True, over the years, we managed many times to breach the social boycott and to get round the measures taken to isolate us, 'outfoxing' the security services. It is not a subject of pride for me – on the contrary, it is shaming that we had to resort to such expedients. In any case, sooner or later, the Egyptian authorities always managed to block loopholes and put a brake on our attempts to break the choking ring of hostility and ostracism that they had established around us.

The heavy feeling of isolation and loneliness which was the lot of the first Israeli team in Egypt – and to a great extent of all the teams that followed it – was magnified many times by the poor cultural life and entertainment possibilities. No classical music and no light western music of any kind, no cinemas (all cinemas were crumbling) and no theaters (all plays were in Arabic), no television and no radio (Voice of Israel broadcasts could not reach Egypt). The only entertainment was eating out at five-star hotels, excursions to tourist sites and occasional visits to swimming pools. To this one should add the cultural events organized by the embassy or the Academic Center for the Israeli staff. Children were more fortunate – the American College was for them a real oasis and most of their daily life evolved around it. There were also periods when, for security reasons, we were compelled to stay at home by ourselves or with friends who lived in the neighborhood. In time, we found various ways to keep ourselves busy: for example, we discovered that at the Al 'Salam (Peace) hotel there was a luxurious cinema that showed western films; we went to public libraries and museums; we played cards (mostly bridge and never for money). Those of us who knew good Arabic also had the privilege to go regularly to shows and read local books and publications.

From this point of view, the situation was better in my second period in Cairo. Many things had improved dramatically: a luxurious opera house had been built and first-class shows were being brought from all over the world (with the exception of Israel, though we repeatedly proposed bringing the Israeli Philharmonic Orchestra at no cost). Old cinemas had been restored and new ones built, excellent restaurants had popped up on every street corner, an enormous conference center had been donated by the Chinese and bloomed with life. The embassy and the Israeli Academic Center had also increased their cultural activities and regularly brought artists over from Israel to entertain the Israelis in Cairo. Above all, most of the staff had installed television dishes on their roofs and could watch the two Israeli television channels as well as many western stations. Furthermore, the foreign ministry had allowed them to travel back home at least once every two months on special leave for 'recharging the batteries'. Once every two weeks, groceries, vegetables and other Israeli products were brought in the embassy van (naturally at their own expense). Life had become easier though still far from ideal. I hope that further improvements have been introduced since I left. However, in one aspect it seems that nothing has changed or will change in the foreseeable future. Eighteen years after the inauguration of the Israeli embassy in Cairo and the consulate-general in Alexandria, Israeli diplomats continue to be ostracized and boycotted socially and culturally. The Egyptian authorities not only continue to enforce, but have also tightened, the measures they have taken from the first day to prevent any kind of socialization with the local population and, indeed, any improvement in the normalization process.

Let me turn now to our fellow diplomats in Egypt. In the first years, it is sad to say that foreign diplomats, including those of the countries most friendly to Israel, behaved in almost the same manner as the Egyptians (most of whom were compelled to act as they did) and sometimes even in a more offensive way. They limited their contacts with us to the minimum. They did not refuse to receive our courtesy calls in their chanceries but refrained from making return visits in conformity with diplomatic protocol. They made it crystal-clear that they were not interested in having professional or social relations with us, exchanging information or reviewing foreign or local political matters as is customary among diplomats. The only invitations to social events we received were to national day receptions (a must between countries that maintain diplomatic relations) or to events to which all the diplomatic corps was invited. Israeli diplomats were seldom invited to informal social gatherings in their colleagues' private residences and this is true, to my great regret, from the ambassador to the most junior Israeli diplomat.

Even when they invited us to formal receptions to which hundreds of diplomats and guests of all categories were invited, our foreign colleagues were reluctant to be seen in our company. In situations that left them no choice, they hardly shook hands with us, exchanged a few words of courtesy and hurried off to less embarrassing company, as if we were plagued with leprosy. I am ashamed to admit that we truly felt leprous and on most occasions remained together isolated in the crowd, conversing amongst ourselves with affected naturalness. However, at one of our staff meetings we decided that we should not dance to the Egyptians' tune and should on such occasions intermingle as much as possible with the other guests. We did not make special efforts in relation to diplomats – it was pointless. We tried again and again to 'glue' ourselves to the Egyptian guests, most of whom we had never met before. The moment they heard that we were Israelis, they turned their backs on us and moved away. Sometimes, we felt like whores shamelessly soliciting customers, notwithstanding their repeated rebuffs and insulting behavior. Naturally, none of us was either a masochist or a fool. We did not enjoy humiliating ourselves!

We simply had a job to do – it was our task to establish relations with the Egyptian people and not only with government officials (as the Egyptians wanted us to do!). On such occasions we did our best to befriend Egyptian individuals, though deep in our souls we felt debased and abhorred each new attempt we made.

I had a few personal friends among the diplomats in Cairo, whom I had met in previous postings and with whom I had developed very close relations. They were very happy to see me again and invited me, at first, to almost all social events they organized, but very soon they noticed that they themselves were being ostracized by the Egyptians. They did not sever contacts with me (we really were friends) but they ceased inviting me to social events at which they had Egyptian guests. They explained to me frankly that their task was to develop friendly relations with Egyptian society and not with Israelis (this was the task of their embassy in Tel Aviv). My presence embarrassed their Egyptian guests even if they supported the peace process fully (mostly, I would say, out of fear from adverse reactions on the part of the security services). I could understand their point of view and I released them from the burden of having to invite me but I continued to invite them quite often, especially when I had Egyptian guests.

In this respect, our greatest disappointment came from our American colleagues, from whom we expected (and were entitled to expect) support and encouragement. If they had wanted, they could have helped us in our first steps in Egypt. It would have been easy for them to create a situation that would have compelled Egyptians to treat us with more courtesy and encouraged other diplomats to establish a normal relationship with us. Instead, they themselves refrained from inviting us and ignored our presence when we met accidentally at various events. Such behavior on the part of the representatives of Israel's staunchest ally and the power that had brokered the peace between Egypt and Israel legitimized the unofficial – but most efficient – social boycott of the Israelis by the Egyptians and other diplomats in Cairo. If the Americans kept their distance from the Israelis, why should others be more forthcoming? And why should the Egyptians fraternize with the 'Zionist enemy'?

The two ambassadors, the American and the Israeli, did meet at least once a month for a professional exchange of views. All meetings took place at the American embassy. I used to meet every second week for lunch, in a restaurant, with the American minister–counselor. They both knew how isolated we were and what were the measures taken by the Egyptian authorities to ostracize us socially. They were aware that, without their help, we could never break the blockade which had been established around us. They preferred to ignore the situation and refrain, as we say in Hebrew, from 'putting a healthy head in a sick bed'. This behavior, which went well beyond the constraints of American diplomacy in Egypt, was strongly resented by our whole team and we waited for an opportunity to voice our bitter disappointment. This opportunity arose in one of the meetings of the joint committee on autonomy, when the head of the American delegation, Ambassador Covalius, asked me, on his own initiative, if it was true that the Egyptians were socially ostracizing the Israeli diplomats and were taking administrative measures to that effect. I answered, straight to the point, that that was indeed the case and that, unfortunately, our American colleagues in Cairo viewed that boycott with complacency. Ambassador Covalius was very surprised by the second part of my answer (the first part he certainly knew from his own sources) and did not push the matter further. He only said that there must have been a misunderstanding that would soon be corrected.

A few days later, the American ambassador of the time, Alfred Atherton, phoned Ambassador Moshe Sasson, told him that he was surprised to hear that Israelis were being socially ostracized by the Egyptians and promised to look personally into the matter. A few days later, he invited him and all the embassy the staff to a dinner at his residence. He added: 'Our Egyptian guests will see with their own eyes that the United States wish the Israeli diplomats well and will understand that they have to change their negative attitude.' We came, full of expectations, to Atherton's residence but to our surprise there were neither Egyptian guests nor foreign diplomats. All the guests present were exclusively staff members of both embassies. From the number of tables and the quantities of food displayed on the buffet, one could see that many more people had been invited and had not come. Atherton did not even hint at such a possibility. On the contrary he emphasized in his welcoming words that he had intentionally invited no one else so that we should feel free of diplomatic constraints. He lifted his glass and declared in a solemn tone: 'This dinner is the first of a long series of social events. I am inaugurating today the establishment in Cairo of the Israeli–American Club. We will be meeting at least once a month, in the two ambassadors' residences alternately.'

The absence of Egyptians and foreign diplomats did not make the evening less enjoyable for us. It was the first of its kind in more than a year, and we were full of hopes for the future. We knew that if the Americans persisted in publicly socializing with us, Egyptians and foreign diplomats would, sooner or later, follow suit. To our great sorrow, the first meeting of the Israeli–American Club in Cairo was also the last. All Moshe Sasson's efforts, and mine, to convene a second meeting, or at least offer a return dinner to Atherthon and his staff, did not bear fruit. There was always a good reason not to accept our invitation and after many attempts it became clear that our American colleagues were not interested in continuing a relationship that might impair their social relations with the Egyptians. To the best of my knowledge, during the next two years Alfred Atherton pampered Moshe Sasson with only one more invitation to dinner. It was on the occasion of President Carter's visit to Egypt. Ignoring the Israeli ambassador on such an occasion would have been unbecoming, especially when President Carter had come to assess by himself how the peace process was progressing.

When I returned to Egypt in 1990, the situation on the diplomatic front was totally different. Peace was already 15 years old; the Israelis had become part of the Egyptian landscape. The foreign diplomats no longer apprehended negative reactions on the part of the Egyptians. It was partly due to a slight improvement in the attitude of the intellectuals and the officials towards peace and towards Israel. Time, 'the great healer', had had its effect. The militancy and wrath of the first days had become less virulent. The stigma of betraying the Palestinian cause had dimmed, the feeling of guilt and the stinging insult of having been vomited out of the Arab world had faded away – most Arab states now toed the Egyptian line, and the Arab League had returned to its seat in Cairo. The well-honed antennae of the diplomats had perceived these incremental changes in the atmosphere and they had begun to treat their Israeli colleagues in a manner more consistent with diplomatic custom and with the friendly relations which their countries maintained with Israel.

For me it was a refreshing change. All ambassadors, to the exclusion of the Arab ones, established an excellent working and social relationship with me. We met regularly on a basis of complete reciprocity, exchanged information, analyzed together the current situation, invited each other to our homes, and so on and so forth. From being ostracized, Israeli diplomats had become an integral part of the diplomatic community and, if I dare say so, they were quite in demand especially as a source of fresh information on the peace process. They maintained regular working and social relations (I have to stress this point again and again) with their counterparts in the various embassies.

I was invited several times to lecture on the prospects of peace and on Israeli policies to the Scandinavian ambassadors and the EEC ambassadors (separately). I was even invited to take part regularly, as an active observer, in an informal forum of non-aligned countries (some of which did not have diplomatic relations with Israel). Particularly friendly were the ambassadors and diplomats of the former eastern bloc, including the Chinese (though we had no diplomatic relations). They were eager to be seen in our company on every occasion and invited us to practically all their social events. Professionally speaking, they were most forthcoming and useful.

Also on the American front, there had been a dramatic change. The US position in the middle east had improved dramatically. American diplomats felt more secure and did not fear negative reactions. The old-school Arabists, who saw everything through the Arab prism, had given way to a new generation of diplomats who had emerged against the background of peace. Furthermore, the massive American assistance and investments, the complete reliance of the Egyptian army on the USA in modernizing itself, the arrival of more than 5,000 American experts in

all fields of economic and social development, gave the American diplomats more self-assurance and erased the complexes of the past. The USA
carried such weight that they no longer needed to fear adverse Egyptian
reactions if they maintained a normal relationship with their Israeli
colleagues or were seen in their company.

The influence of the American ambassador, Frank Wiesner, recalled
in many ways the privileged position of the British ambassador, Sir Miles
Lampson, at the end of the Second World War. In the diplomatic community, he was nicknamed 'the Viceroy'. President Mubarak received him
very often when other ambassadors, including those representing the
most powerful and rich nations, met him only at the presentation of their
credentials, on the eve of their departure or on the occasion of a VIP visit
to Egypt. Wiesner also had almost daily meetings and consultations with
the Egyptian top brass, including the closest advisers to the president and
the senior ministers.

Before I left Jerusalem for Cairo, I was told in the ministry that Frank
Wiesner was very friendly and forthcoming and that I would find in him
all the support and assistance that I needed. Indeed, this was exactly the
case. Throughout my tenure, we met almost every week and he never
failed to do his utmost to help me. I owe him recognition and thanks.
Incidentally, our paths crossed again when we were both transferred to
India.

In spite of our excellent relationship, my first contact with Weisner
was not easy. The day after my arrival in Cairo and even before I officially
became ambassador, I was surprised to receive a phone call from the
ambassador. At first I though that he wanted to congratulate me on my
appointment and wish me good luck. Instead he shouted at me in anger,
almost hysterically: 'how could you do such a thing? What happened to
diplomatic secrecy? You are not worth my trust. From this moment on all
contact between our embassies is severed! I have instructed my people to
cease all meetings with your people and you are requested not to come
to see me.' His wrath was entirely justified. A top-secret telegram sent to
Jerusalem by the minister, Eli Shaked, reporting a highly confidential conversation with Wiesner had been leaked verbatim to the Israeli press.
Even the name of Wiesner's Egyptian sources had been published. I tried
to explain that the telegram had been sent well before my arrival and
that I was absolutely unaware of the whole issue, but Wiesner continued
to shout at me, probably more for Egyptian eavesdroppers than for me. I
did not contact him for almost a whole month in the hope that he would
cool down. Finally, I asked formally for a meeting and he promptly agreed.
We easily straightened out the problem and relations were restored.
Subsequently we maintained an excellent professional and personal
relationship that developed into genuine friendship.

8 · The Egyptian Media

Twenty years of peace did not bring about the slightest change in the attitude of the Egyptian media towards Israel, the Israelis and the Jewish people. As if nothing had changed in the relationship between the two countries, it relentlessly continues to wage against them the same unrestrained and slanderous onslaught which has characterized it for so many years. To this day, the intensity and virulence of the attacks against Israel and the Jews in the Egyptian media are the equal of the warmongering and wild anti-Semitic incitement of the Nasser regime in its darkest period.

Clearly, this unwarranted situation has a cumulative pernicious effect on people-to-people interaction and introduces an element of permanent strain in relations between the two countries. Israeli diplomats in Egypt closely follow the Egyptian media and swallow the daily ration of poisonous venom that they distill – day after day, 365 days a year without a single day of grace. Before going into further detail, it is essential first to present a short insight into the formidable Egyptian information and propaganda machine and the sophisticated way in which it functions, in order to understand fully the dire implications of the situation.

All television channels, radio stations and almost all newspapers and written publications belong to the government. Apparently, independent boards of directors and editors, appointed by the minister of information (after presidential approval) manage them and the authorities claim that the press is absolutely independent and that, as befits a democratic country, the government does not and cannot interfere, directly or indirectly, in its work. They stress that the government has no role whatsoever in what is published or broadcast and that the chief editors and boards of directors enjoy total freedom of action and are the only ones to define the broad policy lines and stands of the press organs they administer. They allegedly encourage genuine pluralism of thought among their staff and allow all journalists to express themselves freely. No journalist is harmed or fired for not toeing the editor's line.

Indeed, the authorities pretend that they are entirely powerless when it comes to the media and point out as proof of their good faith that the government itself, and many prominent political figures, are often attacked in the press and have to suffer insults and heavy criticism. They emphasize that they cannot intervene to restrain or prevent these attacks and that they are helpless, in the same way, when it comes to attacks against foreign countries or personalities. It is inconceivable, they claim, that the government should breach freedom of expression or other civic rights inherent in a democratic society such as the Egyptian one!!!

One has to be very naïve to take these statements at face value. The Egyptian authorities can repeat them a 1,000 times. They can adduce numerous proofs to sustain their contention. Anyone who knows, even superficially, what are the facts of life in Egypt will dismiss them with a sarcastic smile. Political observers worldwide, foreign diplomats and journalists (and certainly Israeli diplomats serving in Egypt) who follow closely what happens, know that the picture is totally different. Even Egyptians – intellectuals and ordinary citizens – will confirm that there is no genuine freedom of press in Egypt and that everything published or broadcast by the media is orchestrated from above in a very minute manner.

The information ministry closely supervises all media organs on a day-to-day basis and, indeed, all journalists and administrative officers are government employees in the fullest sense of the term. The Egyptian information and propaganda setup is comparable to a gigantic octopus. Its arms move in different directions creating the false impression that each arm is a separate entity and has an independent life. In reality, the octopus's head (the ministry of information) regulates everything and the arms (the various media organs) do exactly what they have been instructed by the head to do. They have no life of their own and no free will.

At the top of the information and propaganda pyramid sits the minister of information (for many years, the post has been entrusted to Dr Safuat al Sharif, a graduate of the Nasser regime, who became, and still is, the Egyptian tsar of information and propaganda). He heads an enormous and powerful staff who runs the show in it smallest details. Every morning, without exception, the minister (or his representative) presides over a policy meeting attended by all the chief editors and high officials of the ministry and related propaganda and information institutions. After reviewing current events and assessing the main topics of interest and public opinion trends, clear-cut decisions are taken on how to reflect them in the various media organs and how to explain government policies and stands. The meeting also defines the specific tasks allocated to each organ on a specific day as well as the daily dosage that it should apply in current propaganda and political campaigns related to internal and/or external issues. At the same time, to avoid uniformity and create an impression of diversity and pluralism of thought, a rotation is established among the various organs as to the front page, main titles, editorials, topics to be dealt with, and such like.

The minister of information is also the official spokesman for the government. Besides him, only the president, his political adviser, Osama Elbaz, and the foreign minister may make major political statements or report to the public on government meetings and decisions. The spokesmen of the various ministries and of the presidency itself have a secondary role, which is exclusively limited to technical aspects. In any case, they are all organically linked to the information ministry and are bound by its daily instructions.

In addition, since Nasser's time the president has been accustomed to having a 'court journalist' who has no official standing but acts as his unofficial mouthpiece. Usually, this is a prominent chief editor who commands the respect of the public at large and of his colleagues in the media. He accompanies the president everywhere, participates in the most secret deliberations, has access to confidential information and receives daily intelligence reports and direct briefings from the president and other prominent personalities. Besides acting as a close adviser to the president, the court journalist is entrusted with the task of explaining and defending government policies and political stands. Almost daily, he publishes articles, editorials, political commentaries and interviews that reflect Egyptian policies as established by the highest authority in the country. During most of Nasser's long presidency, Hassanein Heykal, the chief editor of the daily *Al-Ahram* was the court journalist. In Sadat's period, the job went alternately to Ibrahim Saada of the daily *Al Akhbar* and to Anis Mansur of the weekly *October*. President Mubarak first had as his court journalist Ibrahim Nafeh, the chief editor of *Al Ahram* and, after him, Mohamed Akram Mohamed, who replaced him in both functions. Occasionally, the president makes use of the services of other journalists to explain his policies or to test public opinion trends but the court journalist is the only one who expresses the president's views on a daily basis.

'A pen for hire', as the Egyptian journalists themselves call it, is a widespread phenomenon in the Egyptian press community. All opposition newspapers receive, with the authorities' full knowledge and tacit agreement, financial support from various Arab countries and other sources. This obviously influences their journalists' writing and has a major impact on their position in the issues they raise and on their approach to world problems. The financial support for the press organs is often camouflaged as a legitimate payment for advertisements at a tarif well above the regular market price. As for the journalists (including government-employed ones), they are invited to luxurious trips abroad and presented with lavish gifts. Many of them also receive a monthly wage (much bigger than their regular salary) in return for articles and commentaries published in the Arabic press or in their own newspapers.

A prominent chief editor told me that, a few weeks before the Gulf War, President Mubarak went to Iraq to make Saddam Hussein hear the voice of reason. As usual, all chief editors and many outstanding political commentators accompanied him. During their stay, Saddam's emissaries tried to convince them to toe the Iraqi line and publish in their newspaper articles supporting the invasion of Kuwait and hostile to US moves. On the last day, each of them found on the table of his hotel suite a platinum watch worth about $30,000 with a small note bearing the signature of Saddam Hussein: 'In appreciation of your personal contribution to the Arab cause'. But this was only an appetizer. In the course of the press conference, which took place the same evening, the Iraqi president gave each of them a luxurious Mercedes car of the latest model 'in token of my friendship'. The Egyptian journalists were angered by the vulgar attempt to bribe them and brought the matter to President Mubarak's knowledge. He instructed them not to return the gifts in order not to offend Saddam Hussein but specified that while they could keep the watches, they were to transfer the cars to the ownership of the government (later, some of them were allowed to use these cars). The journalists were very happy with the presidential decision and thanked Saddam Hussein profusely. None of them, however, dared write a single line which was incompatible with the official Egyptian position. In less conspicuous cases, the journalists would have kept the gifts and souvenirs without qualms. Most of them would have tried to be forthcoming and meet, at least partially, Saddam's wishes. No one wants to kill 'the goose that lays the golden eggs!'

Egypt has four television channels and several radio stations catering for different publics, inside and outside the country. They all belong to the government and are managed directly by the ministry of information. No effort is made to conceal this fact or to give a semblance of public supervision or independent policy-making. One should stress that, in a country where more than 70 per cent of the population are illiterate or almost illiterate, the electronic media is more important by far for the authorities than the written press. Radio, and to a lesser extent television, reach practically every household in the country and carry tremendous influence. Both are the main instruments for airing the regime's propaganda and mobilizing the masses behind government policies. During Nasser's period, the regime went as far as to install television and radio sets in coffee shops in the popular quarters in big cities and in villages across the country and distributed small battery-operated transistors for free. The Egyptian authorities are not very enthusiastic, to say the least, about exposing their public to foreign independent broadcasts. Only in 1992 did the government yield to CNN pressure and allow it to relay news bulletins several times a day on condition that it use the regular Egyptian television network and agree to a number of restrictions. In recent years, Egyptian citizens have been allowed to install small dish-aerials to view foreign television programs but the cost is still very high for the average pocket and the licensing procedure is lengthy and difficult. One can say that, even in this age of satellite television and open skies, the Egyptian authorities still continue to regulate what the great majority of their citizens are allowed to see, hear and read.

The written press caters mainly to intellectuals and wealthier layers of the population. Propaganda gimmicks and slogans manipulate them less easily and the regime has to resort to various stratagems to create the impression of a free press and of intrinsic differences between one publication and another. Until 1980, all press organs without exception were governmental (in the early 1950s all privately-owned newspapers and weeklies were nationalized and all opposition press banned). However, with the beginning of the democratization process, Sadat, and after him Mubarak, loosened the leash somewhat in order to create the impression of diversity and legitimate controversy. In addition to this supposed freedom of opinion given to the government press, the authorities allowed the publication of a number of opposition newspapers: the Muslim Brotherhood's *Al Daoua* (The Cause), the Liberal Party's *Al Ahrar* (The Liberals), the Wafd Party's *Al Wafd* (The Mission), and the Nasserist–Socialist's *Al Shaab* (The People). These publications were given more leeway but not the liberty to undermine the regime foundations. First and foremost, they were forbidden to attack the president and the military establishment, though they could criticize government policies. For a while, direct censorship was imposed to make sure that opposition publications remained within reasonable boundaries but later more sophisticated means were used to control what they published. If they did not heed voluntarily the limitations hinted at by the authorities, instead of suspending the publication for a while or arresting those responsible the paper allocation would be reduced or canceled as a means of punishment. Considering that the manufacture and import of paper is a government monopoly, this was a deathblow for the rebellious publication. Furthermore, government departments and public enterprises would substantially reduce their advertising thus depriving it of a main source of income. In any case, in the initial stage the allocation of paper allowed the printing of only 20,000–30,000 copies for the entire opposition press. Opposition newspapers were, and still are, very much in demand even among staunch supporters of the regime; they are perceived by the Egyptian public as the only source of information not totally controlled by the state. Now they can easily be found, but I recall periods when they circulated under the table and passed from hand to hand as a very scarce and precious commodity.

The government press on the other hand reaches millions of readers. There are three main dailies sold at a very low price: *Al Gumhurya* (The Republic), *Al Ahram* (The Pyramids) and *Al Akhbar* (The News). They are supplemented by four main weeklies: *Rosa al Yussuf*, *October*, *Al Mussuar* (The Illustrated) and *Ahram al Iktisadi* (an economic offspring of *Al Ahram*). Furthermore, the regime publishes a score of sectarian and professional reviews aimed at different publics which serve its goals in a subtler and less direct manner. As I have previously pointed out, control over the government press is very tight and one can clearly feel the hand that pulls the strings and the synchronization between the various organs orchestrated from above.

Nowadays, the situation is a little better in this respect. President Mubarak is allowing more rope to the written government press (as distinct from the electronic media, which continues to be under absolute government control) and to the opposition press. Still, by western criteria, this is very far from real freedom of expression and liberty of the press. The Egyptian press continues to be supervised and directed by the authorities. Even opposition newspapers take government restrictions into consideration and make sure they do not go beyond the limits imposed on them. The authorities can, at any time, bring back into line newspapers and/or journalists who manifest too much independence or publish attacks that are unacceptable to the government. They have a range of subtle means to achieve their goal and they do not hesitate to use them. On the other hand, the absence of reaction on the part of the authorities is interpreted as tacit agreement with what is being published and, understandably, brings about an increase in the virulence of the attacks. This is exactly what occurs in the case of Israel and anti-Semitism.

In addition to the ministry of information, there is an independent Information Agency (read: propaganda agency) which, though functioning under the aegis of the minister of information, is allowed a wide margin of maneuver and is allocated substantial means. All the network of press and information attachés in the Egyptian embassies as well as the whole propaganda apparatus of the ruling party are under its direct authority. The agency is in charge of all the propaganda and information campaigns, external or internal. Under Nasser, who turned propaganda into a main instrument of government, the agency carried tremendous power. Nowadays it has lost some of its authority, but it is still a formidable instrument of mass manipulation and disinformation. It carries out annual in-depth studies on a wide range of issues, publishes scores of books and publications in Arabic and foreign languages and organizes seminars, mass meetings, international congresses, etc. It is this agency that translates into Arabic and publishes anti-Semitic books such as Hitler's *Mein Kampf* and *The Protocols of the Elders of Zion*. Up to 1982, four years after the signing of the peace treaty and two years after the opening of the embassies, both books and other publications of the kind were exhibited and sold to the public in the agency's official stand at the Cairo International Book Fair. When the Israeli embassy protested, the Egyptian authorities' answer was cynical. We were told that 'these publications are part of an old stock that the agency wants to get rid of'. Here again, one had to be naïve, not to say stupid, to swallow the Egyptian explanation. Alas, to this very day both books and several other anti-Semitic publications can still be found in bookshops across Egypt.

Now that we have taken a short stroll into the intricacies of the Egyptian information apparatus, we can return to our starting point: the ever-continuing slanderous attacks in the Egyptian media against Israel, the Israelis and the Jews almost 20 years after the achievement of peace. Bearing in mind the authorities' *modus operandi* and their complete control over the media, there is only one possible and simple conclusion: whatever we, and the Egyptian people, read in the newspapers, hear on the radio or see on television screens is exactly what the Egyptian government wants us to read, hear and see. This is a carefully designed policy, aimed at achieving goals pre-determined by the government and carried out with the utmost efficiency. In all that pertains to Israel and to the peace process, the media is a tool in the hands of the Egyptian authorities to diffuse the message that Israel is still to be ostracized and that Israelis and Jews are to be feared and despised. It is also an instrument to put pressure, at variable levels of intensity in accordance with the circumstances of the moment, on Israel and world public opinion. It also provides an alibi for freezing the normalization of relations between the two countries and for improving Egypt's image in the Arab world. I have to add that the opinions expressed in the press reflect to a great extent the true inner thoughts of Egyptian policy-makers and their prejudice as well as that of their 'hired pens' (to use the Egyptian expression).

The repeated attempts by the embassy and by Israeli and foreign personalities visiting Egypt to bring these attacks to a stop, or at least to moderate them, have not borne fruit. The ultimate answer has been: 'Egypt is a democratic country. The press is free and the government cannot and will not interfere in what it writes.' Only once did I receive, to my great surprise, a different reply to my bitter protests. It was during my second period in Egypt as ambassador. A leading journalist had attacked Prime Minister Shamir in the most abusive manner, comparing him to a monkey and branding him as 'a murderer of Arab children, a butcher who wallows in their blood like a cruel tiger that feeds on its prey'. This time, I went directly to the foreign minister, Amr Mussa, and made it clear that we could not turn a blind eye to these insults. Within the next few days, I returned to him three times and he finally understood that we would not be satisfied with the usual stereotypical answers. He asked me to convey the apologies of the Egyptian government to Prime Minister Shamir and to assure him that President Mubarak himself had been shocked and had personally instructed the journalist to publish an apology. Indeed, the promised apology was published the very next day but it was not an apology to Prime Minister Shamir, God forbid, but to the monkeys, butchers and tigers for comparing them with Yitshak Shamir, 'who is much worse than they could ever be!' We realized, once again, with whom we were dealing and had no choice but to accept the official apology and remove the matter from the agenda.

As previously said, not a day passes without attacks in the media against Israel, the Israelis and the Jews. However, from time to time, fully-fledged press campaigns are launched. They develop in a very orderly manner and the technique improves from campaign to campaign. Distribution of work between government and opposition press and between the various dailies and weeklies is synchronized in a most skillful manner. It works like a symphony orchestra under the leadership of a great maestro. Usually, the concert begins with short articles in the opposition newspapers. After a few days the government press organs follow suit. Some publish editorials, others commentaries, yet others alleged factual news, and the next day they interchange roles and the size of their titles. The opposition press gets the message and magnifies the attack relying on official sources and adding salt and pepper. Now it is again the turn of the government press to increase the virulence of their attacks. The ball rolls from opposition to government and from government to opposition until the 'maestro' decides that the issue has been exhausted. The onslaught stops as suddenly as it had begun and the press waits for a signal from the maestro to initiate the next campaign against Israel and the Jews (these always go together). Between the campaigns, attacks never cease completely; there is no day without its ration of poison. Only the intensity and the virulence change. Since everything in life is relative, between campaigns the situation is perceived as having improved dramatically, optimistic evaluations are made and then, unexpectedly and with no apparent reason, there begins a new outburst of slander and hatred shattering all evaluations and hopes. The worst part is the anti-Semitic caricatures published from time to time. They are so loathsome and threatening that, I regret to say, the horrendous caricatures published by the Nazi *Der Stürmer* compare favorably. In the foreign ministry's archives, one can find thick folders stuffed with caricatures collected from the Egyptian press since the opening of the Israeli embassy in Cairo in 1980.

In addition to the constant attacks, campaigns and caricatures, we had to endure a series of small but humiliating measures. I will provide only two examples. In the first year after the opening of the embassy, we tried in vain to take out a subscription to the English daily selection of articles and editorials published by the Information Agency. We needed it for Ambassador Ben-Elissar who did not read Arabic and could therefore not receive his daily ration of poison directly from the source. We were flatly refused on the ground that 'the Journalists' Association has passed a resolution calling for the boycott of Israel and Israelis'. The ministry of foreign affairs rejected our repeated complaints invoking as usual 'freedom of the press and civic rights'. We could have obtained the selection through another embassy but this would have meant a public acknowledgement of failure. We preferred to do without it rather than admit that we were encountering difficulties in the first steps of implementation of peace and normalization. At the time, we were still full of expectations and believed, naïvely, that the difficulties we were encountering would find their solutions in the near future with the active support of the Egyptian authorities.

To this very day, not even once has the embassy and/or any Israeli institution and/or any private person succeeded in publishing an advertisement in the Egyptian press – for payment, naturally. Most elementary ads aimed at informing the public of the embassy's new address and phone numbers, or the consulate's working hours or giving details about the holding of cultural events would be flatly rejected by each and every newspaper.

During my first stay, I tried my 'luck' every three months. I used various tricks and stratagems to try to by-pass the interdiction but, whatever I did, I always failed. After two or three days, the ad, and sometimes the payment, would be returned to the embassy with the explanation that 'the competent authorities have not allowed the publication of the ad'. Only once did I succeed in having an ad referring to Israel published in two newspapers. It was a tourism advertisement that had nothing to do with the embassy. It was sent, and paid for, by an Egyptian tourist agency that had a stake in developing tourism between the two countries. I confess that I had prompted the agency to publish the ad in the framework of my quarterly tests. The very next day, the ad disappeared though it had been paid for for a whole week. The tourist agent was summoned to the security services, admonished severely and warned not to continue dealing with Israel.

To be frank, my stubbornness with regard to advertising in the Egyptian press was not prompted by the embassy's functional needs. It was rather a yardstick to check periodically if a positive change had occurred in the policy of social confinement and ostracism implemented by the authorities against us. We would raise the matter quite often in the ministries of foreign affairs and of information, more for its nuisance value than in the hope of finding a satisfactory solution. We knew that we would receive in reply the stereotypical statement about 'freedom of the press and non-intervention on the part of the government'. Sometimes our interlocutors would add a commercial explanation: 'Egyptian newspapers cannot put in jeopardy their substantial returns from the millions of copies they sell in the Arab countries because of the few pounds they could get from Israeli advertisements.' Clearly, this was not the reason – the newspaper edition distributed in the Arab countries is an earlier edition than the one distributed in Egypt itself and there would have been no difficulty in erasing the Israeli advertisements from that edition. The reason was plain and simple: a deliberate government policy, well planned and efficiently enforced, to restrain Israeli activities in Egypt.

On my return to Cairo in 1990, I was informed that the embassy had discontinued the quarterly tests many years before. There was no point in trying, again and again, to circumvent an interdiction that was clearly a government policy. Nevertheless, I decided to try my 'luck' at least one more time. I instructed our administrative officer, Dror Gabay, to publish in the three main dailies an ad informing the public of the embassy's new phone numbers. He went personally to the Government Advertising Agency, where he was received very warmly. He paid in advance for a whole week and was told that the ad would be published as from the beginning of the following week. I was elated by this positive development. I reached the conclusion that time had had a positive effect and that ten years after the inauguration of the Israeli embassy in one of Cairo's main squares, the authorities saw no point any longer in trying to conceal its existence from the public. It had become an open secret. One week, two weeks, three weeks went by. The ad was not published. I sent Gabay to check what was happening. He was told that there had been a slight delay because of technical reasons but that the ad would be published as promised. After two more weeks, Gabay received a phone call asking him to come and receive a refund because 'the competent authorities do not allow the publication of the ad'. The very same explanation that we had heard so many times in the past! Nothing had changed; I should have known better! I abandoned my attempts at climbing steep, slippery walls. My energy, and the little influence that I *did* have, could be put to better use in more important fields. Advertising in the Egyptian press was not essential for the embassy, but nonetheless it was a bitter disappointment for us and a stinging reminder that we were still not welcome in Egypt.

Another aspect of our bizarre relationship with the Egyptian media was the interviews, or more correctly the unpublished interviews, that we granted. From day one, despite the boycott imposed by the journalists' Association, Israeli ambassadors were sought after by Egyptian journalists. After their meetings with Egyptian personalities, journalists flocked around them, waving in their faces tapes, cameras and microphones, and insisting on receiving a statement. They bombarded them with a score of pertinent questions in the most professional manner and even engaged with them in friendly conversations. The next day, there was no reference whatsoever to these long interviews in the written press – not a single word on the radio, not the slightest glimpse on the television screens. *Nada*, nothing! On very rare occasions, a brief sentence – out of context – of what had been said, and sometimes not said, was used to substantiate Egyptian arguments. Mostly, the only reference in the press to our meetings were short press releases issued by the official spokesmen of the various ministries that were far from reflecting the real course of the meetings or the topics discussed. After the first few times, I would joke with the journalists and ask them why they were wasting time and energy interviewing me and bombarding me with questions when they knew in advance that they would not be allowed to publish my statements. They would laugh and answer 'perhaps this time we will have more luck!' I, for my part, played the game and always answered their questions with the utmost seriousness. It was a rare opportunity to explain Israeli positions to public opinion-makers.

Many journalists even approached the embassy spokesman and insisted on being granted a personal interview by the ambassador. We (the successive ambassadors) never refused though we knew that these interviews would not be published. The journalists came well prepared, indicating that they had done their homework and took the interview most seriously. They asked pertinent questions and seemed eager to hear the Israeli side. We answered patiently at length and in detail (for the reasons previously explained). Of the scores of interviews that I have given during my tenure, only once did a woman journalist succeed in publishing in an Egyptian daily a selected part of her interview with me. Paradoxically, over the years, I had more interviews published in the Gulf press than in the Egyptian press. I recall a lengthy interview that I gave to a senior Egyptian journalist for a Saudi newspaper. I did not hide from him my conviction that the interview would not be published and I only asked him to give me his word that, if it were, my words would not be distorted or published out of context. To my great surprise, the interview appeared on two full pages and reflected word for word what I had said. It even included a clear-cut statement emphasizing that Israel would never agree to divide Jerusalem and that the Arabs should desist from their wishful thinking in this respect, if they really wished to give peace a chance.

I would have liked to receive the same treatment from the Egyptian press. I do not point an accusing finger at the journalists. Left to their own professional judgment, they would have acted differently. Many of them developed ties of personal friendship with the Israeli diplomats. But their hands are tied! Forces stronger than they determine the information policy down to its smallest details and enforce it with an iron fist. They have no choice but to follow suit and heed their Master's Voice. I do not however want to give the false impression that all Egyptian journalists are a paragon of virtue and that the blame rests solely on the authorities' shoulders. Many of them, in particular the leftists and the fundamentalists, vehemently oppose the peace established between the two countries and the continuation of the peace process in the region as a whole. They have a genuine revulsion for Israel and Israelis. Some are tinted with active anti-Semitism and abhor all that is Jewish. Nevertheless, as I have said, quite a few journalists maintained fairly good relations with us and, were it not for the authorities' crude intervention, would have tried to balance the picture. For example, Moussa Sabry, the Chief Editor of *Al Akhbar*, allowed us in early 1980 to publish in his newspaper a weekly review of the main events in Israel – a kind of 'Know Your Enemy' page. The editor was a professor of Hebrew language from Ein Shams University who at first strove to be objective and give a true picture of what was happening in Israel. After a few weeks, he was called to order and compelled to give a clear-cut negative character to the Israeli page.

When I became ambassador in 1990, I thought I would be able indirectly to open the Egyptian media for Prime Minister Shamir. President Mubarak, who was interested in addressing the Israeli people directly, had requested through his spokesman that he be interviewed by Israeli television (we had only one channel at the time). As a matter of course, the Israeli authorities agreed and sent a team to Cairo to interview the president. In return, I took advantage of an incidental meeting with him and requested to have Shamir interviewed by Egyptian television. The president agreed without hesitation and told me to speak the next day with the minister of information, Safuat al Sharif, and tie up the technical details. My phone calls and letters to the minister remained unanswered. He did not want to see me. He wanted even less to have Shamir speak to the Egyptian people on Egyptian television. As always, when it came to the media, it was a one-way street!

As I have said, radio and television are the main means of reaching the Egyptian masses and persuading them to support government policies. Happily, Sadat, and after him Mubarak, restricted to a minimum the use of radio and television in the ever-continuing campaign of slander, hatred and demonization (no – this is not too strong a word!) waged against Israel and the Jews in the written press. The rationalization was, and still is, that the very strong impact of radio and television on the illiterate population might create extreme reactions that could boomerang against the regime itself and its policy of peace. (I have to stress at this stage that all that I have explained about Egyptian policies and behavior in no way precludes or diminishes Egypt's commitment to peace and to the peace process. I will clarify this paradox at a later stage.)

Each time we complained to the authorities about the press campaigns against Israel and the Jews, in addition to their ritualistic reply concerning freedom of the press our Egyptian interlocutors would point out that radio and television were not actively participating in these attacks. They added, cynically, that we should be thankful for that as the press reached only a tiny minority of the Egyptian people while the electronic media entered every house and had a very great impact. To illustrate their alleged good will, they told us that in the wake of the Sabra and Shatila massacre in Beirut (perpetrated by the Christian Phalangists), they had allowed the appearance of a few horrendous, realistic pictures only in the press but not on the television. In itself, this was an indirect admission that the authorities indeed controlled both the written and electronic media.

Despite these limitations, radio and television are not totally free of anti-Israeli and anti-Jewish propaganda. That would have been too good to be true! From time to time, television broadcasts feature films and documentary programs depicting Israel and Jews in the darkest shades and glorifying the Arab struggle against them. On the other hand, it also broadcasts campaigns in support of the government's peace policy. As for the radio, most stations do not deal with political issues and limit themselves to news bulletins and short commentaries. Only one station, *Saout al Arab* (the Voice of the Arabs) airs, almost daily, virulent attacks against Israel and Jews. Its programs are mainly directed at the Arab countries and are followed only occasionally by Egyptian listeners. Paradoxically, the Israeli diplomats maintained excellent relations with the radio's Hebrew-speaking station. It did broadcast, many times, material on Israel provided by the embassy. No wonder that it was allowed to do so: the station is directed at the Israeli public and not at Egyptian or Arab audiences.

Israeli diplomats have never been given an opportunity to appear on television (excluding a few accidental takes) or to speak over the radio. They had, however, easy access to the broadcasting authority's building and to the top brass of the electronic media. In 1982, we even signed a Co-operation and Programs Exchange Agreement between the two countries' television authorities. A delegation headed by Tommy Lapid (one of the most outstanding journalists in Israel and presently a member of the Knesset), at the time director-general of the Israeli Broadcast Corporation, was received with red-carpet treatment. After intensive haggling over the small print, an agreement satisfactory to both sides was reached. Tommy signed it with his golden Cartier pen (a gift from his wife on the occasion of their twentieth wedding anniversary) and left it on the table while we all stood to embrace and congratulate each other on the great achievement. When Tommy returned to his place, the pen had vanished. He called me and said aloud: 'Ephraim, someone has stolen my pen. If it is not returned within five minutes, I will make a scandal. I'll call the police, lodge a formal complaint and have them carry out a body search on all participants.' I used all my diplomatic skills to calm him down and begged him not to create a major diplomatic incident. I spoke discreetly to the the Egyptian authority chairman, told him about the pen and requested him to ask his colleagues if one of them had found it. As I expected, the answer was negative; no one had seen the pen. It had disappeared forever in one of the participants' pockets. Tommy swallowed the bitter pill and consoled himself saying: 'The loss of my pen has been worthwhile. At least, we have signed a good agreement. It is a landmark in our relations with Egypt.' I did not want to pour oil on his wound and I refrained from telling him that I was convinced that the agreement would never be implemented. Indeed, none of our efforts to breathe life into it bore any fruit and it remained a dead letter as did all other normalization agreements signed between Israel and Egypt. Signing agreements is one thing, but implementing them is another!

I could tell many more stories about the Egyptian media but I believe that I have already given quite an extensive picture. I cannot conclude this chapter without expressing deep appreciation to the press and cultural counselors who served over the years in the embassy. They all came from Israeli television and volunteered for the job notwithstanding the difficulties, personal dangers and offensive attitude of their Egyptian colleagues. They did an excellent job and, more than any other Israeli diplomat in Egypt, they drank their daily ration of poison to the last drop.

9 · The Remnants of the Jewish Community

At the inception of the State of Israel, there were about 90,000–100,000 Jews in Egypt. Most of them lived in Cairo (around 50,000) and Alexandria (around 30,000). The rest were divided between Port Said, Ismailia and Suez. Only a few hundred resided permanently in villages or small cities. Most of them were engaged in traditional Jewish professions: e.g. wholesale and retail trade, liberal professions, banking, teaching, clerical work, handicrafts. The majority were average middle class and lived quite comfortably. Only a few accumulated great wealth and belonged to the economic and political elite. On the other hand, a few thousand were in a difficult economic situation (not to say poor) and lived very modestly. They concentrated mainly in the Jewish quarters in Cairo and Alexandria (Haret al Yahoud) in the heart of the Muslim working-class districts.

In spite of the millenary presence of Jews in Egypt (there is evidence of a Jewish settlement in the Egyptian city of Yav from the period of the Second Temple), only around 20 per cent had Egyptian citizenship. Almost half had foreign nationalities and the rest were stateless. Most of them knew Arabic but for many of them it was not a mother tongue. Among themselves, the Jews spoke mainly French together with a score of other foreign languages (the average Jew mastered three to four languages).

The Jewish community was tightly-knit and maintained well-organized and active communal and religious institutions (including a rabbinical court). All activities commonly found in well established Jewish communities in the Diaspora existed and functioned smoothly: primary and high schools, beautiful synagogues, sport and social clubs, youth movements, women's guilds, welfare organizations, hospitals and clinics, residences for the elderly, orphanages, cemeteries and such like.

The great majority of the Jews in Egypt belonged to the Sephardi community (originally from Spain and the middle east). About 10,000 belonged to the Ashkenazi community (originally from eastern Europe) who immigrated to Egypt, mostly from Palestine, during the First World

War. There also was a small community of about 5,000 Karaite Jews (a sect which follows exclusively the written biblical precepts) who maintained separate institutions and synagogues. Despite their diversity, there was no antagonism between the various parts of the community and, on the contrary, they were united, shared a common fate, had professional and social interaction, intermarried, attended the same schools and stressed more what they had in common than what separated them.

The Zionist movement functioned openly and unimpeded. Only in May 1948, in the wake of Israel's declaration of independence, did the authorities close its offices and all Jewish youth movements. Over the years, many envoys were sent by the *Yishuv* (Jewish community) in Palestine to help organize youth movements, train self-defense groups and prepare the infrastructure for the emigration to Palestine of Egyptian Jewry.

The relations of the Jews with the authorities and their Muslim neighbors were in general healthy and even cordial. The Jews knew their place and did their best not to be too conspicuous or offensive. With the exception of a very few, they abstained from taking part in local politics, demonstrations or confrontations. For their part, the Egyptian authorities allowed them to freely practice their faith and limited their interference in Jewish communal affairs to an almost imperceptible minimum (at least for the average community member). Their attitude towards the Jews was a mixture of respect and suspicion. They kept a watchful eye on them and established within the Internal Security Service (*Mabakhes*) a Department for Jewish and Zionist Affairs, whose task was to supervise closely what happened in the community.

Active anti-Semitism was not felt in day-to-day life. Latent anti-Semitism, however, was everywhere and Jews were clearly considered second-rank citizens. The situation worsened after the toppling of the king and especially after the Sinai Campaign (1956) and the Six-Day War (1967). Occasionally, sporadic outbursts of violence against the Jews took place, mostly in the Jewish ghettos. Generally, these were spontaneous local disputes between neighboring communities. However, sometimes they were provoked intentionally by Muslim fundamentalist organizations or instigated by the authorities themselves.

During the War of Liberation (1948–49), many hundreds of Jews – members of youth movements, community and Zionist leaders, communist activists and wealthy businessmen – were arrested and placed in internment camps. They were deliberately put together with activists of the Muslim Brotherhood who abused and maltreated them. Sham trials were organized against some of them and they were condemned to heavy prison sentences and hard labor. Furthermore, the authorities sequestered the assets of many community leaders and prominent Jewish businessmen. They also organized a small pogrom in the Jewish ghetto and in the center of Cairo (where the more affluent Jews lived). Then and only then, did the Jews grasp that uncontrollable undercurrents in Egypt were bringing about drastic social and political changes that would certainly affect their lives. For the first time, they realized that they were not welcome any longer and that the comfortable life was coming to an end. Up to that moment, most Jews were satisfied with their situation in Egypt, even if they felt like second- or third-rate citizens, and would have stayed for ever if allowed to do so. They never envisaged emigrating to more clement skies and leaving behind all their worldly possessions and the surroundings to which they were accustomed.

A first wave composed mainly of members of youth movements and of less affluent classes left Egypt at the end of 1949 and in 1950–51. Most of them emigrated to Israel and were quickly absorbed economically and socially. The great majority remained in Egypt, fearing to confront the unknown abroad and hoping against all odds, and notwithstanding the political and social changes taking place under their nose, that the situation would return to normality with the end of hostilities in Palestine. In 1953, when young Jewish activists were caught planting bombs in Cairo and Alexandria (the 'Lavon Affair') and two of them (Dr Moshe Marzuk and Shmuel Azar) were hanged, they turned a blind eye to the writing on the wall. They remained in Egypt in spite of the increased anti-Semitism among the Egyptian masses and the many anti-Jewish measures taken by the authorities.

The inevitable moment of truth arrived in 1956. In the wake of the Sinai Campaign, named by the Egyptians the Trilateral Aggression (Israel, France and Great Britain), Nasser expelled most Jews who held foreign nationality or were stateless together with hundreds of thousands of other foreign nationals. All their assets were nationalized and put under the administration of army officers. A great part came to Israel, found a helping hand and integrated quickly. Many dispersed to the four corners of the world and managed, through their own efforts, to integrate socially and economically in their countries of adoption.

A few thousand, mostly Egyptian citizens, remained behind, by choice or because they had no alternative. Little by little, many of them left and, by 1980, when I came to Egypt for the first time, the remnants of the magnificent Egyptian Jewry counted less than 500 souls, scattered throughout the country (mainly in Cairo and Alexandria). A few hundred more remained anonymous and were not registered in the community. They feared for their personal safety or had intermarried with local citizens and did not want to disclose that they were of Jewish origin. A few of them popped up at the synagogue during Yom Kippur (the Day of Atonement) or when they were desperate for economic assistance.

Before leaving for Egypt, I met in Jerusalem with the acting president of the community, the late Isaac Dana (a lawyer by profession). He had come for a short stay to arrange his two children's emigration to Israel in the framework of *Alyat Hanoar* (a department in the Jewish Agency). He briefed me extensively describing, with the utmost frankness, the distressing situation of the community. He did not try to conceal the hard facts. I thought I was well prepared but when, a few days after my arrival, I paid a courtesy visit to what was left of the community – which I had known in its time of splendor – I was profoundly shocked and moved to tears. The situation was much worse than I had, in my darkest assessment, imagined it to be.

Most remaining Jews were wretched, old, sick and destitute. They lived in awful conditions in the poorest districts or in a residence for the elderly maintained by the community. The Jewish ghetto (Haret al Yahud) was *Judenrein*. Only a single old lady was left. She lived in a small room with a Muslim youngster who took pity on her and looked after her with worthy dedication. Only a handful were well off and lived in the center of Cairo in comfortable flats. They took upon themselves the burden of communal work and, as in any other community, they were divided into small groups and engaged in bitter disputes over the leadership and the control of community properties. They exchanged accusations of corruption, graft and embezzlement. For obvious reasons, I will not elaborate on this point but it seems that in this case there was some truth in the saying 'there is no smoke without fire'. It is a fact that various properties had exchanged hands over the years and not all the moneys were clearly accounted for. There were rumors that even tombstones from the cemetery in Bassatin (near the residential quarter of Maadi) had been sold to construction contractors. This contention has never been proven but the sad reality is that the cemetery is completely ruined and most tombstones (and sometimes the tombs themselves) have disappeared, making it impossible to locate deceased relatives. In this respect the situation is much better in Alexandria, where the community (some 100 souls) is united and well organized. All communal properties are well maintained and every cent is accounted for.

The Jews (especially in Cairo) tried to involve the embassy in their internal affairs and each faction strove to secure its support against the other factions. Israeli diplomats were very careful not to get involved in the 'Wars of the Jews' and not to identify themselves with any faction. The embassy maintained absolute neutrality and made it perfectly clear that it was not authorized to interfere in the internal affairs of the community. Nevertheless, it did not neglect its humanitarian duty to help the poor and the dejected. Nizza Ben Elissar (the first ambassador's wife) created a special fund, to which, the embassy staff and various companies in Israel contributed regularly, in money and material gifts. The residence for elderly people was renovated and a communal restaurant established. Every week the wives of staff members distributed sweets, clothes, medicines and various items that made life easier. The embassy also convinced the JOINT (an American Jewish philanthropic organization) to allocate 45 Egyptian pounds (at the time, about US$30) per month to each member of the community who had no other source of income (around 100 people altogether). The JOINT also agreed to cover hospital expenses and distribute food packages on Jewish festivals. It was not much but it was better than nothing!

When I returned to Cairo in 1990, I noted that the JOINT had not increased the allocations though inflation had substantially diminished the purchase value of the Egyptian pound and its rate against the dollar. It took me strenuous efforts, and many months, to convince JOINT representatives to adjust the allocations to their original dollar value. They also agreed to cover all medical expenses without insisting on the financial participation of the local community (which indeed had very limited sources of income). I also succeeded in persuading the ministry of religions in Israel to extend material and religious assistance to the community. The then minister, Professor Avner Shaki, after a visit to Egypt, gave instructions to his ministry to limit the paper work and do its utmost to help the Jewish community in Egypt.

Understandably, the embassy became a unifying factor and a focal point for extending material support to the community. Each festival, all Jews in Cairo and Alexandria were invited to the celebrations organized either in my house or in the ambassador's residence (in these last years, the celebrations were organized by the embassy in the Great Synagogue in the center of Cairo). The Passover *seder* and the Independence reception were particularly moving. All the Jews, almost without exception, attended – dressed in their best clothes and beaming with pride and joy. It was distressing to see some of them snatching food from the tables and hiding it in their purses and pockets. As a matter of course, we turned a blind eye and sent waiters to replenish the trays. On these festive occasions, and indeed on all occasions, the successive ambassadors and the embassy staff publicly demonstrated their respect for the community leaders and bestowed honors and sympathy upon them. This contributed to strengthening their position in the eyes of the community and the Egyptian authorities.

However, the real bosses of the community are to this very day the officers of the Department for Jewish and Zionist Affairs in the Egyptian security service, which continues to be active even after the number of Jews has become insignificant and their influence irrelevant. These officers have extensive powers. They control communal properties, post numerous guards everywhere, take an active part in all meetings, and intervene in all conversations and decisions. They also determine who sits on the board of the community. Indeed, they know what is going on in the community better than the community leaders themselves. Paradoxically, Jews have to ask for their permission to enter their own synagogues and properties and cannot move a chair – not to say religious artifact or other valuable item – without their patrons giving the green light. They are present at every celebration, religious or secular, and sit in the most central seats.

It was pathetic to see the marks of submission to these officers by their victims and the words of praise poured on them on every occasion (I have no weaker words to describe the situation). After Mr Dana's demise, the authorities compelled Mr Rousso, a retired bank employee, to assume the presidency (he is still functioning). They even tried to make him change the community statutes with a view to barring the membership of foreign nationals and stateless persons. This step would have ruled out more than half the members and stepped up the formal disappearance of the community as a legal entity. In accordance with Egyptian laws, in such circumstances the government is the sole heir of all communal proper- ties. I have to say to Rousso's credit that he withstood courageously all pressures and refused to amend the statutes. I do hope that he continues to stand firm. In any case, sooner or later all the communal properties will go to the Egyptian government.

The authorities have also meticulously registered all the Torah books (scrolls of the Law) and the various religious artifacts in use in the three still functioning synagogues (the Great Synagogue in the Center of Cairo, the Nabi Daniel Synagogue in Alexandria and the Karaite Synagogue in Old Cairo). They have forbidden taking them out of the premises and they carry out a regular inspection to make sure that they have not been sneaked out. More than 60 Torah books and a score of valuable religious artifacts have been confiscated from other synagogues not in use (legally still owned by the Jewish community) and are presently stored in the base- ment of the National Library. All efforts made repeatedly by the embassy and visiting Jewish and Israeli personalities to persuade President Mubarak and the competent authorities to have them transferred to Israel, or to Jewish communities outside Israel, have not borne fruit. All pleas were stubbornly rejected under the pretext that these Torah books and Jewish artifacts belonged to the Egyptian people and were part of its cultural heritage! President Sadat was more understanding; he gave three Torah books to Prime Minister Menahem Begin during his official visit to Egypt and promised to consider favorably releasing the rest. His successor, who continues his peace policy faithfully, seems to be less generous. There are no signs that Egypt will in the foreseeable future return the Torah books and the artifacts to their legitimate owners, Egyptian Jewry. Last year, President Mubarak offered one Torah book to the then minister of foreign affairs, David Levy, in response to his insistent pleas to find a positive solution to this painful issue. Let us hope that it is the first step in the right direction!

It is interesting to note that the Egyptian authorities have acted with great wisdom (and shrewdness) in relation to the communal and private assets of Egyptian Jewry. Though the Jews have been brutally dispossessed of everything they owned, there are no legal grounds for future claims of property restitution or payment of financial compensation. As a first step, the communal assets were sequestrated and administered directly by the government but, a few years later, they were returned to the Jewish community. However, the community was then pressured into selling them at ridiculous prices or leasing them to various government departments at symbolic rents. All schools, hospitals, orphanages, offices and parts of the cemetery came legally under the government's complete control. Synagogues, community offices and cemeteries in use were left in the hands of the Jewish community but, as described, the authorities imposed many limitations and controls turning them into virtual owners of these properties. Once again, everything was legal and done according to the book. Within a few years, the remnants of the Jewish community will go the way of all flesh and the Egyptian government will legally inherit all the communal assets. (Incidentally, the Alexandria community leaders wanted in 1982, and later in 1990, to donate the communal assets to the government of Israel and register them officially in its name. On both occasions, though for different reasons, their wish did not materialize. In my opinion, it is practically impossible to overcome the legal and political difficulties involved in such an endeavor.)

As for the assets of private individuals, they belonged mostly to Jews holding foreign nationality. Many years ago, the Egyptian government settled with the respective governments the issue of compensation for the properties left behind in Egypt by foreign nationals. These governments received a lump sum and took upon themselves the responsibility of settling the claims of their nationals. Indeed, most claimants received token payments (around 20 per cent of the real value) and duly signed a declaration desisting from future claims. Here again, there are no legal grounds for claims against the Egyptian government.

The assets of stateless Jews and of Jews holding Egyptian nationality were covered by a law passed in 1980, shortly before the assassination of President Sadat. It is known as the Law for Returning Confiscated and Nationalized Properties and gives five years to claimants to introduce legal suits before the Egyptian courts for the restitution of their assets. The only problem was that the law stipulated specifically that only claimants residing in Egypt could file such applications. No Jew in his right mind was ready to return to the lion's den! Later, the law was prolonged twice by the High Court of Justice and was in force up to 1995. The Court also abolished the condition that claimants should reside in Egypt as being inconsistent with the purpose of the law. Many Egyptians – non-Jewish – have consequently recuperated their assets though financial assets were practically worthless and real estates were in an advance state of disintegration.

I was in Egypt when the law was amended by the High court of Justice. I found an Egyptian lawyer, who agreed to deal with the embassy in spite of the boycott on Israel declared by the Lawyers' Association, and requested him to obtain from the Custodian Administration the list of Jews who had substantial real estates under sequester. Money, bonds or shares were irrelevant since they were to be refunded at their nominal value despite the raging inflation over the years. I conveyed the list to the Association of Jews from Egypt in Israel and requested them to locate the relevant people or their heirs. Furthermore, I contacted a few individuals I knew personally and put them in contact with the Egyptian lawyer. After I left Egypt for India, I did not follow up developments in this matter but, to the best of my knowledge, not a single Jew from Egypt recuperated even partially the assets he had left behind. If the law has not been prolonged again, one can say unequivocally that the issue of private Jewish assets in Egypt has come to an end. In any case, in accordance with the peace agreement between Israel and Egypt, this issue is to be tackled between the two governments in the framework of their reciprocal claims for compensation. The matter has not been raised during this last 20 years and it seems that it never will be!

Nissim Gaon, a Jewish philanthropist living in Geneva, who was married in the synagogue, restored the Great Synagogue in the center of Cairo in the mid-1980s. He raised more than one million dollars for this purpose and entrusted the planning and supervision of the renovation to the Swiss architect Roger Shaltiel. Throughout the works, there was bickering between the community leaders and Gaon's representatives over what they defined as their sovereign right to administer the raised funds and supervise the restoration works. Gaon did not give in and the synagogue was finally restored to the splendor that it had known in better days.

For the first time in 15 years, a wedding took place in the renovated synagogue. It will probably have been the last since there are no remaining Jewish youngsters in Egypt. The story of the young couple is a modern version of *Romeo and Juliet* with a less tragic end. The bride and groom were the last two Jewish youngsters in Egypt. Both were dashing and well educated, had grown up together, fallen in love and decided to get married. Indeed, they were meant for each other and had practically no other choice. The bride's father (Mr Rousso, the community president already mentioned) vehemently opposed the wedding on the grounds that 'the groom's family belonged to the Karaite community and was of a lower social standing than his'. For three long years, he thus embittered his daughter's life. Finally, my wife and I succeeded in convincing him that it was better to have her marry a Karaite Jewish boy than marry outside the faith later. After the marriage, the young couple emigrated to Israel and I do hope that they will live happily ever after. As for the synagogue, due to lack of proper maintenance, it deteriorated again. The heart bleeds to see how many efforts and how much money went down the drain!

There are only two more functioning synagogues: the one in the Meadi district, maintained by the embassy staff, and the Nabi Daniel Synagogue in Alexandria, which is maintained beautifully by the Jewish community. All other synagogues are closed and neglected. Jewish philanthropists did restore two other synagogues. The Rambam Synagogue in the Jewish ghetto in Cairo (considered to have healing powers) was renovated in the early 1980s by the same Nissim Gaon. It is presently flooded by underground waters and again crumbling. The Ibn Ezra Synagogue in old Cairo, the oldest synagogue in the middle east in which was found the famous *Gniza* (documents kept in the synagogue which give an insight into the lives of the Jews of the period) was renovated by the Bronfman family. It was practically reconstructed and beautifully decorated but it has lost its unique character and looks more like a modern museum than a historical synagogue (indeed, it is presently used as a museum).

The most dramatic issue in this context is the awful situation of the Bassatin Jewish Cemetery in Cairo. As previously said, it is crumbling. Tombstones and tombs have disappeared, garbage is scattered everywhere, thousands of squatters have invaded the cemetery and live permanently on its grounds, desecrating tombs, building shanties, cooking, and raising families. (This a common sight in Cairo, where more than two million people live permanently in cemeteries.) Neighboring factories have also infringed on the cemetery boundaries and occupy thousands of square meters including regions where people are actually buried. As if that were not enough, the Egyptian government was planning to build a main road crossing the cemetery in all its length and involving the destruction of hundreds of tombs. Jewish philanthropists in Israel and the United States have strongly protested and succeeded in delaying the project. Engineers and rabbis were dispatched to Cairo to study alternative solutions including the building of an elevated highway that would limit the desecration of tombs to a minimum. They also pledged to collect all remains and bring them to Israel for burial. The Egyptians agreed to the suggested solution but demanded that the Jews cover all supplementary expenses with compound interest, saying shamelessly 'You Jews are very rich and can afford to pay the cost – it is enough that 20 wealthy men like Rothschild donate a million dollars each.' As a matter of course, this cynical proposal was rejected outright! The pressure continued and the American Congress intervened to help settle the issue. President Mubarak personally pledged to cover all expenses from Egyptian sources. Nevertheless, during the Gulf War a delegation of senators visiting Egypt agreed to have the United States bank the check. At the end of my stay in Egypt, experimental excavations raised the acute problem of desecration of tombs. The works were stopped until adequate measures could be taken. I do not know if the issue has been resolved or is still an open wound.

The burial of deceased members of the community is one more cemetery-related problem. There are no rabbis and no Jewish burial societies. Interment is entrusted to a local Coptic undertaker in return for a very small fee (around US $30). He collects the person's body from the hospital and takes it directly to the cemetery. No religious rites are administered and only seldom are representatives of the community present. The body is put into a hole not too deep (digging more would be costlier) and covered with not well-compacted earth. No tombstone, even the most rudimentary, is ever built on the tomb. Many people have told me that they have seen wandering dogs scratching the fresh tombs and feeding on human bones and body parts. I called the attention of the community leaders to this terrible situation. They confirmed that all I had heard was true but stressed that they had no financial means to organize more elaborate funerals or build tombstones. I tried to raise financial support from external sources but I received refusal after refusal. The JOINT said that its mission was 'to help living Jews and not Jews who have passed away'. The Israeli ministry of religions replied that the burial of Jews abroad was 'beyond the scope of its competence'. The Association of Jews from Egypt tried in vain to collect funds for this purpose but Jewish philanthropists preferred to put their money into more appealing causes. Only Nissim Gaon replied positively and raised around US$100,000, not for improving the standard of burials but for building a fence around the part of the cemetery that had not yet been invaded by squatters.

During the works, a new archive was uncovered in the burial vault of the Mosseri family (one of the richest families). Professor Yossi Ginat, the director of the Israeli Academic Center at the time, succeeded in convincing the Egyptian Department of Archeology to allow the transfer of the archive to a hall specially prepared (at the expense of the center) in the Karaite Synagogue in old Cairo. To the best of my knowledge, tens of bags stuffed with documents are still there untouched, waiting for the authorities' permission to begin sorting and studying them.

In the first months after the embassy's inauguration, we thought that we would be able to transfer the remnants of the Jewish community to Israel. It was a heavy burden but at the same time a sacred duty! Feelers put out to the Egyptian government indicated that it had no objection as long as the transfer was carried out discreetly. We directed our efforts first to the less privileged classes. To our great surprise, the response was minor and very few agreed to emigrate. Most of them returned to Egypt within a few months. They simply did not find their place in Israel and felt like strangers in an environment that was dramatically different from the one they were accustomed to. They were too old to change and learn a new language and new way of life. In Egypt, they knew the language, had friends and lived independently. There was no point in trying to convince them that in the long run they would have been much better off in Israel. We accepted the facts of life and did our best to make their lives in Egypt easier. Over the years, a few emigrated to Israel on their own initiative (mostly the wealthier ones) but the great majority remained in Egypt and will probably end their lives there.

In this respect, let me relate a moving experience of a personal character. When I arrived in Egypt in 1980 I was convinced that I had no

remaining relatives in the country. My mother (she lived in Milan), however, told me in a phone conversation that a first cousin on my father's
side was still residing in Egypt. I recalled that in my youth he lived in one
of the most luxurious hotels in Cairo, Hotel National. I checked whether
it was still existing and inquired over the phone if Albert Aboudi (my
cousin) still resided there. To my great surprise, I was put through to his
room. He remembered me and requested that I come immediately to see
him. He was now 82, in poor health and had lost all his assets; he lived in
a small room for which he paid around $20 per month (the hotel had been
nationalized and was practically crumbling; it was demolished in 1985).
Albert had not paid the rent for the last six months and was to be expelled
the next day. For him, it was God who had sent me! I paid his debts and
six months in advance. I regularly gave him small financial support and
added his name to the list of the JOINT's recipients of financial allocations. Once a week, we would eat together in a restaurant of his choice
or in my house.

After a while, I convinced him to leave behind the filth in which he
was living and emigrate to Israel. I obtained for him the requisite paper-
work from the Egyptian authorities and succeeded in arranging a room
in one of the old people's homes in Israel. One day before the date of his
departure, he informed me that he wanted to stay in Egypt until I left the
country: I was the only relative he had and he wanted to stay with me as
long as I remained in Egypt. Naturally, I concurred with his wishes. One
year later, my tenure in Egypt came to an end. I told my cousin that I
would gladly take him with me. He hesitated and requested me to let him
ponder over the matter for a few days. Three days later, he died painlessly
in his sleep. I have no doubt that he would never have emigrated and
severed himself from the surroundings in which he had lived for so many
years. He kept himself alive as long as I was near him in Egypt and, when
he heard of my prospective departure, he let himself peacefully go to a
better world.

In my second tenure, the issue of *Aliah* (emigration to Israel) was no
longer relevant. It was clear that the last remnants of the once glorious
Egyptian Jewry would end their lives in the country in which they were
born, grew up and then grew old. We Israelis have to accept this fact. It
is our duty to do our best to make life easier for them in the few years
they have left and make sure that, after they pass away, they are given a
decent funeral and are buried in a Jewish and humane manner. It is not
beyond the possibilities of the Jewish people and the State of Israel.

10 · The Struggle for Normalization

There is no doubt that Egypt was interested in making peace with Israel and abandoning the vicious circle of military confrontation. I will elaborate later on the reasons that motivated Egypt. At this stage, I will simply state that, after the Yom Kippur War (1973), Egypt strove desperately to reach a peace agreement with Israel and considered the attaining of it to be a vital national interest. On the other hand, establishing a normal relationship with Israel, as is customary between neighboring countries, was not on its agenda of priorities; on the contrary, this was in opposition to its immediate interests and declared policies. Let me recall the repeated statements of President Sadat and other eminent Egyptian leaders that 'the past cannot be erased in one single stroke. Normalization of relations between the two countries should be left to future generations'.

Egypt, however, grasped at an early phase of the negotiations that Israel was determined to secure most components of normal relations; and would not agree to substantial territorial concessions, let alone total withdrawal from Sinai, without reaching significant and overt progress in this field. Political pragmatism brought Egypt to yield to Israeli pressure and more so to American coaxing. However, from the outset, Egypt was determined to pay the lowest possible price in terms of normalization. After lengthy and bitter haggling, the parties specifically agreed in the Camp David agreement to normalize their relations. The different domains were amply detailed but no clear-cut parameters or timetable were defined. This task was left to joint technical committees, which were to study objectively the possibilities in each field and the pace at which progress was to be made. A mandatory date was fixed only for the opening of the respective embassies and the exchange of ambassadors (January and April 1980 respectively).

As for the military aspects, including the withdrawal of Israeli forces from Sinai and the reciprocal security arrangements, the situation was totally different. They were minutely detailed in the military annex to the agreement. No place was left for varying interpretations or the dodging of commitments. Though it was not specified that the withdrawal of Israel in two phases from Sinai was conditional to the fulfillment of Egyptian commitments, it was clear to both sides – and to the American sponsors – that these were two sides of the same coin.

Egypt set aside its reluctance. Immediately after the signing of the Camp David agreements, joint technical committees were established and began functioning. There were no delays and no artificially created obstacles. It took only a few months to put together the full package of primary arrangements especially in all that pertained to the opening of embassies, the establishment of civil aviation links, trade relations and the promotion of tourism in both directions.

When I arrived in Cairo in mid-1980, Israel had already implemented the first phase of withdrawal to the El Arish–Ras Mohamed line. Many joint committees were functioning and almost every day new committees and sub-committees were being established. They met quite often, alternating between Egypt and Israel. Both sides were conscious that they had to find solutions to all pending issues and embody them in binding agreements before the second phase of withdrawal (24 April 1982). In the first stage, the Egyptians dragged their feet and haggled over each detail. The closer D-day became, the faster was the pace of negotiations – and the Egyptian side, and to a certain extent the Israeli side, became more flexible and less doctrinal. True, Israel still used all the cards in its hands to secure maximum gains and Egypt continued to fight tenaciously to limit its concessions, but both sides were extremely cautious not to reach a zero-sum situation. Paradoxically, all through the negotiations both sides knew that most issues agreed upon would not be implemented in the foreseeable future. Nevertheless, they fought as if their very lives depended on each word. No detail was neglected and no field was left aside. The assumption of both sides was that written agreements had their own dynamics: the more explicit and mandatory they were, the less margin of maneuver was left to the parties and the chances to see them implemented, at least partially, increased.

All aspects of bilateral relations were extensively tackled: civil aviation, tourism, commerce, customs, transport, cultural exchanges, youth relations, agriculture, communications, scientific co-operation, political co-ordination. Furthermore, a joint military committee (officially defined as a liaison office) dealt with the heavy issues such as military withdrawal, security arrangements, borders, missing soldiers. Altogether some 50 agreements and agreed minutes (which did not necessitate a complicated and lengthy procedure of ratification) were signed. From the Israeli standpoint, one of the most salient achievements was the establishment of permanent committees with the task of supervising implementation, smoothing difficulties and studying further possibilities of tightening relations. To show its goodwill and the extent of normalization to which it had agreed (at least on paper), Egypt published on the eve of the second phase of withdrawal a booklet encompassing all the agreements signed between the two countries. It was an impressive booklet covering practically all

111

fields of interaction. To our great sorrow, normalization itself proved to be much less impressive!

The composition of the Israeli and Egyptian delegations to the negotiations was absolutely asymmetrical. Israeli delegations were chaired by the director-general of the relevant ministry and composed of its best experts on the issues under discussion. One or two diplomats from the embassy or the foreign ministry covered the political aspects. Egypt, on the other hand, would send to all meetings, regardless of the issue, the same team of diplomats who were dealing with Israeli affairs in the foreign ministry. A minister plenipotentiary, or at most a junior ambassador, chaired its delegation (only when a minister presided over the Israeli delegation did the Egyptians condescend to raise the rank of their chairman to that of deputy director-general in the foreign ministry). Only one or two technicians from the relevant ministry tackled the professional aspects. The composition of the Israeli delegation changed in accordance with the topic on the agenda; the Egyptian delegation was perennial and only technical experts changed. In other words, while Israel dispatched teams of professionals regarding the issue under discussion, Egypt dispatched experts in Israeli affairs and in negotiating with Israel.

Understandably, the starting point of each side was different. While the Israelis focused on the professional issues and looked for the best technical solutions, the Egyptians focused on the political aspects and looked for ways of limiting unnecessary commitments – even when they were professionally justified. Their only criteria was the policy established by their superiors as to the scope of normalization with Israel. The Egyptians' goal was not to foster normalization but to limit it to a bare minimum. The fact that Egyptian delegations were of relative low ranking allowed them to forestall adoption of obviously justified technical solutions with the excuse that they had to consult with their superiors and with the professionals. The senior composition of the Israeli teams did not allow such flexibility and decisions were taken on the spot.

Incidentally, the Egyptians did not even try to conceal their purpose. Colleagues in the Egyptian foreign ministry with whom I was in daily contact, and with whom I had cordial personal relations (at least on my side), spoke frankly about the parameters that had been set by the highest authorities for the normalization talks. They did not conceal the fact that the composition of their delegations and the pattern they had followed had been established in the light of the too good results achieved in the first few meetings when professionals led the game. They reached the conclusion that technical experts tended to be guided by professional considerations and made unnecessary concessions deviating from Egypt's basic policies.

Another aspect – no less disturbing – was the size of Israeli delegations and their tendency to overstay their welcome and combine pleasure with business. There were neither financial hindrances nor administrative limitations to adding members to a delegation (even if they were not objectively needed) or to extending the number of days of stay beyond actual needs. In accordance with a decision taken in the first stage of the negotiations, each side disbursed all the expenses involved in hosting the other country's delegations. We should not forget that it was still a very early phase and the curiosity to know Egypt and meet Egyptians was very great. Almost every high official (and indeed almost every Israeli) wanted to have the opportunity to see with their own eyes what Egypt was about. The Egyptians were aware of this situation but they never made any negative comment. On the contrary, they gave red-carpet treatment to all Israeli delegations and hosted them lavishly in the best hotels, organized tours of Cairo, Alexandria and Upper Egypt, took them to typical oriental restaurants and night clubs, offered gifts, and so on and so forth.

When their turn to visit Israel arrived, Egyptians would send small delegations (mostly the same diplomats who participated in all the negotiations) and limit their stay to the bare minimum in accordance with the flight schedules. They rejected any program that was not directly linked with the purpose of their visit and preferred to tour the country unaccompanied. In time, they became more flexible. Incidentally, Egyptian functionaries were eager to be sent to Israel. They received full *per-diem* allocations from their government though Israel hosted them and covered all their expenses. They ordered substantial quantities of hard liquor from room service and had lengthy international phone conversations. After a few months of honeymoon, our department of official guests informed them that these two items were not included in our hospitality and would have to be covered by each of them. Let me add that, if the Egyptian side did not follow the Israeli pattern, it was not out of ethical considerations but because their government wanted to prevent undue fraternization and limit contacts to the minimum.

At first, Egyptian delegations refused to reside or hold meetings in Jerusalem because of the negative political connotations entailed. Israel could not turn a blind eye to this provocation. It was counterproductive to stop the negotiations on this ground and we retaliated by refusing to hold meetings in Cairo. We also postponed the convening of joint committees in Israel until the problem found its solution. Bitter discussions and much bickering took place around the issue. It was President Sadat himself who decided upon a compromise solution: Egyptian delegations would be allowed to come to Jerusalem for working meetings but were to reside outside the city. To this day, it is referred to as Sadat's formula (though in reality, I planted the idea during a meeting with the president). Negotiations continued unimpeded and at a stepped-up pace.

Finally, 24 April arrived and the second phase of withdrawal from Sinai (indeed total withdrawal) was implemented. Up to the last moment, Egypt held its breath and lived with the nightmare that Israel might, under any pretext, postpone the withdrawal or, worse, cancel it altogether.

In the final months before the withdrawal, Egypt went out of its way to send positive signals to Israel and multiply goodwill gestures. Suddenly, there was no more foot-dragging, unjustified haggling or bickering. The whole envelope of normalization agreements was concluded within a few weeks via an accelerated procedure.

Only very few agreements, which fitted into the Egyptian policy of normalization, were implemented. The great majority remained a dead letter or were implemented only partially – in total disregard of Egypt's signature on binding international instruments. Clearly, throughout the negotiations Israel was aware that the Egyptians did not intend to live up to all their commitments but it did not think that they would go so far as to practically ignore all of them. In any case, Israel had no choice but to turn a blind eye to the Egyptian infractions. We all hoped that with time the atmosphere would improve and lead to the tightening of relations and to the gradual removal of the obstacles erected by Egypt to prevent normal relations between the two countries. I have to admit that we were wrong. Twenty years after peace, the situation has not improved; on the contrary, it has worsened!

On 25 April 1982, one day after the total withdrawal of Israel from Sinai, I sent (with Ambassador Sasson's approval) to the foreign ministry and to other relevant authorities a long memorandum under the title '25 April and after'. I expounded the collective opinion of the Israeli team in Cairo that the withdrawal would not bring about a breakthrough in the normalization of relations between the two countries. On the contrary, it was to be expected that Egypt would continue to use normalization as a tool of pressure on Israel in bilateral topics in dispute and in issues related to the peace process in general. I pointed out that Egypt would, from time to time, bestow on Israel small doses of normalization with a view to creating an atmosphere conducive to achieving its aims of the moment. Immediately afterwards, it would dodge its commitments and raise new demands. Again, Egypt would make numerous promises and small gestures of goodwill and throw at Israel a few crumbs from the normalization table. But again, as soon as its goals were attained, it would evade its commitments and go on to the next goal and so on and so forth ... I concluded by stressing that as long as Israel continued to show eagerness to foster normalization and was ready to pay again and again for the goods it had already paid for, Egypt would exact an ever-increasing price for every gesture of good will.

I also foretold in the memorandum that after the Taba issue (which was at the time the main issue of contention) found its solution, new demands in the realm of the negotiations with the Palestinians and the Syrians would be brought forward as a precondition for improving normalization. The sky was the limit: recognition of the Palestine Liberation Organization (PLO), direct negotiations with that organization, return to the 1967 cease-fire line, Arab sovereignty in East Jerusalem, withdrawal from the Golan and renunciation by Israel of non-conventional weapons (which, according to the Arabs, Israel possesses). I added the opinion that, even if all these demands were fully met by Israel, the limitations on normalization would still not be abrogated and the machinery, established especially by Egypt to prevent it from developing, would not be dismantled. I explained in the memorandum that Egypt's motivation went well beyond tactical considerations. It genuinely feared that if normalization were not strictly controlled, Israel would gradually push it out of its leading role in the middle east. It also feared that a free flow of information and unsupervised contacts with a neighboring country that had a democratic regime and an open society would increase social and political strife in Egypt. (All these considerations remain valid today.)

In response to the memorandum, we received a mild rebuke from Jerusalem. We were told that our analysis was too pessimistic and that we must have been influenced in our assessments by the atmosphere in Cairo. We knew that we were right but we realized that it would be point-less to engage in endless polemics with the concept that prevailed at the time in Jerusalem. We rolled up our sleeves and went back to the busi-ness of building peace. A few weeks later, the Peace for Galilee campaign opened. Israeli troops entered Lebanon and quickly reached the outskirts of Beirut. This gave Egypt formal justification not to move ahead with normalization, freeze the little that existed and recall its ambassador to Israel for alleged consultations. (I elaborated on this issue in chapter 6.) Our disappointment was great but we consoled ourselves with the assess-ment that, on the other hand, Egypt had proven in a glaring manner its absolute commitment to peace (but not to normalization!). It did not return to military confrontation even when two brother Arab states (Lebanon and Syria) were engaged in a fully-fledged war with Israel.

When I returned to Cairo in 1990, the unending seesaw of the nor-malization committees, which had characterized the first years, had come to a standstill. There was no need to drive almost daily to the airport to receive delegations or escort them back. The seasoning added by the social events, the meetings and the outings that had livened up the delegations' visits (and our life in Cairo), had ceased altogether. The give-and-take process on the substance of the relations between the two countries was practically non-existent. It should not have been so! Many permanent joint committees had been established by virtue of the normalization agreements and should have been convening regularly. Egyptians had no interest in normalization and no will to respond, even seemingly, to Israel's insistence. On the contrary, they had learnt from experience that the convening of a joint committee, and even the setting of a date for it, was an effective tool of pressure and reward. The issue became an important ingredient of the carrot-and-stick policy imple-mented against Israel, which had reaped, time and again, substantial fruit. The scenario evolved as follows: Israel would request the convening of this or that committee to tackle urgent matters (at least in its eyes). For a few weeks the Egyptians would show a deaf ear. After repeated Israeli approaches at different levels, Egyptian colleagues would let us know that the circumstances were not propitious for convening a meeting and would indicate confidentially that if Israel took a certain course of action or moderated its position on a specific issue, the meeting would be scheduled. Firm promises would be made at the most senior level and sometimes a date would be set. Then came repeated last-minute post-ponements under various pretexts. Finally the meeting would be canceled with the pretence that the situation was not conducive to goodwill gestures in the realm of normalization. The entire scenario began again from scratch in an interminable merry-go-round. During the whole two years of my stay in Cairo, I tried intensively to persuade the Egyptians to convene the joint committees for commerce and tourism, losing my self-respect in my own eyes (all in the name of duty!). The topic was raised many times, by me and by visiting Israeli ministers and high officials, at the most senior levels. Each time, firm promises were made but were never kept. Needless to say that the two committees did not convene either during my whole tenure in Cairo, nor for many years after I had left Egypt definitively.

Very soon after my arrival, I grasped that the convening of committees was only the tip of the iceberg and that the pessimistic forecast that I had made in my memorandum to Jerusalem in April 1982 was materializing in full. The Taba issue had been settled to the satisfaction of Egypt, the War of Galilee was well behind us, the peace process was taking a positive turn (it brought about the Madrid conference a year later), many disputes had been resolved and 15 years had gone by since the signing of the peace treaty. Yet Egypt had not changed its policies in regard to the normalization of relations between the two countries. Not only had there been no improvement but, on the contrary, the situation had drastically deteriorated in all fields of interaction. All cultural and social contacts had completely ceased, the volume of trade had fallen from US $80 million in 1982 to a bare $12 million in 1990, the need for an exit visa to Israel (the yellow card) had not been abolished and practically no Egyptian was allowed to visit Israel. Only selected Israeli personalities (regarded as favorable to Egyptian stands) were invited to Cairo. The social boycott on Israeli diplomats had become more stringent, the anti-Semitic and anti-Israeli campaigns in the media more virulent and more frequent, the participation of Israel and Israeli institutions (private or public) in international fairs had been discontinued. Last but not least, the apparatus set up for supervising and hampering normalization had become a well-oiled machine. The Egyptian security services led the game behind the curtain and the Israel department in the foreign ministry (whose task was allegedly to foster relations between the two countries) played a major role in impeding normalization.

Why is Egypt acting in this manner? What is its motivation and what are its hidden goals? As Hamlet said: 'There is a system in this madness.' I will try to explain how Egypt looks upon normalization and what the steps are which it takes to make sure that it is kept within the limits it has determined from the outset of the peace process. As a matter of course, my analysis reflects only my personal opinion, but it is an opinion that is based on the experience of many years (practically from day one) and has been tested, time and again, in the light of reality. I never concealed my views from my superiors in Jerusalem. In the first years, they believed that I was too pessimistic. They were convinced that time would remedy everything and that there was no basic flaw in Egypt's concept of normalization. I believe that today everyone dealing with Egyptian affairs shares the views I expressed in the early 1980s.

I will begin with the half of the glass that is full (I have to stress that the normalization glass is not completely empty). There is no shadow of a doubt that Egypt is absolutely committed to peace and is in this respect more Catholic than the Pope. It strives with all its strength to widen the scope of peace and to reach a global settlement of the Israeli–Arab conflict. However, it is important to know that its concept of peace and the principles on which peace should be founded is altogether different from Israel's approach (I will elaborate on this point at a later stage). I do not foresee any situation in which Egypt would return to military confrontation excluding, naturally, if Israel were to attack it or put in jeopardy its vital interests. Egypt has learned the lesson of its wars against Israel and it will not go back to war for the sake of Palestinians, Lebanese, Syrians or any other factor that is not directly linked to its national interest. This assumption has repeatedly been substantiated in the most blatant manner. Recurrent warring in Lebanon, five long years of the Palestinian *Intifada*, the uncompromising stands of Israel on the Golan and Jerusalem, the stalemate in the peace negotiations, the bombing of the Iraqi nuclear reactor and many other events of the kind did not cause Egypt to revert to arms.

This does not mean that Egypt has forsaken Arab interests and goals, or ceased trying to achieve them. Even after it had signed, against the Arab consensus, a separate peace with Israel and had been ousted from the Arab League, Egypt did not cease to see itself as the leader of the Arab world and to spearhead Arab efforts to achieve their goals. Its bold decision to make peace with Israel was motivated by the conviction (in the light of the outcome of the 1973 war) that it was pointless to continue to try to achieve Arab goals on the battlefield. Much more could be obtained around the negotiating table. Indeed, Egypt recuperated the whole of Sinai without firing a single shot. Furthermore, Egypt believed, and still believes, that the Arab world is strong enough to prevent the total integration of Israel in the region and forestall its taking control of their economic and financial systems. The Arab world can also, with the guidance of Egypt (which considers itself an expert on the matter), limit to a bare minimum the possible damage of Israel's negative example on the social, political and cultural texture of the region. (I will return to this topic in other contexts.) To support my contention, I will provide only two references that clearly reflect the Egyptian approach:

- An editorial by Ibrahim Saada in the daily *Al Akhbar*, published in 1982 immediately after the beginning of the war of Galilee;
- A speech by President Mubarak in 1991 to an audience of students at Cairo University in the wake of increasing public criticism of Egypt's stands in the Gulf crisis.

Ibrahim Saada, who was the court journalist at the time, wrote among other 'pearls' (I quote from memory using my own words):

> Cheating the Jews is a good deed. The Jews are by nature felons and swindlers. Throughout history, they have repeatedly deceived Egypt and done enormous damage to it. This goes back as far as the Jews of Elephantine [a small island in the Nile near Assuan where the ancient city of *Yav* was situated] who betrayed the Pharaoh of the time and opened the gates of Egypt to foreign invaders. The temptation to rescind the Camp David agreements is very strong but we should not let our feelings blind us. We have first to examine, carefully and objectively, whether such a step serves Egyptian interests. It is evident that, if Egypt adopts such a course, it will be branded as the aggressor and accused of breaching its international commitments. The West, which traditionally supports Israel, will stop all assistance, investments and commerce. Since Sinai is demilitarized, in less than 24 hours Israel's tanks will be back on the Suez Canal. This invasion will be considered a legitimate action of self-defense. The cities along the Canal will again be heavily bombarded, the population will flee and the Canal will be closed to international navigation. The oil wells in Sinai will fall into the hands of Israel and the wells in the Red Sea will come to a standstill. The USA will discontinue arms deliveries to the Egyptian armed forces to replace the archaic Russian weaponry. The Soviet Union [still existing at the time] will not come to our rescue and will not provide us with weapons or spare parts. They cannot so easily forget that we refused to join the communist bloc and booted them out of Egypt. Europe, the only other source of sophisticated weapons, will want cash before delivering any goods. As usual, our Arab brethren will not extend any substantial assistance and, on the contrary, will rejoice at our difficulties. To sum up, Egypt will lose more than $12 billion annually and will find itself without arms, defenseless before its enemies (and not only Israel). Gnashing our teeth, we have to draw the logical conclusion from this analysis:

peace with Israel serves Egypt's vital interests. We cannot now afford to rescind the peace treaty with Israel and evade our binding commitments. At this stage, the most Egypt can do is to limit the normalization of relations with Israel to a bare minimum and thus express its abhorrence of Israel and the Jews.

Ten years later (in 1991), in an address to Cairo University students, President Mubarak set aside his written text and, in vernacular Egyptian Arabic, expounded with the utmost frankness his feelings (I am providing from memory a résumé of what he said):

What is all this criticism about? Those who indulge in criticism all the time do not know what they are saying. They have no idea of what was the situation. At the end of 1973, we had gone bankrupt, the treasury was empty and we were not able to pay for the wheat that we had to import for feeding the people. The Egyptian army was in urgent need of spare parts and new weapons. The warehouses were empty. Notwithstanding the glorious October victory [Egyptians present the Yom Kippur War as a great Egyptian victory though they know the historical truth and admit it in private conversations], the war had been very difficult and our armed forces urgently needed thorough reorganization and rehabilitation. The cities on the Suez Canal were in ruins, Sinai was in the hands of the Jews and they sat safely on the Canal banks, prevented navigation and exploited our oil wells. We looked for allies who would assist us. The Soviet Union, which was still in existence, was not ready even to listen to us. The European powers aired numerous statements of friendship and support but, when we asked them to provide us with arms, they said: 'Pay!' Only the USA expressed its willingness to help us and exert its influence on the Jews to return our land [Sinai]. Against us stood the most intelligent people on earth – a people that controls the international press, world economy and world finances. We succeeded in compelling the Jews to do what we wanted; we received all our land back, up to the last grain of sand! We have outwitted them and what did we give them in return? A piece of paper! The Arabs, and those who criticize us from within, were telling us that the Jews would not carry out the second phase of withdrawal and, here, all Sinai has been returned on time. They told us then that the Jews had kept Taba [a small enclave near Eilat] and had double-crossed us and, here, we have succeeded in taking back Taba from the clutches of the Jews. They warned us that the Jews would take control of our economy and our finances, that they would flood us with their goods and their factories, that they would invade us by the thousands and fill our cities and our universities. They warned us that the Jews would penetrate our very souls, corrupt our religion and our cultural

119

values, and lead our youngsters astray … Now, ten years have gone by. Did any of these apocalyptic prophecies materialize? No and no! Look around you and judge! We were shrewder than the shrewdest people on earth! We managed to hamper their steps in every direction. We have established sophisticated machinery to control and limit to the minimum contacts with the Jews. We have proven that making peace with Israel does not entail Jewish domination and that there is no obligation to develop with Israel relations beyond those we desire. With a delay of many years, the Arabs have come to the conclusion that Egypt was right and they are now following in our footsteps. We can guide and direct them in the light of our own experience with the Jews. We have also succeeded in getting closer to the USA, which holds all the cards in its hands. Egypt has become their privileged partner in the middle east.

To the best of my recollection, this part of the speech was not published in the press. The whole ceremony was, however, broadcast live on Egyptian television and I heard it with my own ears. The use of the term 'Jews' and not Israelis is not the fruit of my imagination but an exact quote from the president's words. Incidentally, Egyptians and Arabs in general do not distinguish between Jews and Israelis: they consider them as one. It is important to understand that this was not an anti-Semitic outburst on the part of the president. Paradoxical as it may sound, it reflected, on the contrary, his high esteem for the capabilities of the Jewish people. As for normalization, there was nothing new or surprising for me in the president's remarks. I knew exactly what he was referring to from my daily experiences. For me, the only significant message in President Mubarak's speech was the staunch commitment to peace which he reiterated many times in the very den of the opponents of peace – the University of Cairo.

Egypt's policy towards normalization was established at a very early stage, still in President Sadat's time. The tools and means of action were also devised and put in place during his period. President Mubarak continued to tread the same line and improved upon it. It is difficult to evaluate what would have been the situation today if Sadat had not been assassinated and had continued to rule Egypt. It is a hypothetical assumption; the sad fact is that Sadat stepped down from the stage of history at a very early phase – well before the conclusion of most normalization agreements and the implementation of the second phase of withdrawal from Sinai. Nevertheless, I will not evade the question. In my opinion, the situation with respect to normalization would have been in broad lines exactly the same because it finds its deep motivation in Egyptian genuine interests and anxieties. It is probable that Sadat would have shown more flexibility and that the music accompanying the tune would have been more pleasing to the ear but basically we would have found ourselves in the same situation as the one we are in today.

At the base of Egypt's policy lay the profound conviction that Israel is, first and foremost, interested in keeping a reasonable framework of peace in the region and that, if it has no choice, it will disregard the trimmings of normalization. From the outset, Egypt has defined the scope, depth and range of relations that should be considered the basic level of relations for an undetermined period of time or, as I call it, The Ground Level of Relations. It encompasses what I define as the peace assets of permanent value that cannot be impaired without shaking dangerously the delicate equilibrium created by peace. I will enumerate these components briefly:

- No regression from peace;
- Honoring the military agreements to the dot;
- Maintaining diplomatic and consular relations;
- Free passage of Israeli shipping in the Suez Canal;
- Formal abolition of the Arab boycott and all other discriminating regulations (though trade with Israel is limited to a bare minimum through administrative measures);
- Prevention of terrorist attacks on Israel from the Egyptian border;
- Non-intervention of Egypt's armed forces in armed conflicts between Israel and other Arab states;
- Maintainance of unhampered air, sea and ground communications;
- Sale of crude oil to Israel and maintainance of minimal trade relations with it;
- Allowing (but not encouraging) Israeli tourism to Egypt;
- Maintaining open channels of dialogue between the two countries and persevering in efforts to establish a comprehensive peace in the region.

As previously stressed, these components are most important in themselves. Indeed, they are the essence of peace itself and the backbone of the relations between the two countries. The normalization agreements went much further; they added more components and new dimensions. However, both sides considered, and rightly so, that they were less critical than the basic peace assets. From the outset, Egypt made the assessment that not honoring them would not bring about confrontation or destroy the fragile equilibrium established between the two countries. It was convinced that Israel would not jeopardize peace because of the trimmings of normalization and would have no choice but to accept the situation. This assessment proved to be accurate! Over the years, Egypt succeeded, without taking unnecessary risks, in evading consciously and systematically the implementation of most paragraphs of the normalization agreements. Furthermore, using a method of punishment and reward, it succeeded in making them into a formidable tool for putting pressure on Israel and for sending messages and signals – both positive and negative – to Israel, the Arab states and the Egyptian people.

Israel's yearning for recognition and warmth, its eagerness for normal relations and its obvious readiness to pay, again and again, for the same crumbs from the normalization table encouraged Egypt to increase the use of a tool that had proven its efficiency. The Egyptians learned that smiles have a price and that Israel is willing to pay this price not only once but as many times as it takes. Thus, the meeting of a joint committee, the visit of a personality to either country, the exchange of delegations, the sending of a group of tourists to Israel, co-operation in any field, moderating attacks in the media, easing the security arrangements around the embassy – all these were made into goods to be sold for a price. Similarly, license to publish a bulletin, permission to hold cultural activities, a marginal improvement in the volume of trade, meetings with Egyptian personalities, consent to an invitation to dinner, participation in a trade or cultural fair and a score of similar minor items became a merchandise that had an ever-increasing price. Israel was always ready to buy whatever the Egyptians offered even if it had already bought the very same merchandise numerous times in the past and paid the full price for it each time (with compound interest). This is still the case.

The Ground Level of Relations is not static. The Egyptian authorities allow upward and downward fluctuations as a function of the situation prevailing at the time and Egypt's changing political needs and goals. But, after a relatively short period, they always make sure that it returns to the level that they have determined as the minimum extent of relations needed to avoid rocking the boat and jeopardizing the peace itself (which, as I have repeatedly stressed, Egypt wants to preserve). To clarify things more vividly, let me say that it resembles somewhat the Policy of the Diagonal implemented by the Central Bank of Israel (until recently) for maintaining the rate of the shekel at a certain level corresponding to the economic needs of the country. The Bank, however, allows a leeway of 7 per cent upwards or downwards in accordance with market forces but it intervenes to restore the rate to the determined level as quickly as possible. Egypt does exactly the same: the Ground Level of Relations is the level of the Central Bank dollar. Fluctuations are allowed but only within certain limits! The only difference between the two is that, in Egypt's case, there are no market forces and the fluctuations are due exclusively to the manipulations of the Egyptian authorities themselves.

In the embassy, we used jokingly to call these fluctuations Periods of Smiles and Periods of Anger. During the 'periods of smiles', we strove to achieve some progress in the hope that in the long run we would gradually lift upwards the Ground Level of Relations determined by the Egyptians. We had no illusion that we would be able to bring about dramatic changes but we also did not fear that, in periods of anger, the assets of permanent value would be impaired. In these periods, and they came as surely as night follows day, we armed ourselves with patience and waited for the storm to pass.

It is with profound grief that I have to say that, after more than 20 years of strenuous efforts, patience and forbearance, we have only succeeded in obtaining marginal improvements. The Egyptians blocked our steps in every direction and managed to stick religiously to the parameters they had defined from the outset for the Ground Level of Relations and to prevent time from mending the situation, as we thought that it would. Throughout the years Egypt led the game masterfully. Even now, after more than 20 years of peace, the situation is no better than it was at the beginning. The regulation of the normalization flow remains a well-oiled political tool and a proven means of reward and penalty. It continues to bear fruit to this very day because of Israel's readiness to play the game according to the rules set by Egypt. Israel turns a blind eye to Egypt's continuous breaches of its contractual commitments and continues to hope that with time the situation will improve.

The political and material gains achieved by Egypt's policy of controlling normalization are only a byproduct – a fringe benefit. The prime reason for this policy stems from Egypt's fear that Israel will replace it as the leading power in the region by virtue of the dynamism of its people. Nothing enrages Egypt more than statements on 'a new middle east'. For Egypt, there is nothing wrong with the old middle east – it is its own playground, where it leads the game and carries tremendous influence. Egypt does not understand why it should make Israel into a senior or even junior partner in the region and allow it to compete with Egypt over regional leadership and her own captive markets.

Egypt – people and leadership – genuinely believes that the assumptions underlying *The Protocols of the Elders of Zion* are basically true. It is not sheer anti-Semitism. On the contrary, it stems from a genuine admiration for the Jewish people's national character. Egyptians are convinced that all the Jewish communities, scattered around the world, are closely linked and co-ordinate their actions, making them a mighty force that rules the world and leads the west in general and the USA in particular by the nose. It is useless to try persuading them that world Jewry controls neither the world economies nor the international media. For them, it is a fact or, more exactly, an axiom that need not be proven. I will give only one example to substantiate the extent of this phenomenon. A few days after the Watts riots in Los Angeles, Professor Yusef Wali, the deputy prime minister and secretary-general of the ruling party and one of the most trustworthy supporters of peace, stunned me by saying at one of our many meetings (I quote from memory):

> The riots were not the result of a regrettable police incident as the international press wants us to believe. They were well planned and carried out masterfully. The Jews in the United States pulled the strings. They wanted to teach President Bush a lesson because he refused to give US guarantees for loans for the absorption of the

> Russian immigrants in Israel [\$10 billion] and was threatening to impose sanctions on Israel if Yitshak Shamir did not show more flexibility in the peace process. If Bush does not grasp the hint and change course in time, the Jews have the capacity to prevent his re-election and they will certainly do so.

I tried in vain to make him understand the absurdity of his assessment and prove that it had no factual or logical ground whatsoever. But he did not budge from his opinion and reiterated it again and again. I am sure that Bill Clinton's victory in the presidential elections of 1992 has irremediably strengthened Yusuf Wali in his beliefs.

Paradoxical as it may sound, Egypt genuinely fears that Israel, with the help of world Jewry, will take control of its economy and its financial system and gradually come to pervade all walks of life within Egypt itself. Hence, it considers that the elaborate machinery it has set up to hamper the normal flow of relations between the two countries is a legitimate means of self-defense and is intended to forestall Israeli domination. The whole operation is entrusted to the security services and indeed they control not only the water mains that regulate the broad principles of normalization but also the smallest taps that adjust the minutest details of the process. The dosage that they allow depends on the situation prevailing and on the goals they want to achieve at a determined time.

Egypt also wants to prove to the Arab world that it is possible to maintain relations with Israel and at the same time prevent it from assuming control of the region or of their internal systems. It strives to show that Israel can be mastered and deprived of any accomplishment that does not meet Arab approval. One more aspect for restraining normalization, though less crucial, is the increase of Muslim militancy in Egypt and the opposition of Egyptian intellectuals to peace (not only normalization). As long as the authorities continue to regulate normalization with an iron fist and prevent the outward signs of too great a *rapprochement* with Israel, they use the plausible alibi that peace is a necessary evil that Egypt is compelled to live with. Egypt strives to demonstrate that it is making the most out of peace without endangering its vital interests and without an unbearable degree of intimacy with Israel.

However, as I have said previously, the tendency is always to return to the Ground Level of Relations without impairing the peace assets of permanent value. This is better than nothing and certainly better than military confrontation. That does not mean that I condone Egypt's infractions or approve of their obvious tactics to hamper the normal flow of relations. I have striven here to describe the situation as objectively as I could and give an insight into Egypt's complex reasoning. In my opinion, it was possible in the first stage of peace to, among other things, bring about wider compliance with the normalization agreements and at least to remove blatant absurdities such as the yellow card, the boycott of the trade unions and the public sector, and the commercial restrictions. Truly, we did not neglect these issues but we should have shown more determination, taken more risks and put more pressure on the Egyptian authorities to live up to their commitments, even if it meant renouncing marginal and momentary achievements. Today, it seems to me that our margin for maneuver is much smaller. The patterns of normalization have become a matter of routine that will be very difficult to change. We have also lost any leverage on Egypt that we might have had in the past. We will have, for a very long time, to satisfy ourselves with what Egypt is ready to give us. It is not enough, but it is still quite significant!

I am asked many times what is my opinion on the cold peace with Egypt. I normally answer with sophistry that peace has no temperature. It is a concept that is absolute: either peace exists or it does not exist – there is no middle way. Bilateral relations, on the other hand, can be tighter or looser, more friendly or less friendly, cooler or warmer. However, the nature of the relations does not impair peace itself and its very existence – naturally, as long as both countries have a vital interest in preserving it. It is clear that in the long run strained and cold relations have a cumulative negative effect and, in the long run, could have dangerous implications that might jeopardize the very existence of peace. At this stage, peace is solid and steadfast. Despite the difficulties in the scope of normalization (or rather the absence of normalization) and the ups and downs in the peace process, no grave danger casts its shadow over peace in the foreseeable future. Nevertheless, we should not turn a blind eye to the present situation and dismiss it from our agenda. In the long run, it is fraught with danger. In any case, Israel should not continue to take part in the game according to the rules that Egypt imposes. In spite of its limited margin for maneuver and its eagerness to maintain peace at all costs, Israel has a wide array of possibilities for bringing about significant changes in these rules without endangering 'the bird we have in hand' – PEACE. Yet, in spite of everything, it is a wonderful achievement! It should be preserved at all costs, and enhanced and widened to encompass the whole region.

11 · *Invitations and Visits*

A ny trainee diplomat knows that, in the arsenal of international diplomacy, invitations and visits are among the most favored tools for conveying signals and messages and highlighting the state of relations between two countries at a given time. The same applies to refusing invitations and refraining from visits to the other country. Extending an invitation has in itself an intrinsic value, whether the visit takes place or not. Putting off the date of a visit by one of the two countries after it has been set or manifesting an obvious desire to postpone the visit *sine die* sends dire omens. The character of the visit (official, semi-official, private), the intensity of the program, the list of meetings, the inclusion or non-inclusion of a meeting with the president or the prime minister, are important signals. The number of formal meals, the composition of the attending guests, the exchange of toasts and speeches, the media coverage, and a score of other small details speak for themselves and indicate what winds are blowing on the relations between the two countries.

This kind of signaling is particularly significant in the Israeli–Egyptian context where the web of relations is intricate and delicate. Any signal, any step – positive or negative – is amplified many times and has an impact well beyond its real proportion. To the credit of Egyptian diplomacy, I have to say that it has very quickly grasped the importance of this tool in dealing with Israel and has succeeded in making its usage into a real art. From the first moment, the Egyptians have understood the Israeli soul and sensed the eagerness of Israelis for close relations and external signs of friendship – small as they might be. Mutual visits and invitations became in their experienced hands (like other ingredients of normalization) goods to be exchanged for a price. As for any other merchandise, its value increased in direct proportion to its scarcity on the market. The Egyptians also realized that Israel was ready to pay (again, as for other ingredients of normalization) with gestures of goodwill and tangible concessions and even to pay several times for the same merchandise in the vain hope that it would finally be delivered. Naturally, this Israeli weakness was a golden opportunity for them not only to charge exorbitant prices but also to give a new dimension to their policy of reward and penalty (the stick and the carrot) they had implemented towards Israel from day one. Thus, setting a date for the meeting of a joint committee, extending an invitation to an Israeli personality to visit Egypt or alternatively accepting an invitation to visit Israel, developed gradually from an insignificant side issue to the very essence of bilateral relations between the two countries. Interminable discussions and hard bargaining took place around each invitation or meeting. Egypt avoided giving a clear-cut answer; Israel would persist stubbornly and come back to the matter time after time. It never considered a negative answer to be final.

The Egyptians had the ultimate panacea to ease any tension that clouded relations between the two countries or allegedly to solve any problem of substance. They simply hinted that they might consider setting a date for the convening of a joint committee, or agree to the visit of an Israeli personality, or dispatch an Egyptian delegation to Israel. As time passed, they would evade their commitments applying the theory of stages. First, they would claim that the situation was difficult and did not allow business as usual, then they would hint that if certain preconditions were met they would be more flexible. They would give half a promise and, when Israel's nagging became unbearable in its intensity, they would finally give a fully-fledged commitment and reiterate it in every meeting and at every opportunity – presenting it as a major breakthrough. Sometimes, they would go as far as actually setting a date. Subsequently, they would postpone it time and again. Then they would suggest a new date, pledging that it was final and again find an excuse to avoid keeping their pledge. And the merry-go-round would continue endlessly ... In most cases, they would drag their feet for months and wait for the issue to die quietly. Only very seldom, if it served their purpose of the moment, did they actually live up to their commitment.

For Israel, promises and even half-promises were a significant success. The realization of a visit or the convening of a joint committee was a real breakthrough – even if no concrete results were achieved. Paradoxically, the visits or the meetings were the achievement in themselves! The traffic (of visits) was almost absolutely in one direction. Israeli personalities looked for any opportunity or excuse to visit Egypt. Over the years, practically all ministers, director-generals, top political personalities and high officials visited Egypt in response to an Egyptian invitation or as members of an official delegation. As a matter of course, each visit had its price. Our Egyptian counterparts were also eager to visit Israel, and many of them received official invitations, but their government forbade them (yes, forbade them) to visit Israel or accept invitations (even an invitation to a social event). Only diplomats dealing with Israeli affairs and a few experts (included in Egyptian delegations) were allowed to travel to Israel for very short periods after receiving special authorization (given sparingly) from the security services and other relevant authorities.

It is a well-publicized secret that President Mubarak stubbornly refuses to visit Israel though a score of invitations have been extended to him.

More exactly, he did come to Israel for a few hours on a single occasion. It was on the occasion of Prime Minister Rabin's funeral after his horrendous assassination that shocked the whole world. How sad and how disappointing! All the meetings with Mubarak took place on Egyptian soil or outside of the region. In this respect, Israel – under all its successive governments – desisted totally from the principle of reciprocity, which is the essence of international interaction. Only once did President Weizman threaten not to visit Egypt again if President Mubarak did not reciprocate. However, 'the cup is far from the lips' and, since then, President Weizman went many more times to Egypt for meetings with President Mubarak without having had the pleasure of receiving him in Israel. Mubarak used to reject invitations by saying that he would come to Israel only when the political situation justified his visit (it seems that it never did!). He used the same excuse to refuse meeting in Egypt, or elsewhere, with Menahem Begin and later with his successor, Yitshak Shamir. He made it clear that he would meet with them only after thorough preparations (read: after Israel agreed in advance to the outcome wished by Egypt). Indeed, from Mubarak's accession to the presidency up to the election of the late Yitshak Rabin as prime minister of Israel – for ten long years – no summit conference between the leaders of the two countries took place. To be quite accurate, in this period Begin met Mubarak briefly on the occasion of Sadat's funeral and Shimon Peres was received twice for a one-day visit intended to pave the way to the solution of the Taba problem.

Furthermore, only the Egyptian ministers of foreign affairs, tourism and petrol have been allowed over the years to visit Israel a few times on official business (I do not count the ministers who accompanied Sadat on his historic visit). For all other ministers, Israel is out of bounds! Even the staunch supporter of peace and our great friend, Professor Yussuf Wali, is prevented from visiting Israel though all Israeli ministers of agriculture did visit Egypt more than once at his invitation. Even the pretence that agriculture is a privileged field of co-operation between the two countries did not bring Wali to break the taboo. General (res.) Raphael Eytan (Raful) refused, when he was minister of agriculture in the Shamir government, to accept Wali's repeated invitations as long as he did not first reciprocate and come to Israel. Even the repeated pressures exerted by the Israeli embassy in Cairo, which was interested in the slightest outward sign of relaxation of the very tense situation prevailing at the time, did not make him budge an inch from his position.

The situation in other fields was no less gloomy. Only once was a parliamentary delegation allowed to visit Israel – more than 18 years ago, in the first half of 1981. In accordance with the Egyptian pattern, the visit was scheduled and postponed repeatedly. During his official visit to Egypt, President Yitshak Navon raised the matter directly with President Sadat and urged him to foster contacts between the elected representatives of the two peoples. Only then was the green light given. Within a few weeks a high-level delegation, headed by the chairman of the foreign affairs commission, Mohamed Abdellah, was sent to Israel. Among its members were Dr Mohamed Mahmoud, Chairman of the Health Commission and Minister of Health during the Nasser regime; Mustapha Kamel Murad, President of the Liberal Party and head of the opposition (he was one of the Young Officers who toppled the king in 1952); and Mohamed Abd El Ez, Chairman of the Science Commission and later Minister of Science. Several well-known journalists accompanied the delegation. I was also given special permission to accompany the delegation though the foreign ministry regulations stipulate that the ambassador or chargé d'affaires escorts only presidents, prime ministers or foreign ministers. (Other ministries are more generous and, regardless of the expenses involved, they allow their representatives to accompany all visiting personalities and delegations. The cost is compensated by the personal relationships that are created during the visit and facilitate the representative's work.)

The Egyptian parliamentary delegation was received with red-carpet treatment and the visit ran smoothly. The delegation members, both parliamentarians and journalists, did not expect Israel to be such a developed country (naturally, everything is relative!) and did not believe their eyes. Throughout the visit, they expressed their admiration and enthusiasm repeatedly.

An amusing incident – which accompanied me for many months and passed from mouth to mouth in Cairo – occurred during the visit. I had flown to Israel together with the Egyptian delegation. At Cairo airport, I was introduced to Mustapha Kamel Murad (leader of the opposition) as the minister plenipotentiary in the Israeli embassy. Being hard of hearing, he did not grasp who I exactly was. We spoke Arabic all the time and the members of the delegation conversed freely in my presence. During a trip to Dir al Sultan (a Coptic convent neighboring the Church of the Holy Sepulchre in the Old City of Jerusalem), the conversation became very lively and shifted to very sensitive topics. The political situation in Egypt, the power struggle within the top leadership and the personal feuds among them (especially between the vice-president of the time, Mubarak, and the prime minister, Fuad Mohii El Din) were discussed vividly. Suddenly, Murad shouted furiously that the regime was perverted and expressed the hope that after Sadat – a civilian, not another general – would be elected to the presidency 'thus putting an end to two generations of political manipulation by the army'. One of the delegation members stopped the flow of his diatribe against the regime saying teasingly: 'Mustapha, you have lost control! You are speaking about Egypt's most sensitive problems and you are forgetting who is sitting beside you. We have introduced him to you quite clearly. You should be more cautious.' Murad did not understand what the problem was and said: 'I know who he is. He is the minister plenipotentiary in our embassy in Tel Aviv. He has the right, as do all Egyptians, to know what is going on in his own country and hear what the elected leadership thinks.' Everyone burst into laughter saying: 'Mustapha, you are wrong. The man was born in Egypt and speaks fluent Arabic but he is the minister plenipotentiary of Israel in Cairo and not our minister in Tel Aviv. He has heard every word you have said. You have disclosed Egypt's most sensitive secrets. At the end of the day, he will certainly write a long report to the Mossad and to army intelligence. Poor you if what you have said reaches the ears of the persons you have mentioned or is brought to the knowledge of the army high command.' Murad, sure that they were pulling his leg, turned to me and asked anxiously: 'I swear to you by Allah, is what they say true? You do not only speak and act like one of us but you also look like one of us!' I confirmed that what he had heard from his colleagues was true and I even had to swear that I was an Israeli and not an Egyptian. For a moment, he was embarrassed and stopped speaking, but very quickly the conversation returned to its previous course and they all seemed not to mind that the Israeli minister in Cairo was sitting among them. It was a delicate situation. I could not turn a deaf ear to what they were saying and normally I would have slipped away discreetly but we were in a car travelling at full speed and I am sure that no one expected me to jump out of the window!

In less than an hour we were in Jerusalem. We traveled rapidly through the uncongested streets of the capital and the members of the delegation poured compliments on me about the cleanliness of the city and the beautiful gardening along the streets. When we reached the lane leading to Dir al Sultan, we saw piles of garbage everywhere. One of the members said spontaneously: 'One can easily see that we are arriving in Egyptian territory. Cleanliness is as lacking here as it is in Cairo!' They all laughed loudly. It was difficult for me to restrain myself but I remained as silent as a fish and did not even smile. From experience, I knew that foreign diplomats should never allow themselves to identify with criticism about the country in which they serve, and especially when it is aired by its own citizens. No one likes to hear a foreigner criticizing his own country.

The visit of the parliamentary delegation met with great success and was characterized by openness and warmth. It did not, however, contribute to the tightening of relations between the two parliaments. In Egypt, decisions to improve or cool relations with another country are taken, exclusively, by the highest level of power. Egypt's policy was, and remains, that there should be no relations between parliament and parliament or between people and people. The recommendations of this or that delegation are marginal and seldom have an impact on the decision-making process. From my point of view, however, the visit was very fruitful. It helped me create a personal relationship with the delegation members, both parliamentarians and journalists, and facilitated my work not only for the rest of my first stay in Egypt but also when I returned to Cairo as ambassador many years later. Whatever the circumstances of the moment and whatever the relations' barometer indicated, they were always ready to meet me and listen to what I had to say. Many times, when all other doors were closed, they proved to be a valuable channel for exchanging information, clarifying positions and conveying messages to the highest authorities.

Throughout my second period in Egypt, from 1990–92, not a single Egyptian minister was allowed to visit Israel notwithstanding the many invitations extended to them by your obedient servant or by visiting Israeli personalities. The prohibition was absolute. It included even the ministers of foreign affairs and of petrol who had previously been sparingly allowed to go to Israel for urgent business. The minister of tourism and aviation, Hussein Sultan, fixed five consecutive times a specific date for visiting Israel. Each time, he made sure he received in due time the green light from all the competent authorities and, time after time, he was instructed at the last moment to cancel his departure (these are the terms he himself used). He was very embarrassed and repeatedly apologized for the trouble he had caused 'for reasons beyond my control'. Sultan was a businessman, and not a politician or a high functionary as most other ministers were, and he strongly believed that business and politics should not be mixed. He helped me many times to remove obstacles in his fields of competence, which had purposely been raised by other authorities (read: the security services and the ministry of foreign affairs).

The foreign minister, Amr Mussa, was invited a score of times. He always accepted with a smile (sarcastic, I should say) but he always found an excuse not to live up to his acceptance. During the visit in 1991 of the Israeli foreign minister, David Levy, he himself suggested that we renew the periodic consultations between the foreign ministers and meet at least once every six months. These consultations had been agreed in April 1982 on the eve of the final withdrawal from Sinai, between the then foreign ministers, Yitshak Shamir and Kamal Hassan Ali, and had never been implemented. Amr Mussa also promised to visit Israel on a reciprocity basis within a few weeks. All the reminders, including personal phone calls from David Levy, were of no use and, up to the end of my stay in Egypt, he did not visit Israel. Since then, he has come several times (mostly for one day or a few hours only) when the visit was indispensable for putting increased pressure on Israel or for achieving Egypt's goals of the moment. Almost always, his visits were marked by pungent criticism and harsh rebukes publicly addressed to the Israeli government. During his visit in October 1997, on the occasion of the inauguration of the Peres Center for Peace, he refused to be photographed shaking hands with David Levy (the foreign minister and deputy prime minister) before he was allowed to make a statement to the press criticizing in insulting terms the policies of the Israeli government.

Not only ministers but also high officials and political personalities were strictly forbidden to visit Israel. Even the director of the Israeli department in the foreign ministry, Ambassador Mustapha Hanafi, was not allowed to accept our repeated invitations though supposedly his task was to foster relations with Israel. Only agricultural delegations received, from time to time, the green light at the insistence of Professor Wali, who did his best to compensate for the lack of visits from other ministries. He himself, however, gently declined our invitations and promised to visit Israel 'when the situation is more propitious'.

In the early 1980s, I dealt personally with organizing the visits of Israeli delegations and personalities to Egypt. I had to haggle intensively with my Egyptian counterparts. They strove to lodge the Israeli guests in peripheral hotels (with the intention of making their presence less conspicuous) and to limit the program almost exclusively to tourism. I had to make strenuous efforts to have my interlocutors include working meetings of a professional and political character and agree to lodge their guests at hotels in the center of Cairo. President Sadat, who was more forthcoming, had many times to intervene personally and give clear-cut instructions to meet our requests.

At the time (1980–83), Ambassador Ben Elissar, and after him Ambassador Sasson, were flooded with requests from Israeli ministers to arrange for them invitations to visit Egypt and meet with their counterparts. These visits, especially if the program included a meeting with the president, added political prestige and leverage. The telephones in the embassy did not cease ringing and the requests flowed in. The Egyptians heard every word and toughened their positions accordingly. They were not interested (even then) in showing outward signs of friendship and strove to exact the highest price from each visit. On the other hand, the embassy strove for obvious reasons to obtain as many invitations as possible. It was not an easy task. It necessitated a long process of give-and-take. No reciprocity was demanded; it was a one-way-street! The Egyptians also knew that the ministers could not afford to return to Israel empty-handed: they had to show that their visit had reaped tangible results. They used to tell us mockingly: 'Do not worry, we are going to give your minister enough leeway so that he'll be able, upon his return home, to present positive achievements. We are aware that he needs it for his public image!' The ministers always came with large delegations and scores of journalists to cover the historic event. The Egyptians hosted them lavishly and the whole retinue returned home loaded with excellent impressions, expensive gifts and glittering promises to step up the normalization process, abolish the yellow card (exit visa to Israel), convene a meeting of one of the joint committees, reciprocate with a visit to Israel and so on and so forth. Clearly, all promises remained a dead letter but the minister could always declare solemnly upon his return to Israel that 'the visit has met with great success and will soon reap substantial fruit in the field of normalization and development co-operation'.

In my second period (1990–92), the situation was almost identical. I continued to deal personally with the organization of visits but I was helped by the minister plenipotentiary, Eli Shaked, who dealt with the day-to-day contacts with the foreign ministry. Phones continued to ring and requests to arrange invitations flowed in. The embassy continued to run around trying to induce the Egyptian authorities to extend invitations to Israeli personalities. The haggling around the hotel location and the program's substance was as intensive as in the past. Even the outcome of the visits was practically the same. The Egyptians made sure that their guests enjoyed the visit and returned home with full hands, including the ever-recurring promises (though never implemented or intended to be implemented) to foster normalization. A new negative aspect, however, had been added to the Egyptian policy of reward and punishment. Visits by Israeli personalities who were considered as too 'extremist and irretrievable' by the Egyptians were automatically vetoed. At the same time, they substantially increased extending invitations to political personalities whom they regarded as 'moderates and active supporters of peace'. Ambassador Bassiuni was given a free hand to invite whomever he believed could be brought to tread the Egyptian line. It was clearly a blunt intervention in Israel's internal affairs. As a rule, the Egyptians sent no written invitation. Bassiuni extended verbal invitations, directly to the person concerned, on behalf of the foreign minister, Amr Mussa, or the political adviser to the president, Osama Elbaz. The visit itself was generally limited to a single meeting (without the presence of any Israeli diplomat) with an Egyptian personality (mostly Osama) 'to discuss matters of common interest'. The rest of the program was sheer tourism. No professional aspects whatsoever, no meetings with Egyptian counterparts – not even courtesy calls to political personalities – were included.

After being enlightened by the embassy in Cairo as to the Egyptians' undiplomatic behavior, the majority of the invited personalities politely turned down the invitations and only a very few agreed to come on the conditions dictated by the Egyptians. We could not condone the inadmissible attempt to interfere in Israel's internal affairs and had no alternative but to confront the Egyptians on the issue. We told them clearly, at all levels and on every occasion, that Israel did not look favorably upon Egypt's carrot-and-stick policy and that this policy would not influence Israeli positions – and, on the contrary, would have negative results. At the same time, we insisted that their invitations be extended in writing through the proper channels and that adequate professional and political meetings be included in the visits' program. Both requests were elementary and absolutely in line with diplomatic protocol but the Egyptians ignored them and Ambassador Bassiuni continued to extend invitations verbally and directly to Israeli personalities whom Egypt wished to reward or whose support it wanted to acquire. The Israeli embassy in Cairo did not let go and succeeded in thwarting most visits that did not meet the required diplomatic criteria. After many refusals, and a few visits that did not yield the expected results, the Egyptians understood that it would be more rewarding for them to adopt a middle course and avoid stretching the rope beyond its breaking point. They decided to show more flexibility and began also inviting personalities and officials whose visit was recommended by the Israeli embassy.

In the framework of this change of policy, the first to be invited was the foreign minister, David Levy. The Egyptians went out of their way to please him and gave him royal treatment: streets were closed to traffic hours in advance, policemen in uniform were posted every ten meters, Amr Mussa accompanied the minister everywhere and the president received him three times in two days. The meetings were unusually long and the chemistry between the two men seemed to work very well. David Levy was also received by the presidents of both houses of parliament and had a long session with the parliament's foreign commission. Journalists, Egyptian and foreign, swarmed around him throughout the visit and he was allowed to hold two fully-fledged press conferences attended by a score of Egyptian and foreign journalists (such press conferences were unprecedented). A strange episode occurred after the minister left: the Saudi owners dismissed the French manager of the Meridien Hotel because he had yielded to my insistence to fly the Israeli flag during the minister's stay. Another incident worth relating is the Egyptian foreign ministry's ridiculous efforts to prevent the embassy from inviting more guests to its lunch than the number invited to their own dinner. We were compelled, at the last moment, to cancel several invitations that we had already sent – the Egyptians had made it clear that they would prevent the guests from coming. Despite our yielding to their request, they still did do so with regard to the two presidents of the houses of parliament and a few ministers who had accepted the invitation and were included in the *numerus clausus* imposed upon us (their seats remained conspicuously vacant). The chief of protocol later explained that they had 'accepted the invitation by mistake' – their presence would have been beyond the parameters allowed by foreign minister Amr Mussa and too much for a visiting minister of foreign affairs (read: the Israeli foreign minister).

It is not my intention to review here all the visits that took place during my two periods in Egypt. It would be too fastidious though behind each visit lie many interesting and spicy stories. It is sufficient to touch briefly on visits that have exceptional significance or clearly substantiate the Egyptian *modus operandi*. The first period (1980–83), covering the normalization and autonomy discussions and the negotiations for the establishment of the multinational peacekeeping force was marked by intense activity in the field of visits. For the embassy staff, it was a godsend that alleviated their social isolation. The coming of a personality or a delegation was always marked by hectic activity: meetings, social events and travels throughout Egypt. Up to the final withdrawal from Sinai (April 1982), visits took place at a feverish pace and covered almost the whole political and official spectrum in Israel. Afterwards, these visits dwindled dramatically and from then on, most visits revolved around topics that interested the Egyptians or had been squeezed from them after strenuous efforts.

One of the prominent visits was the reciprocal visit of a Knesset delegation in early 1982. The Egyptians were not very enthusiastic (to say the least) about the visit and refrained for a long time from sending a formal invitation, though they had promised many times to do so. Finally, 24 April approaching (the second phase of withdrawal), the invitation arrived and a large delegation, composed of all factions in parliament and headed by Moshe Arens (at the time chairman of the foreign affairs and defense commission), arrived in Cairo. The Egyptians, who feared what they called 'Arens's extremism', strove to limit the delegation's political contacts to a minimum. Only after heavy pressure did they agree to include in the program a visit to the parliament building and a round-table discussion with the members of the foreign affairs commission in addition to meetings with President Mubarak and Foreign Minister Kamal Hassan Ali. At the round-table, the chairman, Mohamed Abdellah, and after him representatives of the opposition parties and other senior members of the commission expounded in blunt words the Egyptian credo: 'After its decisive victory in the October War, Egypt decided of its own free will to make peace with Israel. It did not sign a separate peace agreement and did not renounce Palestinian legitimate rights or other Arab rights. Israel must withdraw not only from the whole of Sinai but also from all the Arab territories occupied in 1967, recognize the PLO and agree to the establishment of a Palestinian state with Arab Jerusalem as its capital.' These positions were well known to the Israeli diplomats in Cairo; the Egyptians aired them tirelessly on every occasion like a worn-out tune. However, for Arens and the delegation they were a traumatic novelty and triggered a strong reaction.

Arens did not even try to use diplomatic language or conceal his outrage. He stressed in forthright words that the stands expounded by the Egyptian parliamentarians were a flagrant breach of the spirit and letter of the Camp David agreement and were a bad omen for the future. He accused Egypt of systematically violating the normalization agreements and blocking the normal flow of relations between the two peoples through police measures. He voiced his conviction that Egypt was trying to pave its way back to the Arab world by paying in Israeli currency. He presented frankly Israel's stands (of the time, naturally) on the solution of the Palestinian problem and other pending issues. To a direct question on the future of Jerusalem, he answered angrily that Jerusalem was the eternal capital of Israel and the Jewish people and that it would forever remain a united city under Israeli sovereignty. He called upon the Arabs in general, and Egypt in particular, to accept this irreversible fact if they were genuinely interested in promoting peace in the region.

Arens's reaction provoked an immediate backlash and almost torpedoed the continuation of the visit. The embassy immediately moved to limit the damage but the Egyptians refused to hear the voice of reason. However, after canceling a few scheduled events and sulking for a few hours, the Egyptians calmed down, fearing that a major crisis would give an excuse to Israel to postpone and even cancel the second phase of withdrawal from Sinai. We pointed out that Arens had reacted to provocation and had not said anything that was not in line with Israel's declared positions, which were well known to the Egyptian government. The visit continued in a relatively good atmosphere but in the social events that followed parliamentary members were prevented from attending, to the exclusion of Mohamed Abdellah who was the official host and could not reasonably be made to vanish into the air.

An amusing incident during this visit is related paradoxically to the observance of the *Kashrut* (dietary) laws. As usual, the embassy requested that Egyptian protocol make sure that at official meals no meat or meat-based dishes be served to the Israeli guests and that only fish be offered. This time, knowing that Zevulun Hamer (leader of one of the religious parties) would chair the delegation, I personally met with the Egyptian official organizing the visit and explained in detail what kind of food should be served and why. A few hours before the inaugural dinner at one of the most select hotels in Cairo, I came to check the menu and make sure that everything was all right. I was stunned to hear that Chateaubriand steaks and jumbo shrimps (which were the specialty of the house) were to be served. I called the chief of protocol and demanded that the menu be changed. I had to explain again that shrimps were not fish and that *Halal* (Muslim) slaughtering was not equivalent to *kosher* (Jewish) slaughtering. He was deeply offended but promised to change the menu and see to it personally that everything was in order. But as usual, promises and actions were two different things! Huge shrimps in garlic sauce and thick steaks covered with heavy cream were served. Not a single member of the delegation protested or refused to eat. On the contrary, they all ate with obvious pleasure and asked for more. After dinner, the chief of protocol, delighted with the success of the dinner, took me aside and expressed his satisfaction that he had not complied with my demands and had not changed the menu, hinting that my intention had been to sabotage the dinner. I was very embarrassed but I could not explain that the reason for the delegation's unusual appetite was that Zevulun Hamer had canceled his coming. I tried to convince him that I had no hidden intention. I do not think he believed me and I had to put on heavy pressure to have him serve fish during the rest of the visit and at other visits by Israeli personalities.

Another visit that marked the brief honeymoon that prevailed between the two countries before the final withdrawal from Sinai was the official visit of President Yitshak Navon and his wife, Ophira, in early 1981. It was a most successful visit by any standards – both in respect of the substance and the outward etiquette that went well beyond the exigencies of diplomatic protocol. President Sadat and his wife Jihan went out of their way to create throughout the visit an atmosphere of warm friendship. They instructed the foreign ministry and the protocol department in the presidential office not to spare any effort or material means in ensuring the success of the visit. President Navon thoroughly prepared himself for the visit, brushed up his Arabic, read a score of books by many eminent Egyptian writers, ploughed into ancient and modern Egyptian history and studied in depth all aspects of Israeli–Egyptian relations.

Two or three days before his arrival, Ambassador Ben-Elissar fell sick with acute jaundice and had to lie in bed for the duration of the visit (and a long time after it). I replaced Ben-Elissar as chargé d'affaires a.i. and accompanied the president in his meetings and tours. The Israeli press, and in its wake the Egyptian press, did not spare criticism of Ben-Elissar and accused him of pretending to be sick so as to be unable to welcome a president who did not belong to his own party (the Likud). There is no truth whatsoever in these accusations; Ben Elissar was genuinely sick and missed the opportunity of his life. For him, the official visit of the president of state – the symbol of its sovereignty – was to be the high point of his tenure and glaring proof of the success of his mission. Instead, he gnashed his teeth and lay down helplessly in bed. He followed the visit in its smallest detail. Every day, late at night, I would come to his bedside, report on the events of the day and ask his advice about the next day's program. He also requested his wife Nizza to accompany me at all official events. This created a protocol problem since Nizza had no official standing and my own wife Sarah was accompanying me. We overcame the difficulty in the best of spirits and, in spite of the reluctance of Egyptian protocol, we managed to give Nizza priority in all the events in which she participated. Nevertheless, I felt uncomfortable throughout the visit because I was unwillingly stealing the show from Ben-Elissar.

President Navon arrived in a chartered plane accompanied by a retinue of more than 100 members (including security guards). President Sadat and his wife received him at the airport in a fully-fledged military ceremony attended by Vice-President Mubarak and his wife, all ministers, the army chief of staff, religious personalities and so on. The president and a few aides, Yossi Hadas (at the time deputy director-general for Egyptian affairs), Nizza, my wife and myself were lodged in a wing of the Abdin Palace (the official residence of the kings of Egypt and the seat of Sadat's cabinet). The rest of the retinue was lodged at the Hilton Hotel in the center of Cairo. The program was intensive and included several meetings with President Sadat as well as a helicopter trip to the village where he was born, Mit Abu el Kom. A long meeting with Vice-President Mubarak was also arranged (it was the first significant discussion with Mubarak, who was to become, within a few months, the president of Egypt and was until then a complete mystery to us). The program also included meetings with the chairmen of both houses of parliament, the chief editors of all media organs, and the board of the writers' association. President Navon almost cancelled this last meeting because several of the writers he had expected to attend (and whose books he had especially read) had refused to do so. I finally succeeded in convincing him to go through with the meeting and it met with tremendous success – the participating writers simply fell in love with him. It was the first, and probably the last, meeting of an Israeli personality with a substantial number of eminent Egyptian writers.

President Navon also addressed the leadership of the ruling party in the party's seat. He stressed in particular the strong bond of the Jewish people to the Land of Israel and its inalienable historical rights and triggered an improvised reply from Mustapha Khalil, the former prime minister who, at the time, was acting vice-president of the party for external affairs. (I will go into the substance of this most indicative reply in another chapter.) Incidentally, the meeting was scheduled instead of an address to both houses of parliament that the embassy had insisted on including in Navon's program. At first, the Egyptians claimed that it was contrary to diplomatic protocol and was contrary to local custom. When we reminded them that President Sadat had addressed the Knesset and insisted that Navon address the Egyptian parliament, they put forward the excuse that the opposition might make use of the opportunity and organize anti-peace demonstrations. We finally compromised on the meeting in the party's seat.

During the visit, two official dinners took place, the first offered by President Sadat and his wife in honor of the guests, and the second offered by President Navon and his wife. In reality, the two dinners were organized by Egyptian protocol and took place in the same hall at the Abdin Palace. The entire Egyptian Who's Who participated in the dinners and the two presidents emphasized 'the growing friendship between the two peoples and the two countries'. A slight incident threw a shadow on the preparations for Navon's return dinner – the Egyptians compelled us to cancel invitations that we had sent to a few Egyptian businessmen working with Israel and practically dictated the list of guests. They also refused to invite Israeli journalists accompanying President Navon alleging Egyptian protocol. Navon insisted on inviting Mira Avrekh of the daily *Yediot Akhronot* and we had to sneak her in as the wife of one of our diplomats. We had to do the same for the late Leon Taman (a Jewish businessman and personal friend of Navon) and his wife who had arrived at the last minute.

As a matter of course, tourism was not forgotten – in addition to the main archeological sites in Cairo, the entire retinue was flown in Sadat's personal plane to Abu Simbel, Aswan and Luxor. Throughout the visit, Jihan Sadat accompanied Ophira Navon and took her to see an orphanage that she was sponsoring (Wafaa oua Amal). This is linked to another amusing incident: President Navon had brought with him, as a gift to the

Egyptian people, an ultra-modern laser surgical instrument manufactured in Israel (no such instrument existed in Egypt at the time). The Egyptians did not want to attract attention to Israel's technical superiority and were reluctant to install it in one of their hospitals. They could not, however, refuse to accept the gift and they decided to install it in Jihan Sadat's orphanage though it was totally useless there and could not even be connected to electricity. It remained in the dispensary for many years, untouched and rusting. I do not know if it is still there or if it has been finally transferred to one of the hospitals and put to better use.

The chemistry between the two presidents proved to be excellent and Navon raised a series of issues that had not found their solution at lower levels or had not been implemented despite repeated promises. Among other things, he obtained from Sadat fresh promises to allow the establishment of a bus line between Tel Aviv and Cairo, increase commercial flights, foster youngsters' exchanges, open academic centers in the respective capitals and step up cultural exchanges. In addition, he received the usual worn-out promises that all restrictions on trade between the two countries would be removed, the yellow card abolished and the work of the normalization committees stepped up. Only very few of Sadat's promises were implemented after strenuous efforts on our part and most remained a dead letter. It was better than nothing! In any case, the visit was in itself a tremendous success and President Navon made a strong impression on all those who had the privilege to meet him.

For my wife and me, both born in Egypt, it was a moving and unforgettable experience. In our wildest dreams we never imagined entering the Abdin Palace, not to say residing in it. In our youth, as members of a Zionist youth movement, we were under strict instructions never to go near the palace or even its immediate neighborhood. We feared arousing suspicion accidentally and being arrested, thus endangering the whole Zionist movement in Egypt (which was legal at the time). I recall only three other events that moved me as much: arriving in Egypt after 32 years of absence, participating in an official remembrance ceremony on the anniversary of Gamal Abd el Nasser's death and presenting my credentials as ambassador to President Mubarak in 1990.

Another important visit in that period was the official visit of the then chief of staff, General Raphael Eytan (Raful). After great pressure, he was invited by the then minister of defense, Marshal Abu Ghazala, on special instructions from President Sadat, 'to tighten the ties between the two armies'. General David Ivri (then the air force chief) and a few high-ranking officers came with him. The Egyptians demanded that they refrain from wearing uniforms. Raful categorically refused and threatened to return home on the next flight. Finally, a compromise with the Egyptians was brokered by the embassy: the Israeli officers would wear their uniforms at official events and on visits to military camps; in private events and tourist tours they would change to civilian clothes.

The whole discussion was no more than 'a storm in a glass of water'. Once the Egyptians established the principle, they lost interest in the matter and they did not mind that our officers went around in their uniforms. Indeed, it would have been very difficult to implement the compromise since the official events and the tourist tours were interwoven. The delegation laid a wreath at the tomb of the Unknown Soldier in a fully-fledged military ceremony and was received with ostentatious warmth at the army headquarters and at the Egyptian Military Academy. Our officers were impressed to see that the sand tables in the various military installations they visited were oriented towards a possible clash with Libya and not with Israel. The visit was cut short on its third day. The chief of staff was urgently called back owing to increasing tension on the northern border. The delegation was escorted to the airport by all the top brass of the Egyptian army who insisted that they should resume their visit as soon as the situation cleared up. This did not happen. This was the first and last top Israeli military delegation to pay an official visit to Egypt (to the exclusion of regular meetings of the joint military committee and some unpublished visits). Let me add that Raful's visit has never been reciprocated.

Ezer Weizman (who was to become the president of Israel from 1993–2000) visited Egypt three times during this period (1980–83). The first, in his capacity of minister of defense, took place a few weeks after my arrival. He met for lengthy discussions with President Sadat, the foreign minister, Kamal Hassan Ali, and the defense minister, Abu Ghazala. The two other visits took place after he had resigned from government. In the first, he arrived in a small chartered plane to present his condolences to Jihan Sadat. Boutros Boutros Ghali came to the airport to receive him and it gave me the opportunity, because of an unexpected delay of Ezer's plane, to chat informally with him for almost three hours (I will touch on our conversation in another chapter). As a matter of course, he was also received by President Mubarak and Foreign Minister Kamal Hassan Ali. The third time, he came with his family as the guests of the foreign minister and, as always, he was received with open arms and with all due honors. Ezer acquired not only the confidence of the Egyptian top leadership but also their affection. They appreciated his straightforward approach to the most difficult problems and the creative solutions he suggested. They used to call him, and certainly still do, with ostentatious admiration and sympathy 'Ezra Weissmann' (with a strong Egyptian accent). In his third visit, he embarrassed me somewhat. I had accompanied him to a meeting with Kamal Hassan Ali during which the difficulties encountered in establishing the multinational force arose. Ezer, in his characteristically direct manner, said suddenly: 'If I were still Israel's defense minister, I would have renounced that force completely. It is totally redundant – between friendly countries, there is no need for artificial buffer zones. In any case, international forces are totally powerless to prevent wars and military confrontations.' At that time, we were still having bitter negotiations on the issue and we were under instructions to make it clear to the Egyptians that if the establishment of the force were delayed, the second phase of withdrawal would be postponed accordingly. I had no alternative but to contradict Ezer and express the official stand.

Moshe Dayan and his wife Rachel also came in this period for a short visit and were the guests of the Egyptian government. Dayan was received with red-carpet treatment (though with less warmth than Ezer Weizman) despite the fact that he had resigned from the government and had no official position. Sadat and Kamal Hassan Ali received him for long and friendly conversations. Boutros Ghali and Ben-Elissar offered dinners in his honor which were attended by many Egyptian top leaders. Because of his fatal illness, Moshe was already a shadow of himself but he was still full of charm and wit and he deeply impressed everyone with his sharpness and power of analysis. At one of the social events, when we were in small committee, Boutros asked Moshe why, in his opinion, Israel refused to recognize the PLO and enter into direct negotiations with it. Moshe answered by detailing the usual Israeli arguments of the time – but Boutros interrupted him with some impatience and asked bluntly whether Israel would be ready to talk to the PLO if it rescinded its covenant, ceased definitively all types of terrorist activities and renounced the right of return. Moshe replied that he did not think that this would happen in the foreseeable future and there was no point in considering hypothetical situations. Boutros insisted and, finally, Moshe said that 'if a miracle occurs and the PLO meets the conditions voiced by Boutros, I do not see why Israel would not enter into negotiations with it since, to the exclusion of the name, it would be an altogether different organization.' He added, with a sarcastic smile: 'If you take a ferocious tiger, pull his claws and teeth out, and give him a strong sedative to make sure that he has no unexpected reactions, then it is no longer a tiger but an inoffensive cat. With such a cat, I have no objection to negotiate.' Boutros did not laugh as we all did and said angrily: 'It will happen sooner than you think!' Time is relative: what seemed impossible in early 1982 became ten years later the official policy of the government of Israel. Egypt from the outset, even before the Camp David agreement, strove patiently to bring about this drastic change in the Israeli approach to the Palestinian leadership. It did not conceal its goal and reiterated its credo on each occasion.

In that period, I also dealt with the visit of Shimon Peres (at the time leader of the opposition). He came with a delegation of the Labor Party composed of Abba Eban, Haim Bar Lev, Yossi Beilin, and Israel Gat. As usual a number of journalists accompanied them. The ruling party in Egypt had formally invited the delegation but it was in reality the guest of the Egyptian government. For obvious reasons, the embassy was not involved in setting up the details of the program. In any case, there was no need to haggle or pressurize; the hosts themselves made sure that the program would include ingredients that were not usually made available to official

Israeli delegations. Ambassador Ben-Elissar did not look favorably on the coming of the delegation a few months before the 1981 elections and viewed it as blatant intrusion on the part of Egypt in Israel's internal affairs. Polls gave a substantial lead to Labor and it was obvious that the Egyptians wished to send a clear signal to the voters in Israel that they favored that party. They did not conceal the fact that they believed that Labor was less committed to ideology *per se* and would be a more pragmatic partner in moving ahead with the peace process. Ben-Elissar refused to receive the delegation at the airport and to be involved in their program. The task fell on me. I received the delegation, briefed them in depth on bilateral relations and gave a reception in their honor attended by all the Israelis in Cairo (including Ben-Elissar and his wife). I finally escorted them back to the airport. I abstained, however, from attending their meetings with the Egyptians in order not to embarrass the hosts and also the guests who had their own agenda.

I recall this visit in a rather picturesque manner. The delegation had arrived at a very late hour and the airport was almost deserted. Abba Eban, who looked profoundly moved, paced rapidly towards the VIP's hall, leaving behind the rest of the group, and seeming to be literally striding on the 'wings of history'. But that was not to be! A few days before the elections at the end of June 1981, President Sadat decided, against the advice of his closest collaborators, to balance the picture. He agreed to meet with Menahem Begin in Sharm el Sheikh though he realized that the summit might be construed as an indirect service to the election campaign of the Likud Party. In his great wisdom, he had come to the conclusion that Egypt should take out an insurance policy in case, against all the odds (and polls), Labor did not win the elections and the Likud were returned to power. Indeed, the Likud won the elections but Sadat did not reap the fruit of his political foresight; a few months later, in October 1981, he was assassinated. And in the interim, the Sharm el Sheikh summit brought him only embarrassment and anger: a few days after the meeting, Israel bombed the Iraqi reactor and the whole world got the impression that the summit had been intended to bring Israel's intentions to Egypt's knowledge and receive its tacit agreement. Sadat boiled with rage as did the whole Egyptian leadership and intelligentsia. The press did not fail to condemn Israel's 'treacherousness and slyness'. Egypt initiated a hectic and vociferous diplomatic campaign to cleanse itself of the suspicion of such an unholy collusion with Israel against a sister Arab country and took the lead in the international arena with initiatives to condemn Israel. Ambassador Sasson (who had by then replaced Ben-Elissar) was very upset by the turn of events; he feared that the peace process would come to a standstill and that all our strenuous efforts to build a semblance of normalization between the two countries would go down the drain. He was relieved when President Sadat agreed to receive him a few days later. It was a good omen but the president was still furious and gave Ambassador

Sasson a piece of his mind. He did not, however, close the door or threaten to take extreme steps; on the contrary, he made it clear that the incident would not have any after-effects that could not be overcome in due time. Paradoxically, notwithstanding all the fuss and uproar, the Egyptians were pleased that a major potential danger to the whole region – and to them – had been removed. They were cautious not to voice their satisfaction publicly but they more than hinted at it in private conversations.

In the early 1980s, General (res.) Ariel Sharon (Arik) came many times to Egypt and his visits always aroused great interest and much coverage in the Israeli press (he was always accompanied by a score of Israeli journalists). The Egyptian press, on instructions from above, ignored his visits or mentioned them briefly although throughout the visit many Egyptian journalists joined his retinue, interviewed him at length and bombarded him with questions (this was the case with most visiting Israeli personalities and delegations). Understandably I cannot go into all Sharon's visits and I will limit myself here to his first and last visits, which were the most significant in terms of their substance. The attitude of the Egyptians towards Arik was ambivalent: on the one hand, they respected and admired him for his dominant personality and his out-standing capacity as a military and political leader; on the other hand, they felt deep anxiety at what they referred to in their conversations with us as his forcefulness and the impossibility of foreseeing his actions.

On his first visit, Sharon came in his capacity as minister of agriculture in response to an invitation by his Egyptian counterpart, Professor Daoud. I was then acting as chargé d'affaires a.i. after the departure of Ben-Elissar and I prepared the visit in all its details. I persuaded Moshe Sasson, who had just been appointed, to avail himself of the visit by making the acquaintance of a substantial number of top Egyptian person-alities whom, normally, it would take him several months to meet (if ever!). Moshe arrived one day before the beginning of the visit and pre-sented his credentials to President Sadat the next day. Arik waited in the next room during the presentation and was deeply moved to hear the *Hatikva* (the Israeli national anthem) resounding in the presidential palace. A few minutes later, the president received the whole delegation and Moshe took part in the meeting as the fully-fledged ambassador of Israel to Egypt. The main purpose of Sharon's visit was to foster agricul-tural co-operation – the Israeli government had allocated $1 million for this aim – but the Egyptians were dragging their feet, notwithstanding Daoud's ostensible goodwill and genuine interest. At the time, we were still naïve enough to believe that the reason for the procrastination in starting the various projects, which had been decided upon by the joint agricultural commission, was red tape and Daoud's personal helplessness. We thought that if a detailed plan of action were approved at the highest level of power, it would start the ball rolling and compel the agricultural establishment to move ahead with more efficiency and energy.

Sharon's delegation was composed of several eminent agricultural experts, among them Professor Shmuel Pohorilis, the head of agricultural planning in Israel whose professional capacity was highly respected in Egypt. He brought with him not only detailed projects of co-operation but also more than 30 crates of juicy melons of the Tal Haemek variety (not known in Egypt at the time; today Egypt exports this variety to many Arab countries), which he offered to the personalities he met. They all appreciated (and enjoyed eating) Sharon's original gift and most of them requested him to send them melon seeds so that they could grow them in their private farms.

The meeting with Sadat lasted much longer than scheduled and was characterized by a special warmth. The president agreed in broad outline to all the projects we presented. His only substantial remark was that we should give more attention to the new lands (lands redeemed from the desert) and not focus on the more developed Delta lands where the *fellah* (peasant) would be reluctant to adopt modern methods of cultivation. At the same time, he instructed the minister of agriculture, Professor Daoud, to move ahead simultaneously with all the projects and remove all administrative constraints. In the concluding meeting in the embassy, Sharon gave the same instructions to his staff and stressed that they should not be deterred by financial considerations. He took it upon himself to raise the necessary funds (much beyond the million dollars allocated by the government). Arik returned to Israel carrying with him positive impressions and convinced that things would now move rapidly on the agricultural front. In the embassy we were all elated at the visit's success and we began, immediately after Sharon's departure, to tackle vigorously with the Egyptians the technical details involved in the implementation of the various projects. Very quickly, it became clear that there was a great discrepancy between words and deeds and that, so long as Egypt's basic normalization policies were not officially abrogated or drastically amended, the lower scales of the Egyptian civil service would continue to put spokes in the wheels of co-operation. Most of the projects agreed with Sadat remained on paper (I will go into further details in Chapter 14).

Sharon's last visit to Egypt was in his capacity as minister of defense, directly responsible for the arrangements related to Israel's final withdrawal from Sinai. It had historic significance of the highest order. The Egyptians lived in the anxiety that Israel might at the last moment jump out of the moving train, and waited impatiently for Arik's visit. He decided to make the most of this fact and informed them (through the embassy) that he intended to come by car using the central road in Sinai, Nitzana-Suez (that was, at the time, still closed to traffic), and visit the various sites where he had fought. He also requested (demanded) to visit El Alamein and Marsa Matroukh on the border with Libya in the western desert. The Egyptians rejected both requests explaining that

1. The first Consul General in Alexandria, Shaul Bar-Haim, flying the Israeli flag on the building of the consulate.

2. The first four ambassadors to Egypt, from right to left: Eliahu Ben Elissar, Moshe Sasson, Shimon Shamir and Ephraim Dowek.

3. The first building of the Embassy in Cairo and the heavy security apparatus around it.

4. The first and only visit of an Egyptian parliamentary delegation to the Knesset (1981). From right to left: Mustapha Kamel Murad, Ephraim Dowek, Mohamad Mahmud, Nathanel Lorch, Mohamad Abdellah, a Knesset guide, Saad Murtada, Yossef Hadass and other members of the Egyptian delegation.

5. The then Minister of Commerce and Industry, Gideon Pat, at a press conference in Cairo in 1982 (a very uncommon event). With him are the then Minister Plenipotentiary Dowek, the Press Counselor Eli Laniado and the Commercial Counselor Yossef Porat.

6. The then (1991) Minister of Religions, Professor Avner Shaki, and the author receiving a token gift from the Baba Shenuda, Head of the Egyptian Coptic Church.

7. The author with the Director of the Israeli Department, Ambassador Ismat Reda, in one of their frequent meetings at the Egyptian Foreign Ministry.

9. The then (1991) President of Israel, Yitshak Navon, during his state visit to Egypt, with the Pyramids as a backdrop.

11. The author laying a wreath on President Sadat's Memorial a few weeks after his arrival in Egypt as Israeli Ambassador.

8. The Israeli children in Cairo on the occasion of the celebration of the Tabernacle Feast at the ambassador's residence.

10. The then (1992) Deputy-Minister of Religion, Bibi, being received by the Egyptian Deputy-Prime Minister and Minister of Agriculture, Yussuf Wali.

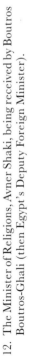

12. The Minister of Religions, Avner Shaki, being received by Boutros Boutros-Ghali (then Egypt's Deputy Foreign Minister).

13. The author pointing out, during an official visit to the Egyptian Museum of Antiquities, the inscription in hieroglyphs on a memorial stone, where the Pharaoh of the time brags: 'I have eradicated for ever the seed of Israel from the face of the earth'.

14. The author with Mustapha Kamel Murad, the Liberal Party President, and Sheikh Ahmad Al Kadar from Sudan during the Independence Day reception.

15. The author receiving a token gift from the hands of students trained in Israel, in the presence of the USA Ambassador, Pelletreau. In the picture also: Fuad Abu Hadab, the Minister of Agriculture, Yussuf Wali's right-hand man and co-ordinator of the Israeli programs and Moshe Dana, the Israeli Commercial Counselor.

16. The author being cordially received by students and officials in one of the students' agricultural settlements.

17. The author and the Cultural Counselor Yitshak Bar-Moshe with the famous Egyptian writer and journalist Anis Mansur.

18. The author and his wife with the Egyptian Minister of Petroleum, Mohamad Kanil, and the famous journalist the late Abd-El-Satar Tawila.

19. The author and his wife at their farewell reception with USA Ambassador Pelletreau and his wife.

20. The late Prime Minister Yitshak Rabin during a visit to the main Synagogue in
Cairo. Near him are the author, the President of the Jewish Community Rousso,
and the Deputy-Director General for Egyptian Affairs David Sultan (who later
replaced the author as ambassador to Cairo).

the central road was physically impracticable and that, in view of their strained relations with Libya, Sharon's visit to the western desert would be interpreted as a provocation. I conveyed the Egyptian response to Sharon's cabinet and received instructions to persist with the two requests. After a series of meetings and bitter discussions, neither the Egyptians nor we would budge an inch from our respective positions. Finally, they informed us that they had brought the matter before the president himself and, 'out of concern for Sharon's safety', he had vetoed both requests and therefore from their standpoint 'the matter was closed'. I informed Jerusalem (by phone) and recommended that we drop both requests and did not ride our high horses because of such a marginal issue. In parallel, even before receiving a reply, I informed the Egyptians that Sharon would cancel his visit if they did not agree to both his requests. Obviously, the Egyptians were aware that it was a tactical move on my part that had no covering from Jerusalem. They replied bluntly that they were not ready to back down since 'Sharon's personal safety is at stake'.

I again phoned Jerusalem and requested definitive instructions before a meeting with the Egyptians scheduled for the next hour. A few minutes later, Sharon himself was on the phone and he instructed me to inform the Egyptians officially that he was postponing his visit 'until the central road becomes practicable'. I went to the meeting and informed my inter-locutor, Ambassador Fawzi al Ibrashi (responsible for the Israeli desk in the foreign minister's cabinet), of Sharon's final position. He was not particularly impressed and again reiterated, like a broken record, the Egyptian stand. A junior diplomat handed him a small note. Ibrashi stopped speaking, read the note carefully and, with a somber face, apol-ogized for the fact that the minister was calling him on an urgent matter. After almost half an hour, he returned to his office, apologized again and brought to my knowledge the good news that President Mubarak had reviewed the matter again and had agreed to Sharon's com-ing by the central road though it entailed strenuous preparations. Ibrashi added that the president had, however, requested that Sharon renounce going to the western desert because of the delicate situation with Libya. Clearly, the Egyptians knew that this time my threat to cancel Sharon's visit had the fullest backing from Jerusalem and changed their position accordingly. I did not show any outward sign of satisfaction in having finally succeeded in twisting their arm. On the contrary, I thanked Al Ibrashi and requested him to convey to the president 'the appreciation of the government of Israel for being so forthcoming and understanding'. I also agreed, on the spot, to drop the visit to the western desert. I had not received instructions to that effect from Sharon but, from my phone conversation with him, I had gained the impression that he would not insist on that part of the program. In any case, it was a risk that I had to take because I felt that we should not overplay our hand and rock the boat further.

145

As expected, Sharon dropped his visit to the western desert. He came by the central road as he had wished. The Egyptians yielded to his dictate. He was accompanied by a small army of journalists and photographers, stopped at every site where battles had taken place (and in Sinai there are a great number of such sites), explained what had happened at each spot, and had plenty of snapshots taken. He arrived at Suez with more than three hours' delay where all the region's top brass were waiting patiently to welcome him. Moshe Sasson and I were sitting on pins but the Egyptians swallowed the snub with a smile. They received Arik with all due honors and went well beyond the call of duty and oriental courtesy. They crowded around him, wanting to shake his hand and exchange a few words with him. The meal originally scheduled as a lunch turned into a dinner (happily the food remained edible in spite of the torrid heat). Speeches were exchanged and beautiful presents were offered to Sharon on behalf of the City of Suez and the Canal Region. Sasson and I sat quietly, observing the fuss around Arik and wondering at the upheavals of history. Who would have believed in his wildest dreams that General Ariel Sharon would be received in Suez as if he had liberated the city and not almost erased it from the map?!

The rest of the visit ran according to the agreed schedule. Throughout the visit, Sharon was treated as a king and no one mentioned or hinted at the central road incident. He met with the president, the defense and foreign ministers and the army chief of staff. In his meeting with the foreign minister, Kamal Hassan Ali, Arik touched upon the situation on the northern front and stressed that if the PLO did not cease its terrorist attacks against civilian targets, Israel could not indefinitely exercise self-restraint and would have to take the necessary steps. Kamal grasped the hint immediately and warned Sharon not to get involved in the Lebanese quagmire. A few months later, Israel launched the Peace for Galilee operation and Kamal's warning proved to be right! Eighteen years later, Israel was still stuck in Lebanon and had paid a heavy price in an interminable guerilla war. For many years, Sharon also personally bore the consequences. Now happily, after 18 long years, Israel has unilaterally withdrawn to the 1923 international boarder.

Incidentally, the Yamit (a small Israeli city built by Israel in Sinai) issue, which at the time was a major topic in the press both in Israel and Egypt, was not raised in the discussions. The Egyptians were aware that Israel had decided to erase the city completely though for several weeks a detailed negotiation had taken place on the sale to Egypt of the city's buildings and installations in conformity with a previous understanding between the two countries. The Egyptians resigned themselves to the inevitable and kept silent on the official level but in private conversations they did not conceal their bitterness. At the center of the discussions stood the Taba issue. Each side claimed that the one-square kilometer enclave belonged to them. Finally, it was decided to establish a special committee to try and find a solution before 25 April 1982 – the date scheduled for completing the withdrawal from Sinai.

A regrettable bungle occurred to me during the visit, which upset me for a long time. On Sharon's arrival, I was given a thick folder classified top secret containing studies and position papers that had been prepared for the discussions by the ministry of defense. I read the documents with great attention, made a few comments and returned the folder to the security officer. In the meeting with the Egyptians, the folder was again handed to me and I put it before me on the table. After three hours of intensive discussions, we were all worn out and left in a hurry for an official lunch. Arriving at my car, I suddenly noticed that I had forgotten the folder on the table and rushed back, in a total panic, to the meeting hall in the foreign ministry. I spoke to the guards in Arabic and they allowed me in, thinking that I was one of the Egyptian participants. I went directly to my seat and felt as if I had been struck by lightning: the folder had vanished! I yelled at the guards, introduced myself as the Israeli minister plenipotentiary and threatened them with dire sanctions if they did not immediately return the folder. They swore that they had seen nothing and taken nothing. The chief security officer was urgently summoned. He gently tried to calm me down and assured me that he had locked the doors himself and that there was no folder left on the table. I shouted and threatened; the man panicked even more than I did but insisted that the table was clean of any document. I had no alternative but to resign myself to the evidence: I had lost a top secret folder and it was now probably in the hands of the Egyptian security services. I went back to the embassy preoccupied and shameful (I had lost my appetite and skipped the lunch). I informed our security officer of what had happened. He smiled and said: 'Calm down, no need to worry, the folder is here!' He explained that the standing procedure was that, after a meeting, security officers made sure that no document or even bits of torn paper were left behind. I breathed in relief but it was not easy to overcome the trauma that I had undergone. For many days I felt as if I had escaped a major accident that had endangered my very life.

In my second period in Egypt (1990–92), after the Egyptians had been induced to soften the ban on Israeli officials and political personalities that they considered irretrievable from their point of view, several interesting visits took place. The most important, as a matter of course, was the official visit of the then foreign minister, David Levy. It was the first visit of an Israeli foreign minister after a long period of estrangement between the upper levels of government (President Mubarak was adamant not to meet Prime Minister Shamir and Levy's visit was the second best from our point of view). I have already touched on this visit and I will only repeat that, though it was a great success in itself, it did not bring about a breakthrough in relations between the two countries.

The visit of Professor Avner Shaki, the then minister of religions, was of particular significance though it too did not have the impact we had hoped for on relations with Egypt. In an unprecedented gesture of good-will, the Egyptians arranged for him meetings with the Great Mufti of Egypt, the head of the El Azhar University and the Copt Patriarch, Baba Shenuda. The latter had declared a binding boycott on Israel and Israeli representatives in protest against the Israeli position in the Dir al Sultan conflict with the Ethiopian church. Naturally, the foreign minister, Amr Mussa, also received him but President Mubarak refrained from doing so. Up to the last moment, the Egyptians waived the possibility of a meeting with the president (in Egyptian eyes, a most valuable remuneration that should be bestowed on an Israeli guest only if it was worthwhile). It seems that, according to the Egyptian scale of values, Shaki was not flexible enough to receive such a high honor.

A delegation of Knesset members from the Likud Party was also invited for a two-day visit. Eliahu Ben-Elissar, the first ambassador to Egypt, headed the delegation (at the time he chaired the foreign affairs and defense commission). This delegation too was not found worthy of being received by President Mubarak. It was a public snub, especially for Ben-Elissar. The delegation met with the foreign minister, the presidents of both houses of parliament and the board of the Institute for Middle Eastern Studies (a body sponsored and financed by the Egyptian authorities). The Institute organized a round-table to exchange views on ways and means to solve the Israeli–Arab conflict and promote a comprehensive peace in the region. The delegation was stunned to hear in the most explicit language that there would be no real peace as long as Israel did not totally stop Jewish immigration and did not dismantle its nuclear arsenal (for the Egyptians it is an incontestable fact that Israel possesses such weapons). This, in addition to agreeing to the establishment of a Palestinian state and the return of the refugees, total withdrawal from all the occupied territories including east Jerusalem and so on and so forth.

The ruling party invited a delegation of Labor's youth wing and received them with great warmth. The embassy convinced Professor Wali (in his capacity as secretary-general of the party) to also invite a small delegation of the Likud Party to balance the picture. Officially, the embassy was not responsible for these two visits but behind the scenes it helped organize every detail. The Likud delegation was not received in the party's headquarters but only in small branches in the suburbs of Cairo and Alexandria. A very cordial dialogue was established with the Egyptians but the authorities thought that the meetings had got out of hand and did not allow the party activists to attend a reception offered by me in their honor.

A visit of an altogether different kind was that of a group of about 20 cadets from our Diplomatic School. We had to work very hard to get the invitation and even harder to translate it into action. For the first time, the Egyptians allowed a direct contact with their trainee diplomats and young political researchers. Surprisingly, they even allowed them to attend a reception I offered in my residence and to fraternize with the Israeli trainees. However, all our repeated invitations for a reciprocal visit remained unanswered. Even our readiness to cover all expenses including air fares did not lure the Egyptians.

In addition to the official and semi-official visits, there was a stream of private visits, especially from the left of the political spectrum in Israel. The embassy was not involved in arranging these visits or in escorting the visitors, but it always received notice of their coming and relatively up-to-date briefings on their meetings. The embassy made a point of welcoming Israeli guests, from right or left, and of facilitating their stay in Egypt. My door was always open to them and most of them were invited to my table. I looked with a favorable eye on any sort of contacts with the Egyptians that might increase the interaction between the two countries and lead to a better understanding. In this field, the pro-peace movements were most active. They regularly organized seminars, round-tables and tours with the financial help of international factors interested in fostering peace in the region. In opposition to the Israelis who were totally independent and openly took stands opposed to the government's policy, on the Egyptian side every initiative and every step was co-ordinated with the authorities. There was no spontaneity or deviation from the official line; every move was made under strict supervision from above. In the period that preceded the Madrid conference, one could clearly feel the Egyptians' disappointment at the inability of the Israeli left to deliver the goods. They strove to widen the circle of pro-peace activists and made various approaches to enrol elements of the right close to the Israeli government of the time. They hoped that these elements would be able to shift pro-peace activities from interminable verbosity to a more tangible track. It partly explains the sudden flexibility of the Egyptian authorities in their policy regarding invitations and visits and their readiness to invite personalities and groupings that were considered extremists and were until this change of policy *persona non grata* in Egypt.

In parallel, Egypt continued its transparent attempts to interfere in Israel's internal affairs and directly influence its political process. As always, the favorite tool remained invitations and visits. Close to the 1992 elections, a large delegation of leaders of all Arab parties in Israel was invited to Cairo with a view to convincing them to run on a single list and thus improve their prospects in the elections. To the Egyptians' bitter disappointment, their efforts at persuasion did not reap fruit. Similarly, leaders of the orthodox religious parties were invited (each one on himself) to persuade them that they should relinquish their support for the government and join a peace coalition or, in plainer words, a coalition led by the Labor Party. The leader of Degel Hatorah (a small orthodox faction) and at the time deputy minister of housing, Rabbi Abraham Ravitz, was invited for talks by Osama Elbaz, the political adviser to President Mubarak. The explicit precondition for extending the invitation was that the Israeli ambassador in Cairo would not be present at the meeting. Ambassador Bassiuni convinced Rabbi Ravitz, an intelligent and decent politician who was still new to international diplomacy, to agree to that humiliating condition. On his arrival, I explained to him the absurdity of the situation and he decided that I should accompany him to all his meetings. When the message was conveyed to Osama, he threatened to cancel the meeting (he could not reasonably say what he had in mind in the presence of the ambassador of Israel) and pointed out that Ravitz had been invited on a clear-cut condition. The minister was perplexed and did not know how to react. I advised him to live up to his own commitment and hear what Osama had to say. After the meeting, Ravitz gave me a detailed report, which was almost identical to what I had told him that he would hear. I was punished for my cheek in trying to impose my presence; my invitation to a lunch in the minister's honor was cancelled on the pretence that the event had been postponed and that Osama would host Ravitz to a one-on-one lunch. It was clear that the lunch would take place as scheduled and that all guests, to the exclusion of the ambassador of Israel, would be present. Again, Ravitz did not know what to do. Paradoxically, I had to convince him to go to the lunch and 'not throw out the baby with the bath water'.

Over the years, I had grown a thick skin to this kind of snub. However, I could not turn a blind eye to such rude behavior, which stood in flagrant breach of diplomatic protocol, not to say elementary politeness. I presented an official protest to the foreign ministry and requested that they convey to Osama Elbaz a verbal message: 'The government of Israel provides its ambassador in Cairo with a salary that is sufficient for all his meals – breakfast, lunch, dinner and in-between. The ambassador was sad that his invitation to the lunch in honor of the Israeli deputy minister of housing was cancelled in such a rude manner, but he did not starve to death and will certainly survive.' I added to the message a piece of my mind in the most explicit words. Ravitz's visit left me with a bitter taste and intensified my anger at the Egyptians' crude behavior. I was not offended for myself. I could not support the idea, and still cannot, that Israel accepts with no reaction whatsoever that an Egyptian civil servant, high as his position may be, has the cheek to extend invitations to Israeli ministers and high-ranking political personalities, and dictates conditions, threatens and presents ultimatums. Elbaz is not to blame; he only takes advantage of Israeli weaknesses and makes the most out of them. No doubt the Israeli side of the equation is more at fault! Were it not for our eagerness to rub shoulders with the Egyptians, the whole system of penalty and reward (of which visits and invitations are an integral part) conceived and put in place by the Egyptians would have been totally ineffective and probably discontinued.

Let me add that Osama Elbaz has never received any serving Israeli ambassador for an exchange of views, a courtesy call or for any other purpose. All of us have tried to establish a working relationship with him but to no avail. On the other hand, his door is always open to visiting Israeli personalities, especially those he has invited to Cairo with the intention of persuading them to toe the Egyptian line or those who are ready to collaborate with him. On this subject, Ambassador Sasson related to me a very characteristic event: on the occasion of the official visit of a top Israeli minister, he was put by protocol in the same car as Elbaz. He took advantage of the opportunity to express wonder that his repeated requests for a meeting had remained unanswered while many visiting Israelis had been received. Osama answered straight to the point and without blushing: 'I have no time for diplomatic conversations or small talk. I am ready to meet with you only if you agree to establish a useful collaboration with me.' Sasson was profoundly offended and answered dryly: 'You are forgetting that I am the ambassador of the State of Israel. I have a useful collaboration only with the government of Israel!'

Another Orthodox leader invited to Cairo, through the good offices of Ambassador Bassiuni and upon his recommendation, was Rabbi Mehachem Porosh, the head of the Agudat Israel Party and a key player in Israeli politics. It was on the eve of the 1992 elections and Egypt was very keen to persuade him to shift allegiances and support a Peace Government (read: a Labor-led government). Exceptionally, the invitation was extended on behalf of President Mubarak himself, who at the time was on vacation in Alexandria. Porosh and Ambassador Bassiuni (who accompanied him personally as if he were the prime minister) were taken by special plane to Alexandria. Since it was an official visit that included a meeting with the president, I also came by car and waited for the honored guest together with the chief of protocol. The plane was delayed by three hours because of a technical problem. Usually, in such cases the meeting with the president (which is viewed in Egypt as a royal event) is cancelled or postponed for another day – there can be no delays or excuses! This time, Mubarak waited patiently and received Porosh immediately upon his arrival and, in accordance with diplomatic protocol, I participated in the meeting. It was unusually long – more than two hours. The president poured on Porosh smiles and outward manifestations of sympathy and, though he did not speak straight to the point, he made clear what was his purpose in inviting him. Bassiuni was more straightforward.

Porosh strongly rejected the president's condemnation of the policies and personality of Prime Minister Shamir and tried (in vain) to persuade him that Shamir was doing his utmost to bring about a comprehensive peace and was ready to make substantial concessions to this end. He reminded the president that Shamir had called many times for a summit between them to discuss frankly and in detail all issues of contention. He (Mubarak) had refused to meet Shamir, alleging that 'nothing can be achieved with Shamir' and that 'such a summit will reach a dead-end and complicate the situation even more'. Towards the end of the meeting Porosh raised, at my request, a few pending issues but the president, apparently disappointed and angry at having wasted his time, rejected all our requests. It was clear that he had been expecting another kind of reaction from Rabbi Porosh. It seems that Elbaz and Bassiuni had led him to believe that if he personally dedicated time to Porosh, he would easily be brought to cross the line. Nevertheless, Mubarak concealed his feelings and parted cordially from Porosh stressing that contacts with him would continue through Ambassador Bassiuni. Bassiuni seemed devastated and tried up to the last moment to reverse the situation but Mubarak scolded him saying in Arabic: 'Enough, enough, don't you see that there is no hope!'

The Egyptians also used their reward and punishment policy towards Israeli journalists. They rarely invited them as official guests and seldom agreed to cover their expenses (in the framework of the understanding whereby each side covers hospitality expenses in his country) when they came with Israeli official delegations. In general, Israeli journalists came to Egypt on professional duties and their expenses were fully covered by their employers. The Egyptians knew that, in any case, it was impossible to influence serious journalists with visits and invitations. They were more subtle and looked for weak spots that would give them leverage on the journalists. For example, they exploited the fact that the Israeli media organs had not appointed resident correspondents in Egypt and covered events by sending ad hoc teams. Journalists who wrote in too offensive a manner encountered difficulties in receiving their accreditation cards from the government press office (without which it was practically impossible to cover events in Egypt). The journalists were made to come and go and the embassy's press counselor to run, on their behalf, from one official to another. Sometimes, the card would not be issued at all; at times it would be issued after the conclusion of the main events; at other times it would not allow entry to the presidency where the most important press conferences took place. A more drastic means to punish a recalcitrant journalist was to delay the issuing of his visa or even to deny him the visa altogether. In my two periods in Egypt, the embassy tried in vain to persuade the Egyptian authorities to issue annual visas (allowing multiple entries) and permanent press cards to Israeli journalists covering the middle east. The Egyptians flatly refused – they had *prima facie* a good excuse that made sense: 'Israeli journalists who want to cover Egypt permanently should reside in the country as hundreds of other foreign journalists do.' The real reason for their refusal was less candid: they simply were not ready to forfeit an efficient tool of pressure on the Israeli journalists.

There were other and more original ways to punish a stubborn journalist. For a certain period, he would be denied interviews with leading Egyptian personalities such as the president and the foreign minister.

Worse still, exclusive interviews would be given to journalists working for competing organs. It was a double-edged weapon: on the one hand, a sanction against the recalcitrant journalist and, on the other, a reward to other journalists and media organs. Clearly, journalists punished in such a manner would go out of their way to be granted an interview with a top Egyptian leader (especially the president) and requested Ambassador Bassiuni and all their relations in Egypt (including in the embassy) to interfere on their behalf. Consciously or not, this situation must have had an impact on their writing.

The most drastic sanction against a hard-boiled journalist was to declare him *persona non grata* and ban him definitively from entering Egypt. For a journalist covering the middle east, this was literally a deathblow. I recall one such case, during my second period (1990–92). The chief editor of a foreign-language daily had written an article about Israeli– Egyptian relations in which he had made a reference to President Mubarak that was not to the president's liking. (Take my word, it was a very mild criticism that was absolutely innocuous compared with the slanderous attacks published daily in the Egyptian press.) He was officially notified by the Egyptian embassy in Tel Aviv that he had been permanently banned from entering Egypt. The editor, who was indeed a staunch supporter of peace and saw Egypt as a bridge to the Arab world, was devastated – his entire world had suddenly collapsed! He requested me to intervene personally and do my utmost to have the draconian and unwarranted measure abrogated. At first, I flatly refused; I did not want to be part of the Egyptian game. However, he was an old friend since my Beit-Shaan days (1953–63) and when I was prompted to help him by various political figures in Israel, I arranged his coming to Cairo. The press counselor accompanied him to several meetings with top Egyptian leaders and spoke on his behalf. All misunderstandings were removed!

Naturally, besides the above-mentioned means, Egyptians did not neglect all the customary tricks used in a government–press relationship. They leaked information to journalists they wanted to favor and withheld it from those who did not toe the Egyptian line. They would allow the former to maintain free telephone contacts with top personalities, facilitate their visits, and grant them exclusive interviews or coverage of major events. The others would be kept at a distance and meet with petty difficulties in the accomplishment of their duties. Certainly, most (not to say all) Israeli journalists covering the middle east are experienced, decent and outstanding professionals. None of these Egyptian stratagems could make them write against their conscience and their professional judgment. However, there is no doubt that in their subconscience, it must have had at least a restraining influence. I discussed the matter several times with journalist friends and they did not conceal that it was a factor they had to take into consideration, though it was not a decisive one. I could easily understand what they meant and I am sure the reader does too.

After the change of government in Israel in July 1992, I helped arrange the first visit of Yitshak Rabin as prime minister. I will relate the details and analyze the implications of this visit in Chapter 17. I also dealt with the first visit of Dr Yossi Beilin as deputy foreign minister (I had already been appointed ambassador to India and was on the verge of ending my tenure in Egypt). Beilin was a welcome guest in Egypt and as always he was received with great warmth. His schedule included only two meetings: with Osama Elbaz (the political adviser to the president) and with Amr Mussa (the foreign minister). I did not participate in the first meeting for reasons explained earlier in this chapter. The meeting with Mussa took place on a Saturday (the Jewish Sabbath) and we were compelled for religious reasons (or more exactly, coalition reasons) to walk a long distance across the city, attracting much press coverage both in Egypt and Israel.

Beilin explained thoroughly to Amr Mussa the policies of the new government and stressed its determination to move ahead promptly with the peace process – simultaneously on the Palestinian and Syrian tracks. He requested that Egypt refrain from opening additional fronts and exert its influence in restraining other Arab countries from doing so. He especially requested that Egypt discontinue its repeated attacks on Israel for refusing to adhere to the NPT (Non-Proliferation Treaty) and cease to raise the issue in the multinational track of the Madrid conference. Amr Mussa listened carefully, said a few words of encouragement but gave no clear-cut commitment. At the end of the meeting, I told Beilin that there was no chance that Egypt would comply with his request and cease to fan tension around the nuclear issue. I stressed that, on the contrary, Egypt would make it a major issue of contention in the months to come and explained the Egyptian motivation and goals (I will deal at length separately with this very important topic). The two ministers decided to revive the (stillborn) periodic consultations at the level of foreign minister, and to convene meetings every three months instead of every six months as had been decided upon (but never implemented) during David Levy's visit. I called Beilin's attention to the fact that if that decision were really implemented this time, it would empty the mission of the ambassador to Egypt of substance. Beilin smiled and replied: 'Why do you mind? It will be long after you have left Egypt. In India you will have plenty of work and be totally on your own ...'

To understand the full scope of Egypt's policies in respect of visits and invitations, the visits that did not take place are no less interesting, and sometimes even more interesting, than those that *did* take place. After the tragic assassination of President Sadat, Prime Minister Begin attended the state funeral and met with President Mubarak for a short exchange of views. They both expressed their staunch commitment to the peace process and pledged to respect fully all agreements that had been signed in the past. They decided to meet in the near future for more comprehensive talks at a date that would be decided upon through diplomatic channels. For obvious reasons, Begin was interested in holding the meeting as soon as possible and was ready to come to Cairo immediately. He was anxious to know Mubarak better and personally assess what his intentions were. A few days after the funeral, the embassy began contacting the Egyptians in order to arrange a summit between the two leaders as decided. As usual, there began an interminable and exhausting seesaw. We received evasive answers, then half-answers and finally a clear-cut answer: 'In the wake of Begin's insulting statements to the effect that he has the intention of demanding that Egypt reiterate its commitment to live up to its obligations in conformity with the peace treaty provisions, President Mubarak refuses to hold the meeting under pressure.' True, Begin had made statements to that effect but they were more than justified in the circumstances of the time and had nothing offensive or injurious in them. The Egyptians, however, pretended that Mubarak had been profoundly offended and decided to postpone the meeting 'until time heals the wound and the President cools down from the unwarranted affront to his personal credibility and to Egypt's honor'.

We reported to Jerusalem and were instructed to continue the pressure. Aware of the historic importance of such a meeting, we continued to nag the Egyptians notwithstanding the unpleasantness involved (the Egyptians are usually very nice but they can also be rude and blunt when they want to be). Even after we hinted that the postponement of the meeting might lead to a postponement of the second phase of withdrawal from Sinai (an Egyptian nightmare), they did not budge from their position. During this time, Mubarak presented his first government to the Egyptian public and the ceremony was broadcast live on all television channels (I followed it closely). Finally, Mubarak, with his ministers around him, stood on the palace staircase for an inaugural snapshot and then answered questions from the press. One of the first questions was whether there was any truth in the rumor that Begin insisted on coming to Egypt in the near future and whether the president would receive him in spite of his offensive statements. Mubarak laughed scornfully and answered in an Egyptian dialect: 'If he wants to come, *Ahlan wa Sahlan* (welcome), Egypt is open to everyone.' All the ministers and the whole public burst into laughter. The foreign correspondents, who did not grasp the scorn in the president's reply, reported that 'Mubarak has invited Begin to visit Egypt' ...

The reaction did not take long in arriving. A few hours later, the prime minister's office contacted me over the phone and complained that we in the embassy were sabotaging the peace process and did not know what was taking place under our own nose. I was given strict instructions to immediately inform the Egyptians that Begin accepted Mubarak's invitation and was ready to come in the next few days at a date convenient for the president. I explained strenuously the background behind the alleged invitation, described the disdainful laughter and begged to preserve

Begin's dignity. All my supplications and explanations were to no avail but what saved the situation was the inaugural picture on the palace stairs. It had been published on the cover of the weekly *Al Mussawar* and one could clearly see the president and all his ministers bursting into laughter. I faxed the picture, adding a brief comment: 'This is the exact moment when the president extended his invitation to the prime minister.' The message was received and finally understood and the topic was removed from the agenda for a few weeks.

When we resumed our nagging, the Egyptians informed us that President Mubarak was ready to go to Israel but he demanded that all meetings and social events, including meetings with the president and prime minister, take place outside Jerusalem. We were eager to receive President Mubarak and were ready to do our utmost to make the visit possible. We could not, however, bend completely and we insisted that at least the meeting with the president should take place in Jerusalem. The Egyptians categorically refused and again pretended to be offended to the depths of their being: 'You are trying to dictate to the President of Egypt that he should act against his will and compel him to visit Jerusalem. He has, therefore, decided to cancel the visit!'

Many years later, the Egyptians still claimed that Mubarak had wished to visit Israel but that Israel had profoundly offended him. The truth is that Mubarak did not want for his own reasons (probably as part of the reward and punishment policy) to establish an open relationship with the Israeli prime minister of the time and he stubbornly refused to set foot in Israel. Not only did Begin's visit never take place but Mubarak also refused to meet Prime Minister Shamir in Egypt or elsewhere. For ten long years, from 1982 to 1992, indeed from Mubarak's accession to the presidency until Rabin's election as prime minister, not a single summit took place. Rabin's first visit as prime minister abroad was to Egypt and he came many times afterwards. Shimon Peres, President Ezer Weizman, Benjamin Netanyahu and Ehud Barak also met with President Mubarak in Egypt several times but he never made a gesture of goodwill and reciprocated. Paradoxically, he did come to Israel and even went to Jerusalem! That was on the occasion of Rabin's funeral.

Mubarak's refusal to meet Shamir during his six years as prime minister (1986–92) focused world attention. Israeli and foreign personalities tried in vain to persuade Mubarak that such a meeting was essential for fostering peace and establishing a climate of understanding. Mubarak dodged the pressures with half-promises: 'The meeting will take place when conditions are ripe and conducive to a real dialogue ... the meeting should be thoroughly prepared to make sure that it will lead to positive results ...' Sometimes he added his version on how Begin had allegedly offended him in 1982, tried to force him to a meeting and humiliated him by doubting Egypt's commitment to peace. To stress his goodwill, he also told his interlocutors how Begin had thwarted his visit to Israel and tried to compel him to come to Jerusalem and thus recognize Israeli sovereignty over the city. To sum up, no visit and no meeting ever came out of these approaches. The situation became tenser every day and, as usual, the Egyptians turned the issue into a bargaining card to exert pressure on Israel.

I have to confess that I also tried my luck, using my best diplomatic skills. In the situation prevailing at the time, the convening of a Mubarak–Shamir summit would have been the consecration of my mission to Egypt. I raised the matter as early as in my first conversation with the president, immediately after presenting my credentials, when I tried to persuade him to meet with Shamir and discuss all pending issues face to face. I stressed that Shamir was keen to put relations with Egypt on the right track and foster the peace process in the region but that it was not reasonable to expect him to accept Egypt's positions in return for a meeting or a visit. I added that there should be no preconditions on either side and that everything should be open for discussion. Mubarak replied at length, more or less on the same lines as I have described earlier. The bottom line was that he did not trust Shamir and did not believe that he genuinely wanted a comprehensive peace in the region or was ready to pay the price for securing it. He did not see the usefulness of such a meeting and believed that it would be counterproductive and worsen the relations between the two countries. Between the lines, I could clearly read that he was in no hurry and was ready to wait until the government in Israel changed.

Throughout my stay in Egypt, I did not relinquish the matter and tried discreetly to bring about a summit between the two leaders. There was a moment when I believed that the official visit of Foreign Minister David Levy (which I had arranged after strenuous efforts) would lead to a visit by Shamir but my expectations never materialized. At this point, I have to stress that Shamir never requested me – and to my knowledge never requested anyone else – to arrange a summit between him and Mubarak. It is clear that he would have welcomed such a summit but he refused to play the game according to the rules dictated by the Egyptians and pay (in advance …) the price, in political or other concessions, for the pleasure and honor of shaking Mubarak's hand.

After I persuaded the Egyptians to remove the ban on visits of Israeli ministers and personalities perceived as extremists, I tried to have them invite Benjamin Netanyahu, at the time deputy minister of foreign affairs. I stressed that he was just starting his political career and would go far and that it was important for them to know him better and let him know their views. It was a non-starter; they refused to discuss the matter. It was a categorical No with a capital N! They were convinced that he was a lost cause and that inviting him would serve no useful purpose. They defined him as 'a second Yitshak Shamir and worse'! They also feared, though they did not say so openly, that inviting him to Egypt would strengthen his position, internally and internationally. A profound knowledge of the Israeli mind and years of experience at that game strengthened them in the belief that, for the average Israeli politician, an invitation to visit Egypt had tremendous weight. The Egyptians did not want to receive Netanyahu as deputy minister – though since then they have received him many times, and with a red carpet, as prime minister!

There was a single case in the reverse direction, i.e. of the Egyptians requesting an Israeli invitation for an Egyptian delegation to visit Israel and meet with their counterparts. As a matter of fact, from the outset, we did our utmost to increase the number of Egyptian guests and to foster Egyptian tourism to Israel. In this case, however, we surprisingly took a different course. In one of my endless meetings with the director of the Israeli department in the foreign ministry, Ambassador Hanafi, I complained about the standstill in the work of the joint committees and requested the urgent convening of the trade committee. He replied that this matter was under consideration and that we should first convene in Israel the archeology committee in conformity with the understanding between Foreign Minister Levy and Ambassador Bassiuni. I was not aware of the existence of such a committee and of any problem between the two countries in this field. I tried to be evasive and get as much information as possible from Hanafi without showing my complete ignorance in a matter important enough for the Egyptians to take the initiative of sending a delegation to Israel. After a few indirect questions, the picture became clear: in the 1970s, the Israeli department of archeology had conducted excavations in Sinai and taken several archeological findings to Israel. On instructions from Cairo, Bassiuni had raised the matter several times and requested the prompt return of the findings. Minister Levy had invited an Egyptian delegation to come and discuss the modalities.

I told Hanafi that I did not foresee any difficulty and that Egyptian delegations were always welcome in Israel. I hurried back to the embassy and asked for confirmation of what Hanafi had told me. Indeed, it was true. Someone had forgotten to brief me! The department of archeology had been requested to set a date for the coming of the delegation as soon as possible. I relayed the answer to Hanafi and in the following months he did not cease to inquire if a date had already been set. I did not see any reason to hurry and did not put pressure on Jerusalem to set a date. I gave Hanafi evasive answers and invented new excuses each time. I enjoyed the situation tremendously but, after almost six months, I thought that it was high time to give the Egyptians a clear-cut answer and I began bombarding the ministry with cables. Finally, I received an answer that the department of archeology was not prepared to return the findings before concluding the scientific researches involved and was demanding from the foreign ministry an allocation of one million dollars for this purpose. I was requested not to bring this information to the knowledge of the Egyptians and co-ordinate with them a date in three months' time. The Egyptians had no alternative but to accept the date I suggested.

One month before the scheduled date, they formed a delegation that included the director of their own department of archeology and my friend Ambassador Hanafi, who until then had not been allowed to visit Israel (indeed, his inclusion was meant to be an enticement). Without any prompting from the embassy, they even hurried to send the passports to the embassy to obtain visas (an unprecedented event!). We issued the visas but, on the same occasion, we informed them that the visit had been postponed for a further two months. Then came more and more postponements (the reason was that no source of funding had been found for the million dollars). I confess that I enjoyed feeding the Egyptians with the same food they were feeding us but I thought that we were going too far. I cabled the ministry that the department of archeology could not hold the whole State of Israel captive to its whims and that we should either bring the matter to the cabinet for urgent decision or officially inform the Egyptians that the returning of the findings would be delayed. I received a laconic answer: 'The matter will be brought before the cabinet in due time. Continue to procrastinate.'

As a good soldier, I continued to postpone the visit from date to date. In the meantime, Foreign Minister Levy arrived in Cairo for an official visit and Amr Mussa, the Egyptian foreign minister, raised the matter in their first meeting and on every occasion during the visit. He complained of foot-dragging on Israel's part and accused it of avoiding returning the findings in flagrant breach of international law. Levy assured him that there was no basis for such accusations and promised that, immediately upon his return to Israel, he would personally make sure that a date for the visit was set. But until I left Cairo for India, almost a year later, the visit had not yet taken place. I had exhausted my stock of excuses and I simply briefly informed the Egyptians of each new delay and of each new date. As I said, our unusual behavior was due to an internal conflict within our own administration but, unintentionally, a message was sent to the Egyptians that in matters of visits and invitations there was a double-track road. Israel *could* pay Egypt in its own currency if it wanted to!

12 · Tourism and Transport

Immediately after the signing of the Camp David agreement and well before the exchange of embassies, a number of joint committees began functioning to establish the first peaceful relationship between Egypt and Israel after more than 30 years of war. The committee for tourism functioned swiftly and efficiently. Most of our Egyptian interlocutors were high officials in the ministry of tourism and did not try to hinder the negotiations' course as happened later in other committees. Their approach was professional and free of political considerations. Very quickly, an agreement was reached, recognizing the principle of free flow of tourists in both directions and establishing the foundations of close co-operation between the two countries in attracting tourists from other countries to the region. Furthermore, it was decided to open tourist offices in the two capitals on a basis of reciprocity. In parallel, the transportation and aviation committees, after a year of hard bargaining and many more months of detailed discussions in subcommittees, agreed on the immediate establishment of air, sea and land links between the two countries and defined the modalities of their functioning. The Egyptian approach was still professional and decisions were taken in function of the objective needs of the two sides. Among other items, the creation of a bus service between the two countries, the detailed arrangements for the crossing of private cars and the transport of goods in both directions were decided upon. Furthermore, with the aim of solving promptly any problem that might arise, direct contacts between the aviation authorities and the transport ministries of the two countries were clearly defined.

Tourism being one of the main economic fields in Egypt, the professionals were understandably interested in stepping up the flow of tourists from Israel and from other countries (mainly Jewish tourists) through Israel. If they had been left to their own devices, the agreements would have been implemented rapidly and faithfully. In my two periods in Egypt, I always found them helpful and understanding and on many occasions they removed obstacles left by other authorities – the security services and the foreign ministry. The latter are entrusted, almost exclusively, with the implementation of the policies of hampering the normal flow of relations with Israel and of keeping these relations within the parameters decided by the highest levels of power. From the first moment, a veto was put on direct contacts between the professional authorities; everything had to be channeled through the embassies and foreign ministries. Even in a matter as elementary as maintaining working contacts between the flight control towers of the two capitals' airports, the Egyptians wanted us to use diplomatic channels. We had to struggle for many months until we obtained their tacit acceptance of direct contacts between the two towers, which is a must in such a sensitive area.

As for Israeli tourism to Egypt, the instructions from above were to regulate the flow of tourists by a series of administrative steps. For example, while the Israeli embassies, in Cairo and elsewhere in the world, were authorized to issue on-the-spot visas to Egyptian citizens, all Egyptian embassies – to the exclusion of the embassy in Tel Aviv – were strictly forbidden to issue visas to Israeli citizens. Even the embassy in Tel Aviv was not allowed to issue visas on the spot; it had to send all applications to Cairo for decision despite the delay of three to four weeks involved. Furthermore, the number of visas was limited to a few hundred per week and to a single entry to Egypt. This last measure was intended to hamper Israeli businessmen traveling to Egypt and complicate the transiting of Israelis through Egypt to other countries. The immigration authorities at the airport were instructed not to issue transit visas on the spot to Israelis arriving without a valid visa as is customary with citizens of other countries. Israelis in this situation, most of whom had transited through Egypt to another destination and were on their way back, were summarily arrested, treated with the utmost harshness and expelled from the country on the first plane to Israel (obviously at their own expense). Our consular officers were very often summoned to the airport by Israelis in difficulty (and not by the Egyptian authorities, as should have been the case in accordance with international law). The only thing they could do was to try easing the conditions of detention and have them expelled as soon as possible. Naturally, the embassy also protested repeatedly and expressed disappointment concerning the rough treatment of Israeli citizens contrary to the minimal rules of courtesy and to Egypt's own interest in increasing tourism to the country.

After more than a year, we succeeded in convincing the Egyptians to reduce the delay in issuing visas and to increase their number substantially. In my second period in Egypt (1990–92), taking advantage of a period of 'smiles', I finally persuaded the authorities to allow two entries to Israelis transiting to a third country, on the condition that they presented air tickets proving that they were compelled to return through Egypt. In spite of all my efforts, I could not bring them to make more flexible (not to say rescind) the instructions to the Egyptian embassies and to the immigration authorities not to issue visas to Israeli citizens. I do believe that the situation today is pretty much the same and visa restrictions continue to be part of Egypt's diplomatic arsenal in its attrition campaign against Israel.

Immediately after the inauguration of the embassy, Israel opened a tourist office in one of the most select streets in Cairo and appointed Maurice Cassuto, a successful Egyptian-born tourism promoter, as director general. He quit his flourishing business and volunteered for the job in the firm belief that tourism would be a steadfast bridge between the two countries and the two peoples. He stormed the Egyptian tourist market and quickly established a working and personal relationship with tens of tourist agents and hotel managers. He helped them find counterparts in Israel and conclude co-operation agreements. Maurice also developed good relations with the Egyptian officials in the ministry of tourism and planned with them ways and means of increasing the flow of tourists in both directions and attracting tourists from other countries. Later, for budgetary reasons, the tourist office was moved to a separate accommodation in the building where we had our chancery. The Egyptians, for their part, did not reciprocate and indeed have not opened a tourist office in Israel to this very day. For obvious reasons, the Israeli tourist office in Cairo took upon itself the fostering of Israeli tourism to Egypt as well as Egyptian tourism to Israel (as it was meant to do).

Paradoxically, the Egyptian tourist agencies were very enthusiastic. They organized themselves to receive Israeli groups and take Egyptian groups to Israel. Israeli tourists began to flock in, the only limitation being the number of visas issued by the Egyptians. In the first few months, a few organized Egyptian groups visited Israel and returned absolutely enchanted with the country and the welcome they had received. The backlash was immediate: the Egyptian tourists were summoned to the security services and advised not to speak to anyone about their impressions of Israel. The tourist agencies were also instructed to focus on bringing Israeli tourists to Egypt and refrain from encouraging Egyptians to visit Israel. To make sure that these instructions were not bypassed, the authorities took – at a very early stage – a series of precautionary measures. Egyptians who wished to travel to Israel were to apply for an exit visa (the 'yellow card') and receive a new passport 'valid for Israel only'. The authorities were far from forthcoming: new passports were issued only after interminable formalities and the very few who managed to overcome this obstacle were denied the yellow card. Those who insisted were taken, late at night, to the not too alluring premises of the security services and persuaded that the time was not propitious for visiting Israel. The little tourism that had slipped away in the first few months was totally stopped. Only officials on missions, businessmen, tourist agents (allowed to work with Israel) and Palestinians visiting parents in the Gaza Strip received the green light. From time to time, when the authorities wished to send positive signals to Israel, organized groups were also allowed to go to Israel (purportedly on a mission). They were warned that upon their return they should refrain from public statements and from sharing their impressions with friends or relatives.

Israel obviously could not turn a blind eye to this direct blow to the very essence of peace and we raised the issue on every occasion. At first, the Egyptians denied everything. When we brought incontrovertible evidence to sustain our contention, they claimed that we did not understand the way bureaucracy functioned in Egypt. They added brazenly that the only reasons that kept Egyptians from visiting Israel were the extravagant cost of living and the abhorrence of the Egyptian people at the inhuman treatment of the Palestinians. In 1991, in an interview with the Israeli daily *Maariv*, President Mubarak added a few more explanations for the lack of Egyptian tourism: there is nothing to see in Israel; besides we have in Egypt beautiful beaches and a score of interesting archeological sites that are infinitely superior to what Israel has to offer. However, the most insulting justification advanced by the Egyptians, after they could no longer deny the reality, was that all the measures they imposed were meant to protect Israel from being invaded by thousands of unemployed workers and infiltrated by terrorists under cover of tourism. They turned down our requests to let us decide for ourselves what was good for us and apply to Israel the same treatment they applied to any other country. We gradually escalated our protests and demanded that the government allow Egyptians who wanted to 'throw their money out of the window' and go to Israel without having to confront insurmountable bureaucratic obstacles. The Egyptians were not impressed by our arguments and did not budge an inch. They continued to feed us with lies and deceit (and still do so). The only improvement we obtained was compelling them to rescind the need for Egyptians allowed to travel to Israel to change their regular passports; we simply notified them that we would stamp visas only on regular Egyptian passports validated for Israel. We reminded them that they had recognized Israel and maintained with it fully-fledged diplomatic relations. I should explain here that, at the time, regular Egyptian passports still bore the stamp 'not valid' for Israel and South Africa.

As to the yellow card, it is required to this very day. President Mubarak has personally promised, many times and on many occasions, that he will give instructions to abolish it once and for all. Since they are still in use, and no one in Egypt would dare infringe the president's instructions, one has to reach the inevitable conclusion that no such instructions have ever been given! At first, Israel was in good company. Egyptian citizens wishing to travel to the Soviet Union (still in existence at the time) also had to apply for exit visas. The small, but rather important, difference was that in most cases they received the visa within a few days and were not harassed after their return. With the improvement of relations with the Soviet Union and the change of regime in South Africa, the need for exit visas was abolished and Israel remained in splendid isolation – the only country in the whole world for which an Egyptian citizen requires special permission to visit. Obtaining such permission is – almost always – a Mission Impossible!

It is sufficient to cite one example that speaks for itself. At the beginning of 1989, a bus transporting Israeli tourists was attacked by terrorists some 50 kilometers from Cairo. An Egyptian chemical engineer who was traveling behind the bus in his Mercedes car transported a number of the injured to the nearest hospital, thus saving their lives. Day after day, he came to see them and brought flowers and oriental sweets. Obviously, bonds of friendship were woven between the casualties and their savior. Upon their return, wanting to pay back a little of what he had done for them, the Israelis invited his wife and him to visit them in Israel. He applied for the famous yellow card but his applications were turned down time after time. He stubbornly persisted because he believed that it was his right, and his duty, to visit people whose lives he had saved. The security authorities were of a different opinion and pressured him to abandon what they saw as a stupid idea. Finally, I decided to speak directly to the interior minister, Abd el Halim Mussa, and request his intervention. The minister denied, with a wide smile, that exit visas for Israel were still required but he phoned, in my presence, the internal security chief and requested him to make the necessary arrangements. The reader will already have guessed that the yellow card was not issued and that the chemical engineer could not respond to an invitation he had received from private persons (whose life he had saved) and not, God forbid, from the government of Israel. I considered speaking again with the interior minister but I decided not to do so, fearing that the authorities might take measures against this noble Egyptian. Only in 1994, five years after the terrorist attack, was the engineer finally authorized to visit his friends in Israel on the occasion of the unveiling of a monument in memory of Israeli tourists murdered on Egyptian soil. He was allowed to go a second time in early 1995. Let me make it clear that both permissions were granted during periods of 'smiles' in relations between the two countries, when the Egyptian government wanted to send positive signals to Israel. As amazing as it may sound, many people in Israel described this tiny gesture (after five years of persistence!) as a major success and expressed gratitude to the Egyptian authorities ...

To the undeclared but stringent ban on tourism to Israel enforced by the Egyptian government, many organizations added their own boycott and threatened with expulsion any member who infringed it. Such was (and is) the case of the trade unions and all professional associations (e.g. doctors, lawyers, journalists, academics, students). The Coptic church also strictly forbade, in the early 1980s, its members (around four million according to official sources and well beyond 12 million according to church sources) to visit Israel. This was meant as a means of pressure on the Israeli government to intervene in favor of the Egyptian church in the conflict between the Egyptian and Ethiopian Coptic churches on the Dir el Sultan issue (a monastery in the old city of Jerusalem). In the early 1970s, monks belonging to the Ethiopian church had taken advantage of the Easter holidays to squat, late at night, in the monastery's yard and change the lock of a door giving direct access to the Holy Sepulchre Church. The Egyptian monks lodged a formal complaint but the Israeli police refused to intervene because of the sensitivity of the issue and the long history of clashes between the two sister churches on controlling the yard. (At the time I was deputy director of the African department and personally involved in the matter.) The Egyptians appealed to the High Court of Justice for an order against the Israeli authorities. The Court accepted their application and criticized the police for not taking immediate steps. However, because of the political aspects involved, it left the final decision to the Israeli government. As usual in such delicate matters, a committee was established to strive to work out a compromise between the two churches. The Egyptians refused to move from their categorical demands. Baba (Pope) Shenuda, a retired army officer and eminent scholar who rules his flock with an iron fist and has no fear of the authorities or the Muslim establishment, was removed from office in early 1982 by President Sadat for having organized a Coptic self-defense militia. He was exiled to a remote convent and later reprieved by President Mubarak and reinstated in his functions. He reiterated the ban to visit Israel until such time as Dir El Sultan be returned to the control of his church, insisting that Israel use force to evict the Ethiopian monks. He mobilized the support of Boutros Boutros Ghali (himself a Copt) and of many other eminent Egyptian personalities who did not miss an opportunity to demand the return of Dir El Sultan to its legitimate owners. Israel preferred not to put a healthy head into a sick bed (the last thing Israel wants to do is to use force against monks) and continued to call for a negotiated compromise between the two churches. When I returned to Cairo in 1990, I tried to establish contact with Baba Shenuda with the intention of convincing him to lift the boycott and accept a compromise on Dir El Sultan with the Ethiopian church. I knew that Coptic tourism to Israel depended, first and foremost, on removing the restrictions imposed by the Egyptian authorities but there was no harm in trying to improve relations with the Coptic church. In any case, Baba Shenuda refused to receive me. I finally met him on the occasion of the visit of our minister of religions, Professor Avner Shaki, and most of the conversation turned around the Dir el Sultan issue. Baba Shenuda did not budge from his demand that the Israeli government use force to evict the Ethiopian monks and return the monastery to the Egyptian Coptic church. The matter is still unresolved and until this very day the yard is controlled by the Ethiopians. The Egyptians still raise the issue from time to time though with less intensity and frequency than when Boutros Ghali was in the foreign ministry.

Israel maintained for many years its tourist office in Cairo despite all the difficulties and the non-reciprocity by the Egyptians. For obvious reasons, it dealt, almost exclusively, with the promotion of Israeli tourism to Egypt. From the political standpoint, one-way tourism is better than no tourism at all. Finally, our ministry of tourism refused to continue banking the check for what it viewed as a political tourist office that exported Israeli tourists rather than importing Egyptian ones. When I returned in 1990, the office had already been closed – while the restrictions on Egyptian tourism to Israel had been made even more stringent. Up to my departure, at the end of 1992, the situation did not change (even incrementally) despite all the efforts exerted by the embassy. Statistics indicated that thousands of visas were issued every year but a quick scrutiny showed that, as in the past, the overwhelming majority of visas were issued to Palestinians from the Gaza Strip, holders of an Egyptian *Laissez-Passer* and Egyptian citizens visiting relatives in the territories or dispatched on official missions. The situation is more or less the same today.

In the field of aviation, the results were much better in the early 1990s. We succeeded in increasing the number of El Al weekly flights to Cairo from three to four and in securing rights for Arkia (a small airline) to make two weekly flights to Sharm el Sheikh in Sinai. During the Gulf War, to minimize the risk of Iraqi ground-to-air missiles, we obtained permission for El Al to flyover Egyptian territory on its way to and back from Africa. Towards the end of 1999, the Egyptians, alleging administrative irregularities, compelled Israeli aircraft bound for Africa to turn back notwithstanding the permission that had earlier been issued to them. It is probably part of the harassment game constantly played by the Egyptian authorities to fan tension between the two countries and put pressure on Israel. I do not believe that they would now go so far as to rescind or limit the aviation agreements between the two countries, which they themselves view as part of the plane of minimal relations essential to preserving peace.

However, things were much less rosy in the early 1980s. The aviation protocol signed at the time stipulated that the aviation rights of both sides would be equal and symmetrical and that each side would operate two weekly flights. El Al promptly organized itself and inaugurated its flight to Egypt immediately. At first, these flights were not mentioned on the flight boards or in spoken announcements at Cairo airport. After repeated protests, El Al's name appeared on the boards but the flights were marked to fictitious destinations and not to Tel Aviv. We continued to put on the pressure (at the time, we still had some leverage since most of Sinai was still in Israeli hands) and finally – after almost two years of efforts – the flight boards and spoken announcements began to reflect reality. It was heartwarming to hear, all over the airport, the loudspeakers announcing the arrival and departure of El Al flights to and from Tel Aviv. The El Al counters were also moved to a more central location, next to the Saudi Airline counters. Indeed, these were very insignificant achievements but the Egyptians made us feel as if we had conquered Everest. I must confess that each time I came to the airport, and I had plenty of opportunities to do so, the symbolism of what my eyes saw and my ears heard made me feel deeply emotional. At last, we were in the heart of the Arab world and rubbing shoulders with Arabs from 22 Arab states – even if they were still at war with Israel!

Misr Air, the Egyptian national airline, on the other hand, got cold feet and refused to fly under its own name to Israel, fearing a boycott by the Arab countries (notwithstanding the boycott against Egypt, flights to and from the Arab states were never discontinued). It leased planes from foreign companies and flew them to Israel without any identification marks in breach of international aviation regulations. We were compelled to agree to this odd procedure and, for several months, planes painted from head to toe in glittering silver without any identification marks landed twice a week at Ben Gurion airport. In our conversations with the Egyptians, we used to describe them jokingly as ghost planes. The Egyptians realized that this situation could not continue indefinitely and they finally established a Misr Air subsidiary, named Sinai Air, to operate the line to Israel. In the blink of an eye, the planes were repainted in the regular Egyptian colors and given proper identification marks and the logo of the new company. Everyone – in Egypt and the entire Arab world – knew that it was a sham company but they turned a blind eye to reality. If the Arabs were satisfied with such a blatant camouflage, we had no reason for our part to oppose it. We did not mind them using the fig-leaf that they needed so badly!

I will not detail here all the difficulties we met, over the years, in making the security arrangements essential for flying to Cairo and Sharm el Sheikh. The embassy had to intervene to smooth out misunderstandings each time that a new difficulty arose. More than once, it had to threaten to discontinue the flights if the El Al security personnel was not allowed to take measures, in addition to those of Egyptian security, to ensure the safety of its passengers and planes. We acknowledged that on Egyptian soil the prime responsibility for security rested with the local authorities but, as in any other country in the world where El Al flies, a certain amount of Israeli involvement was essential for reasons obvious to everyone. The Egyptians yielded only when Israel made it clear that it was a *sine-qua-non* for the establishment of air links between the two countries.

I will add only two more interesting topics related to aviation. Up to this very day, the Tel Aviv–Cairo line remains a monopoly of the two national airlines. No other airline is allowed to transport passengers from Cairo to Tel Aviv and vice versa. In 1991, an exception was made for the American airline TWA. It did not affect the monopolistic situation and air fares remained substantially higher than on similar stretches. In the early 1980s, Israel pressured Egypt to grant rights to El Al for operating charter flights to Etsion-Gaber airport in Sinai (which had been built by the Israeli air force and handed over to Egypt in the first phase of withdrawal). After much haggling, an agreement to that effect was reached between the two countries. El Al, however, never used these rights since it would have meant scoring an own goal. In accordance with international aviation regulations, all airlines flying to Egypt would automatically have received the same rights and would have had indirect access to the Israeli charter market.

In the field of land transportation, the situation was even more complicated. From the outset, Egypt was not interested in the free movement of vehicles in both directions. Israel, on the other hand, strove to have open borders with Egypt in the fullest sense of the concept. The negotiations lasted for several months and were acrimonious. The Egyptians raised one obstacle after the other. At first, they claimed that the Israeli cars might be sold in Egypt and demanded that Israeli drivers deposit a bank guarantee for the full amount of customs duties and related taxes. They also laid down conditions that made the mutual recognition of driving licenses and insurance policies (especially third-party insurance) virtually unfeasible. Finally, both parties agreed on procedures that theoretically enforced the principle of free movement but in reality made it almost impossible to cross from one country to the other in a private car. Drivers were to go through time-consuming formalities. They had to secure special permits from the respective embassies and automobile clubs, contract third-party insurance with a local company, translate and have certified the car's documents and driving license and, furthermore, give a personal guarantee in the amount of the full customs duties and other taxes. In practice, these restrictions hindered only Israeli drivers; they were irrelevant to Egyptian car-owners who, in any case, were forbidden to travel to Israel as were all Egyptians. At the Egyptian border, Israeli drivers had, in addition, to put up with a thorough and lengthy inspection of their cars and luggage. One had to be very stubborn to endure all these difficulties for the dubious pleasure of driving one's car into Egypt. But Israelis being what they are, in the first months after the signing of the agreement several cars *did* succeed in reaching Cairo.

The Israeli drivers quickly realized that it was not easy to cope with the hectic Egyptian traffic. They parked their cars near their hotels and moved about in taxis (the fares of which were very cheap). The whole issue died a painless death and fell into oblivion. When I returned to Cairo in 1990, the topic was not on the agenda; it had become irrelevant and no one was interested in raising the matter as long as the principle of open borders was outwardly safeguarded. Today, there is almost no crossing of private cars between the two countries to the exclusion of a few diplomatic, UN and international force cars (Israeli traffic to the Taba enclave is a special case, which will be treated separately).

The trucks and heavy vehicles issue was much simpler. Israel too was not keen to have Egyptian lorries cross into its territory. It feared accidents and undue competition with the Israeli transporters whose tariffs were much higher. We suggested that trailers, which would change tow-trucks at the border, transport merchandise between the two countries. This proved to be unfeasible because of technical discrepancies between the trailers of the two countries. Finally, it was decided by common agreement that the transport of merchandise be carried out back-to-back i.e. transported by Israeli or Egyptian trucks on the portion of the road in their own territory and shifted at the border to the other country's trucks.

As for buses, Israel strove to allow tourist buses to cross the border and transport their passengers throughout their tour. But Egypt did not want to have Israeli buses crisscrossing the country without adequate supervision. They also knew – as we discovered later – that there would be no significant Egyptian tourism to Israel and that the whole issue was irrelevant from their standpoint. Understandably, they preferred that the back-to-back arrangement be applied also to tourist buses thus providing more employment for their own buses (out of the 520 kilometers between Tel Aviv and Cairo, almost 400 are in Egyptian territory). We finally accepted the Egyptian position hoping that the cheap tariffs of the Egyptian buses would encourage popular tourism in both directions. To make the pill more palatable and create a perception of open borders, the Egyptians agreed to establish a public bus service between Cairo and Tel Aviv that would be allowed to transport passengers from point to point. Later, they also agreed to establish a similar bus service from Eilat to Noueiba and Sharm el Sheikh. A joint company was established between Egged (the main bus company in Israel) and an Egyptian public sector company, which operated four runs weekly in each direction – two by Israeli buses and two by Egyptian buses. The return fare was fixed at $35 and indeed attracted many passengers, mostly Israelis, foreign tourists and Palestinians visiting their families in the Gaza Strip. The few Egyptians who were allowed to travel to Israel preferred to fly at the cost of $250, which, in most cases, was covered by their government.

The fact that Egypt agreed to allow Israeli buses to reach Cairo was in itself highly significant but the Egyptians found ways to make them less conspicuous. The buses were prevented from stopping at the main bus station in the center of Cairo and were instead directed to a small side station where they attracted less attention. They were also forbidden to take the passengers to their hotels as the Egyptian buses did. Our requests to change this unacceptable situation fell on deaf ears. We nevertheless continued to run the bus service for many years out of political considerations. When I returned to Egypt in 1990, the situation of the bus line was desperate. The buses traveled almost empty, losing money on each run. Understandably, the number of weekly runs had fallen to two – one by an Israeli bus and one by an Egyptian bus. This time, it was the Egyptians who raised the matter with me and sought a positive solution. They complained that Egged was also operating a tourist bus company that competed with the public buses. They requested me to use my good offices with Egged and persuade them to discontinue directing passengers to that company. Again, because the very existence of the public bus line was politically important, I tried to convince Egged's management. They explained that, after so many years of running at a loss, they had to give priority to economic considerations over political ones. They also pointed out that it was the Egyptians themselves who had created a situation where it was more profitable, and more comfortable, to use the back-to-back system.

The line from Eilat to Noueiba and Sharam al Sheik had been discontinued a few years earlier. The Taba agreement was already in operation and the Egyptians – this time rightly – preferred Israeli tourists to cross the border on foot and continue to their destinations in Egyptian public buses or taxis. They saw no valid reason to share with an Israeli company the profits of a bus line that ran exclusively on Egyptian territory.

Roads linking Israel to Egypt were also, in the early 1980s, a major topic of hard bargaining between the two countries. Israel wanted the three major roads, crossing the Sinai peninsula in all its length, to be promptly opened to both private and public traffic (the western shore road through Gaza and El Arish to Kantara on the Suez Canal, the central road from Nitzana to Suez, and the eastern shore road from Eilat through Noueiba and Sharam el Sheik to Ras Mohamed). Israel also wanted all the roads crisscrossing Sinai to be opened to unhindered Israeli traffic. On the face of it, Egypt was not opposed to opening the three main roads but it was not prepared – and rightly so – to let Israel dictate what it should do on its own territory and at what pace. They claimed that the central road was in a poor condition and needed extensive repairs (which was true, although the road was easily useable); not being on their list of national priorities, these repairs would therefore be delayed for several years. As for the transversal and side roads, they flatly refused, alleging that these were narrow roads in bad shape that could not cope with international traffic (in reality, they were almost exclusively used by the Egyptian army to access various restricted military installations).

The negotiations took place in the first two years, when the cards were still in our hands and the Egyptians were compelled to make their position more flexible – at least on paper. They formally agreed to open the three roads to Israeli traffic but did not commit themselves to a definite date for repairing the central road and only pledged solemnly that they would do so as swiftly as they could. As for the transversal and side roads, a face-saving compromise was devised: Israelis would be treated on an equal footing with the nationals of other countries and allowed to travel on roads open to foreign traffic. Indeed, this was almost tantamount to barring traffic on these side roads since, throughout Egypt, foreigners were forbidden to leave the main roads without a special permit from the security authorities. In the first period, Israelis turned a blind eye to the conspicuous boards forbidding foreigners to leave the main road. Consequently, the Egyptian police arrested many of them and the embassy had to work very hard to have them released. The Arab affairs correspondent from the Israeli Broadcasting Authority, Ehud Yaari, was arrested with a team of cameramen on a side road near a military installation. They were released after several hours of detention but it was no easy task to convince the authorities that they had lost their way and were not engaged in spying or any other illegal activity.

Very quickly the issue of the linking roads between the two countries became marginal. The western shore road was (and remains) the main link between Israel and Egypt. The central road lost its importance – even after it was repaired and officially opened to traffic – since it was mainly used by trucks and the back-to-back system had made it irrelevant for Israeli traffic. The eastern shore road was opened to Israeli private cars only in 1989 after the implementation of the Taba agreement; however, it never became a linking road between the two countries since Israeli cars are forbidden to go beyond Ras Mohamed. Let me add, for curiosity's sake, that the Egyptians used the western shore road built by Israel for a few months only; a few meters away and parallel to it, they built a new road of exactly the same width and standard. The old road was left to disappear, as if it had never existed, under thick layers of desert sand. I must confess that, to this very day, I do not understand what brought Egypt to scuttle the Israeli road (which they had paid for with good money) and waste millions of dollars on building a new road instead of widening the original road. It is possible that they wished to erase all traces of the Israeli occupation but, if that was their motive, then why do they preserve to this very day several other infrastructure installations built by the Israelis?

The negotiations on the construction of border facilities and the arrangements for crossing from one country to the other were concluded relatively rapidly. The main elements of the agreement were self-evident and did not necessitate lengthy discussions. Immediately after the first phase of withdrawal, Israel built temporary terminals a few miles from El Arish (the main city in Sinai, which was still in Israeli hands). It consisted of a few wooden shacks, poor-looking and lacking minimal comfort. On the eve of the second phase of withdrawal, permanent terminals were built a few kilometers from Rafiah (a small border city). On each side of the border, at a distance of some three kilometers from each other, identical compounds were erected – still wooden shacks, though the finishing of the Israeli installations was much better and the buildings much more spacious and functional. To the best of my recollection, an Israeli contractor carried out the works on both sides of the border, each country bearing half of the cost. The only difference between the two terminals was the day-to-day maintenance and the gardening around the buildings: Israel invested substantial means on these two items.

In parallel, terminals were built at Nitzana on the central road. They were intended exclusively for merchandise and were adapted to the back-to-back system. The Egyptians did not allow the crossing of persons and only exceptionally, after the embassy's intervention, did they agree to let a few persons cross the border on foot and continue to their destinations by taxi. For a transitory period (until the road was repaired and facilities built along it) trucks used a side road connecting the terminal to the western shore road. The reader has no doubt inferred that the trucks were exclusively Egyptian.

As for the shore road, up until the transfer of the Taba enclave to Egyptian sovereignty in 1989, the crossing from Taba into Egyptian territory (still in Israeli hands) took place through narrow openings in the barbed-wire fences separating the two territories. In order not to create a *fait accompli*, the Egyptians did not agree to operate temporary terminals and to erect even rudimentary shacks. Only after the signing of the Taba agreement were the terminals built on both sides of the border. Again, Israel invested additional means to make the place more pleasant to the eye and more comfortable for those passing through it (many of whom were in private cars). A few years later, the Egyptian authorities dramatically improved their terminal to cope with the ever-increasing flow of Israeli and foreign tourists crossing the border as a result of the more liberal regime laid down in the Taba agreement.

Significantly, Egypt never mentioned that the terminals were located on the border with Israel or even that the border itself was leading to Israeli territory. On all the road signs, the only mention was (and still is) 'Border Ahead'! On the occasion of the inauguration of the Rafiah terminal, the Egyptian authorities published an official announcement saying that a terminal on the border between Egypt and the countries to the east had been inaugurated on that day. Naturally, we asked the foreign ministry what countries to the east meant in the Egyptian lexicon. We were stunned to hear that the intention was to point out that when comprehensive peace prevailed in the region, the Rafiah terminal would be a crossing-point to Israel, the Gaza Strip, the West Bank, Jordan, Lebanon, Syria, and even to far-away Turkey. We had to swallow this far-fetched explanation and the sarcastic smiles that accompanied it. We knew perfectly well that the reason behind this odd formulation was to imply that the Rafiah terminal – and others still to come – were to be crossing-points to the future Palestinian state and not to Israel. For Egypt, neither the Gaza Strip nor the West Bank – and not even the Negev – were not part of Israel. No wonder! According to the official atlas published by the ministry of education for use in all secondary schools in Egypt, Israel did not exist at all. On all the maps of the middle east, between the Mediterranean Sea to the Jordan River only the word Palestine appeared. Despite our repeated protests, up to the highest levels of power, the Egyptians did not change the situation and Israel remained unmentioned in their maps – even within the pre-1967 borders. The official excuse was that the government printing house published an atlas every few years after it had exhausted all its old stock. The excuse came accompanied by a solemn promise to make the necessary correction in the next edition. But, as I have already said, in Egypt promises and actions are two different things. Up to the end of 1992, when I left Egypt for India, Egyptian atlases printed by the government – 14 years after the establishment of peace – still completely ignored Israel's existence. The same was the case with atlases published by private publishing houses. I do not know what is the situation nowadays but it is more than probable that nothing has changed in this respect.

Incidentally, immediately after the second phase of withdrawal in 1982, the Egyptian government decided to relocate the offices of the governor of the Gaza Strip to El Arish. For more than 20 years, these offices had been kept in Cairo, where they had fallen practically into oblivion. At that juncture, the transfer was meant to be a symbolic gesture highlighting Egypt's determination to reject the *fait accompli*. We protested vigorously and repeatedly but the Egyptians ignored our protests. They claimed that they had commitments and obligations towards the Palestinians – especially those living in Egypt – and that it was easier for them to tackle their needs from El Arish rather than from Cairo. On the face of it, there were objective grounds to these explanations but, in reality, the real motive of the Egyptians was political and not administrative, as they wanted us to believe. The resurrection of the governor of the Gaza Strip and the return of his offices to El Arish was to emphasize that – notwithstanding the fact that Egypt no longer controlled the Gaza Strip physically – it still considered itself responsible for that territory until the Palestinian problem found its solution. Today, things have changed dramatically and the whole issue is no longer on the national or international agenda. Indeed by 1995, in the wake of the Oslo agreement, the Gaza Strip had already been handed over to the Palestinian Authority under the chairmanship of Yasser Arafat, the PLO leader.

An issue which highlights an interesting and characteristic aspect of Egypt's longstanding policies and its *modus operandi* towards Israel arose in the early 1980s. In the wake of the *Infitach* (economic liberalization), imports and exports had substantially increased and the archaic port installations, especially in Alexandria harbor, could not cope with the booming maritime traffic. Ships were compelled to anchor in the high sea for 20 to 30 days, waiting for their turn to enter the harbor – and several more days were needed for the handling of the cargo. The damage to the Egyptian economy reached the proportions of a national catastrophe. Israel expressed its readiness to put the Ashdod harbor at Egypt's disposition at no cost, and to allow the transit of merchandise to Egypt through its territory. The direct and indirect advantages to the Egyptian economy would have been tremendous but Egypt rejected the Israeli offer out of hand. The Egyptians gave no explanation and did not comment on its economic feasibility – it was clear that they did not want to be dependent on Israel in such a crucial field, even for a transitional period. Again, as with many other issues, political considerations overshadowed economic calculations. When I returned to Egypt in 1990, the situation of the

Egyptian ports had substantially improved. There was no point in raising the issue again though – economically speaking – it made sense (and even now makes sense!) to handle the maritime freight for Sinai and southern Egypt through the Ashdod harbor. In any case, I knew for certain that any suggestion to that effect was a non-starter with the Egyptians and I preferred to deal with acute and urgent matters that were endangering the very texture of peace.

Incidentally, Zim, the Israeli national maritime company, succeeded at a very early stage in squeezing itself through the Egyptian restrictions, and the volume of its operations now reaches several million dollars a year. I will not elaborate on how it was done and what the reasons were for this very positive achievement, which contrasts so favourably with some aspects of the Arab boycott on Israeli navigation that are still enforced by Egypt (I will deal with this matter later on). The Egyptians also allowed ships flying the Israeli flag to pass unhindered through the Suez Canal on their way to and from the Far East. The only restriction they imposed in breach of international regulations was to forbid Israeli sailors from going ashore without a visa. Sailors of all other nationalities, even if they were on board Israeli ships, were allowed to disembark without superfluous formalities. It was not a crucial problem but it did irritate! In addition, military vessels, Israeli and others, had to give via the diplomatic channels and in writing, two weeks' notice of the date of their passage through the canal. This Egyptian requirement was a flagrant breach of the Montreux Convention but all countries abided by it under protest and Israel had to follow suit. To the credit of the Egyptians, I have to specify that in urgent cases – including in periods of war and tension – they allowed the passage of Israeli military vessels at much shorter notice.

Another point of contention – which was only partially defused in 1991 – was Egypt's unjustified restrictions on Israeli navigation in its territorial waters in the Red Sea and the very harsh manner in which these restrictions were enforced. It never reached the proportions of a maritime boycott or disruption of free passage in an international waterway. However, it consisted of a series of actions designed to display Egypt's sovereignty and keep Israel under pressure within the framework of their carrot-and-stick policy. Israel recognized Egypt's sovereignty over its territorial waters and had no intention of infringing it; nor did it want to dictate to Egypt rules of behavior that were in opposition either to its interests or its best judgement. Israel only insisted on the application of the international sea regulations to its vessels and on the implementation of the maritime agreements freely contracted, after lengthy and detailed negotiations, by the two countries. By virtue of these agreements, small Israeli tourist boats and private yachts had the right to sail in Egyptian territorial waters in the Red Sea and transport passengers to the Corals Island and other sea resorts in Sinai. A few months after the handing back of Taba to Egypt, the difficulties began. The Egyptian authorities demanded that all Israeli vessels wishing to anchor anywhere along the Egyptian coast pass the customs and emigration formalities, both on their arrival and departure, in Sharm el Sheikh and in Sharm el Sheikh only – some 200 km down the coast from Eilat. For Israeli tourism operators and the private boat owners who intended to visit the Corals Island or have a swim in Taba or Noueiba, this meant 800 km (in both directions) of tiresome, costly and time-consuming sailing. If you add to that the lengthy and unpleasant customs and police inspections in Sharm el Sheikh, it was literally a deathblow to Israeli tourist navigation in the Red Sea. Furthermore, visitors from Israel (including foreigners) to the Corals Island (the main attraction in the Red Sea) had to comply with a very uncomfortable timetable. Israeli vessels were also required to sail at a distance of 3 km from the Egyptian coast in daylight and 5 km after dark. They were strictly warned not to deviate from these instructions under any circumstances, even in case of bad weather that endangered the vessel and its passengers. Fishing, even for pleasure, was strictly prohibited and the damaging of corals (even by accident) was defined as a major offense entailing heavy fines and long prison sentences. The authorities enforced these restrictions in their tiniest detail with a heavy hand well beyond what was reasonable. Several Israeli vessels were hailed at sea by Egyptian gunboats or in Egyptian sea resorts and confiscated for long periods. They were finally released after lengthy judicial procedure and vigorous diplomatic intervention, but in the meantime everything on board that could be dismantled and transported had been stolen. The boat owners and their passengers were kept in custody for many days, brought before courts and released only after the payment of heavy fines and exorbitant anchorage fees. On some occasions, light vessels, which had found refuge from raging storms on the Egyptian coast, were threatened with seizure and forced back to sea regardless of what might happen to them and their passengers.

When I returned to Egypt in 1990, the situation in this field was as bad, if not worse. After several more incidents, the yacht owners and the municipality of Eilat organized protest demonstrations and demanded the intervention of the Israeli government. They invited me to Eilat, complained bitterly at the blatant violations of agreements by Egypt and protested at the rough behavior of the Egyptian authorities. I tried my best to calm them down and I even justified some of the Egyptian measures that were objectively warranted. I promised to give top priority to the issue and do my best with the Egyptian authorities to make the restrictions more flexible and have them enforced in a more humane manner as is proper between two neighboring countries maintaining fully-fledged peaceful relations. Indeed, I raised the matter in the strongest terms on every occasion and made sure that every visiting Israeli personality and delegation also raised it in the same terms. My main goal was to persuade the Egyptians that, if they persisted in their harsh policies, they would give a deathblow to tourism along the Sinai coast and imperil, against their best interests, the influx of foreign (not just Israeli) tourists to the resorts in Sinai. There was no point in insisting on respect for binding agreements, fairness, humane behavior or other niceties: it would have led nowhere. It seems that the Egyptians finally got the message and gradually eased some of the strictest measures. The permitted sailing distance from the coast was reduced to 1 km in daylight and to 2 km at night, vessels were allowed to seek refuge on the Egyptian coast in case of storms or life-endangering accidents and guards were posted on seized vessels to prevent thefts. The Egyptians also pledged they would improve the treatment of arrested persons and expedite judicial procedures. They even promised to allow more entrance points, besides Sharm el Sheikh, for customs and police formalities and started planning the building of port facilities in Taba and Noueiba. It was the maximum we could get out of them. I do not know if the Egyptians have lived up to all their promises and what exactly the situation is at the present time but, as I have already mentioned, no one wants to kill the goose that lays the golden eggs – things probably have improved. For the sake of fairness, I have to specify that all Israeli yachtsmen did not always behave properly. Some of them scattered litter on the coast and in the sea, broke and even stole corals, anchored wherever they wished, fished and broke Egyptian laws. But none of these infringements justified the harsh policy of the Egyptian authorities. Their motivation was, no doubt, political and political only.

In spite of all these problems (most of which were unknown to the general public), Israeli tourists flocked to Egypt in the early 1980s in their thousands. In less than one year, Israel became the third biggest source of tourists after the USA and Germany. Out of obvious political considerations, the Israeli government and the embassy in Cairo did their utmost – despite the one-sided tourism – to increase the flow. Israelis travelling to Egypt were exempted from the travel tax (about $200) that was levied at the time thus giving a great boost to tourism to Egypt (it was an indirect subsidy practically covering the air fare). El Al and several travel agencies published promotional ads in the press, and newspapers published articles praising Egypt's hospitality and encouraging Israelis to visit its unique archeological sites and tourist resorts. The embassy in Cairo gave the highest priority to help solve all the problems confronting Israeli tourists (and there were many). It dispelled fears in tense political situations and in the wake of vicious attacks in the Egyptian press, and loudly praised the hospitality and kindness of the Egyptian people.

In the first two years, there were no serious mishaps to the exclusion of the visa-related problems and the harsh treatment of the immigration and customs authorities at the entrance points. Understandably, in periods of political tension the number of Israeli tourists dropped but it gradually resumed when the situation cooled down. During my first three years in

Egypt (1980–83) there were no terrorist attacks on Israeli tourists. The two major deadly attacks – in Ras Burka and near Cairo – took place after I had left Egypt. They did not bring Israeli tourism to a standstill but, added to the dwindling curiosity and the emergence of new poles of attraction for popular tourism, they brought about a significant drop. When I came back in 1990, Israeli tourism had stabilized at a yearly 40,000–50,000 (not including the Taba region) and, as a consequence, the relative weight of Israel in the eyes of the Egyptian tourist authorities had decreased substantially.

In this period, three main problems troubled the Israeli tourists and kept the embassy busy: the counterfeit dollars, the smuggling of weapons, and drugs-related problems. These three problems hung over the head of each Israeli tourist like a Sword of Damocles.

Let us begin with the counterfeit dollars. In the early 1980s, Egypt had stringent controls on foreign currency. All foreigners arriving in Egypt had to declare the amount of foreign currency they were carrying and change at least US$50 into Egyptian currency at the official rate. They were also to settle their hotel bills in foreign currency and show upon their departure the remainder of the currency they had brought in. The black market functioned almost openly and was considered semi-legitimate by the authorities. At the time, more than 100,000 Israeli tourists visited Egypt every year. They filled the streets of Cairo with their shouts and bought anything they could find – paying (like all other foreign tourists) in dollars at the black market rate. Many shops, grasping the mentality of the common Israeli tourist, hung boards in Hebrew saying: 'Here we sell at cheap prices. Haggling is allowed or good exchange rates.' During this entire period, no complaint as to foreign currency infringements ever arose and not a single counterfeit note was ever found.

In the early 1990s, all restrictions on foreign currency were officially rescinded; the rate of the Egyptian pound stabilized and the black market was practically non-existent. Customs were instructed not to check in- and out-going tourists for foreign currency and the settling of hotel bills in Egyptian pounds was allowed. In most hotels, exchange bureaux were opened and functioned 24 hours a day. Only at the Rafiah terminal – and only there – did things remain exactly as they were in the 1980s and even worsen. Customs and emigration formalities lasted for hours and hours; incoming and exiting Israelis, with no exceptions whatsoever, were required to show all the foreign currency in their possession. Nationals of other countries were exempted even when they and Israelis were travelling in the same bus.

Suddenly, counterfeit US$100 notes began to pop up at a rate of four–five per week. At the Rafiah terminal, there was no electronic appliance and the examination was carried out exclusively by hand. One of the customs inspectors, who regarded himself (and was regarded by his superiors) as an expert in identifying forged dollars, bullied Israeli incomers, checked every single note and regularly found forged notes. Interestingly enough, it was always $100 notes! Even more interestingly, banks, shops, hotels – where the Israeli tourists exchanged hundreds of thousands of dollars – never found a single counterfeit note. Only at the Rafiah terminal did the expert continue (and probably still continues) to find them, at a regular pace. The poor tourist, on whom the alleged counterfeit note (in most cases, only one!) was found, was arrested on the spot even if he presented documents proving that he had bought the dollars in a reliable Israeli bank. All his dollars, and not only the suspect note, were impounded as judicial evidence without even giving him an official receipt. After a few hours of a humiliating inquiry, he (and sometimes she) was taken to the El Arish prison and transferred after a few days, under police escort, to El Kantara (at a distance of 200 km) to stand trial. Ironically, the arrested Israeli tourist had to pay out of his own pocket for the car ride and for the policemen's meals. In El Kantara, he was kept in the local prison and brought the next day before a judge who released him on bail and, in the same breath, issued an order expelling him from Egypt. The poor tourist, after one more night in the El Kantara jail, was taken to the border (again, at his own expense) and booted out saying goodbye forever to Egypt and to his dollars – forged or genuine. If he dared inquire about their fate, he was told with a sarcastic smile (sometimes accompanied by threats and insults) that they would be returned to him after his trial. Understandably, no one took the risk of playing Russian roulette and putting Egyptian justice to the test!

As a matter of standing procedure, the embassy took immediate steps to help arrested tourists. The administrative officer (first Dror Gabay and after him Roni Porat), who also had the function of consul, became an expert in the matter. Immediately upon receiving notice, they left for El Arish at a distance of 400 km from Cairo, together with our Egyptian lawyer Sherif (the one who began his career in the embassy as my personal driver). There, they arranged – the reader will guess how – the immediate transfer of the arrested tourist to a hotel and accompanied him (or her) the next day to El Kantara, making sure that the police escort was 'kept satisfied and happy' and that the case was expedited. Many times they succeeded in returning to the Israeli border on the same day, sparing the poor tourist one more nightmarish night.

In parallel, on my side of the line, I embarked on a diplomatic crusade to try and change the situation. I met several times with the ministers of the interior and of foreign affairs, the governor of northern Sinai, and the police chiefs at the central and regional levels. I protested about the harsh and unwarranted treatment at the Rafiah terminal and pointed to the discriminating practice of checking – only in that terminal – incoming tourists (exclusively the Israelis among them) for foreign currency. I stressed that this was the only place in the whole of Egypt where Israeli tourists were caught with counterfeit $100 bills. I did not refrain from pointing an accusing finger at the expert in Rafiah and bluntly voiced my doubts as to his expertise and motivation. Nothing helped! I was wasting my breath! My Egyptian interlocutors swore that there was no discrimination and no hidden intentions. They stressed that Egyptian laws were very strict about the smuggling of forged currency into Egypt and presented the expulsion of the offenders before the completion of their trials as an act of humanity and friendship. The maximum I could obtain was a promise to instruct the relevant authorities to act promptly and treat the arrested tourists decently. It was better than nothing!

The Egyptian press did not fold their arms. From time to time they initiated orchestrated campaigns denouncing the wanton sabotage by the Jews of the Egyptian economy through flooding the country with forged foreign currency, and demanding an immediate ban on Israeli tourism to Egypt. Despite our repeated protests the authorities did not intervene to stop the incitement against innocent tourists. The obvious truth was that even if all the banknotes discovered by the famous expert in Rafiah had really been forged bills (and I maintain that the great majority were not), it amounted over the years to a few thousand dollars. Such a small amount could in no way jeopardize, even marginally, the Egyptian economy and was chickenfeed when compared with the tens of millions of good American dollars injected every year by the Israeli tourists into the Egyptian economy. Neither the authorities nor the press wanted to be confused by facts. The attacks became increasingly virulent and heinous. No wonder – the topic was part of the carrot-and-stick policy and was meant to fan tension and put pressure on Israel. In periods of 'smiles', when the Egyptians wished to reward Israel or ease tension before it reached breaking point, no forged dollars were found for one or two months. The embassy staff breathed in relief but did not delude themselves that the topic had been removed permanently from the agenda. It knew for certain that when tension resumed for any reason (and this was bound to happen as surely as night follows day) the forged dollars would again suddenly pop up and the slanderous press campaigns rage once more against the sabotaging of the Egyptian economy by the Jews.

After I despaired of convinciong the Egyptian authorities to stop this cruel game, I turned to our side of the border and tried to block the loopholes. I suggested that the Israeli customs check electronically the $100 notes that were carried by our tourists and issue a certificate, bearing the note's serial numbers, attesting to their authenticity. I hoped that this would discourage the expert at the Rafiah terminal from discovering more forged notes and convince the authorities that the game was too obvious to be continued. However, after several months of discussion, the Israeli customs refused because they were liable to bear legal responsibility towards the tourists if they were arrested at the border for smuggling forged notes. I also suggested that the Israeli police investigate tourists accused by the Egyptians of carrying forged dollars to ascertain if there were any objective grounds to the accusation. Here also my suggestion was turned down on the grounds that the offense (if any) had been made abroad and did not fall under Israeli jurisdiction. I refused to accept this explanation and I persevered stubbornly. Finally, the police agreed to check a few cases and requested the embassy to send them the banknotes alleged to be counterfeit in order to facilitate the opening of an inquiry (they were ready to settle even for photocopies). The Egyptians refused to co-operate, claiming that it was impossible to remove judicial exhibits from Egypt as long as the trials had not been concluded (and, for obvious reasons, none had been, nor ever would be). Finally, the only positive step that was taken was to hang announcements all over the Israeli terminal calling on outgoing tourists to check their dollars thoroughly and make sure that they carried no forged notes. The tourists themselves also took precautionary steps: they shifted to other currencies and travelers' checks or ceased to bring $100 notes and, if they did, they made sure to bring with them receipts from their bank bearing the notes' serial numbers. Nothing doing – none of this deterred the expert at the Rafiah terminal from continuing to discover forged notes. He proudly declared that his hands were more reliable than the most sophisticated electronic device and accused the employees of the Israeli banks of planting the forged notes to make personal profits and sabotage the Egyptian economy.

The second problem confronting Israeli tourists was of a similar nature but, in this case, the Egyptians' accusations were absolutely justified although the sanctions they took were out of all proportion to the gravity of the offenses. Every now and then, in the routine inspection of private cars entering Egypt at the Taba terminal, bullets and sometimes small weapons were found (it is known that virtually everyone in Israel carries some weapon for self-defense). It was enough for the Egyptian customs to find a single bullet to arrest the driver and all the passengers in the car, accuse them of trying to smuggle arms into Egypt and treat them with the utmost harshness. After a few days of intensive and most unpleasant interrogation, the passengers were expelled from the country (with the car). The car owners were kept in custody until their appearance before an Egyptian court. Generally, they were taken to El Tur (the main city in southern Sinai at about 200 km from Taba) and kept for many days in awful conditions in the local prison. In these cases, the embassy could not protest to the Egyptians, it could only intervene to ease the conditions of imprisonment and speed up the investigation and judicial procedure. Naturally, it appointed Sherif (my ex-driver who worked full-time in the embassy as legal adviser) to defend them. He usually succeeded in having them released on bail and expelled from Egypt after a few more days of detention, which for the poor tourists seemed an eternity.

The Egyptian authorities reacted with the utmost severity though they knew for certain that the weapons or the bullets had been left in the car inadvertently and that there was no criminal intention. We tried to convince them to expel the cars and people involved on the spot, before they entered Egypt. They rejected our pleas claiming that Egyptian laws did not allow expulsions from the country without due legal procedure. They stressed that the courts were already showing unusual leniency by releasing the offenders on bail or fining them instead of condemning them to heavy prison sentences in accordance with Egyptian laws. Indeed, such offences are punishable in Egypt by up to five years' imprisonment with hard labor and things could have been much worse. However, had the Egyptians gone that far, it would have brought to a complete stand-still Israeli tourism to southern Sinai (which is the backbone of foreign tourism to that region) and as such would have been counter-productive to the Egyptians.

Here too, I tried to patch up the gaps on our side of the border. I demanded that the Israeli customs carry out a thorough inspection of outgoing cars and ensure that no arms or bullets were forgotten. The customs authorities refused, claiming that such a procedure was time-consuming and would anger the outgoing tourists. The argument was far from convincing – on their side of the border the Egyptian customs took all the time they needed to search the cars and found arms that, under Israeli laws and regulations, should not have been allowed out of the country by the Israeli customs! Here also, as in Rafiah, the panacea was the hanging of announcements warning car owners that taking weapons or bullets into Egypt was a severe offense and calling on them to search their cars thoroughly before crossing the border.

The third problem is drugs. The problem is acute especially in south-ern Sinai, where drugs are notoriously easy to find (mostly grass known in Egypt as hashish). A few Israeli youngsters are tempted to buy relatively small quantities for personal consumption from the Bedouins in the region. What they are not aware of is that the suppliers are generally double agents: they sell the drugs to the tourists with one hand, and with the other, they notify the Egyptian police in return for their protection. The police do not always act on the information but occasionally they catch the offenders red-handed. Often the matter is concluded with the seizure of the drugs and a few pounds exchanging hands. However, in a few cases, the offenders are arrested and brought to trial. In the case of drugs, once the file is opened and the inquiry officially started, it is practically impos-sible to stop the procedure or release the offenders on bail as in the forged dollars and arms smuggling cases. Egyptian laws are very strict in this matter: sentences are very severe and no reprieve or reduction of penalty is possible. Indeed, to the best of my knowledge, no drugs offender – Egyptian or foreigner – has ever had his sentence commuted.

Luckily for us, very few Israelis were prosecuted and brought to trial. The most notorious case – but by no means the only one – was that of Yariv Ben Herut, who was condemned to seven years' hard labor and served his sentence to the last day. All our attempts to obtain for him a reprieve or a diminution of punishment did not bear fruit. Another Israeli drug offender is Joseph Tahan, who was caught at Cairo airport transporting a substantial quantity of heavy drugs and was sentenced to death. Israel did (and is doing) its utmost to obtain a reprieve or at least to have the death penalty commuted. President Mubarak is still considering the reprieve request and, as long as he does not take a decision, Tahan's life is not in danger. Indeed, because of his case, the enforcement of death sentences pending against drug offenders was put on hold for a long period. The opposition press repeatedly accused the president of discriminating in favor of an Israeli criminal for political considerations. If I may be permitted to give advice to the Israeli press, the less they meddle in the matter, the safer Tahan's life is – digging publicly into his case could well be counter productive. Incidentally, Tahan's is a case that is not typical of the difficulties confronting the Israeli tourist in Egypt. The embassy has treated him like any other Israeli in trouble and has tried, over the years, to help him to the best of its ability.

A secondary, but by no means unimportant, difficulty are the periodic campaigns in the Egyptian press warning against the dire dangers to Egypt posed by the invasion of tens of thousands of Israeli tourists. In general, the campaign begins in the opposition newspapers in the wake of the incarceration of an Israeli tourist – whether on genuine or false grounds. It develops into a series of completely unfounded and slanderous accusations. The government press organs follow suit, adding imaginary accusations of their own and relating in the smallest detail events that never took place. All Israeli tourists are depicted as spies roaming all over Egypt with sophisticated cameras, photographing military installations and stealing economic secrets. The Israeli government is accused of implementing a monstrous scheme to weaken Egypt by subverting its economy and perverting its youth. The press shamelessly alleges that it is flooding the country with forged dollars and heavy drugs and sending beautiful Jewish women carrying Aids or venereal diseases to contaminate Egyptian youngsters. This last accusation was even the theme of a show that ran for several months in one of Cairo's main theaters. It was also the subject of a film that is still shown from time to time by the Egyptian television stations.

These campaigns are not known to the common Israeli tourists (at least not in their details and intensity) and do not have a negative impact on their eagerness to visit Egypt. On the other hand, happily until now they have not had a negative impact on the warm manner in which the Egyptian masses receive the Israeli tourists. I doubt if anyone in Egypt in his right mind believes the phantasmagoric accusations repeatedly published in the press. However, in the long run, they are bound to have a cumulative and pernicious effect. The embassy could not turn a blind eye to these press campaigns against innocent Israeli tourists. It protested vigorously in the wake of each campaign, demanding its immediate discontinuation and the publication of an official denial on the part of the competent authorities. As expected (and we knew exactly what to expect), our protests were rejected on the grounds of freedom of the press. Our inter-locutors knew for certain that, almost whatever they did, Israel would not take steps to stop or diminish the flow of its tourists to Egypt.

In my second period in Egypt (1990–92), an exceptional event took place which could have given the deathblow to Israeli tourism to Egypt. Four Israeli citizens – three Arabs and one Jew – were detained on the charge of espionage. As usual, a campaign of slander and misinformation was waged. It was unprecedented in its intensity and wickedness even for the Egyptian press. As always, the first indication appeared in one of the opposition newspapers. It was a small article on an inside page claim-ing that according to security services sources, a network of Israeli spies had been dismantled. It was said that the network operated from a rented apartment in Heliopolis (a select quarter in Cairo), befriended army officers and collected sensitive military and civilian information. The newspaper added that a radio transmitter and other sophisticated spying equipment had been seized and that one of the spies had broken a leg when jumping from the balcony to escape arrest. As usual, the next day the government press followed suit. Every day, new hair-raising details were published.

Let me sum up the general outlines of the story as it was reported in the Egyptian press, supposedly relying on sources in the security services, day after day for many long weeks. The Mussarati family, an Arab and deeply religious Muslim family residing in Lod in Israel, had been recruited by Israeli intelligence (the Mossad). It was sent to Egypt on a spying mis-sion and, among other tasks, was ordered to assassinate Boutros Ghali and other Egyptian personalities. They were given a huge amount of cash in dollars to cover their expenses and lead a lavish life-style. Upon their arrival, they deposited the money in an Egyptian bank, rented a luxurious apartment and threw extravagant parties. They used the family's daugh-ter, the beautiful 18-year-old Faiza, to entice army officers to participate in sex and drugs orgies. Consequently, they blackmailed the officers and extorted from them highly classified documents and confidential infor-mation that were relayed to Israel, using a most sophisticated radio trans-mitter. But that was not all! Faiza carried Aids and contaminated all the persons with whom she had sex. The father, taking advantage of his Libyan origin, had infiltrated into Libya with the aim of murdering the Libyan leader Ghadaffi and was arrested at the border on his return to Egypt. A high-ranking Israeli intelligence officer operated the network and had visited Egypt several times bringing with him funds and instruc-tions. His identity was known to the Egyptian security services and he was soon to be arrested. Before I continue with the phantasmagorial story, I have to point out a few blatant discrepancies. Beauty was not one of the main attributes of the poor Faiza and medical examinations, which were carried out at the embassy's demand, certified that she was not sick with aids and was still a virgin. No sophisticated transmitter (it was an ordinary transistor) or other spying equipment was ever found. The huge funds were a few hundred dollars which were sparingly exchanged from time to time in the local bank where they were deposited. The father was arrested in his apartment and not at the Libyan border. The alleged Israeli intelligence officer, who was indeed arrested the next day as predicted by the press, was nothing but a petty merchant of used furniture in the Jaffa flea market.

His name was David Ovitz. He had participated in a tender by the American embassy in Cairo for the sale of used furniture and had come to Cairo to acquire a sum that he had deposited as a guarantee and which the embassy had refused to refund him because of some procedural problem. He came to the embassy and requested the commercial counselor, Moshe Dana, to intervene on his behalf with the American embassy. He indicated that he had the impression that he was being followed and that his phone calls were being bugged. It also appeared that he had business and personal relations with the Mussarati family and was not aware that the Egyptian authorities had arrested them. Moshe Dana reported to me and, realizing that he might be the person to whom the Egyptian press was referring, I instructed him to persuade Ovitz to fly back to Israel the same day. I stressed that he should not touch on the events in order not to entangle the embassy in case the Egyptians arrested him. Dana handled the matter as instructed and Ovitz left the embassy on his way to the El Al office to purchase a ticket for the same day's flight. The next day we phoned El Al to check if he had boarded the flight but it appeared that he did not go to El Al and was not registered on any flight. Instead, as we later learnt, he decided not to waste his trip to Egypt and went to Alexandria to collect some furniture he had ordered. On his way back, he was arrested near Cairo for grave spying and remanded in custody.

The embassy acted immediately and within 24 hours our consul, Roni Porat, was allowed to visit Ovitz and the Mussarati family in jail. It appeared that Faiza had broken down under interrogation and said whatever the interrogators had wanted her to say. She did not grasp that, by doing so, she was literally tightening the noose round her family's neck and her own (Egyptian laws providing only for the death penalty in cases of espionage). On my side, I met several times with the foreign and interior ministers and with the director of the *Mabakhes* (the civilian security service). I pointed out the absurdity of the accusations and the blatant discrepancies and contradictions in the stories leaked to the press. I demanded the immediate release of all the arrested Israeli citizens and the immediate discontinuation of the press campaign against Israel.

My interlocutors refused to get involved in the case, hiding behind considerations of state security. They alleged that the matter was handled

exclusively by army intelligence and no other administration could interfere. The Mussarati family and David Ovitz were indicted for grave spying and brought before the Tribunal for the Security of the State, a body
that has very wide powers and whose sentences cannot be appealed. In
accordance with Egyptian law, there is no need to substantiate accusations in this court beyond any doubt as is customary in regular criminal
courts and it is enough that the judges are reasonably convinced that
the defendants are guilty. In cases of grave espionage, the only possible
sentence is the death penalty. The sentence is brought for approval to the
president of Egypt and he can either confirm or rescind it – there is no
middle course. Ovitz's family appointed an Egyptian lawyer to defend him
(he accepted the case notwithstanding the Bar Association's boycott on
Israelis and, clearly, much money was involved). They also appointed a
leading Israeli lawyer, Uri Salonis, to follow the case. In parallel, the
family launched a press campaign to mobilize public opinion both in Israel
and the United States.

Before the opening of the trial, a rather amusing incident took place
(in retrospective it was amusing but, at the time, we did not laugh or even
smile!). One evening, after working hours, the phone rang in Roni Porat's
office. On the line was a man who identified himself as a junior partner
in the Egyptian lawyer's firm and requested that we settle the tribunal
fee immediately in order to meet the deadline for appointing a defender.
He demanded that we put a rather large sum of money in a white envelope (not bearing any identification) and deposit it the same evening
under his name in the tribunal's secretariat so that he would be able, early
the next morning, to go through the necessary formalities. Roni prepared
the envelope and rushed to brief me before he went to the tribunal. The
request and the manner in which it was put forward aroused my suspi-
cions. I instructed Roni to put everything on hold until he checked the
matter with the lawyer himself. The next day it turned out that it was a
not too sophisticated attempt to extort money from the embassy.

The trial continued for several weeks. The consulate kept in permanent touch with the defendants, comforted them and provided for their
basic needs. Nevertheless, the very difficult conditions in jail and the
tremendous nervous tension adversely affected their health and their
ability to cope with the situation. Yitshak Shamir, the then prime minister,
spoke several times on the phone with President Mubarak and requested
him to release the prisoners, assuring him personally that their hands
were clean and that they had no relation whatsoever with Israeli intelligence. The Egyptian press publicized these repeated requests, stressing
that President Mubarak refused to interfere in a judicial procedure. The
newspapers stressed that in Egypt there was a clear separation between
the three branches of power and lauded the judicial system for its independence and clean hands. It did not prevent them from calling, in the
same breath, for an exemplary penalty for the Zionist spies.

Suddenly, the affair, which had erupted so vociferously, ended in a deathly silence! General Hani, the man responsible for Israeli and Jewish matters in the civilian security service, requested to meet me urgently. I received him immediately and I was stunned to hear that President Mubarak had decided to release all the four prisoners immediately and put an end to an affair that was exacting a heavy toll on relations between the two countries. The very same day – to save face – the prisoners were brought before the Tribunal for the Security of the State and released on bail on their personal guarantee. Then they were taken by helicopter to Cairo airport, kept for a few hours in confinement (in a room and not in jail) and put on an El Al flight to Israel, accompanied by the Israeli consul, Roni Porat. The press campaign stopped miraculously and the case was never again mentioned. A few weeks later, the embassy even succeeded in recuperating David Ovitz's deposit from the American embassy as well as the furniture and the transistor that had been seized by the Egyptian authorities.

It is interesting to point out that a few weeks before the eruption of the Mussarati–Ovitz case, an Egyptian Bedouin, who had infiltrated into Israel, was accused of spying. He was kept for a long time in jail without giving notice to the Egyptian consulate in Eilat and without authorizing the consul to visit him. In the wake of the unexpected release of the Israeli spies, Egypt requested the release of the Bedouin. After a few months, he was indeed released without trial and sent back to Egypt. I do not know if there is a circumstantial link between the two cases but the proximity between the two events is rather disturbing. High-level Egyptian officials close to the security authorities assumed that the entire Ovitz–Musarati affair had been concocted by one of the secret branches of army intelligence with the aim of fanning tension between the two countries. The case was defused when President Mubarak realized that the accusations were groundless and ordered the release of the arrested Israelis – demanding in exchange the release of the Bedouin incarcerated in Israel. The extraordinary publicity around the case and the daily leaks from the investigators' and prosecutors' desks – which had no factual basis whatsoever – were attributed to the urge of some of the officers to gain bombastic headlines and catch the public eye. Knowing how the system functions, it is difficult for me to accept at face value this rationalization of the events but I can say for certain that if the affair had not finished with a happy end, it would have badly impaired Israeli tourism to Egypt. At the peak of the case, it literally came to a standstill and, even after the prisoners' release, it took many months and much effort to bring Israeli tourism back to a reasonable size. To be accused of espionage, at the whim of an Egyptian official or at the pleasure of the authorities, is a much more serious problem than being accused of carrying forged dollars. No one in their right mind would have such a risk hovering over their head – with all it entails in terms of mistreatment and humiliation – for the mere pleasure of visiting Egypt.

There are other cases of abusive treatment under various pretenses, involving Israelis who had been established in Egypt for a while rather than the usual tourists. I will give only a few examples. An Israeli woman (whose name I will not cite) was hired by a local tourist agency to look after its Israeli clients. She fell in love with an Egyptian colleague, converted to Islam, married and gave birth to two children. One night in mid-1991 she was apprehended by the security service in her own house and taken to jail despite her husband's protests and her children's tears. No explanation was given to the family as to the reasons for the arrest. The very next day, I met the interior minister, Abd el Halim Mussa, and appealed for the poor woman's release using my best diplomatic skills. At first, the minister said that it was a matter of state security and rejected my plea. When I continued to insist, depicting the family's heartbreaking situation in detail, he phoned the chief of the *Mabakhes* and pretended to inquire if anything could be done to meet the request of our friend the Israeli ambassador. After a few minutes, he turned to me and said that the woman was accused of prostitution (a very serious offense in Egypt). He added that, because I had personally intervened in her favor, he was ready to consider expelling her from the country together with her children instead of bringing her before a court, that would certainly send her to prison for a long time. I read the minister's message between the lines and thanked him for his generosity and comprehension: insisting would have meant having the poor woman separated from her family and thrown into prison. She was better off in Israel! Clearly, this harsh treatment had nothing to do with state security or prostitution (I can vouch for that); the woman's only 'fault' was that she was too deeply intermingled with Egyptian society, forgetting that she was an Israeli citizen and as such forbidden to do so. Big Brother did not forget and did not hesitate breaking up a family!

A similar case was that of Dvorah Ganani, an entrepreneur who established an import–export business with Egyptian partners and was on the line between Tel Aviv and Cairo. In late 1996, she was arrested at Cairo airport and accused of imaginary security offenses. Luckily for her, at the time the leader of the Labor Party, Ehud Barak, was on an official visit to Egypt. He appealed directly to President Mubarak and refused to leave without her. After a few hours of tense negotiations, she was allowed to fly back to Israel on the same plane as Barak. She had to leave behind everything she had built up over years of strenuous effort, but at least she was spared a lengthy vacation in Egyptian jails and the ordeals that had been concocted for her. Who knows, she might also have been accused of prostitution!

The latest case, which has not yet found a happy ending, is that of Azam Azam, an Israeli Druze (a small religious sect of Arab origin) who worked as a textile expert in an Israeli–Egyptian joint venture (one of the very few). He was arrested in early 1997 for espionage. The entire Who's

Who in Israel interceded on his behalf and Israeli intelligence, in an unprecedented step, gave firm public assurances that he was not, and had never been, one of their agents. This time, nothing helped; the Egyptians were determined to go to the bitter end. Azam was tried and condemned to a very heavy prison sentence. He is still decaying in jail and let us hope that he will soon be released. Like so many other innocent Israelis thrown into Egyptian prisons on trumped-up charges or as a result of blown-up cases, he is the victim of Egypt's policies. They were conceived from the outset with the aim of maintaining a reasonable degree of tension between the two countries, demonstrating Arab militancy and sending political signals, internally and externally.

I have described at length the difficulties with which Israeli tourists to Egypt are confronted because I am convinced beyond the slightest doubt that they are not due to routine, bureaucracy or mere coincidence but are deliberately orchestrated by the Egyptian authorities. It is not my intention to discourage Israeli tourists from visiting Egypt or to frighten them. On the contrary, I have always done my utmost to foster Israeli tourism to Egypt, even in periods of great tension and serious physical danger. I believed, and still do, that tourism is an essential factor for strengthening the peace and bringing together the two peoples. In retrospect, out of the hundreds of thousands of Israelis who have visited Egypt since the establishment of diplomatic relations in 1980, only a relatively small number have fallen victim to the whims of the Egyptian authorities. All others were received with open arms and enjoyed every minute of their stay in Egypt. Sinai is bustling with Israeli tourists all the year round, including in periods of tension such as during the Israeli Grapes of Wrath military operation in Lebanon. Indeed, my own daughter, Tali, who resided in Egypt for a few years, loves Sinai and the Egyptians. She travels there at every opportunity and always returns with favorable impressions and full of praise for Egyptian hospitality.

As I have said, Israel sees tourism – even one-way tourism – as a bridge between the two peoples and a means to skirt the obstacles scattered by the Egyptian authorities so as to reduce normalization to a bare minimum. Clearly, there is a large gap between Israeli expectations and Egyptian readiness to allow the fulfillment of these expectations. Let me tell you an amusing story that illustrates clearly what I mean. One year after the signature of the tourism agreement (1981), the embassy decided to organize an Israeli Week in one of the great hotels with the aim of giving a foretaste of Israel to prospective Egyptian tourists. The Nile Hilton was more than happy to host the event and began, together with us, to make plans for it. El Al and the ministry of tourism agreed to cover all expenses. We planned to make use of the great ballroom and all adjacent halls and bring from Israel first-class artists, chefs, food products, handicrafts, tourism films, slides and the like. A large delegation of tourist operators, headed by the then minister of tourism, Avraham Sharir, was to come for the whole week and strengthen relations with their Egyptian counterparts. In the course of the preparations, we received a cable from Jerusalem signed by the minister himself (I doubt if he really knew about its content). It suggested that the Israeli Week be scheduled for Hanuka (a Jewish festival commemorating the heroic stand of the Maccabis against the Roman conquerors) and that representatives of the Maccabi movement from the world over join the official delegation and parade in the streets of Cairo. Several troops of Israeli folkdancers would enliven the parade that would march from Liberation Square (where the Hilton is located) to the pyramids. There, a great popular celebration would take place in the presence of President Sadat and the Egyptian élite.

The project was clearly a non-starter. We replied in diplomatic language that the suggested program could not be realized in the conditions prevailing in Egypt and that it would be more practical to stick to the original planning. We received an angry answer threatening that the minister would cancel the budgetary allocation if the embassy were unable to organize the suggested program. I repeatedly phoned Jerusalem, explained the facts and the limitations imposed upon us and tried to convey my conviction that there was not a remote possibility that the Egyptians would agree. All my diplomatic efforts were in vain. Finally I lost my temper and sent (with the ambassador's approval) the following cable: 'The suggested program is preposterous. The feast of Hanuka does not mean anything to the Egyptians and the bravery of the Maccabis does not arouse in them either admiration or enthusiasm. Though Egypt has signed a peace treaty with Israel, it has not yet joined the Zionist Organization ... The Embassy has stopped all preparations for Israeli Week.' There was no direct reply: after several days' silence we received confirmation of the budgetary allocation and the green light to proceed with the original program.

By now, the reader must have guessed that the embassy had been over-optimistic and that the Egyptian authorities did not approve even of the original program, which was much less ambitious and conspicuous. Such an event did not fit their vision of normalization. They did not say so officially and did not make any comment or suggestion. Some two weeks before the scheduled date, the Nile Hilton notified us that the ballroom, and all other halls, had unexpectedly been reserved by the Egyptian government and to their great sorrow, they were unable to host Israeli Week. We tried all other hotels in Cairo and received the same stereotyped reply: 'Sorry, all our halls are reserved for the next six months.' It was crystal-clear that Big Brother's hand was behind the Hilton's last-minute cancellation and the series of refusals that we had received. Obviously, the Israeli Week never took place and it seems that seeing Israeli dancers perform against the background of the pyramids is to be postponed until the Messiah comes!

Nevertheless, when one picks the right time (a period of 'smiles') and has the right connections, things *can* be achieved well before that fateful event. In my second stay in Cairo (1990–92), I had the pleasure of witnessing beautiful Israeli models present together with (no less beautiful) Egyptian models the Gotex (a leading Israeli swimwear firm) collection at a private hotel with the pyramids in the background. Furthermore, the entire next season's Gotex catalogue was photographed against the background of the main Egyptian archeological sites in and around Cairo. The embassy did not lift a finger and indeed did not even dream that such an event was feasible. It was the achievement of an Egyptian businessman who had the right connections and knew how to twist arms and make the impossible become possible!

To conclude this chapter on a positive note, let me say that, despite the limitations and difficulties, the Egyptian authorities in general do make an effort to attract Israeli and Jewish tourists to Egypt, especially in the Taba region. The warm reception offered by the Egyptian people and the encounter with the man-in-the-street are in themselves a refreshing and delightful experience. Egypt offers a profusion of fascinating tourist sites and outstanding archeological monuments which not surprisingly are strong poles of attraction. True, one never knows where, when and on whose neck the Sword of Damocles will fall as a result of the carrot-and-stick policy, but even then the overwhelming majority of the Israeli tourists have an interesting and pleasant stay in Egypt. It is not surprising that thousands of Israelis, who have already been to Egypt, return time and again.

One can learn about the authorities' desire to attract Jewish tourism from the thorough manner in which they maintain the tomb of Rabbi Abu Hasira and organize the pilgrimage to his shrine. He was a Moroccan rabbi who is believed to have had supernatural powers and performed miracles. He is buried in Damanhur (a city in the Delta, not far from Alexandria) and his tomb is a pilgrimage site for Jews of Moroccan origin. In 1981, very soon after the opening of the embassy, Aharon Abu Hasira, the then Israeli minister of religions and a great-grandson of the legendary rabbi, organized the first group of pilgrims (some 40–50). The tomb, and indeed the entire Jewish cemetery in Damanhur (there are no more Jews in the city), were in a terrible state of neglect and the earth-lane access to the tomb was covered with thick herb. The pilgrims – and the embassy and consulate staff – rolled up their sleeves, cleaned, weeded, hoed, leveled the road, whitewashed the rabbi's tomb and neighboring graves, erected a large tent and passed the night there singing and praying. The pilgrimage became a tradition and every year the number of visitors increased. When I returned in 1990, the number of pilgrims had reached several hundred. The Egyptian authorities had restored the cemetery, opened a new earth-road and built various facilities for the comfort of the pilgrims. They also took upon themselves the organization of the festivities and provided transportation and lodging as well as tight security measures.

In 1991, the then minister of religions, Professor Avner Shaki, and many high officials of his ministry decided to join the pilgrimage to the revered rabbi's tomb. A few days beforehand, I personally went to Damanhur to co-ordinate the minister's visit with the local authorities and make sure that everything in the cemetery was all right. On the same day, heavy rains had fallen and the road to the shrine was one big puddle of mud. We had to leave our cars and walk a few kilometers in the mud, literally up to our ankles. The Egyptians, though they had already made all the preparations, requested me to persuade the minister not to participate in the pilgrimage in order to spare him the difficult walk. I rejected the suggestion and assured them that the minister would walk in the mud like all the other pilgrims. On the day of the pilgrimage, on our way to Damanhur, I informed the minister of the situation and prepared him for sinking into the mud up to his ankles. At the entrance to the city, the regional governor received us and to our great surprise we drove straight to the cemetery (almost to the rabbi's tomb) on an excellent asphalt road. The governor, very pleased with our manifest surprise, explained with pride that after I had informed him of the minister's determination to participate in the pilgrimage, he had instructed his department of public works to build a 4 km asphalt road to the cemetery. The road was built in less than four days! The obvious conclusion is that when the Egyptian authorities wish to please, they know exactly what to do and are capable of doing it in the shortest time. I am sure that the reader understands by now what I am hinting at ...

13 · Commerce and Economy

Negotiations on the establishment of trade, economic and financial relations between the two countries were also initiated before the opening of the embassies. Israel attached great importance to these fields – more out of political than economic considerations. It was clear that, for objective reasons, Egypt would never become a major commercial partner for Israel. Israeli experts in foreign trade estimated, that within three to five years, the volume of trade with Egypt (not including oil) would reach annually around $150–200 million, representing less than one per cent of Israel's global trade (today, less than 0.5 per cent). They believed that, with time, there might arise additional opportunities for joint ventures with the Egyptian public and private sectors. They also hoped that Egypt would become a transit point for indirect trade with Arab and Muslim countries which did not maintain diplomatic relations with Israel and implemented the Arab commercial boycott.

The geographic nearness and the short distance by good roads between the two countries gave Israel a relative advantage over overseas competitors – maritime freight costs as well as the substantial expenses involved in repeated handling of goods and land transportation to and from the ports could be spared. Altogether, only 520 kilometers separate Jerusalem from Cairo (of which 400 are on Egyptian soil). From the main Israeli industrial centers the distance was much shorter and did not significantly exceed the distance from Alexandria to Cairo (270 kilometers). In the early days, the road was narrow and heavily congested (in the late 1980s, a super-highway was built) and, furthermore, Alexandria harbor was overcrowded and the long waiting time made the costs of maritime freight even heavier. But all this proved to be irrelevant in the light of the Egyptian policies aimed at reducing trade with Israel to the bare minimum, even if it was economically advantageous for Egypt.

With the opening of the embassies, Israel strove to accelerate the economic negotiations and reach, as quickly as possible, mutually agreed solutions on all relevant issues. It raised the need for arrangements in the fields of: trade exchanges, goods transportation, customs facilities, anchoring rights, access to public sector tenders, banking and financial links, direct relations between the two central banks, encouragement of joint ventures and reciprocal investments, prevention of double taxation, and participation in trade and industrial fairs. First and foremost, it demanded the termination of Egypt's adherence to the Arab boycott and the abrogation of all related laws and regulations.

Egypt was in no hurry. It dragged its feet on every issue and made the convening of subcommittees (established under Israeli pressure) into a complex and time-consuming diplomatic operation. Discussions were acrimonious and went into the smallest details. Elementary matters, which would have been settled in a few hours with any other country, were turned by the Egyptians into cardinal issues necessitating endless discussions and which seldom found a satisfactory solution. Only a few weeks before the decisive date – the second phase of withdrawal from Sinai – did the Egyptians (fearing an Israeli backlash) condescend to conclude a few framework agreements and agree to establish a permanent joint committee for trade, economic and financial affairs. We knew that the prospects that Egypt would live up to its commitments were very slim. The character of the negotiations clearly indicated that Egypt was more interested in preventing the normal development of economic relations between the two countries than in fostering them. Nevertheless, we had no alternative but to bow gracefully to the Egyptian positions and hope for the best. We still believed that time was the best healer and would bring about pragmatic solutions through inertia.

Our optimism was not groundless. Egyptian businessmen came by the hundreds to the embassy, inquiring about possibilities of trade and joint ventures and putting forward feasible proposals of co-operation. They were eager to enter into serious business relations with their Israeli counterparts. They believed that it was a unique opportunity for them to secure advanced technology, avail themselves of the Israeli marketing network worldwide and develop trilateral trade. In the first few months, the authorities were still very forthcoming and allowed them free access to the embassy. Several businessmen were even authorized to travel to Israel and look in to the possibilities of establishing business links with Israeli companies.

For their part, Israeli businessmen flocked to Egypt looking for commercial opportunities and suitable partners. Many of them even appointed agents to act on their behalf in Egypt or received distribution rights for Egyptian goods in Israel. The Koor Company (one of the major Israeli industrial and commercial concerns) opened an office in Cairo and posted one of its top men to manage it.

Despite the haggling in the joint committees, the Egyptian external trade ministry seemed, for a short while, to deal objectively with applications for import or export licenses to and from Israel (universally required at the time) and applied to Israel the same rules and criteria as those applied to all other countries. Trade between the two countries developed fairly well and within a year the volume of exchanges reached $85 million. Israel was allowed to participate for two consecutive years in the international trade fair and the international book fair held annually in Cairo. In the book fair, the organizers, or more accurately the authorities, made sure they placed the Israeli stand near the Palestinian one for the sake of balance and more so to create friction that would signal to Israel that it was not welcome. In the trade fair, the authorities were even more cynical: in the second year, they induced Israel to build at its expense a permanent pavilion though they knew that they would not allow it to participate in future events.

The economic honeymoon soon ended and already in the second year troubles began. We saw that the authorities had made a drastic turnabout and were taking stringent measures to contain the normal flow of trade. Businessmen coming to the embassy were meticulously filtered and only a few were allowed to reach the embassy. Most of them were interrogated at length and warned to terminate their contacts with the embassy. Those who persisted were summoned to the security services for a more thorough investigation and persuaded to renounce their intention of working with Israel even if it meant forfeiting money they had already invested.

In parallel, invitations to participate in fairs and exhibitions were discontinued under the pretence that the Egyptian government could not vouch for the Israeli participants' security. Our repeated efforts to convince the Egyptians to change their positions remained fruitless. We were given explanations that did not hold water and aroused only anger and frustration. During my tenure as ambassador in the early 1990s, I became sick and tired of the Egyptian behavior and recommended that we cease to beg year after year for invitations to international events which would never be sent. I pointed out that the Egyptians saw our threats to retaliate as toothless (each year, as the last resort, we hinted that Israel might retaliate) and would dismiss our pleas with cynical and humiliating answers. I insisted that our running after invitations simply gave more leverage to their stick-and-carrot policy by allowing them to turn marginal issues into means of pressure on Israel. I added that the very fact that we repeatedly accepted the *fait accompli* of their refusal to invite Israel without significant retaliation on our part (despite our repeated threats) sent the Egyptians a clear signal that Israel was protesting only for lipservice. They knew for certain (and rightly so) that Israel would eventually move ahead as if nothing had happened.

My recommendation was overruled and I was told that we should not make the task easier for the Egyptians. I was compelled to continue pleading with them to invite Israel to international events held in Egypt in conformity with their contractual obligation and to present toothless ultimatums. As a good soldier, I did it with the utmost earnestness, at various levels and in all relevant ministries – but it was to no avail!

The Egyptians dismissed my repeated representations with cynical smiles and vague promises that 'Israel will be invited when the circumstances allow it'.

But let me come back to the first years. In the framework of their nuts-and-bolts tightening of relations, the Egyptian authorities established a special track for import and export licensing to and from Israel and made the procedures much more complicated and frustrating. An Israeli desk was especially established in the external trade ministry to supervise all dealings with Israel. Complicated application forms for import or export licenses had to be completed in great detail and were to be presented to the Israeli desk together with a cash deposit of four per cent of the transaction's presumed value. After numerous meetings and lengthy discussions, the application forms were referred to the security services on condition that the desk's director found the transaction commercially valid. From there, after several more weeks, the forms were sent to the Israel department in the foreign ministry for political clearance. In the event that both administrations gave the green light, the applications were brought before a special professional committee (which seldom convened) for objective commercial scrutiny. If it found that the transaction met the professional criteria, the application was brought before the director general of the external trade ministry. His decisions were final and could not be contested or reviewed. The entire procedure took many months and in the meantime the deposit was held hostage in the ministry. In the event of refusal, it was refunded after several more months. In a country where bank interest was as high as 22 per cent and inflation 30 per cent (official statistics were lower), this meant a substantial financial loss for the applicants.

At first, Egyptian businessmen continued to flood the external trade ministry with applications for both import and export licenses. However, as the Egyptian authorities became less and less generous and the security services more and more pugnacious, the number of applications substantially decreased with time. No one in their right mind was prepared to throw away good money *and* confront the authorities' wrath. Israel made official representations and received the ridiculous reply that the new measures taken by the Egyptian government were aimed at facilitating trade between the two countries ... In the initial months, the embassy tried to step up the procedure and contacted all relevant authorities repeatedly. For a short while, we had some positive results but, after the implementation of the second stage of withdrawal from Sinai, these interventions became counterproductive and endangered the businessmen involved.

The Egyptian steps alleged to foster trade between the two countries rapidly bore fruit: the volume of trade fell drastically. We thought, in the first stage, that this was a temporary reaction to the Galilee Operation in Lebanon but very soon we reached the conclusion that it was a long-range policy on the part of the Egyptian government. Indeed, despite the revolutionary liberalization of foreign trade and the total abolition of licensing from 1983 onwards, special regulations concerning trade with Israel were published in the Official Gazette. Israel was defined as a special case, which continued to be subject to licensing through the same procedures as those enforced in the past. Furthermore, the regulations strictly and specifically forbade the public sector (around 85 per cent of the Egyptian economy) to trade or have business relations with Israel. In practice, this did not change much: from the outset this prohibition had been enforced unofficially and no Israeli firm could ever win a public sector tender (even when its prices were the lowest and its Egyptian agents most influential). Nevertheless, we were stunned because, for the first time, the Egyptians had expressed their discriminating policies towards us overtly and flouted all their commitments openly. When we protested, the Egyptians at first denied the existence of such regulations and, when we confronted them with the Official Gazette, they brazenly affirmed that we were missing the point and that the regulations were aimed at fostering economic relations between the two countries ...

When I returned to Egypt in 1990, the volume of trade had fallen to $12 million and Egyptian businessmen had given up their efforts to develop trade and joint ventures with Israel. Only a very few still had limited relations with their Israeli counterparts and met difficulties and harassment at every step. The Israeli trade ministry had lost hope and refused to continue covering the economic counselor's salary and expenses; out of political considerations, the foreign ministry decided to bank the bill instead. I decided to give first priority to this aspect of our relations with Egypt and to try to improve the situation rapidly. In addition to Moshe Dana, the able and dedicated economic counselor, I harnessed the whole staff to this task. The results were very slim. Two years later, at the end of my stay in 1992, the volume of trade between the two countries had risen to $18 million only and its composition had changed in favor of the Egyptian side. I have to admit that it was a battle lost in advance: nothing the embassy did, or could do, was any match for the formidable machinery put in place by the Egyptian authorities to prevent the free flow of trade.

In reality, the volume of trade between the two countries is higher than the figure shown in official statistics. There is an indirect trade, which has gradually developed and is not reflected in the statistics. Over the years, Israeli and Egyptian businessmen have found ways – with the knowledge and tacit blessing of the Egyptian authorities – to bypass the Egyptian restrictions with the help of third-country businessmen who act as middle men. Israeli goods are officially exported to that country and from there dispatched to Egypt with a certificate of origin showing that the merchandise was manufactured on its territory. According to rough estimates (accurate statistics being impossible), the annual volume of this indirect trade is around $25 million. Some consider that an achievement. I personally do not see in it anything to be pleased about. Israel has always

had a substantial indirect trade with several countries that do not maintain diplomatic relations with it and/or adhere formally to the Arab boycott. There is no justification for allowing Egypt to act as if it were one
of them; after all, it has signed with Israel a fully-fledged peace treaty and
several normalization agreements for which Israel has paid a heavy price.

But even if we put aside principles and add the figures of direct and
indirect trade with Egypt, we reach a volume of $43 million. This figure
still does not represent half the volume of the direct trade attained in the
first two years (80–85 million) when the Egyptian authorities did not
crudely intervene to curb it by administrative means. It is also very far
from reflecting the immense possibilities of commercial interaction
between two neighboring countries that have complementary economies.
Is it possible that Egypt can find nothing to purchase in Israel – a country
that exports goods and services worth billions of dollars to more than 100
countries? Is it logical that Egypt has nothing to sell to Israel in addition
to oil? Is it natural that the volume of trade between two countries linked
by short and excellent roads is so insignificant? The answer to these
disturbing questions is no with a capital N.

Even non-Israeli Jewish businessmen who were interested in promoting trilateral joint ventures (Egyptian initiative, foreign capital and
Israeli technology) found it difficult to overcome the obstacles erected by
the Egyptian authorities. Baron de Rothschild from the French branch of
the family organized a group of potential investors and created a special
fund with an initial capital of $10 million in response to a request from
President Sadat a few weeks before his assassination. He appointed
Aharon Gafni (the former governor of the Central Bank of Israel) to head
the fund and Mohamed Abdel Megid (the former Egyptian minister of
finance and Ismat Abdel Megid's brother) to represent the fund in Egypt.
Over the years, tens of projects were put forward but not a single one ever
reached fruition. When I returned to Egypt ten years later, the fund had
gone into deep freeze.

A related problem was the total absence of direct relations between
the banking systems of the two countries, which made the development
and free flow of commercial relations very difficult. Despite all signed
agreements and verbal pledges and notwithstanding Israeli's unceasing
pressures, Egypt stubbornly refused to allow any sort of links between the
two central banks and the establishment of a financial clearing system
between the two countries. During my two periods in Egypt, I met several
times with the successive governors of the Egyptian Central Bank and
raised forcefully Israel's demand to establish a minimal banking relationship. They always received me politely, heard attentively what I had to
say, offered me coffee and oriental sweets, but refused to address the problem – stressing that it was a political issue which rested in the government's hands. After long nagging, I succeeded in arranging a meeting in
1991 between the governors of the two central banks on the occasion of

a conference of the World Monetary Fund, when our then governor, Moshe Mandelbaum, visited Egypt at his colleague's invitation. The Egyptian governor never returned the visit despite repeated invitations and solemn pledges by the Egyptian foreign ministry that the visit would soon take place. As I have explained, visits and invitations were (and still are) part of the Egyptian diplomatic arsenal against Israel.

Indeed, nothing ever moved in the field of banking and, when in 1992 the Egyptians expressed a desire to resume their banks' activities in the Gaza Strip and the West Bank, I recommended that we condition our acceptance on the establishment of official links between the two central banks. This time, my recommendation fell on receptive ears and I was instructed to relay accordingly a message to the Egyptians. I confess that I did so with pleasure. The Egyptians protested loudly and pretended they were profoundly offended. We insisted that the road could not always remain one-way and that the matter should be tackled in the framework of broader issues at the next meeting of the economic joint committee (the convening of which the Egyptians postponed time after time). When I left Egypt at the end of 1993, the next meeting had not taken place. I did not follow what happened later, but I know for sure that the Egyptian banks are presently functioning in the territories and that, to this very day, no formal relations exist between the two central banks.

As unbelievable as it may sound, for years (and to the best of my knowledge, to the present day), elementary financial activities such as opening letters of credit, transfer of payments are bank guarantees are a Mission Impossible. No local bank ever agreed to deal directly with its Israeli counterparts. In the early 1980s President Sadat had to intervene personally to persuade the Bank of Suez to allow one of its branches to deal with Israel through banks in Great Britain and Switzerland.

Even more unbelievable is the fact that not a single Egyptian bank ever allowed the Israeli embassy in Cairo or the consulate in Alexandria to open a check account – or for that matter any kind of account. We were compelled to open a dollar account with City Bank, an American offshore bank that was not allowed to manage accounts in Egyptian currency. Each time the embassy and the staff needed cash or had to make payments, we exchanged dollars for Egyptian pounds and carried them around in suitcases to settle our bills. Seven years later, when I returned to Egypt, this was still the situation – matters had even deteriorated, but this time the Egyptian authorities were not at fault. The Israeli staff, fearing that their money might be confiscated in the event of a sudden worsening of relations, had closed their accounts with City Bank and received their salaries in cash in dollars, which they kept under the mattress until they had an opportunity to deposit them in an Israeli bank. I could not condone such an approach. I reassured the staff as to our relations with Egypt and persuaded them to reopen their personal accounts with City Bank and receive their salaries by bank transfer as is customary in Israeli embassies throughout the world and as we used to do in Egypt in the first days.

In parallel, I decided to check if, after more than 12 years of peaceful relations, it was now possible to open an account in an Egyptian bank. I requested our administrative officer, Dror Gabay, to enter any bank casually, open an account in the embassy's name and deposit a large sum in it. He did so and returned to report that he had encountered no difficulty and that the branch manager had asked him if he also wanted to open a dollar account. I was less enthusiastic and waited to see what would happen in the next few days. Indeed, the very next day Gabay was summoned to the bank and informed that the head management (read: the authorities) had not approved the opening of the account. Our money was refunded and we continued to run about carrying suitcases stuffed with Egyptian pounds. I hope that a more creative solution has been found since I left Cairo. But to be frank, I doubt if the problem has found its solution or will do so in the near future.

Even the mutual sale and dispatching of newspapers and magazines was a complicated task. True, a local distributor was allowed to import a small number of leading Israeli newspapers and export Egyptian publications to Israel. At first, the Israeli newspapers regularly reached the stands in the main hotels but with time they disappeared (read: were not allowed to be displayed and sold). The transfer of newspapers, in both directions, was carried out by the public bus line functioning between the two countries. There were many difficulties at the border and the newspapers often reached their destination after several days, but the main problem was the mutual settlement of bills since no Egyptian bank was ready to deal with Israel. The embassy had to take upon itself the channeling of the small sums involved as if the sale of newspapers were a cultural exchange program. When I returned to Egypt, the embassy had dropped out of the picture. The entire operation continued to function thanks to the Egyptian distributor who made a few pounds on the transaction and was allowed to travel to Israel from time to time. A small number of Israeli newspapers still arrived but they went exclusively to the various security services, which understandably were interested in receiving publications from Israel regularly. I accepted this situation as a fact of life and did not lift a finger to try and change it despite the pressure of the Egyptian distributor (a personal friend) to return to the previous arrangement, which was more profitable for him.

As for the Arab boycott, we had in the two first years (1980–82) a significant success – at least on paper. After brief hesitation, and many reminders on our part, the Egyptian parliament passed a law abrogating in the clearest language the enforcement in Egypt of the Arab boycott regulations. The law became final immediately after its publication in the Official Gazette. We also reminded the foreign ministry that adequate notification should be sent to the United Nations secretariat and to all international economic organizations. We requested that, on the same occasion, the Egyptian government notify the UN that it was canceling all the reservations concerning Israel in its ratification of international instruments. Again, we had to nag the Egyptians for a few months but finally they complied and sent official notification to all relevant international bodies. It was an historic turnabout. After 40 years of warring, Egypt had formally withdrawn from the vicious circle of the Arab boycott. On the face of it, there is no doubt that Egypt has gone quite far in this respect. It allows Israeli shipping to cross the Suez Canal and anchor in Egyptian ports, it has established regular land and air links with Israel, welcomes Israeli tourists, sells oil to Israel in substantial quantities and maintains with it a semblance of commercial exchanges.

However, things are not that simple and not all remnants of the past have been erased. Egypt, for its own reasons and independently of the provisions of the Arab boycott, has established a selective boycott on Israel. To sustain this contention, it is enough to recall the famous yellow card, the need for import and export licenses or the special procedure for trading with Israel. We can also add the total absence of relations between the two banking and financial systems, the banning of Israel from economic events taking place in Egypt and the prohibition imposed officially on the public sector from having any kind of exchanges with Israel. This is quite an impressive list though regrettably not an exhaustive one. In spite of the breakthrough that cannot be denied, real comprehensive normalization of economic relations between the two countries is still a long way off.

To my great regret, problems in this field are not limited to the topics I have cited. They are much wider and deeper. Throughout the period from the opening of the embassy in 1980 to my final departure from Egypt in 1993, not a single serious joint venture was established. There was no lack of projects; on the contrary, tens of projects – mostly put forward by Egyptian promoters and allegedly approved by the authorities – were discussed in detail but never reached fruition. I will provide here only a few examples that speak for themselves. On the flight taking me to Cairo to take up my post as ambassador to Egypt, I met a top delegation of Chemicals for Israel (one of the main Israeli companies). They informed me with pride that they were coming to sign an agreement with an Egyptian public-sector company for establishing a liquid fertilizer factory in Egypt. From my previous experience, I knew that Egypt was not keen on having joint ventures with Israeli companies and that the public sector was out-of-bounds for Israel (indeed, as I have written, there are regulations to that effect). I tried to dampen their enthusiasm and explained the way things work in Egypt. I told them the Egyptians had killed a proposal to establish a joint company for supplying acetylene gas (a by product of one of their factories) to Israel and preferred to let it dissipate in the air from the factory funnels. My interlocutors thought I was out of touch with what was happening in Egypt. Indeed, the agreement was signed the next day but two years later the project was still stuck in the tangles of Egyptian bureaucracy where it still remains.

Immediately after my arrival in Cairo, the economic counselor, Moshe Dana, briefed me on his approach to developing trade with Egypt. He believed that the only way was the indirect one, i.e. encouraging the establishment of joint ventures which would, as a matter of course, have to import prime material and machinery from Israel. He detailed a few projects that were in the pipeline and were realistic (or so he thought ...). He insisted on the inauguration as soon as possible of an Israeli agricultural exhibition hall in the center of Cairo that was intended to be a shop window for the marketing of Israeli agricultural products and equipment. He stressed that the initiative had come from the Egyptian minister of agriculture, our friend Professor Wali, who had already received all the necessary authorizations from the security services and the foreign ministry. I did not hide from Dana that I was much less optimistic than he and that his approach seemed to me tantamount to driving in neutral since the Egyptians were even keener on preventing joint ventures than on reducing trade. I pointed out that this had always been their policy; and that I seriously doubted whether it would be possible to circumvent the measures they had taken to that effect and present them with a *fait accompli*. Nevertheless, I encouraged him to persevere in his efforts and promised all my support. In any case, we had no better alternative and it was worth a try. It is superfluous to say that not even one of the many projects he had detailed ever took shape and that the exhibition hall never became a reality.

For historical accuracy, I have to specify that two small joint ventures did materialize before 1992 – an assembly workshop for solar powered boilers and a water pump factory. Both were registered as entirely Egyptian undertakings and the necessary components were imported through a third country. It is difficult to regard them as genuine joint ventures.

And one more example ... In the late 1970s, at the initiative of President Sadat, large farms were established some 40 kilometers from Cairo. Enormous sums were invested in bringing water for irrigation and improving the quality of the sandy soil. In the early 1990s, most of these farms went untilled and the desert was winning the soil back. In the spirit of the time, the Egyptian government decided to privatize them and lease them to individual promoters. I was summoned to the minister of agriculture, Professor Wali. He went straight to the point and requested me to locate a few Israeli agricultural companies that would assume the task of rehabilitating the farms and redeeming the land. He brushed aside my doubts as to the feasibility of his request in view of the security services' opposition and insisted that only Israel could save the situation. As for possible obstruction on the part of other government departments, he assured me that he would 'personally remove any problem that may arise'. He also suggested the establishment of joint agricultural companies, which 'will be registered in Egypt and have a predominant Egyptian majority to prevent slanderous accusations that the Israelis are taking control of Egyptian lands'. The idea appealed to me, especially because it was put forward by the minister directly responsible for the farms and who was in addition the first deputy prime minister and secretary-general of the ruling party. I invited to Cairo the representatives of a few companies and had them meet with Wali so that they could hear his proposals directly from him. They came out of the meeting charmed and full of motivation but as usual nothing concrete ever materialized.

This was not the first time that Israel was barred from participating in a large-scale agricultural project in Egypt. Already in 1979, during Begin's first visit to Egypt, the late Shaul Eisenberg (a leading Israeli promoter) who was accompanying him, put forward to President Sadat a proposal to develop 400,000 acres of barren land and resettle several thousand *fellahs* (peasants) who would be transferred from the overcrowded Delta. Sadat was enthused by the proposal and on the spot gave the green light to go ahead. He requested to receive as soon as possible a detailed feasibility study covering all aspects of the project including the sources of financing. Eisenberg immediately sent a team of experts from Tahal (the main agricultural planning company in Israel) to conduct a detailed study on the ground. The first draft was relayed through the embassy to the Egyptian minister of construction and land development, Kafraoui, who had been appointed by Sadat to follow the project through. The Egyptian experts massacred the study and criticized especially the financial setup. They pointed out that Eisenberg's financial contribution was of some 10 per cent only (around $100 million) and the rest of the funding was to come from various international donors and funding establishments. They stressed that Egypt did not need Eisenberg for raising money on the international market and that it could do so on its own. It is possible that they were right but the fact is that the project never materialized. If Eisenberg's proposal had been finalized at the time, the 400,000 acres would have been redeemed and settled a long time ago instead of remaining barren desert land to this very day. But even at that time, the real reason for barring the project was not economic but political. After Eisenberg had clarified the financial issue, the Egyptian experts made more and more excuses, clearly demonstrating that they did not want the project to materialize (I believe that Sadat personally was genuinely interested in the project but that it was forestalled by the security service apparatus).

As for the Arab boycott, in 1991, more than ten years after Egypt had officially abrogated its adherence to the boycott, we discovered that this was not the case when it came to maritime freight. We received from the Anti-Defamation League in the USA copies of more than 80 reports by the American trade department's commission which monitored compliance of American firms with the Arab boycott regulations. We were stunned to discover that all the reports were about Egyptian companies. In their tenders, they still included a provision specifying that the company that would be chosen would have to undertake in writing that it would not ship the merchandise on Israeli ships or on ships that were partially owned by Israeli firms. Furthermore, they were to undertake that the ships would not anchor in Israeli ports before or after the shipment to Egypt. The provision was taken word for word from the Arab boycott regulations; in other words, Egypt was still clearly implementing the Arab boycott. Before taking any step, we requested our embassy in Washington to double-check the reports and provide us with additional information. We received a number of similar reports and documents clearly bearing the signature and stamp of the Egyptian firms (mostly from the public sector).

The case was clear beyond any doubt. I lodged a formal complaint with the foreign ministry and, in parallel, I requested the then American ambassador in Cairo, Frank Wiesner, to verify the information directly with the department of trade and raise the matter with the Egyptian authorities. A few days later, Wiesner informed me that the trade department had closed the files since all the American companies concerned had refused to comply with the Egyptian dictate and therefore the American embassy had no legal standing in the matter. I explained that this was not the point: the only relevant issue was that after ten years of a peace brokered by the USA, Egypt was still enforcing the Arab boycott. Wiesner looked embarrassed and tried to evade my pressures by sticking to legal arguments but he finally promised to raise the matter with President Mubarak himself and with the minister of external trade. He did live up to his promise and after a few weeks he informed me solemnly that the Egyptians had looked into the matter and told him that the tender forms were old forms that had been used for economy's sake and inadvertently without deleting the boycott provisions. I received exactly the same answer from the foreign minister, Amr Mussa, who also promised that these old forms would be withdrawn from circulation. We accepted the official explanation and moved on to other matters on the agenda though we had received reliable information from Australian sources that Egypt had made conditional the purchase of sheep from Australia on the same Arab boycott provisions.

Again, to be quite accurate, I have to point out that in one of the forms the boycott provision had been crossed out and that it was written in handwriting that the provision was no longer relevant. But this specific form dealt with the shipping of oil and, as is well-known, Egypt had been selling large quantities of oil to Israel. Indeed, in the economic field, the sale of oil is the only item that works like a Swiss watch. The Egyptian commitment (given in Camp David) to sell annually one million tons of oil to Israel for five consecutive years at international market prices has elapsed long ago. However, Egyptian oil continues to flow to Israel in ever-increasing quantities – naturally for hard cash. In the meantime, a fair relationship has been established and an excellent working procedure worked out by mutual consent. In the most strained situations, even when Israel was engaged in military operations against other Arab states, Egypt did not discontinue the supply of oil and did not threaten (or hint) that it would bring it to an end or even postpone shipments until the situation improved.

Every year, an Israeli delegation from the fuel administration comes to Cairo for a two-day visit and concludes with the Egyptian ministry of petrol all relevant details: quantities, prices and schedule of shipments. Half the quantity is purchased directly from the ministry and the other half on the 'spot market', where transactions are not officially accounted for. Mustapha Khalil, who was prime minister in the Camp David period, once told me with pride that he had been the architect of the oil agreement between the two countries. He stressed that it was still enforced smoothly because, at the time, he had insisted that it should be based on economic principles and market prices without taking into consideration political or other pressures. He praised the Israeli negotiators for not having used the political leverage they had at the time to pressure Egypt to concede privileged treatment to Israel. Paradoxically, in the early 1990s the Egyptian authorities made serious efforts to persuade Israel to purchase more oil from Egypt and it was Israel that refused. Professor Yuval Neeman, the then Israeli minister of energy, did not wish to become too dependent on Egyptian oil and preferred to diversify sources of supply.

In the same period, his adviser, Shaul Haramati, requested me to look into the possibilities of buying industrial gas in Egypt. I met a few times with the petrol minister, Dr Bambi, and he repeatedly stressed that Egypt did not produce enough gas to meet its own needs. I thought that, once again, I was receiving a political answer, which had no economic grounds. That was not the case; I checked the issue thoroughly and the information I gathered confirmed the minister's reply. I had an even more crushing confirmation at a dinner in my own house. I had invited, among other guests, Dr Bambi and Fikri Abaza, the electricity minister. During dinner, the latter angrily addressed the former: 'Bambi, you are not living up to your promises – when will I finally receive the gas? The turbines I have installed stand idle and the factories still have to use oil!' Bambi explained at length that there was a scarcity of gas and the two ministers discussed the matter the entire evening. Incidentally, it seems that, only a few years later, Egypt surprisingly had not only gas to cover its own ever-expanding needs, but also had a substantial surplus that it was ready to sell to Israel – and even built a special pipeline to supply Israel. Here too things are not entirely clear – at least to me. In any event, several years have gone by and no gas has materialized to this very day. At the same time, Egypt continues to use the issue as a means of pressure on Israel and, as late as April 2000, the Israeli minister of infrastructure, Eliahu Souissa, met in Cairo with President Mubarak to discuss the issue. In January 2001, the board of the Israeli electricity corporation decided to purchase $1.5 billion worth of gas from Egypt over the next five years. Let us hope that this transaction materializes.

Strangely, Egypt also agreed in 1999 to the building of a refinery by a group of Israeli, Egyptian and European investors at a cost of more than $500 million. I doubt if this project will materialize in the near future and – if it does – whether the Israeli partners will remain. The project stands in flagrant contradiction with the Egyptian *modus operandi* over the years and it is difficult to believe that Egypt will entrust Israel with refining its oil when it refuses to co-operate with it in the most minor matters.

Let me add that Egypt never agreed to include oil in the balance of trade between the two countries. Israel pointed out many times the immense discrepancy in favor of Egypt due to its massive oil imports, but the Egyptians claimed that oil had 'nothing to do with regular trade relations'. Incidentally, many people in Israel maintain that all the problems that we confront in our economic relationship with Egypt are dwarfed by the regular supply of oil by Egypt and maintain that we should close our eyes to Egypt's infringements in less important matters. Personally, I do not share this opinion. I firmly believe that Egypt sells oil to Israel because this meets its own commercial interests and, if it only wanted to, it could have developed the same kind of relations in all other commercial sectors. It is not true that it has to fear an Arab backlash or violent reactions from the Egyptian masses. A country that sells oil – a strategic commodity – to Israel for billions of dollars annually can without fear sell to Israel, or buy from it, much less important commodities that would not add up to more than a few million dollars. As I see it, it is the small sum involved that allows Egypt to use trade as a weapon in its arsenal of pressures on Israel – it can reap political and diplomatic returns without having to sustain serious economic damage.

To conclude, let me mention one more item for curiosity's sake. From time to time, the Egyptian press makes an outcry about Israel's alleged intention of taking control of the Nile waters and warns the government against yielding to Israeli pressures. True, more than 70 per cent of the Nile waters flow into the sea and are totally wasted but Israel never raised the issue, directly or indirectly. It was Sadat who, at one of their meetings, offered Begin to supply the Negev with Nile waters but Begin politely turned down the offer. The only proposals raised by Israel in this field have nothing to do with Nile waters; they focus on the possibility of creating new sources of water by desalinization and other processes. For example, the Israeli businessman Yaakov Nimrodi had in mind a project to build desalinization plants in northern Sinai that would provide the Gaza Strip, Sinai and the Negev with irrigation water, using Russian nuclear reactors to produce the electricity needed for their functioning. He even asked my opinion as to whether the Egyptian government would be interested in such a project. I answered that, knowing the Egyptian apprehension as to the Israeli presence in Sinai, I did not believe there was the slightest chance that Egypt would give a positive answer, especially when the project involved the operating of nuclear reactors by Israeli technicians. I added that Egypt had enough water of its own and was on the point of inaugurating a pipeline transporting Nile waters to Sinai. Nevertheless, I encouraged him to raise the matter with the Egyptian authorities and hear their reaction 'from the horse's mouth'. I do not know if Nimrodi heeded my advice and, if he did so, what the Egyptian reply was. In any case, the fact is that neither any reactor nor any desalinization plant have ever been built and I am ready to prophesy that they will never be – at least not with direct Israeli involvement.

14 · Development Co-operation

With the establishment of diplomatic relations, the Israeli government set development co-operation with Egypt as a high-priority target. It allocated one million dollars, in addition to the sums normally channeled through the department of co-operation in the foreign ministry, to initiating a meaningful program of co-operation, especially in the field of agriculture. It lifted, exceptionally, all restrictions on the transfer of the latest technologies and improved seeds to Egypt, despite the possibility that it might become a potential competitor to Israel. The government also encouraged the private sector to harness itself to this task and disregard petty financial considerations. Already on his first visit to Egypt in 1979, Menahem Begin included in his retinue the late Shaul Eisenberg and other prominent businessmen.

Obviously, the Israeli government had no illusions about Egypt's technological capability and did not look upon co-operation with Egypt as a means of enriching Israel's own technology. It was moved by a genuine desire to help Egypt overcome its enormous economic difficulties and contribute to the best of its ability to modernizing its agriculture (the backbone of Egypt's economy). As someone who was deeply involved in the matter – both as a diplomat to Egypt and as head of the Israeli international co-operation – I can certify that Israel had no selfish intentions. It did not strive to make a link between development co-operation and political (or other) issues and never tried to make technical co-operation with Egypt conditional on any prior commitment on its part. The Israeli government believed that the improvement of economic conditions in Egypt would strengthen stability and peace in the region. It also believed that close co-operation between the professional elite of the two countries would create bonds of friendship between them, help erase the vestiges of enmity and speed up the normalization process between the two peoples.

The USA – the sponsor of the Camp David agreements – also saw development co-operation as an important tool for cementing the newborn peace. It encouraged co-operation between the two countries by allocating substantial funds. In the first stage, Congress earmarked an annual $5 million for direct trilateral co-operation and a further $5 million for student exchanges between Israel and the Arab states (not just Egypt).

American Jewry also established a special fund, named after Albert Einstein, with a view to fostering technological co-operation between Israel and Egypt.

At first, we thought that the security services would receive instructions not to hinder the emerging co-operation because of its special significance for the Egyptian economy. We also thought that Egyptian professionals would strive to make the most out of it. Intensive negotiations were held to define the parameters of the technical co-operation between the two countries and a set of principles and patterns of work were agreed upon with a view to accommodating Egyptian sensitivities:

- Co-operation would be a two-directional venture serving Israel and Egypt in equal measure;
- Courses and further training activities would be formally defined as joint seminars and workshops for the exchange of information between the experts of the two countries;
- Israeli experts working in Egypt would be sent by Israeli private companies, which would, for their part, be contracted directly by the Egyptian authorities (obviously, free of charge);
- No formal co-operation agreements would be signed between the two governments, and neither foreign ministry would be openly involved;
- Activities financed by the USA or Jewish funds would be administered as independent entities by trilateral steering committees functioning under Egyptian chairmanship, and Egypt would have a right of veto;
- Technical co-operation would be channeled through Israeli universities or private companies even in cases where funding came exclusively from the Israeli government or other official agencies.

These were not ideal arrangements but they were aimed at overcoming Egyptian sensitivities and preventing internal opposition. Egypt, which itself is a donor country, did not want to be portrayed as being in need of Israeli technical assistance. Israel, for its part, had no intention of patronizing or humiliating Egypt. It promptly agreed to all Egyptian demands in this respect though they made the co-operation process cumbersome and difficult. In this field as in others, we still hoped at that stage that time – the great healer – would help remove artificial barriers and gradually foster less formal ties and procedures.

Within a very short time, it became clear that everything was eyewash. Egyptian universities, and certainly Arab universities, were barred to Israeli students. No Egyptian student was allowed to study in Israel. The American Scholarships Fund remained untouched for many years and it was finally transferred to other, more realistic purposes. The Albert Einstein fund bowed to Egyptian dictates and appointed a Venezuelan manager for the farm it had established near Alexandria. It also refrained from open contacts with Israel though the Israeli department of co-operation had advanced a substantial amount to allow it to begin its activities before it had raised the necessary funds. The American Agency for International Development (AID) financial allocations were not used for establishing tangible joint projects in the field – either in Israel or in Egypt. The money was partially spent on convening scientists' meetings in exotic locations around the world and on so-called joint research projects. In fact, the money was divided, almost equally, between the three partners for financing the research programs of their respective universities. The only human contacts between the Israeli and Egyptian scientists were two or three annual meetings in which participated the same group of scientists who had contrived to use the American funds for their exclusive benefit. Under Egyptian pressure, the trilateral program gradually became a purely Egyptian–American one and Israel was totally excluded from its daily management.

In my three first years (1980–83) in Cairo, neither I nor any other Israeli diplomat knew exactly what was going on in the framework of this program. The embassy as such was not involved and we were vaguely aware that some limited trilateral research co-operation was taking place. To the credit of the American program, it continued to function in periods of great tension even when the Egyptians froze the little normalization that existed. It seems that none of the three partners wanted to slaughter the 'goose that lays the golden eggs' and forfeit the opportunity to travel around the world on expenses. In the last 18 years, the USA has invested about $90 million in this program without achieving any concrete realization. This is exactly what the Egyptians wanted – the trilateral research program fitted perfectly their concept of co-operation (or rather non-co-operation) with Israel and it is why it has continued unhampered for so many years.

In the bilateral area, things were no more heart-warming. As I have mentioned, Shaul Eisenberg's proposal to develop 400,000 acres of desert land was angrily rejected for purely political reasons without even the semblance of serious debate. Up to 1993, no Israeli firm – private or public – was allowed to enter into direct and open co-operation with its Egyptian counterparts with regard to transferring technology or establishing joint ventures. However, in the positive period that prevailed in the wake of the change of governments in Israel (Rabin's period) and the beginning of negotiations with the PLO, a few companies did manage to reach arrangements in this realm, directly or through third parties. The volume of interaction was and remains insignificant. The little co-operation that exists depends totally on the Egyptian government's whims and its ever-fluctuating attitude towards Israel in the framework of its stick-and-carrot policy.

In the early 1980s, development co-operation was limited to a single Israeli agricultural expert whose task was to help diversify crops in the Suez region and introduce modern technologies. The Egyptians were aware that the Israeli government was financing the whole operation and that the expert carried a service passport and was working in close co-operation with the embassy in Cairo. Nevertheless, they insisted on camouflaging these facts and signed a sham contract with Agridev (an Israeli public-sector agricultural firm) that had been contracted for this purpose by the Israeli department of international co-operation. This firm became, and remains to this day, the official channel for agricultural co-operation with Egypt though every one knows that the government of Israel is behind all its operations and finances them partly or in full.

The Israeli expert in the early 1980s, Baradon, was allowed to move freely in the Suez region and was allocated a small experimental plot in one of the governmental farms near Ismailiah to carry out agricultural trials. However, he was not given minimal means and did not enjoy the genuine collaboration of his Egyptian counterparts. On several occasions, they intentionally cut the water supply to the Israeli plot or did not send tractors and other equipment to till the land. Once, after heavy rain, Baradon complained that his plot had been flooded because of lack of adequate drainage and demanded that immediate steps be taken to save the crops. His Egyptian colleagues said that he was raving since drainage pipes had been laid down a few months before winter. To substantiate their claim, they showed him cesspools scattered in the plot but he was not convinced – if the fields had been flooded it was obvious that the drainage system was not operational. The same night, he dug around the cesspools and was stunned to find that they were not connected to any pipes at all. The contractor who had carried out the drainage works had simply decided that pipes were superfluous and the supervisors did not notice their absence or perhaps had good reason to turn a blind eye. In another case, Baradon sent a few workers to spray pesticides ... After a few hours, he discovered that they were spraying pure Nile water and that the pesticides had vanished. He rushed to the embassy in Cairo threatening to bring the matter before the minister of agriculture himself. We calmed him down and instructed him to refrain from being the Keeper of Egyptian Morality – what the Egyptians did in their own country was not his or our business. No wonder that, under such conditions, agricultural results were slim despite all his efforts and skills. The political returns, on the other hand, compensated for this drawback. Every few months, Baradon plucked his crops and distributed crates of excellent vegetables to Egypt's elite (at the time, good-quality vegetables were lacking in Egypt). At our meetings with the ministers and high officials, they poured compliments on us and praised the allegedly wonderful work Israel was doing for Egypt. Baradon stayed three full years in Egypt and he could have made a dramatic improvement in vegetable-growing in the Suez region but this did not occur for reasons beyond his control and beyond that of the Israeli embassy in Cairo. The Egyptian authorities and his Egyptian counterparts were not interested for clearly political reasons and shortsighted considerations.

In the first months after our withdrawal from the greater part of Sinai, we candidly offered to help Egypt run, for a transitional period, a few farms that we had created in the desert at great effort. We suggested leaving our experts on the ground so that they transferred the farms in an orderly manner to their Egyptian counterparts and guided them on cultivation in difficult desert conditions. The Egyptians politely refused and said that they doubted if they could upkeep the farms because of lack of funds and marketing outlets. We volunteered to put at their disposal our agricultural marketing network throughout the world as well as the Eilat airport facilities to make the farms more efficient and economically sound. We even found Jewish investors (not Israelis) who were ready not only to finance the whole operation on a joint-venture basis but also undertake to buy the whole farms' production at international market prices. To our great surprise, the Egyptians dragged their feet and we could not understand why – logically, they should have jumped at the opportunity. Finally, high officials in the foreign ministry counseled us, in informal friendly conversations, not to insist because the real reason for Egypt's procrastination was that 'the Israelis have been in Sinai too long and have grown into the habit of considering it theirs'. Egypt preferred that they keep out of Sinai for a few years. They swore 'on all that is dear to us' that there was no hidden intention and that Egypt did not want to forestall agriculture co-operation with Israel. They brought as ultimate evidence of their truthfulness the fruitful co-operation in the Suez region and the wonderful work the Israeli expert was supposedly doing! This time, we got the message loud and clear and we stopped nagging the Egyptians. Soon, the matter became irrelevant and the desert gained back the few acres we had snatched from it.

We tried our luck in other fields but the results were no less frustrating and the Egyptians' behavior no less offensive. Let me provide only a few examples. In the first stage, we offered to co-operate in the field of health – a field of prime necessity for Egypt. After great efforts and much nagging, the Egyptians allowed us to bring a delegation of top Israeli experts to discuss possibilities of co-operation with the Egyptian ministry of health. The negotiations with the Egyptian professionals were thorough, straightforward and friendly. A detailed program of co-operation was drawn up. After months of pointless discussions, the Egyptian foreign ministry informed the embassy that 'the implementation of the program that has been agreed upon is impossible because the Medical Association has banned all contacts with Israel'.

We suggested informal co-operation between the universities of the two countries, in addition to the American Scholarships Program. Again, we found much interest on the face of it and began preparing detailed plans of action but finally, after months of discussions, we received exactly the same answer. We were told that 'the Academics' Association is boycotting co-operation with Israel and the idea is therefore not feasible.

In a country "respectful" of academic freedoms like Egypt, it is impossible to compel universities to act against their will and best judgement.'

We suggested co-operation in the field of youth activities so that the new generations should learn to work together in a spirit of understanding and friendship. This proposal was rejected outright without any pretense of going through the motions – the Egyptians were not ready to allow even minimal contacts between the youngsters of the two countries. We took advantage of President Navon's visit to Egypt (early 1981) to raise the matter again directly with President Sadat himself. He immediately agreed to an exchange of youth delegations and to the holding of joint summer camps and seminars. The bureaucracy had to bow to the President's direct instructions and a delegation of Israeli secondary school students was allowed to come to Egypt. They were received very well and the Egyptian students showed them much warmth and friendship. However, it proved to be a one-shot operation – there was no return visit by the Egyptians and all other planned joint youth activities remained on paper.

The Israeli police force proposed to collaborate professionally with the Egyptian police in the fields of information exchange and combating crime and especially drug-smuggling. After many efforts, and as usual much nagging, the embassy succeeded in receiving an agreement in principle from the foreign and interior ministries. We thought that in such a sensitive field in which the benefit would be significant for both countries, the Egyptians would not pull our leg, and that police co-operation would soon start for real. However, the efforts exerted by the Israeli police to infuse life into the agreement were foiled. All repeated attempts to establish contact with the Egyptian police – either directly or through the embassy – remained unanswered. The foreign ministry informed us that the Israeli police should go through Interpol channels 'since relations between the two police forces have an international aspect'. When no reply came through Interpol, we were told (again by the same high officials in the foreign ministry) that the Israeli police should have contacted the Egyptian police directly 'since the relations are to be essentially bilateral and Interpol is not directly involved'. We again complied despite the obvious contradiction but the interminable merry-go-round continued. We finally succeeded in squeezing from the Egyptians an invitation to dispatch to Cairo an Israeli police delegation to work out a joint program of co-operation. As always, the delegation was received with the best Egyptian hospitality and had fruitful discussions with its Egyptian counterparts. Positive results were reached – relatively easily – on a series of important topics: e.g. co-operation in the struggle against drugs, prevention of goods smuggling, exchange of information. Channels for direct and close contacts between the two police forces were also established. Everything seemed to be perfect, but the reader must already have guessed that not a single item of this program was ever implemented. The Egyptians could not, this time, claim that the Egyptian police was boycotting Israel like the private professional associations, but in informal conversations they advised us not to insist further. They explained that 'at this stage, co-operation with the Israeli police will be viewed by Arab public opinion as aimed against the Palestinians and will substantiate the slanderous allegations that Egypt has betrayed the Arab cause and ceased to uphold Palestinian legitimate rights.'

Israel suggested fostering co-operation between the local authorities and promoting twinning between cities in Egypt and Israel. The Egyptians agreed to host a sizable delegation of Israeli mayors and interior ministry high officials. They were received not only lavishly but also very cordially and had discussions with their Egyptian counterparts, up to the small hours of the morning, defining a series of fields of interaction and co-operation. And again, as with previous Israeli delegations, immediately after the visit all that had been decided upon went into oblivion and never became reality. All our efforts to bring about at least a return visit to Israel by the Egyptian local authorities remained fruitless.

So many frustrated (and frustrating) efforts in such a wide range of fields made it crystal-clear that Egypt was not interested in technical co-operation with Israel and that this was the outcome of a policy deter-mined at the highest levels of power. After a few more months and a few more failed attempts, we grasped the hard facts of life but we nevertheless persisted in our efforts to promote development co-operation, hoping that we would find a gleam of light at the end of the tunnel. The Egyptians encouraged us to continue and, from time to time, made their positions apparently more flexible and fanned our hopes. To be quite frank, both sides were interested in continuing the game. They had a common inter-est in creating the perception that relations between the two countries were developing rapidly and that they had established a fruitful rela-tionship in a series of fields. The numerous normalization committees that were at the time working full steam ahead were also meant to strengthen this unfounded perception and project to internal and inter-national public opinion a positive image of the peace process. As the reader is certainly aware, perceptions are no less important than reality and are frequently even more important.

In fact, after much nagging on our part, the Egyptians solved (and also disposed of) any new proposal for co-operation by agreeing to the visit of an Israeli delegation to discuss the possibilities directly with the relevant professional authorities. For us, even such a slim result was an important success since it allowed the embassy staff to diversify its interaction with the Egyptian top bureaucracy, which was normally inaccessible to Israeli diplomats. As I have pointed out, we interacted mostly with the foreign ministry officials in the normalization committees and other realms, and we seldom had opportunities to meet with the professional bureaucracy. At the time, we still thought naïvely that expanding the scope of our human contacts and deepening our relations with the Egyptian bureau-cracy would create a dynamic of its own that would, in the long run, break the wall of hostility that surrounded us. We also hoped that, through a series of incremental changes, we would gradually succeed in raising the Ground Level of Relations that had been determined by the Egyptians from the outset. We never despaired. If we found a door closed or if it was slammed in our face, we simply tried another door and, when all doors were apparently inaccessible, we tried the windows and the hatches. And when these were also locked and nailed down, we continued to look for some crack through which we could get in. It was not a rewarding or pleasant task, but this was the job for which we had been sent to Egypt, and was what was expected from us.

However, we clearly had no chance. The Egyptian approach to devel-opment and technical co-operation with Israel – like everything else pertaining to relations with Israel – had obviously been decided at the highest levels. The entire Egyptian bureaucracy was under strict instruc-tions to stick to the established line of conduct and not deviate from it by a single inch without specific authorization. No doubt Sadat – and after him Mubarak – were not only aware of the situation, but also condoned the stringent manner in which this policy was implemented by the bureaucracy. Sadat, contrary to Mubarak, left some room for flexibility and a few safety valves to release mounting pressure. He personally inter-vened several times and instructed the bureaucracy to be more accom-modating on specific issues (but he never went as far as to change the overall policy). More than once, his intervention did not help, or helped only temporarily. In the last resort, the bureaucracy always succeeded in bypassing instructions and reverting to the basic line of conduct (prob-ably with Sadat's tacit agreement).

Let me be a little more specific. When we complained to President Sadat about the slow progress of agricultural co-operation despite his instructions, he did not overrule the bureaucracy or put pressure on it to mend its ways. He merely suggested that the best way of showing everyone that the highest authority in Egypt was in favor of technical co-operation with Israel and had faith in its expertise was to have Israeli experts plant a citrus grove in his private farm in Mit Abu Elkom (his native village). We jumped at the suggestion and, in record time, we brought the most advanced irrigation systems and planted several acres of Israeli citrus saplings in Sadat's farm. As one could expect, it did not have any impact – even marginal – on the general Egyptian approach to co-operation with Israel. Nevertheless, both sides were happy to point to the citrus grove in the president's farm as tangible testimony of the harmonious co-operation that had developed between the two countries since the establishment of peace. In Sadat's farm, the situation was not so rosy. The Israeli expert supervising the professional aspects met with difficulties at each step and did not obtain the collaboration he needed from the farm's staff and Sadat's household. The grove deteriorated and, after his tragic death, our expert continued for a few weeks until we received a hint that it was now proper to discontinue the project; for obvious reasons, we promptly complied. I do not know in what state the grove is today and whether it still exists. During my second stay in Egypt (1990–93), I did not visit Sadat's village and, though I met several times with his gracious wife, Jihan, I did not ask her about the grove, not wanting 'to sprinkle salt on her wounds' (she had been badly abused and slandered after Sadat's assassination).

I confess that, after I left Egypt in 1983, I did not follow closely what was taking place in the realm of technical co-operation with Egypt. I was completely immersed in my work as permanent representative to the UN in Geneva. Frankly speaking, I never gave special weight to that aspect of our interaction with Egypt since I was convinced that Egypt had no interest in fostering co-operation with Israel. Indeed, this was the conviction of most of the Israeli diplomats in Cairo – after the first few months and several disappointments, we had awoken from our rosy dreams and reached the conclusion that we were facing a concerted Egyptian policy. The efforts exerted in this field by the embassy staff – I among them – stemmed from the dynamics of the situation and our dedication to our mission. Zvi Mazel, the then political counselor (and current Israeli ambassador to Egypt) was in charge of promoting co-operation with Egypt and dealing with the day-to-day problems. He frequently lost his temper over the Egyptian behavior. I too lost my temper quite a few times, not so much because of the Egyptians' procrastination and last-minute refusals but because I was deeply offended by their *modus operandi*. They misled us repeatedly, gave us obvious pretexts and treated us as if we were retarded children unable to understand what was going on under our noses. We played the game because we had no alternative but, needless to say, we did not take pleasure in it.

Towards the end of 1986, I was appointed head of the department of international co-operation in the foreign ministry and I had to devote my attention to co-operation matters. I was directly responsible for Israeli co-operation worldwide, including with Egypt. I decided, in conjunction with Moshe Sasson (my ambassador) who was still in Egypt, to try and stimulate development co-operation and put it on the right track. I received the enthusiastic approval of the then director-general, General (res.) Avraham (Avrasha) Tamir, to give priority to Egypt (budget-wise) and try to remove the obstacles placed by the Egyptian authorities. Moshe recommended putting special emphasis on agricultural co-operation. He had developed a close personal friendship with the minister of agriculture, Professor Yusuf Wali, who, since I had left Egypt in 1983, had been promoted to deputy prime minister and appointed secretary-general of the ruling party. He believed that, with Wali's help, it would be easier for us to overcome bureaucratic and political difficulties. It was also his assessment, in the light of a few deals with the private sector approved by the Egyptian government, that there might have been a change in the basic Egyptian policy on agricultural co-operation with Israel. Professor Wali himself was (and always had been) genuinely interested in fostering co-operation – and not in throwing sand in our eyes as many of his colleagues did. Moshe and I had very high expectations and hoped that he would seriously promote important agricultural joint projects. We decided that I would come to Egypt on the first possible occasion and work out a detailed plan of action with Wali and Moshe.

Ambassador Sasson informed Wali of my appointment and requested him to convene the agricultural joint committee to study new concepts of co-operation between the two countries and several ideas for joint projects. It was the only joint committee that still met regularly, once or twice a year, owing to Wali's active support (and maybe to cover up putting all other committees in deep freeze). I came with a big delegation that included renowned agricultural experts, among them the director of the Israeli Agricultural Planning Authority, Professor Shmuel Pohorilis, who for many years had chaired the joint committee and was a close friend of Wali. For the first time, the head of the department of international co-operation in the foreign ministry (myself) and Itshak Abt, the director of Sinadco (the department's agricultural branch), were allowed to take part. After many years during which agricultural co-operation with Egypt was camouflaged as a private-sector venture, we could finally step out of the closet.

As always, Wali was full of compliments about the Israeli experts' so-called outstanding achievements and he stated emphatically that Israel had practically saved Egyptian agriculture and caused it to progress dramatically. He took us personally to see by ourselves the marvelous things that the Israeli experts were doing. In reality, there was very little to see. There were no more than 10 acres of joint-experiment plots scattered over a few experimental stations, financed by American grants. Agridev (the private agricultural firm allegedly contracted directly by the Egyptian government) was active in two government farms, the first in Gumeisa in the Delta region, some 120 kilometers from Cairo, and the second in Nubaria, some 50 kilometers from Alexandria. The allegedly wonderful project in the Suez region was so wonderful that it had been discontinued. We kept one Israeli expert in each of the two locations but their hands were tied and their Egyptian counterparts hampered their work at each step. In Gumeisa, a farm of some 40,000 acres, less than 25 acres had been allocated to our expert to carry out his experiments. In Nubaria, also a farm of about 50,000 acres of desert land, a plot of around 50 acres had been allocated to the Israeli expert. In both plots, only one third of the land was under actual cultivation and one could notice no substantial difference as to yields, farming methods or equipment, in comparison with other fields in the neighborhood. Incidentally, as the reader already knows, the Israeli government, through the department of international co-operation in the foreign ministry, financed the whole operation.

During the visit to Gumeisa, the farm manager told me bluntly, pointing to the Israeli plot: 'This field is totally unnecessary. We do not need it. It is not an agricultural field; it is a political one! It exists only because the agriculture minister, Professor Wali, wants it to be here.' He added that 'he did not need Israeli experts who were less competent than he and received a salary 50 times bigger than his'. In Nubaria on the other hand, the farm manager, Fuad Abu Hadab (one of Wali's closest collaborators), was most enthusiastic and urged us to increase the scope of co-operation. He urged us to invest more money, equipment and expertise in developing the entire farm and not only the experimental plot. Wali strongly supported his request and stressed that he would personally remove any political obstacle that other government departments (read: the security services) might raise.

From Nubaria, we rode with the minister and Fuad a few kilometers further, to the farm that had been established by the Einstein Fund under the management of a Venezuelan expert. There was literally nothing to see, though hundreds of thousands of dollars had been poured into the farm. Wali, literally choking with rage, threatened to discontinue the whole project saying: 'The Einstein people think they can run a farm in the desert from a five-star hotel in Cairo, sipping iced beer. They should learn from you, the Israelis, how to work!' I tried to calm the minister down but he decided that, from that very moment, the Einstein farm had ceased to be an independent entity and would come under the scope of the Israeli–Egyptian agricultural co-operation program with the direct involvement of Israeli experts.

Notwithstanding Wali's repeated praise of Israel's 'outstanding contribution to Egyptian agriculture' and the compliments he poured on the Israeli experts, I realized that the situation in the field was dreadful and far from justifying the minister's enthusiasm. In substance, the manner in which our experts worked was not very different from the Einstein Fund pattern. Our two experts resided in Cairo and had to travel thousands of kilometers each week to reach the farms where they worked. Understandably, they stayed there only for a few hours and found good reasons not to come as much as they reasonably could. The average annual cost of an expert was about $150,000, not including the investment and running expenses of his plot. Over the years, substantial sums were spent (and if we add American contributions, we reach astronomical amounts) without any tangible results and this despite the fact that the Egyptians claimed that there were no restrictions on agricultural co-operation with Israel and praised it loudly. The reality was totally different; there were more statements about co-operation and its wonderful results than real co-operation in the field that were substantiated by perceptible achievements. True, Egypt bought some seeds and agricultural equipment from Israel and allowed Israeli agricultural companies to work in Egypt with private Egyptian companies. It did so, however, only because of Professor Wali's personal support and the unceasing pressure he exerted on the system to alleviate the restrictions on agricultural co-operation. From a political standpoint the Egyptians used the little agricultural co-operation that existed as an alibi to cover the almost total lack of co-operation in other fields. Each time we voiced complaints that Egypt purposely foiled each and every co-operation project that Israel put forward, they brandished the supposedly thriving agricultural co-operation between the two countries as the best testimony for their good faith and goodwill. They also never failed in their meetings with the Americans and Europeans to praise the excellence of the agricultural co-operation with Israel and stress the good and open relationship that was allegedly developing between the two countries as indicated by this co-operation.

At the end of our visit to the 'Israeli farms', I shared my misgivings with Wali frankly (in practically the same terms that I have used here). In view of our good personal relationship, I could allow myself to put aside diplomatic language and speak straight to the point. I made it crystal-clear that if he really wanted to foster genuine agricultural co-operation between Egypt and Israel, he had to change Egypt's basic approach to development co-operation with Israel, remove all artificial barriers and reach a bilateral agreement with the Israeli government and not through proxies. Furthermore, he should allow the Israeli department of international co-operation to co-ordinate and manage directly and openly, together with the Egyptian agriculture ministry, all joint projects including the American research program, the Einstein farm and the Israeli projects. I also hinted that he should consider entrusting co-operation with Israel to officials who believed that it served Egypt's best interests and keep away those who had been hampering its expansion from the first.

As I had expected, the minister's reaction was positive and he asked me for concrete ideas. I presented a detailed plan of action that had been thoroughly prepared by Professor Pohirilis and Itschak Abt in co-ordination with Ambassador Sasson and me. The centerpiece was the planting of a 300-acre orchard in Nubaria and the developing of 200 more acres, half for grapes and half for melon and vegetable cultivation. I also suggested putting the Einstein farm under Israeli management as he had wanted (in co-ordination with the Einstein Fund) and settling there several hundred unemployed agricultural school graduates. The plan included:

- Establishing three modern saplings and seed nurseries fully equipped by Israel;
- Distributing free of charge improved seeds and saplings to the traditional farmers;

- Building 300 greenhouses for vegetable production;
- Introducing modern irrigation systems in the Delta region;
- Improving cattle, goat and sheep herds with Israeli stock and breeding methods;
- Increasing the milk production of several thousand cows that had been purchased in Israel in the early 1980s;
- Organizing in Egypt a series of on-the-spot courses and middle-level seminars;
- Organizing in Israel high-level seminars and further training for top officers;
- Training in the Kibbutz and the Moshav (two settlement methods specific to Israel) hundreds of secondary-school graduates with the purpose of preparing them to settle in the new lands;
- Substantially increasing the number of Israeli experts in Egypt to meet the needs of the new projects and the expansion of the old ones;
- Creating a regional agricultural machinery complex to service the needs of the traditional farmers and act as a prototype for other regions.

Wali listened attentively, asked a few questions, added a few ideas of his own and approved the whole plan of action as I had presented it. He requested me to prepare a summary in writing for formal approval by the agricultural joint committee in their session the following day so that we could move ahead rapidly. Pohirilis, Abt and myself worked feverishly the whole night and prepared in handwriting a comprehensive and detailed document. We feared that we would not have time to type it before the meeting but the minister instructed his chief of cabinet to take care of the matter and within a few hours the document was ready just in time for the committee's session.

At the meeting, we were stunned to note that Wali had dismissed the Egyptian co-chairman of the committee, the deputy minister of agriculture Adel Biltagy (one of the opponents of co-operation with Israel to whom I had hinted in my conversation with the minister). To our great pleasure, he had appointed in his place Fuad Abu Hadab, the manager of the Nubaria farm and his close friend. In his opening statement, the minister frankly disclosed that he had removed Biltagy because he was against widening co-operation with Israel and would have sabotaged the whole program of co-operation had he stayed in charge of it. He added that, from now on, he would appoint to work with Israel only officials who were dedicated to peace and convinced beyond any doubt that it was in Egypt's interest to co-operate with Israel in the realm of agriculture. He described them as 'the believers'. Towards the end of the meeting, Ambassador Sasson joined us and was very pleased when the committee unanimously approved the document that we had prepared without changing a single word. In a short ceremony, attended by the minister, both co-chairmen signed a protocol finalizing the plan of action and calling for its prompt implementation.

After the signing, I requested Wali to give me two letters – one for the American AID and the second for the Dutch ministry of co-operation – by which he authorized the Israeli department of international co-operation to seek their financial support for the approved projects. He agreed without hesitation and asked me to prepare a draft. I did so willingly and the same evening, at a dinner in his private house, he handed me the two letters duly bearing his signature and the seal of the agriculture ministry. He told me that he had also sent copies to the Egyptian foreign ministry and to the ambassadors of the USA and Holland in Cairo, with whom he intended to meet personally and stress the importance of the projects for Egypt.

For the first time since the opening of the embassy in Cairo, a significant program of co-operation had been agreed upon. If it had been implemented (even partially), it would have changed drastically the relationship between Egypt and Israel in the agricultural field and would no doubt have reflected positively on the whole spectrum of relations between the two countries. This was exactly what Egypt did not want and, from the first day, the implementation of the program – despite Wali's unceasing support and active assistance – met with foot-dragging, bad will and sabotaging. For our part, we took the matter very seriously: Pohirilis and Abt began urgently to prepare implementation plans for each of the projects and to recruit the necessary experts; and I flew to Washington and Amsterdam to raise part of the funding. I was stunned when my interlocutors showed me a letter from Biltagy in which he wrote explicitly – in his capacity as the official responsible for foreign relations in the Egyptian agriculture ministry – that they were to discard his minister's letter. He claimed that Wali had been induced by deceit to sign it and did not realize what he was signing. Naturally, my interlocutors knew that there was no foundation whatsoever to such allegations. They clearly understood that a minister of Wali's stature could not have been lured into signing a letter that did not reflect his own wishes exactly. Furthermore, their ambassadors in Cairo had reported that he had personally summoned them and requested their support for the Israeli–Egyptian projects. Nevertheless, they could not disregard Biltagy's official letter and had to act with caution. They gave me an agreement in principle to help in financing the projects but they demanded a formal request from the Egyptian foreign ministry in order to avoid misunderstandings and possible diplomatic clashes.

I relayed to Moshe Sasson what had happened and how embarrassed I felt. He met immediately with Wali, who claimed to be as stunned as I had been by Biltagy's letter and promised to instruct the foreign ministry to send an official request for financial support to Washington and Amsterdam. The reader will not be surprised to read that this request was never sent and that Sasson, and his successor Shimon Shamir, received promise after promise which, as usual, were not kept. It seems that Wali had gone too far when he had agreed to the plan of action presented by Israel. Alibi or no alibi – he had been overruled by a higher authority that would not permit Israel to break out of the narrow framework of relations that had been decided upon from the outset. During the rest of my tenure in the international co-operation department, I managed to push forward only a tiny part of the program that had been established with Wali. In 1989, I was transferred to the UN in New York and again lost active interest in the matter.

Upon my return to Egypt in 1990, I found that very little progress had been made. The students' settlement project had been frozen. The Einstein farm had become an experimental site for greenhouse vegetables under the guidance of an Israeli expert but the Egyptians had no interest in the experiments: there was no serious scientific follow-up, no recording of results and no attempt at popularizing cultivation methods. We had left the Gumeisa farm in the Delta (during my tenure in the international co-operation department) because the Egyptians had refused to let us develop there a significant project, and there was no point in maintaining a 'political field' as the Egyptians described it. A number of courses and seminars had been held over the years but no graduates had been allowed to train in Israel (though arrangements to receive them had been made several times at Wali's request). There were no visible sign of the greenhouse project, although (during my tenure) we had provided 100 fully-equipped greenhouses and had delegated the head of the greenhouse department in our ministry of agriculture to help the Egyptians for a three-month mission. Indeed, to this very day, I do not know what happened to the greenhouses that we donated; no one in Egypt seemed to be aware that they had ever reached that country. The livestock projects never took off. The modern irrigation project in the traditional villages was vetoed by the Egyptian security services on the grounds that they could not guarantee our experts' safety (I later learned that the real reason was that the Egyptians did not want an Israeli presence in the over-populated Delta region). Sophisticated irrigation equipment for several thousand dollars (donated by the department of international co-operation during my tenure) lay in the stores of the Egyptian agriculture ministry as if it were useless scrap iron. The joint research projects, financed by the Americans, continued to be conducted along the same lines as in the past and remained an entirely American program, with no tangible realizations in the field. The three nurseries had not been implemented and as a consequence the distribution of improved seeds and saplings to the traditional farmers never began. The livestock and cows projects, as well as the establishment of a regional agricultural machinery complex, never went beyond the blueprint stage.

The only ray of light was the Nubaria farm where part of the project agreed upon had been implemented. Fuad Abu Hadab, the manager, had the ambition and the drive to develop his farm and he succeeded in removing several obstacles. He found in us a reliable and efficient partner. During my tenure in the department of international co-operation, Israel provided seed money and we had planted some 200 acres of plum, apricot, apple and pear trees. Later, the orchard size was slightly increased and other components of the project were partially implemented. However, the department of international co-operation had been formally pushed out of the picture (though not in reality). The deputy minister for agriculture, Adel Biltagy, had had the last word and the project had been entrusted to Agridev, just as it had in the past. Yet, despite all the obstacles, we had succeeded in creating in the desert an impressive monument to Egyptian–Israeli agricultural co-operation.

During my tenure as ambassador to Egypt (1990–93), I tried strenuously, but with no significant success, to revive some of the projects and develop those which had started. I found in my successor in the department of international co-operation, Shlomo Binou, an attentive ear and a helping hand. As always, the problem was not at the Israeli end but at the Egyptian end. Egypt's basic policy towards technical co-operation (or should I say non-co-operation) with Israel had not changed and, on the contrary, had become more stringent. Notwithstanding the support of the agriculture minister, Professor Wali, and his genuine interest in fostering co-operation – using all the leverage he had as deputy prime minister and secretary-general of the party – all I could achieve was of a temporary nature and did not leave any tangible trace in the field. One monument marking Israeli–Egyptian co-operation (the Nubaria orchard) was more than enough for the Egyptians. The number of reciprocal agricultural visits increased substantially and hundreds of school graduates went for short periods of training in Israel (and came back enthusiastic). Yet despite all our efforts, no real project of significance took off. Since the embassy staff had been reduced, I entrusted co-operation matters to the economic counselor, Moshe Dana. He fulfilled this task with efficiency and grace but no real progress was made.

I have to confess that my failure to promote significant agricultural co-operation (and indeed any kind of co-operation in any field whatsoever) during my tenure as ambassador distressed me, even though it was through no fault of mine. It was simply impossible to fight the watertight system established by the Egyptians to prevent co-operation from developing and foil any attempt to foster it. Nevertheless, I had a few rewarding incidents related to development co-operation that gave me immense pleasure. The agriculture minister, Professor Wali, organized a visit to the new land settlements for the then American ambassador Robert Pelletreau (later, the under-secretary of state for the middle east) and myself. Wali's goal was to show Pelletreau the wonderful work Israel was doing and motivate him to support financially some new joint projects (that never came about!). When we reached the most important settlement, the settlers (most of them graduates from agricultural schools) received us with great enthusiasm. Within a few minutes, the American ambassador was forgotten and all the students fussed around me and requested me to give them in Arabic a short insight into Israel. I complied willingly, not forgetting to praise my American colleague and the USA for their tremendous support for Egyptian agriculture and the Israeli–Egyptian programs. The settlers bombarded me with questions and some of them, who had been to training courses in Israel, spoke warmly of their recollections of Israel and stressed the relevance of its experience for Egypt. They also offered me as a token of friendship a beautifully engraved copper plate manufactured by one of them, and poured on me from every side embraces and marks of friendship. I confess that I was profoundly touched but Pelletreau was literally flabbergasted. He never imagined that the ambassador of Israel would be received with such warmth by hundreds of Egyptian graduates (universities in Egypt are hotbeds of hatred towards Israel). I was somewhat embarrassed that the ambassador of the USA, which donated billions of dollars to Egypt each year and invested in the economy billions of dollars more, had been neglected for the representative of a small country like Israel but, deep inside, I could not refrain from feeling pride and satisfaction.

One other incident of the kind, which gave me even more pleasure, was when Wali dismissed his deputy, Adel Biltagy, and restored him to his previous anonymous job. It was an open secret that he opposed co-operation with Israel, put spokes in the wheels of each and every project, and torpedoed all agreements reached with his minister. Well informed persons also knew that, a few days earlier, I had requested an urgent meeting with Wali and had complained about Biltagy's systematic sabotaging of Israeli projects. They also knew that this time I had not only hinted that he should be kept away from dealing with Israeli co-operation, but had also requested that the minister take immediate steps. Biltagy's sudden dismissal, only a few days after my meeting with the minister, convinced everyone that the dismissal was the direct outcome of that meeting and should be attributed to me. In reality, that was not the case – Wally, notwithstanding his political weight, could never have afforded to dismiss Biltagy on an Israel-related matter. A few times in the past, he had removed him from dealing with Israeli projects but he had always reinstated him after a short while. Wali – better than any one else – knew that Biltagy was indeed implementing the official Egyptian policy towards Israel set by the highest level of power and was merely following instructions. As cynical as it might sound, it is my earnest belief that there was a distribution of work between the two with respect to Israel. The minister was always the good guy, who went out of his way to promote co-operation with Israel, and his deputy Biltagy was the bad guy whose unpleasant task was to prevent the minister's promises from becoming a reality. In his function as the official responsible for the foreign relations of the agriculture ministry, he was the watchdog and his task was to prevent co-operation with Israel from overstepping the parameters decided at the highest level. It is a fact that Wali did not dismiss Biltagy even after he had written officially to the American and Dutch governments depicting him as someone who did not know what he was doing.

The real reason for Biltagy's dismissal was contain in an incident to do with relations with Canada. Wali had appointed a delegation to represent Egypt in an agricultural congress and had written a personal letter to the Canadian ambassador in Cairo urgently requesting him to grant visas to the delegation members. Biltagy, who did not approve of the delegation's composition, wrote an official letter to the ambassador requesting him to deny the visas because the composition of the delega-tion had not been approved beforehand by the Egyptian government. The delegation did not go to Canada and Egypt did not participate in the con-gress. This time Wali could not swallow the affront without losing face and jeopardizing his position. His reaction was immediate and crushing: Biltagy was dismissed and returned to the minor position of director of the agricultural research department – far from the decision-making center and deprived of all the fringe benefits that came with the position of deputy minister. (For those who do not know, I have to specify again that most ministers in Egypt stem from the civil service and resume their regular positions after they conclude their term of office.) I confess that I was pleased with Biltagy's predicament – over the years, he had made many problems for me. I did not deny that his dismissal was the result of his negative attitude towards co-operation with Israel and of my personal influence with the minister; I let the rumor circulate unhindered in government and diplomatic circles. In any case, no one in Egypt would have believed my denials just as no one believed my repeated denials of the preposterous and totally unfounded Egyptian contention that the Jews ruled the world.

In conclusion I have to point out, with great sorrow, that almost 20 years since the establishment of diplomatic relations and more than 22 years since the conclusion of a fully-fledged peace accord, Israel has not succeeded in getting Egypt to develop minimal technical co-operation between the two countries. Here and there (especially in agriculture) one can find a relatively small number of facts that seem to contradict this assertion but, if one digs deeper, one will reach the inevitable conclusion that these are exceptions that confirm the rule. Egypt, for its own con-siderations, is not interested in any kind of co-operation with Israel and it has taken – and still takes – all necessary measures to prevent any significant co-operation from developing, both at the private and govern-mental levels. The little that has been achieved in agriculture is the result of strenuous efforts by Israel and the constant support of the Egyptian agriculture minister, Professor Wali, who is, as he himself puts it, a 'believer'. However, these small achievements are from reflecting the enormous potential that exists in this sector, despite the fact that they are used by the Egyptians to cover up for the total lack of co-operation in other sectors. President Mubarak, in his conversations with foreign personalities, often points to the 'close and fruitful agricultural co-operation' with Israel as excellent evidence of the 'good relations existing between the two countries'. With all due respect to President Mubarak, such satisfaction is entirely unfounded. I maintain my contention that there is practically no technical co-operation between the two countries and that Egypt is solely to blame for this situation. Equally, the loss is also solely hers. Israel has done its utmost to develop technical co-operation with Egypt in each and every possible field but, as the saying goes, one can take a horse to water but one cannot make it drink.

15 · Negotiating Palestinian Autonomy

The subject matter of this book is the relations between Israel and Egypt. I will not, therefore, deal with matters related to the granting of autonomous status to the Palestinians in the territories occupied by Israel in 1967, as embedded in the Camp David accords. Neither will I deal with the arguments or counter-arguments put forward by Egypt and Israel in almost three years of negotiations on the issue. As is well known, the Palestinians themselves categorically refused to take part in any negotiations based on these accords. In fact, the discussions were held between the best man (Egypt) and the bride (Israel) without the participation of the groom (the Palestinians), who had made it quite clear that he had no interest whatsoever in the marriage. I will restrict myself here to those elements that have a bearing on the bilateral relationship between Israel and Egypt: the real positions of the two sides, their negotiating tactics, and the impact of these on their interaction.

Very few people have taken the trouble to read the Camp David accords in full. World public opinion, and to a great extent the United Nations and most foreign ministries (not only in the Arab states), perceived the accords as aimed at establishing a separate peace between Egypt and Israel. They were seen as exclusively tackling those aspects of the Arab–Israeli conflict directly relating to the two countries, and the setting up of mechanisms for cementing and preserving peace between them. No doubt, this was basically the principal purpose of the Camp David process, but it was far from being the only purpose. This fact can be seen immediately in the accords' heading, 'The Camp David Accords for Comprehensive Peace in the Middle East'. A quick glance across the contents would also show that, in addition to the bilateral aspects, the accords clearly specified the principles on which a comprehensive peace in the region would be based. They also defined in great detail the ways and means for attaining this goal on the Palestinian and Jordanian sides. For the first time, Israel explicitly recognized the legitimate rights of the Palestinian people and abandoned the narrow formulation 'the rights of the Arab population in Judea, Samaria and the Gaza Strip' (the biblical Hebrew names of the territories) which it had used until then. Basically, the agreement determined that Egypt, Jordan and Israel would conduct negotiations to find an agreed solution to the Palestinian issue in all its aspects. Furthermore, it was clearly specified that the Palestinians residing in the West Bank and Gaza Strip and other Palestinians to be agreed upon (hinting at the participation of the Palestinian diaspora) would be included in the Jordanian delegation.

It also stipulated that the negotiations would have two phases and defined the chronological-framework and the scope of each phase. The first phase was to focus on the establishment of Palestinian autonomy – for a transitional period of five years – and on the powers that would be transferred to the Palestinians with the aim of giving them full control of their internal affairs. Furthermore, in this phase were to be determined the modalities for electing a Palestinian self-governing authority which would replace the Israeli military government and its civil administration. In the second phase, that was to begin no later than three years after the election and empowerment of the Palestinian authority, negotiations – on the basis of UN Security Council 242 and 338 – were to be held on the final status of the West Bank and the Gaza Strip. It was explicitly stated that, in this second phase, a delegation representing the Palestinian authority would participate in the negotiations – in its own right and not as part of the Jordanian delegation as in the first phase. The Camp David agreement also stipulated that, in parallel, Jordan and Israel would conduct negotiations with the aim of signing a fully-fledged peace agreement between the two of them. In this agreement, the parties were to determine not only the borders between the two countries and the substance and scope of the relations between them, but also the security measures that would be taken for preserving the peace indefinitely.

In order to conclude the bilateral aspects of the agreement, the multilateral aspects, on which Egypt and Israel were still far apart, were purposely drafted with a certain vagueness and included key words that allowed each side to interpret them in a manner reflecting its own approach. The detailed negotiation on the real significance of the Palestinian clauses, as well as those referring to third parties (Syria and Jordan), was left to the future. However, throughout the discussions, both sides did not conceal that they were in diametrical disagreement on their interpretation of the multilateral issues. For Israel, the granting of a rather limited autonomy to the Palestinians – residing in the territories (and only to them) – was an adequate solution to the Palestinian issue and a final word on the matter. It was the maximum it was ready to concede – the problem of the Palestinian exiles was to be resolved exclusively within an Arab framework. Israel also adamantly rejected any possibility of transferring sovereignty on all or part of the territories to the Palestinians and it was determined to proceed unimpeded with its settlement policy. It upheld the opinion that Jerusalem was not negotiable under any circumstances and vehemently opposed recognizing the PLO as a legitimate political entity or negotiating, directly or indirectly, with it. For Egypt, on the other hand, autonomy was to be the waiting room for statehood, sovereignty and independence, and was to lead ineluctably to the establishment of a Palestinian state in all the territories occupied by Israel in 1967, including East Jerusalem. Egypt also demanded the immediate discontinuation of the building of new Israeli settlements in the territories or extending the existing ones. It held the opinion that Israel should recognize the PLO and enter into direct negotiations with it – both on the transitional period and the final-status issues. In Egypt's eyes, its stand represented a major concession when compared to the Arab traditional positions, which Israel should grab with both hands. Until then, all Arab states (including Egypt) had negated the very right of Israel to exist and rejected any peaceful solution not based on the 1947 partition resolution of the UN General Assembly (which allocated much less territory to Israel).

Both Egypt and Israel were adamant they would not budge from their respective stands and expressed their reservations and different interpretations in separate letters to President Carter. These letters were attached to the main body of the accords to mark the divergences between the parties and to avoid future misunderstandings. Egypt did not conceal or camouflage its position – from the first moment, it stated in clear-cut words and on every occasion (in the negotiations, in public statements and in private conversations) its stand on the Palestinian issue and the solutions it advocated. Israel, probably because of its eagerness to foster peace with Egypt (and maybe out of political shortsightedness), chose to believe that Egypt did not mean what it was advocating and that its extreme stand was no more than a fig leaf for the benefit of its Arab brethren. Israel was convinced that, in return for its own land (Sinai – a territory three times larger than the whole of mandatory Palestine), Egypt would tacitly give a free hand to Israel in the West Bank and the Gaza Strip. The embassy in Cairo was not of that opinion – several times, in writing and verbally, it warned that Egypt meant exactly what it was saying publicly and that, after Israel completed its withdrawal from Sinai, it would have no interest or incentive to make its position more flexible. It also expressed the conviction that Egypt, in all that pertained to the Palestinians, would not only support the most extreme anti-Israeli stand in the international arena but would also take the lead in the Arab diplomatic onslaught on Israel. Clearly, Egypt's main concern was to cleanse itself of the stigma of having betrayed the Arab cause and pave its way back into the Arab world. But beyond these selfish considerations, it also genuinely supported the Palestinians and was determined to do its utmost on their behalf – to the exclusion of a reversal to military confrontation.

There could be no misunderstanding, no haziness in interpreting the Egyptian messages. The Palestinian issue was on the table, at the initiative of our Egyptian interlocutors, at each and every meeting in the foreign ministry and in practically every conversation we had with high officials, political personalities, journalists and intellectuals. They expounded, frankly and in detail, their views and their stand. They did not conceal that they had very little sympathy (I am using a mild euphemism in comparison with the very strong words they used) for the Palestinians in general and for the PLO in particular. They stressed, however, their conviction that there could be no real peace in the region as long as Palestinian expectations were not met and that nothing less than a Palestinian state in all the territories occupied by Israel in 1967 (including East Jerusalem) would ever satisfy the Palestinians. They also expressed the conviction that Israel would, in the long run, have no alternative but to recognize the PLO and negotiate with it directly on this basis (recent history has proven that they were right!) and they urged us to do so – the sooner the better. The Egyptians conceded that Jerusalem was a most sensitive issue, which carried a heavy emotional load for the Israelis and the Jewish people, but they pointed out that this was also the case for 200 million Arabs and one billion Muslims throughout the world. They advocated that discussions on the fate of Jerusalem should be left to the end of the process and that, in the meantime, Israel should refrain from provocative statements and administrative steps, which were bound to provoke violent reactions and compel the parties to give first priority to the matter. President Sadat, in a meeting with Ben-Elissar, went so far as to say that 'time should be given to time and that, if the problem is not artificially exacerbated, it will find its solution in 50 years – probably by flying a Saudi or Jordanian flag over the El Aksa mosque'.

It was a most important development and Ben-Elissar hurriedly sent a report on his conversation with Sadat, which he classified top secret. To avoid any possible indiscretion, he specified in the cable that utmost precautions should be taken to prevent leakage of the report to the press and warned that no reference to its content should be made either privately or publicly. He stressed that 'a breach of Sadat's confidence would be catastrophic and lead to the collapse of communication with the President'. The very same day, in the news bulletin of the Voice of Israel, Ben-Elissar's report was quoted in its broad outlines by the political commentator Shimon Shifer. Ben-Elissar, choking with rage, sent a cable of protest the opening sentence of which was 'A villainy has been perpetrated!' The next day, on the 6 o'clock bulletin, Shimon Shifer not only quoted Ben-Elissar's cable but this time read it word for word.

Let me make a small digression. During my two periods in Cairo, leakage of restricted information from the embassy reports was a common feature. Several times, our diplomats were put in the most embarrassing situations that made more difficult the limited interaction we had with government officials, local personalities and foreign diplomats in Cairo. No one in his right mind was ready to take the risk that information or opinions that he had aired in informal conversations would leak to the Israeli press and work as a boomerang against him. In chapter seven,

I related the shameful leak of a conversation with the American ambassador, Frank Wiesner, which took me months to mend. During my tenure as ambassador, there were several more cases but it would be fruitless to relate them all. I tried in vain to have the plague of leaks stopped but the phenomenon was too deeply-rooted in the system to be eradicated. Finally, I was counseled by high officials in the ministry to send confidential reports either by non-restricted cables or by letters in the diplomatic pouch addressed to a single correspondent. The rationalization was that the journalists did not attach importance to unrestricted reports and, therefore, they would not find their way to the press. No doubt this was true but, in the same manner, these reports would not have found their way to top officials – within and outside the ministry – and would not have had an impact on the decision-making process. As for me, I considered this weird method of preventing leaks a dereliction of duty and I instructed the embassy staff to stick religiously to the regular classification of documents in operation in the ministry. This meant that leaks would continue and that we had to live with them and pay the ever-increasing price they entailed.

Let me return to Palestinian autonomy and to our dealings with the Egyptians on the issue. As is known, the United Nations and most countries rejected the Camp David agreement in all its components. Even the West supported it reluctantly. The Arab states saw in it the personification of Egypt's betrayal and the source of all evils (at a later stage, even in Egypt itself, Camp David became a dirty expression and disappeared from the Egyptian lexicon). Understandably, an overwhelming majority in the United Nations and other international institutions adopted numerous resolutions condemning separate agreements and declaring them null and void year after year. During my tenure at the UN – both in Geneva and New York – I took the floor several times and expressed revulsion that an organization supposedly dedicated to preserving world peace and fostering understanding between nations rejected a peace treaty signed between two sovereign countries of their own free will. I also expressed amazement that it rejected an agreement putting an end to many generations of warring and, for the first time in history, opened a serious possibility of solving the protracted and tragic Palestinian problem and establishing a just and lasting peace in the middle east. In private conversations with UN colleagues, I received many expressions of identification with my views but never did any of my UN colleagues take the floor and publicly express support for these views. They also never changed their pattern of voting and stuck to the instructions that they had previously received from their ministries. In the UN, good speeches and strong arguments have no impact on the predetermined positions of the various delegations as defined, long before the opening of the debate, in their respective capitals. After days of an unceasing flow of verbosity, votes are cast – not on the merits of the case or as a result of what has been said – but solely in accordance with national interests or considerations of expediency.

In reality, international support or lack of support for the Camp David accords was irrelevant and would not have affected the course of events. If all the parties involved had been determined to move forward on their own, nothing and no one could have hampered the implementation of the accords. The enforcement of the bilateral clauses, despite international rejection, is the best evidence of this. But Jordan and the Palestinians refused to join the peace process on the basis of Camp David and joined the vociferous chorus of condemnation. President Sadat was surprised at the violence of their reactions and their rejection of the agreement in its entirety. However, he remained optimistic and was sure that, sooner or later, they would grasp the overall significance of the agreement and the underlying breakthrough that it represented for the Palestinians and for peace in the region. For weeks, he tried to convince them through quiet diplomatic efforts and, when he felt that the ground had been sufficiently prepared, at the end of 1979 he invited all parties concerned – including the PLO – to a conference in Cairo. To his great disappointment, with the exception of the Oman and Egyptian delegations, not a single Arab delegation showed up. The Israeli delegation, headed by Eliahu Ben-Elissar (at the time director-general of the prime minister's office), was not aware that Sadat had invited the PLO and was flabbergasted to see the Israeli flag flying next to the PLO's flag over the Mena House Hotel near the pyramids. The delegation pondered if it should immediately fly back to Israel but it was spared the need to take a decision when it became clear that the PLO had not come. It went into the conference hall as if it was reconciled with the idea that the PLO would attend. Years afterwards, the Egyptian still recalled this incident. They praised Israel for showing its goodwill and blamed the Palestinians for having missed an historic opportunity to achieve recognition and forward their interests in the direction they wished.

Notwithstanding the stinging affront, Sadat continued his efforts and tried to weld an alternative Palestinian leadership from among the residents of the West Bank and the Gaza Strip in place of the PLO. He invited to Cairo around 40 eminent personalities to discuss ways and means of solving the Palestinian issue. Less than half accepted the invitation and only some 12 actually came to meet with Sadat. They stated, publicly and privately, that they had responded to the invitation only out of respect for Sadat and that the PLO was, in their eyes and in the eyes of all Palestinians, the only legitimate representative of the Palestinian people. They rejected unequivocally all pressures and entreaties to take part in a process that had not received the blessing of the PLO and the Arab consensus. Despite the staunch loyalty they had shown to the PLO, many were assassinated within the few months after their return from Cairo.

Sadat choked with wrath at what he described as 'the stupid obstinacy of the Palestinian leaders and their total lack of wisdom and foresight'. He decided that, since these leaders were acting against the Palestinian people's best interests, Egypt would temporarily assume the representation of the Palestinians in the framework of the Camp David process. He stressed that Egypt was legitimately entitled to do so as the largest Arab state and the nation that had always shouldered the heaviest burden in the Arab struggle on behalf of Palestinian rights. He also pledged to do his utmost to move ahead rapidly and reach a comprehensive solution that would secure all legitimate Palestinian rights. Understandably, Sadat's decision could not have a practical significance or moral validity. Assuming the Palestinian representation, without their acceptance and without co-ordinating positions with them, obviously could not yield serious results. No decision taken without the participation of the Palestinians themselves, and to a lesser extent that of Jordan, could ever be enforced against the wishes of two million Palestinians residing in the territories. Israel, and Egypt itself, realized these hard facts but – for reasons inherent in the bilateral negotiations between them – they decided to establish a special committee for Palestinian autonomy and initiated a negotiating process that lasted more than three years.

Both sides hoped that, if the negotiations were conducted seriously, the Palestinians and Jordanians would join in. Very quickly, it became clear that this was wishful thinking. Both countries appointed a minister to head their respective delegations. Egypt appointed General Kamal Hassan Ali, the foreign minister of the time, while Israel appointed Yosef Burg, the interior minister. The rest of the Egyptian delegation was composed of the foreign ministry officials who dealt regularly with Israeli affairs in all their aspects. The Israeli delegation was composed, again as usual, of senior ministers (foreign affairs, defense, justice, and commerce and industry) and, in their absence, of the directors-general of their respective ministries. Practical work was to be done by civil servants and army officers who dealt with Palestinian affairs. It was also decided that the committee meetings would be held alternately in Egypt and Israel.

Incidentally, Burg's appointment provoked a major crisis between the prime minister, Menahem Begin, and the then foreign minister, Moshe Dayan. The reason was not personal rivalries; it reflected divergent approaches to the Palestinian issue. Begin wanted to demonstrate clearly that the granting of autonomy to the Palestinians was an internal Israeli problem and therefore it was to be dealt with by the interior minister. Dayan opposed this approach and believed that it would create an atmosphere which would prevent significant progress. As a sign of displeasure, he instructed the embassy in Cairo not to take part in the talks but, after a few weeks, he resigned from the government (mainly on these grounds) and his replacement, Yitshak Shamir, rescinded Dayan's instructions.

The USA was not formally a member of the autonomy committee but it participated in all meetings with observer status. Indeed, it acted throughout the talks as a neutral intermediary and helped (mainly on procedural matters) the two negotiating parties, Israel and Egypt, to bridge their views. It was represented by a high-powered delegation composed of senior diplomats and legal experts. After the first few meetings and the opening moves, the committee convened at long intervals and the discussions proceeded very slowly. The Egyptians used, and misused, it – as they did with all other joint committees – in the framework of their policy of reward and punishment for sending messages and signals to Israel and/or the Arab states and/or their own internal public opinion. They would either agree to convene the committee or postpone its meetings as a function of their needs of the moment on the bilateral or regional front and demanded a price for each meeting.

In the negotiations, the Egyptian tactics were transparent. From the first moment, they did not see themselves as authorized to reach agreements or operative conclusions – even in broad outline – in the absence of the Palestinians. They clearly had no intention of adopting a practical approach and, in private conversations, they did not conceal this fact. They stressed that 'as long as the divergences between us are so enormous, Egypt cannot tie the Palestinians' hands in matters vital to their future and, in any case, it will be impossible to enforce arrangements that do not meet with Palestinian approval'. In less diplomatic language, our Egyptian interlocutors meant that, if Israel agreed that the negotiations would finally lead to the establishment of a Palestinian state, Egypt would find it easier to persuade the Palestinians to agree to a transitional period along the lines of Camp David. From the outset, Egypt strove to change the order of the negotiating phases as they had been defined, after long and bitter discussions, in the Camp David accords and tackle first the final status of the territories, leaving the transitional period (autonomy) to the second phase. Obviously, Israel refused to 'put the cart before the horse'. It insisted on abiding with the agreed timetable: a first phase to work out matters related to the transitional period and a second phase to work out the final settlement in all its components, after the election and empowerment of a self-governing Palestinian authority.

Indeed, from the outset, there was no minimal common denominator between the two sides and the autonomy talks were still-born. Nevertheless, they dragged on over a period of more than three years. Many discussions were held at ministerial level and several others at the level of directors-general and experts. Egypt went through the motions because it feared that formally discontinuing the talks might give Israel a pretext to delay, or even cancel, its withdrawal from Sinai. Up to the very last moment, almost everyone in Egypt was convinced that Israel would not live up to its commitments and that it was looking for an excuse which would sound reasonable to international public opinion to avoid implementation of the second phase of withdrawal. Egypt tried, therefore, to give the talks a semblance of seriousness until after the withdrawal but, clearly, it had no intention of letting them lead anywhere.

All along, the Egyptians kept in close contact with the PLO and briefed them faithfully on the content of the talks. Despite the official severance of relations, the PLO had maintained a representation in Egypt at ambassadorial level and many PLO leaders, including Arafat's brother and Nabil Shaat, continued to reside in the country and conduct their activities normally. There were rumors that the PLO ambassador to Egypt was an agent of the Egyptian security services (there is no doubt that he received a financial contribution from them) but he was an efficient channel of communication between the two parties. He was not replaced, even after relations between Egypt and the PLO were officially resumed, at the highest level, during the Galilee campaign in 1983. He was still ambassador to Cairo when I returned in 1990.

At first, the consultations were aimed at keeping the PLO in the picture and convincing the Palestinians to join the peace process, if only indirectly. After Sadat's assassination, relations with the PLO became more cordial and the consultations became a means for co-ordinating positions and tactical moves and reassuring the PLO about Egypt's real intentions as to the autonomy talks. Egypt made it clear that, because of tactical needs, it would have to drag them out until after the Israeli withdrawal from Sinai and that it had no intention of reaching any agreement with Israel without the prior approval of the PLO.

The first meetings of the autonomy committee pinpointed the topics that were to be discussed. I will cite here only a few of these:

- What was the substance of the autonomy – would it be territorial (as the Egyptians wanted) or personal (as the Israelis wanted)?
- What would be the legal source of the powers defined for the Palestinian self-governing authority?
- What powers would factually be transferred by Israel and what powers would remain in its hands?
- Would the Palestinian authority be a legislative or executive body?
- How would the day-to-day security problems be tackled and where would the Israeli armed forces be stationed in the territories?
- What would become of the settlements and what would be the judicial status of the settlers? Whose laws would be applied to them?
- Would the Palestinian authority have a separate customs administration? A central bank? A currency of its own? The right to legislate and levy taxes?
- How would elections of the self-governing authority be organized? Who would supervise them? Who would have the right to elect and be elected? (The Egyptians wanted Palestinians throughout the world to be given both rights.)

- What would be the civil rights of the Arab residents of Jerusalem? Would they be dependent on the Palestinian or Israeli authorities? Would they have the right to vote and be elected to the Palestinian authority?
- Who would control the sources of water in the territories? Who would be responsible for their allocation and distribution?
- Who would control the land reserves? Who would decide on land allocations and to whom would they be allocated?
- How would the Palestinian police be established? What weapons would it be allowed to carry?
- Who would control the entrance points to the autonomy and who would control the borders?
- To what extent would the autonomy and Israeli authorities co-ordinate their actions, especially in those areas that had a bearing on both parts of the population (Jews and Arabs)?

I will not go any further. The list that I have provided seems long and heavy but it is only a very partial list of the items that were to be tackled by the autonomy committee in the first phase of negotiations. I also have no intention of entering into the details of either side's positions or describing the haggling that took place throughout the period. It is enough to stress again that there was no lowest common denominator between Egypt and Israel and that there was no chance (and no intention) of reaching agreement on any of the topics under discussion.

In the course of the negotiations, Egypt changed its position and reasoning many times – going from one extreme to another according to its tactical needs of the moment. Even when agreement was apparently reached on procedural matters (on the substance itself the parties always remained far from each other), the Egyptians suddenly rejected all that had been previously achieved and reopened the discussion from scratch. For example, they would request to debate a certain topic in-depth and in detail. Israel would agree and send to the next meeting experts on the topic to be discussed. After a thorough Israeli presentation, the Egyptian delegation would say that there was no point in debating a single topic before they heard from Israel its overall concept on autonomy and where it would lead. Again, Israel agreed and, at the next meeting, its delegation would present an overall view on how autonomy would function and request to hear Egypt's reaction and its own concept. The Egyptians would pledge to do so at the next meeting but instead they would revert to their previous arguments. They would claim brazenly that, after having studied the Israeli presentation, they had reached the conclusion that it was futile to discuss overall concepts without first going into the details and debating each topic separately. Israel would accede and a topic for discussion at the next meeting would be defined (it was generally suggested by the Egyptians themselves). A delegation of relevant Israeli experts would make a presentation and, again, the Egyptians would request to discuss the overall concept and so on and so forth ... An interminable merry-go-round.

One should recall that, on the Egyptian side, almost exclusively the same team of foreign ministry diplomats who dealt with relations with Israel participated in the talks. Only seldom did experts on the topic under discussion join in. Israel, on the other hand, thoroughly prepared the technical aspects and dispatched top experts in the field under review. The Americans seldom took the floor in the official meetings. However, they were very active behind the scenes, exerting strenuous efforts to build a bridge between the diverging stands and doing their utmost to prevent the collapse of the talks. On the substance of the negotiations, it was clear that they were closer to the Egyptian standpoint than the Israeli one. Only once did I see them lose patience in a formal meeting with Osama Elbaz (who, exceptionally, headed the Egyptian delegation). In the same session, he reversed his position on a minor procedural issue time and again with the purpose of taunting the Israeli delegation. The Americans suddenly intervened in the discussion and told Osama dryly that he was exaggerating, pointing out that he had once more changed his position and asked in the same breath for one thing and its opposite. Osama replied arrogantly, puffing on a thick Cuban cigar: 'Yes, we have changed our opinion again, so what! Egypt is a sovereign country and can change its opinions and positions as many times as it wishes and when it wishes!' The Americans (and the Israelis) swallowed the pill, gnashed their teeth and yielded again to Osama's demands.

The question is why Israel agreed to participate in this farce when it was clear from the outset that the talks would lead nowhere. I believe that, until Sadat's assassination, Israel still hoped that he would succeed in persuading the Palestinians and the Jordanians to join in the negotiations. When this did not materialize, they genuinely thought that Egypt would truly assume the Palestinian responsibilities and conduct serious negotiations which would lead to the adoption of the Israeli stand (at least partially). This wishful thinking was in line with the belief (which proved to be groundless) prevailing at the time among Israeli decision-makers that Egypt would give a free hand to Israel in the occupied territories in return for its own land. Later, though Israel had come to the obvious conclusion that the talks were a non-starter, it continued to go through the motions, not wanting to break the utensils (as we say in Hebrew). Israel needed the autonomy talks – as much as Egypt – to create the perception that the Camp David process was leading to a comprehensive peace in the region and that everything was proceeding according to plan. The show had to go on (both for autonomy and normalization) even if no tangible results were to be expected and even if the prospects that Egypt would live up to its commitments were slim. For Israel, the dynamics of negotiation and the ongoing dialogue with Egypt were no less important than the ingredients of peace itself!

From December 1981 onwards – with the withdrawal date (25 April 1982) approaching – the embassy in Cairo repeatedly called the decision-makers' attention to the need to put pressure on Egypt to reach a binding agreement on autonomy before the withdrawal, just as Israel was doing on the normalization. The embassy warned that, after forfeiting the cards that were in our hands (read: Sinai), there was no prospect whatsoever of concluding the autonomy talks in a manner satisfactory to Israel. I personally raised the matter with the foreign minister, Yitshak Shamir, and with the defense minister, Ariel Sharon, on the occasion of two separate visits to Egypt on the eve of withdrawal. I urged them to put pressure on the Egyptians before it was too late. Their reactions were surprisingly similar, despite the difference between them in temperaments and style. Shamir said laconically that Israel had no interest in reaching an agreement with Egypt on a matter that did not concern Egypt directly and which clearly had no chance of being enforced because of Palestinian opposition. He added that, sooner or later, negotiations with the Palestinians themselves would have to take place and the agreement with Egypt would be taken as the starting point for pressuring Israel into further concessions. After I had presented my case, Sharon asked me for my assessment of the possibility of Egypt's reversion to military confrontation and in what circumstances it might do so. I replied that, to the best of my judgement, for the foreseeable future this eventuality was to be ruled out unless Israel itself launched a military attack on Egypt or wantonly harmed its vital interests. Naturally, I detailed the reasons that lead me to that outright evaluation. I quoted an article in the daily *Al Akhbar* by Ibrahim Saada (the court journalist of the time) in which he reached the conclusion that peace served the best interests of Egypt (I have gone into the details of this article in chapter ten). Sharon then asked me a straightforward question that left no room for diplomatic wording: 'Would Egypt go to war if Israel annexed the West Bank and the Gaza Strip?' I answered in the negative and said that the most extreme step that Egypt would take would be to recall its ambassador for consultations and keep him in Cairo for a long period (this is exactly what Egypt did, one year later, after the Sabra and Shatila massacre in Beirut). I also stressed my conviction that Egypt would not sever diplomatic relations and would not let itself be dragged again into a war for the Palestinians or any Arab country – it had paid a heavy price in the past and had learned the lesson thoroughly. Sharon concluded that, in the light of my own assessment, there was no reason to pressure Egypt into reaching an agreement that would bring no benefits to Israel and would only tie its hands in the future. He added that Israel controlled the territories and could do whatever it chose without Egypt's benediction or approval. In order to avoid misunderstandings, I have to emphasize that Sharon made it clear that Israel had no intention of annexing the occupied territories and that the questions he was putting to me were of a hypothetical nature and were only meant to substantiate his arguments. Shamir had also clearly specified in our conversation that Israel was not contemplating the annexation of the territories.

The last meeting of the autonomy committee before the Israeli withdrawal from Sinai took place in Cairo in very difficult circumstances. Tension was at its highest – a few days before the meeting, there had been a number of strong Israeli statements about building new settlements in the territories and extending the existing ones. Furthermore, the Knesset had passed a law applying Israeli legislation to the settlers in the territories and was on the eve of adopting the Jerusalem Law, which in Arab eyes was tantamount to the annexation of the eastern part of the city. The press in both countries dealt intensively with both topics, the Egyptian press voicing sharp criticism of the Israeli provocation and unilateral steps. Were it not for the impending withdrawal, the Egyptians would have cancelled the meeting and demanded a firm undertaking that Israel refrain from unilateral steps as a precondition for convening the meeting in the remote future. But, appreciating that Israel would retaliate by postponing the withdrawal, they expressed eagerness to hold the meeting and upgraded their delegation to include the three top men in the Egyptian foreign ministry: Kamal Hassan Ali, Boutros Boutros Ghali and Osama Elbaz.

In the first informal encounter, Kamal Hassan Ali expressed Egypt's resentment at Israel's unilateral step and wondered aloud what was the need for convening the autonomy committee after such a *fait accompli*. He voiced disappointment that, on the eve of the meeting, Israel not only ignored Egypt but also embarked on a fully-fledged public campaign around such sensitive topics as Jerusalem and the settlements. As usual, Yosef Burg, the Israeli interior minister, responded wittily stressing that Israel had not gone beyond the parameters it had expounded frankly and publicly since the beginning of the Camp David process. Kamal Hassan Ali was not appeased by Burg's reaction and requested Boutros Ghali to provide quotes from the Israeli press to substantiate what he meant. Burg stopped him and asked Boutros's permission to tell a short anecdote:

> A businessman who had been abroad for a long time finally returned home. Wishing to buy a local newspaper, he asked the vendor for the price. The latter, thinking that he was dealing with a tourist, quoted a price ten times higher than the real one. The businessman paid, took the newspaper and began reading. By chance, he noticed the price printed on the first page and realized that he had been cheated. He returned to the stand, brandishing the newspaper and shouting angrily: 'How dare you charge a price ten times higher than the one published in the newspaper?' The vendor answered calmly: 'Do not believe everything that is published in the newspapers. They lie and cheat as they breathe!'

Everyone burst into laughter and the tension was defused.

All following meetings, including one with President Mubarak, ran in a relaxed and friendly atmosphere. Each side refrained from unnecessary confrontation: Israel did not put on pressure to reach an agreement (even in broad outline) and Egypt did not raise Israel's unilateral steps. As expected (and as usual), there were no concrete results excluding a decision to convene as soon as possible a meeting in Israel to tackle the issues of the settlements and the redeployment of the Israeli armed forces in the territories. This meeting never took place and indeed the Cairo meeting proved to be the swan song of the autonomy committee. After having regained the whole of Sinai, Egypt had no further incentive to keep the autonomy talks alive artificially. The autonomy committee entered into deep hibernation, as did the normalization committees and all related agreements.

As usual, the Israeli embassy in Cairo did not spare any effort in setting a date for convening the autonomy committee as had been decided by the ministerial meeting in Cairo. After much nagging, the Egyptians finally agreed to set a date. But, at the same time, they casually informed us that they had decided not to attend working meetings in Jerusalem (in breach of the Sadat formula, which was elaborated in early 1981). Let me specify that, in any case, most autonomy meetings took place in Herzlia. It was a wanton provocation and the embassy was instructed to inform the Egyptian foreign ministry that Israel insisted on the Sadat formula, according to which the Egyptian delegations to Israel resided in Tel Aviv but participated in working meetings in Jerusalem. The embassy tried to persuade the ministry not to let the Egyptian provocation drag Israel into a reaction that would enable Egypt to cancel the meeting altogether and make Israel bear the blame. The embassy stressed that Egypt had no intention of continuing with the autonomy talks in any case whatever the location of the working meetings and that, tactically speaking, it was better to let Egypt bear the sole responsibility for discontinuing the talks in a blatant breach of the Camp David agreement. Regrettably, the ministry was in no mood for diplomatic games and the embassy was given strict instructions to inform the Egyptians unequivocally that all working meetings would take place in Jerusalem. As expected, the Egyptians reacted by canceling the scheduled meeting and putting the blame on Israel's intransigence. That was the end of the autonomy talks with the Egyptians but not the end of the autonomy concept embedded in the Camp David accords.

For its nuisance value, the embassy continued to raise the issue from time to time, even after the beginning of the Peace for Galilee campaign in mid-1982 and the subsequent recalling for consultations of the Egyptian ambassador, Saad Mortada. Israel had no real interest in reviving a forum that clearly would not lead to concrete results. We would simply embarrass our Egyptian interlocutors by blaming them for aggravating the Palestinians' plight by the irrational manner in which they had conducted the autonomy talks. They had stalled the talks on unimportant details of the transitional phase instead of adopting all of the Israeli proposals and going immediately to the negotiations on final status – which was the only real issue. We poured salt on their wounds by pointing out that several years had gone by and, in the meantime, irreversible facts had been created in the territories, which would undoubtedly be a major factor in the shaping of any solution. We added casually that an autonomous self-governing authority – whatever its scope and character – was better from the Palestinian standpoint than military government by the occupying power. We reminded them that the transitional phase was to last for no more than five years, years that had been wasted, in any case, by Egypt in futile negotiations. The Egyptians did not contest our arguments. They retorted that the Palestinians themselves were to blame for the lost opportunity since they had threatened that they would foil by force any arrangement made in the framework of the Camp David accords. The Egyptians would also return the ball to the Israeli court and blame Israel for having negotiated in bad faith and taken advantage of the wasted time to strengthen its grip on the territories. They warned us that, whatever the situation in the field, Egypt and the Arabs would never accept a *fait accompli*.

When I returned to Cairo in 1990, the autonomy issue was not directly on the agenda but was still very much alive. At the center of the intense diplomatic activity stood the efforts to work out an alternative formula to the Camp David process which led to the convening of the Madrid conference in 1991. Like us, our Egyptian interlocutors expressed regret that more than ten years had been wasted and that we had to begin from scratch while the factual situation in the territories had become much more complicated. As I have mentioned, the Camp David agreement had gone out of fashion in Egypt. President Mubarak expressed several times the need to find another formula that could be worked out with the Palestinians and the Arab states and take into account their sensitivities and expectations. However, he never expressed reservations about the bilateral clauses of the agreement. In private conversations, Mubarak and other top Egyptian interlocutors reassured us that Egypt remained faithful to the spirit of the Camp David accords and continued to support the underlying principles embedded in them. They believed, however, that since the very words Camp David were perceived by the Arabs as tantamount to betrayal, it was essential to present the same ideas in another packaging, i.e. under a new title. The Egyptians urged us, as they had done from day one, to recognize the PLO and enter into direct negotiations with it, which would inevitably lead to the establishment of an independent Palestinian state on all the territories occupied in 1967, including East Jerusalem. On this last issue, they were much more demanding than in the early 1980s and it was clear that it had become a top-priority issue for them (at least for propaganda's sake).

Furthermore, after a few fruitless attempts to establish a Palestinian leadership that would replace the PLO, Egypt had reconciled itself to Yasser Arafat's leadership and had become his most active supporter (following the saying 'if you can't beat them, join them!'). Even then, many Israeli leaders still believed that Egypt would back a Jordanian solution (the establishment, under the Hashemite crown, of a federation or confederation between Jordan and the Palestinians). Indeed, there were a few Egyptian public statements to that effect and in private conversations the Egyptian leaders sometimes voiced support for that solution. However, from my own experience and contacts, I have no doubt whatsoever that Egypt would never passively have allowed the Jordanian solution to become reality. Clearly, Egypt considered it not only as unfeasible but also as contradictory to overall Arab interests and to its own interests in the region. I repeatedly warned the decision-makers in Jerusalem not to take at face value Egyptian statements supporting the Jordanian solution, which in my opinion were voiced for tactical reasons to please Israeli ears.

A few months after my return, the Madrid conference took place and all parties concerned adopted the Madrid process. It was a kind of mishmash that bridged the Arab demand for a binding international conference with the Israeli demand for direct negotiations. However, in respect of all that pertained to the Palestinian issue, the principles embedded in the Camp David agreement were maintained by the Madrid conference (and later by the Washington talks). The Palestinian delegation was composed of residents of the territories and included a few non-residents approved by all parties involved (including Israel). It was formally part of the Jordanian delegation though, at a later stage, negotiations were conducted along separate Jordanian and Palestinian lines. The procedures followed in looking for a solution to the Palestinian issue also found their inspiration in the Camp David accords. There was to be a transitional phase of five years during which the Palestinians would have autonomous status (details of which were to be worked out in the negotiations) and elect a self-governing authority (the election modalities and the scope of its powers were also to be worked out). In a second phase, no later than three years after the election and empowerment of the Palestinian authority, negotiations on the final status were to start. All this must sound familiar to the reader. Indeed, to the exclusion of the words Camp David, it was exactly the same formula adopted 13 years earlier and it was practically a resumption of the autonomy talks from the very same point at which they had stopped – this time with the participation of the Palestinians and Jordanians. The Egyptians realized this fact and, in their conversations with us, they mocked the Palestinians who, after wasting 13 precious years, had agreed, almost word for word, to the Camp David formula, which they had earlier rejected as a vicious betrayal on the part of Egypt. The Egyptian government and opposition press, generally fanatically pro-Palestinian, went all out to ridicule the Arab states and the Palestinians for their shortsightedness and to praise Egypt for having chosen the right path despite the unwarranted Arab slander. Nevertheless, Egypt continued to consider itself the Palestinians' guardian and did not spare them advice, material assistance or diplomatic support. It also made it clear that the multilateral track of the negotiations, which was decided upon by the Madrid conference with the aim of fostering regional co-operation, was organically linked to the bilateral track and did not stand independently. The Egyptians went through the motions but in reality they made sure they prevented any progress on the multilateral track. Gradually, they succeeded in transforming the negotiations into a symposium for exchanging ideas rather than a forum for reaching practical decisions and co-ordinating regional development projects. Egypt also stood at the forefront of the Arab onslaught on Israel, especially in the subcommittees for disarmament, water resources and refugees.

In retaliation, Israel refused to yield to Egypt's entreaties to convene the international conference in Cairo and preferred Madrid (meeting in Cairo would have been for Egypt the ultimate rehabilitation from the stigma of betrayal and a sweet revenge on its Arab detractors). Later, Israel also refused to hold bilateral meetings in Egypt with the Syrians, Jordanians or Palestinians. The official explanation, which we gave to the Egyptians and to other intermediaries, was that the climate in Cairo was extremely hostile to Israel and that the Egyptian press would make the negotiating process more difficult. Furthermore, Israel ruled out Egyptian participation in the bilateral track despite its insistence and American entreaties, arguing that Egypt had already signed a peace treaty with Israel and had ceased to be a confrontation state. Israel also emphasized that it did not consider Egypt to be a neutral mediator or an honest broker.

These Israeli stands provoked much resentment in Egypt and shattered its hopes of using the Madrid process as a lever for regaining a leadership position in the Arab world and presenting itself to international and Egyptian public opinion as the main driving force behind the peace process. I was summoned several times to the ministry of foreign affairs (including by the foreign minister, Amr Mussa) with the aim of persuading Israel to make its position more flexible. In parallel, quite a few foreign ambassadors met with me, at Egypt's request or at their own initiative, and expressed the opinion that Israel was showing too much inflexibility on this matter. They insisted that Israel should strive to strengthen Egypt's position – internally and vis-à-vis the Arab states – as a moderating factor in the region. Paradoxically, some of them also volunteered to host the international conference if Israel persisted in its rejection of the Cairo venue. I faithfully reported to Jerusalem the Egyptian and foreign approaches and I even tried, in one of my periodic meetings with the then prime minister, Yitshak Shamir, to persuade him to make a gesture of goodwill towards the Egyptians. As ambassador to Cairo, it was my prime duty to re-establish, after years of almost complete standstill, the dialogue with Egypt and I believed that Egypt's eagerness to host the international conference and/or the bilateral discussions could provide us with an excellent lever to reach that goal. But it was not to be – Shamir flatly refused. I explained to the Egyptians and to the foreign ambassadors who had approached me that, since Egypt stood with its two feet in the Arab camp and was leading the Arab diplomatic onslaught on Israel, it could not have its cake and eat it. I also pointed out that the Egyptian government had discontinued any meaningful dialogue with Israel and was condoning (and probably instigating) the ever-increasing poisonous attacks in the Egyptian press against Israel and the Jewish people.

After the elections in Israel in the summer of 1992 and the accession to power of a Labor government, the atmosphere in Cairo improved dramatically. The first visit abroad of the new prime minister, the late Yitshak Rabin, was to Egypt. I will elaborate on this visit in another chapter but, at this point, it is important to specify that the visit was intended to mark a drastic change of attitude towards Egypt on Israel's part. For the first time, Israel was ready to see in Egypt a leading factor in the peace process and a partner with whom it could co-ordinate action. Israel's goodwill gesture was not returned. In the wake of Rabin's visit – despite the improved atmosphere – several attempts to co-ordinate positions with Egypt brought no positive results. Nor did Egypt heed Israeli pleas for a lower profile on a number of sensitive issues in the multilateral track, and to use its influence to moderate the Arab diplomatic onslaught on Israel (which, indeed, was led and initiated by Egypt itself). While Egypt paid lip service to the need for political co-ordination with Israel, in reality it had its own agenda and continued to take one-sided positions and to pour oil on the fire.

A few months after I left Cairo at the end of 1992 and took up my new posting as ambassador to India, the Oslo process began, bringing mutual recognition between Israel and the PLO and the adoption of the Gaza and Jericho First formula. In broad outline, autonomy and the two phases of negotiations remained at the basis of the process, though the overall goals of the two agreements are of a very different nature. Camp David might have led, at the most, to extended autonomous status for the Palestinians, while the Oslo process will probably lead, sooner or later, to the establishment of an independent and sovereign Palestinian state. The self-governing Palestinian authority has now been in place for six years and is led by the PLO with Yasser Arafat as chairman. It is difficult to forecast how things will develop in the next few years and where they will lead (especially in view of the political upheavals in Israel). In any case, the positions upheld by Egypt since the onset of the peace process have been vindicated and are nowadays shared, to a great extent, by all the parties involved in the solution of the Palestinian issue, including

Israel itself. Paradoxically, Egypt's positions have also evolved and have become more extreme. In many ways, Egypt seems now to be more vociferous than the Palestinians themselves and more Catholic than the Pope! In any case, it continues to play a leading role and, after the cold winds that blew during the Netanyahu government (a Likud-led coalition), it seems that the Barak government (a Labor-led coalition) is again trying to co-ordinate action with Egypt and seeking its good offices. Egypt and the USA brokered the timetable for the implementation of the Wye Plantation Agreement with the Palestinians in October 1999. Subsequent agreements remained a dead-letter, contributing to the increasing tension and violence, disintegrating the Barak coalition and compelling him to resign and call new elections. Notwithstanding all this, I rest firm in my conviction that Egypt cannot be an honest broker in all that pertains to the Palestinian issue or to Arab interests, and that it is preposterous to believe that Israel can rely on Egypt or collude with it. It is tantamount to expecting the cat to keep a watch on the milk. For the time being, it seems that the developments of this last year completely confirm my assessment and Egypt is inciting the Palestinians, Syria and Lebanon to take extreme stands. I would be very happy to be proven wrong!

16 · *Strategy and Defense*

The military annex of the Camp David accords detailed the phases of withdrawal from Sinai, the future deployment of both armies, the security arrangements, and the machinery for supervising the faithful implementation of its provisions and assessing possible infractions by the parties. Indeed, it was the only document that was drafted in the clearest possible language and did not leave any leeway for interpretations and haggling in the implementation phase. The drafting process was meticulous and the wording absolutely clear and unambiguous. The negotiators dug deep into the substance of the matter, covered the smallest detail and consistently avoided haziness and double meanings. They did not strive to bridge unbridgeable differences by sophisticated diplomatic wording and did not leave to the future possible clashes of interpretation. On the contrary, the annex was drafted in the clearest language and the various paragraphs were purposely inter-linked like the rings of a single chain in a manner that ensured the faithful enforcement of all the provisions by both sides. The implementation of a given commitment by one of the parties depended on the other side's implementing his commitments in a previous phase of the process and so on – from one ring of the chain to the other. The breaking of one of the rings would have resulted in the disintegration of the whole chain. In less picturesque language, evading the enforcement of one of the provisions by Egypt would have automatically entailed the cancellation of the Israeli withdrawal, in its first or second phase, and even more drastic counter-measures. Furthermore, it was implicit that any major infraction by Egypt would lead to the discontinuation of US military assistance to Egypt, thus impeding the quick rehabilitation of the Egyptian army which had been badly damaged by the Yom Kippur War.

Notwithstanding these underlying assumptions, there were no solid guarantees that the military annex would be respected and its provisions faithfully implemented. Clear wording or not, had Egypt not wished to live up to its commitments – fully or partially – it would have found a score of pretexts as it did with respect to the normalization agreements, some of which had been drafted no less meticulously than the military annex. However, from the first moment, Egypt respected the various provisions to the last detail and did not strive to evade their implementation or drag its feet. It did not engage in futile exercises of deceit or procrastination as it did in other fields. No doubt the Egyptians had in mind the considerations that I have detailed here but it is my firm belief that their longstanding compliance with the military annex goes well beyond these considerations. They have lived up to their commitments many years since the restitution of Sinai to the last grain of sand and in very tense situations such as the bombing of the Iraqi nuclear reactor, the Peace for Galilee campaign and five long years of the Palestinian *Intifada*. Clearly, Egypt has grasped that peace will live or die on the basis of the faithful implementation of all the provisions of the military annex and that neither Israel nor the USA would turn a blind eye to breaches of this annex as they do to the numerous breaches of the normalization agreements. This is why Egypt has put faithful adherence to the military aspects of the Camp David accords at the forefront of the assets of permanent value which it is ready to grant Israel – whatever the political situation – in order not to endanger peace itself. Egypt needs peace as much as Israel and understands that it has to pay a price to prevent a deterioration of the situation that might drag the region back into military confrontation with all the risks that that entails.

During both my periods in Egypt, the Israeli defense establishment complained from time to time about breaches of the military annex. The complaints focused mainly on the size and weaponry of the Egyptian forces stationed in zone C of Sinai (a narrow belt along the Suez Canal) and the nature of the fortifications that had been built there. As a matter of course, I would relay formally these complaints to the Egyptian foreign ministry, as well as to various political personalities, and forcefully demand their immediate correction. In parallel, I would call the attention of the authorities in Israel to the fact that the English text of the military annex (the only binding text) was formulated in a manner that gave leeway to Egypt to decide, on its own, the quantities of weapons in zone C and the nature of fortifications. Whilst for zone A (the belt along the Israeli border) the presence of military forces and building of fortifications were strictly prohibited, and for zone B (most of Sinai) the quantities of weapons and fortifications allowed were detailed in a clear-cut specification, for zone C this was not the case. Here the annex stipulated that Egypt was allowed to station a certain number of military units with their statutory weaponry.

Naturally, my Egyptian interlocutors maintained that there had been no breaches on their part and brought the same argumentation to refute the Israeli complaints. I retorted that I was well aware of the formulation in the English text and pointed out that it not only limited the number of units to be stationed in zone C but also clearly specified that the weaponry would be the statutory one. I added that the norms in operation in the Egyptian army, which were well-known, had been widely exceeded in zone C. My interlocutors did not try to deny the facts, as they did with respect to other agreements, and did not claim that Egypt was a sovereign state free to do whatever it wished on its own territory. On the contrary, they went out of their way to alleviate tension and explained that the Egyptian army was going through a process of reorganization that entailed, among other measures, a change of the statutory quantities and types of arms of the various units throughout the national territory. Consequently, the units stationed in zone C had been issued, as allowed by the military annex, the new statutory weaponry. I must say that I was convinced by this explanation and favorably impressed by the Egyptians' eagerness to justify their steps and prevent misunderstandings in this very sensitive field. I relayed to Jerusalem the Egyptian arguments (which were in line with my own interpretation of the annex) as well as my opinion that they had acted in good faith and were clearly not trying to deceive us. There were no reactions from the relevant authorities in Israel and one may assume that they too were persuaded. In any case, the weapons and fortifications involved in the Israeli complaints were minor in quantity and scope and did not change, even marginally, the military balance in the field. Our complaints were meant to signal to the Egyptians that we kept a vigilant eye and would not accept infringements of the military annex.

In my second period in Cairo, I was instructed to lodge a complaint about the entry of uniformed Egyptian army officers into zone A in breach of the provision stipulating that only a limited contingent of policemen was allowed to be present in that zone. The Egyptians choked with rage but explained that, at an inspection at a nearby location, the commander-in-chief of the air force had used a small airport in zone A to fly back to Cairo where he had been urgently summoned. They emphasized that he had done so openly and in broad daylight and that, in the circumstances, this should not be regarded as a breach. We insisted that, with all due respect to the air force chief, this was a blatant breach of the military annex and should not be repeated in order to avoid unnecessary tension. To the best of my knowledge, until my departure from Egypt towards the end of 1992, no more breaches of that kind (and indeed of any kind) occurred. In any case, I did not receive any further instructions to complain about breaches of the military annex by the Egyptians.

It was not a one-way street; Egypt also had complaints and reservations. In both my periods in Cairo, I was summoned several times to the foreign ministry and received verbal representations about Israeli infringements of Egyptian airspace by air force planes. In the first years, there were almost daily infringements but, with time, their number decreased substantially. They did not however cease completely as the Egyptians, rightly, demanded. The embassy had to explain time and again that Israeli air space was very small and that, at supersonic speeds, pilots could not determine the border's exact location and crossed into Egyptian air space by mistake. Clearly, the Egyptians did not swallow this far-fetched explanation.

They were sure that there was no mistake and that the purpose of the Israeli airforce was to take operational pictures of the region. They considered the repeated breaches of their air space a blatant violation of Egyptian sovereignty bordering on contempt, but they never threatened to take action against the Israeli planes or to retaliate by evading their own military commitments.

There were also Israeli complaints and protests in the wake of offensive statements by top Egyptian military leaders. In speeches to the armed forces or to the nation on the occasion of military celebrations, the Egyptian minister of defense – whoever he was at the time – and other top-ranking officers praised the capability and state of alertness of the Egyptian army. They called for stepping up Egypt's rearmament to enable it to cope with the external dangers posed by its immediate neighbors. Sometimes, they specified Israel by name as the source of the potential dangers, and stressed that Egypt had to prepare itself in view of Israel's ever-increasing military might. In time, they went so far as to state that Egypt had to muster enough strength to fulfill its mission in the framework of the Arab mutual defense pact 'as the shield of the entire Arab Nation against Israeli territorial ambitions'. The Egyptian press amplified these statements out of all proportion and embarked on alarming descriptions of the alleged dangers to Egypt from Israel (which existed only in their wildest imagination).

These statements contradicted not only the spirit of the Camp David accords but were also a flagrant breach of the written text, which specified that Egypt's obligations stemming from the accords had precedence over any other Egyptian commitments. In other words, Egypt's obligations towards Israel had precedence over its military commitments towards its Arab brethren. Whenever the reference in the press to Israel was too crude, the embassy was instructed to make a verbal protest. Several times, I requested urgent meetings with Egyptian political personalities and top officials in the foreign ministry and expressed Israel's concern at these statements, which depicted Israel as the main danger to Egypt as if the two countries were still at war. My interlocutors dismissed our concern as being totally out of proportion and claimed that Israel was mentioned only to cover up for the fact that the statements were in reality aimed at Libya and Sudan (Arab brotherhood did not allow them to point an accusing finger at fellow Arabs, but slandering Israel was legitimate!).

The most picturesque answer I was ever given in this context was by the chairman of the foreign affairs committee, Mohamed Abdellah, during my first period in Egypt. In the most difficult of times, his door was always open to me. This time, he received me at the peak of the Peace for Galilee campaign, when all other politicians and high officials had totally severed the limited contacts they maintained with us. I read to him a statement by the then minister of defense, Marshal Abu Ghazala, on the occasion of Revolution Day (23 July), the Egyptian national festival, in which he had attacked Israel and pledged that Egypt would defend all Arab states against it. I expressed my resentment that such a statement had been made only a few months after Israel had shown, in the most tangible manner, its adherence to peace by completing the withdrawal from Sinai. I stressed that it had done so despite the fact that Egypt did not live up to its commitments in the realm of normalization. Abdellah laughed and replied:

> Don't be impressed by this statement or by similar statements from other military personalities. They are a symptom of weakness, not strength. If Egypt had really considered Israel a potential danger, it would have dashed to the rescue of Lebanon and gone to war against Israel. On the contrary, it has adhered religiously to peace and withstood all Arab pressures either to intervene militarily in the conflict, or to at least threaten Israel by mustering forces on the border. Similarly, it has not availed itself of the opportunity to rescind the Camp David military annex and has not re-deployed its armed forces in Sinai. The fact that Egypt is striving to step up its rearmament has nothing to do with Israel – it is not even aimed at establishing a balance of forces with it. The dangers to Egypt come from other directions – Libya and Sudan. It has to take these dangers into account and prepare itself adequately. One need not be a military strategist to know that, in any case, Israel can easily beat all the Arab armies combined as it did in the past. It has atomic weapons and enormous conventional forces, the whole of Sinai is demilitarized and Israel can overrun it within a few hours and again reach the banks of the Suez Canal. If someone in Israel goes crazy again [he meant Arik Sharon] and decides to go to war against Egypt, all that Egypt wants is to be able to resist for a few days until the international community intervenes and stops the fighting. Please do convey to your government Egypt's assurances that there is nothing to be worried about and that it should pay no attention to such statements in the future.

During my second period in Egypt, this kind of statement had become more explicit and more militant, but the answers I received to my protests from various Egyptian personalities, including Abdellah himself (still in the same functions), were exactly in the same vein and almost in the same wording. I would retort that I was absolutely convinced that Egypt had no intention of going back to military confrontation with Israel and would not initiate a war against it and added that, like them, I believed that the real danger to Egypt was from its Arab neighbors. I emphasized however that this was not the point at all and that they were turning a blind eye to the dangers of continuing to depict Israel, at each and every opportunity, as an incarnation of Satan and Egypt's main enemy. I drew their attention to the pernicious cumulative impact of such statements and to the sediments of hatred that they left in the Egyptian people, especially among the intellectuals who read the newspapers and listened to their leaders' statements. I reminded them that a fully-fledged peace treaty had been signed between the two countries 15 years earlier and that Israel had lived up to each and every one of its commitments, including withdrawal from the whole of Sinai to the last grain of sand. Personally, I was profoundly disturbed by the systematic indoctrination of the masses against Israel and I tried my best, throughout my stay in Egypt, to explain to the Egyptian leaders the long-range effects of such hate propaganda. Regrettably, I never succeeded in making them heed the voice of reason and they stubbornly persisted in the course they had set for themselves – it was no doubt part of a concerted policy.

Topics of a military nature were not directly tackled by the embassy. They were entrusted to a joint military committee that had been established in accordance with the military annex of the Camp David accords and had entered into operation immediately after its signature. As a matter of course, the embassy did follow the committee's work closely and was the channel of communication between the two sides from meeting to meeting. In serious cases, the embassy was instructed to raise at the political level matters that did not find their solution at the military level, and to formally approach the foreign ministry. The Egyptians also would bring serious cases to the political level and several times they summoned the ambassador or the minister plenipotentiary to the foreign ministry to convey a complaint or a request that necessitated a political decision (as in the case of the infringement of Egyptian air space).

Throughout the years, the relationship between the military committee and the embassy was excellent and the co-operation between them close and fruitful. I have to add that this was the only joint committee that was taken seriously by the Egyptians and functioned – whatever the political situation – as efficiently as a Swiss watch. Meetings took place at regular intervals (every four to six weeks), alternately in Egypt and Israel, and only seldom were they postponed for short periods because of political constraints. There were also many ad hoc meetings to deal with specific issues which generally took place at the border terminals. Furthermore, both sides kept liaison officers at the terminals who maintained daily contact with each other, in contrast with the civilian border authorities who were, against all logic, almost completely cut off from each other. Contact between the latter was made by phone and only in very urgent cases was the director of the Israeli terminal allowed to cross to the Egyptian terminal and meet with his Egyptian counterpart.

The two chairmen of the joint military committee (in the 1980s, Admiral Hamdy and Brigadier-General Dov Sion) maintained excellent personal relations and were in constant touch by phone. The teams on both sides were professional and efficient and meetings ran in a relaxed and businesslike atmosphere in spite of the profound differences of views and the sensitivity of the issues dealt with. In the mid-1980s, the Egyptians claimed that the military committee was not needed any longer. They agreed however to establish in its place a liaison office between the two armies that would continue to tackle military issues. The name was different but the substance and the functioning remained the same (and I will continue to use the term military committee for the rest of the chapter).

When I returned to Egypt in 1990 I found that, on the Israeli side, Brigadier-General Yiftakh had replaced Dov Şion, but on the Egyptian side, Admiral Hamdy was still holding the position (a few months later he was replaced by his deputy). In the early 1980s, in my position as minister plenipotentiary, I had no difficulty in maintaining contact with the Egyptian members of the military committee and especially with the chairman, but as ambassador, it took me many weeks until I succeeded in re-establishing the contact. The Egyptians claimed that the military liaison office could maintain relations only with the military attaché in the embassy and not with its civilian staff. Incidentally, there was no military attaché in Cairo and indeed, to this very day, the Egyptians have not agreed to the exchange of military representations, and the offices prepared since 1981 in the Israeli chancery for this purpose remain vacant.

After I failed to get the lower ranks of the Egyptian foreign ministry to take action on the matter, I asked to see urgently the foreign minister, Amr Mussa. I complained that I was being prevented from fulfilling my duties and that, in the absence of an Israeli military attaché, it was essential that I be allowed to maintain a working relationship with the military committee. I added casually that Ambassador Bassiuni was a welcome and frequent visitor to the Israeli ministry of defense: Brigadier-General Yiftakh and other army officers, including the chief of staff, the head of army intelligence and the co-ordinator of the civil administration in the territories always received him with all due honors. It was an unmannerly hint that if the military boycott on me were not removed, Bassiuni might encounter similar difficulties in his contacts with the military authorities in Israel and not only with the military committee. It was a long shot on my part. I had no illusions that, in our political and social structure, my veiled threat could ever become a reality and I knew for certain that, whatever the treatment accorded to the Israeli ambassador in Cairo, dancing around Bassiuni would continue. I also raised the issue along the same lines with the interior minister, Abdel Halim Mussa, and with the army chief of staff, Marshal Tantaoui (at a social event).

The three personalities did not comment on the substance of my complaint and only comforted me with a few polite words that things would, sooner or later, be resolved. I was surprised when a few days later my secretary received a phone call from the army liaison office that Admiral Hamdy would be delighted to receive the ambassador at his convenience.

I was indeed received with all due honors and had an excellent exchange of views with Admiral Hamdy and his staff. Finally the ice was broken and from then on, I encountered no more difficulties in maintaining regular contacts with him (and later with his replacement). Let me specify that, as a general rule, Egyptian army officers were (and certainly still are) under strict orders not to have any contact with Israeli diplomats and not to respond to their invitations to social events, including the national day reception. Furthermore, Israeli diplomats were barred from entering military social clubs – even when they were invited to events organized by civilians (who rented the premises) and all the participants were civilians (I related a most indicative case in a previous chapter). The only exceptions were the formal social events organized by the Egyptians on the occasion of meetings of the military committee.

The agenda of the meetings encompassed a wide range of items that changed in line with the circumstances. A few items, however, were perennial and were raised at every meeting without exception. The most important and sensitive one was that of the missing Israeli soldiers who had disappeared on Egypt's territory or near its coasts, during the many years of war between the two countries. From the first moment, the Egyptians turned the issue into a bargaining chip to achieve various goals. Indeed, their behavior was not too different from that of other Arab countries, which shamelessly engaged in the commerce of corpses of fallen Israeli soldiers. As long as we were still in Sinai, we had a lever to induce the Egyptians to collaborate fairly efficiently in the searches and several corpses were located and returned to Israel for burial.

After the withdrawal, the Egyptians' attitude became much more inflexible. They claimed that the searches had been exhaustive and that there was nothing more that could be done. They did not volunteer any further information, did not investigate possible clues and found a score of pretexts to make the searches more difficult. At each meeting, after intensive debates, they pledged they would plough deeper into the matter and report at the next meeting but they never brought the slightest information. In parallel, the embassy raised the issue forcefully and repeatedly in the foreign ministry and made sure that it was put on the agenda of every visit of an Israeli personality to Egypt and in every conversation with the Egyptian leadership, including the president himself. These constant pressures, both on the military and civilian tracks, induced the Egyptians to agree, seemingly, to renew their efforts and allow a team of Israeli experts to visit various locations in Egypt, interrogate witnesses and gather information. The tangible results were very slim but the material collected by our experts indicated clearly that, with a little goodwill on the part of the Egyptian authorities, it would be possible to locate the sites where most of our missing soldiers were buried.

When I returned to Egypt in 1990, very little progress had been achieved and the problem was still on the agenda. There were still some 24 missing soldiers in addition to the crew of the submarine Dakar that had disappeared near the Egyptian coast. Before I left for Cairo, Brigadier-General Yiftakh (the Israeli chairman of the military committee) organized a meeting devoted exclusively to the issue, in which participated the officers in charge and the mother of one of the missing soldiers, Betty Cohen, an 80-year-old lady from Degania B'. She and our experts were adamant that the Egyptians knew exactly where the bodies of the missing soldiers were and that all their foot-dragging was intended to increase the price and taunt Israel. (Indeed, after I left Egypt, in the positive period that followed the change of government in Israel, the body of Betty's son, Aran Cohen, a flight navigator whose Phantom plane was shot down during the Yom Kippur War, was suddenly found and brought to Israel for burial.) At the meeting, I received an updated briefing from our experts on their discussions with the Egyptians and detailed information on the case of each of the missing soldiers. In conclusion, they all requested me to give the highest priority to the issue. I did not need prompting – the problem of the missing soldiers was not new to me: I had dealt with it intensively during my first stay in Cairo and at the UN, both in Geneva and New York. I was determined to do my utmost to prevent the Egyptians from continuing to use the issue as a bargaining chip in their ongoing give-and-take with Israel.

In fact, the problem of the missing soldiers was one of the main reasons for my wanting to establish contact with the military liaison office immediately upon my arrival in Cairo. In the first meeting with Admiral Hamdy, I insisted so much that he finally agreed to allow one more visit of our experts and pledged to facilitate their work, though he did not budge from his position that there was nothing more that could be done. Indeed, a few weeks later (after two or three postponements) the team of experts arrived but was not allowed to go out of Cairo or interrogate anyone. A single working meeting was held and, as usual, the Egyptians expressed their readiness to continue on their own with the searches and report at a future meeting. Again, the Egyptians demonstrated their bad will and, despite my reluctance to play into their hands, I had no alternative but to continue to raise the issue on every occasion. The coming of an Israeli team of experts and the scope of their visit became a topic of endless haggling, similar to what occurred with all the joint normalization committees. In 'smiling' periods, the Egyptians promised to allow the team to carry out extensive searches and to help solve the issue once and for all. In 'frowning' periods, promises were forgotten and the Egyptians insisted that Israel would have to accept that the missing soldiers would never be found. Israel made it clear repeatedly and unequivocally – through me and in the military committee – that it would never cease its efforts until the last of its missing soldiers was located and brought home for burial. Nevertheless, we were very careful not to burn our bridges since the active co-operation of the Egyptian authorities was essential for continuing the searches and reaching positive results.

After Admiral Hamdy left the liaison office, I met with his replacement (formerly his deputy) and again raised the missing soldier issue with passion. I expressed my outrage at Egypt's manifest bad will in such a sensitive humanitarian issue and explained the religious aspects involved, especially for the parents. I stressed that it was obvious that none of the soldiers was still alive but that, until we found their bodies, for every one in Israel they would be missing and not dead. My interlocutor assured me that he, personally, was genuinely interested in solving the problem in the shortest possible time (in some cases almost 20 years had already gone by). However, he emphasized that he believed that the army had exhausted its possibilities and by contrast with the civilian authorities, was not equipped to conduct a deeper investigation of the entire national territory. He advised me to use my good relations with the interior minister and to request of him that the *Mabakhes* (internal intelligence) take over from where the army had left off. I pointed out that the civilian authorities would never agree to intervene in matters that pertained to the army without receiving through the relevant channels the army's green light. He agreed and promised to take all necessary steps, including allowing the civilian authorities to enter military installations, carry out searches in closed military areas and interrogate military personnel. Obviously, I was not authorized to give him a positive answer without consulting both the foreign and defense ministries and I requested him to give me a few days to ponder over his proposal. I also stressed that, whatever my answer, Israel would continue to consider the Egyptian army as the major institution responsible for solving the issue of the missing soldiers. To me, it was clear that the army was determined to cease its involvement in a matter that had been dragging on for years and threw a heavy shadow on its credibility. We had no choice; the alternative would have been a total standstill in the searches. I sent a detailed report to Jerusalem, recommending following the liaison chief's advice and exploring a new approach that might eventually lead to better results. To be quite frank, knowing the Egyptian overall attitude on the issue, I was not optimistic about the final outcome but I firmly believed that we had to go through the motions and exhaust all possibilities.

I received authorization to give a positive answer and discuss the modalities directly with the interior minister, Abdel Halim Mussa. I was also instructed to suggest that the search be entrusted to a recently retired police general who would dedicate all his time to the investigation and co-ordinate action with the relevant military and civilian authorities. I was even authorized to hint that Israel would be ready to cover his salary and expenses. I knew for certain that such a proposal was an absolute non-starter but, as a good soldier, I carried out my instructions. I informed the chief of the liaison office of my decision to follow his advice and requested him to convey the army's green light to the civilian authorities. Some two weeks later, I met with the interior minister and briefed him on the missing soldiers issue as well as on our suggestion on how to handle it. From the minister's reactions, I realized that the liaison chief had briefed him thoroughly but he replied that he could not give a definitive answer before speaking personally with the defense minister and other relevant authorities (read: the president and the security services). He added that he had doubts about the efficiency of a police investigation after such a long period and stressed that, in any case, Egypt would never agree to one of its officers – retired or not – receiving a salary from a foreign power. Furthermore, he pointed out that an officer who was not on active duty would find it very difficult to activate police units throughout the country or to interrogate civilians and army officers. To leave the door open for continuing the dialogue, I formally asked the minister to entrust the matter directly to the civilian security services (*Mabakhes*) and to organize the continuation of the searches in any manner that he saw fit. In conclusion, the minister promised to study my proposal with the defense minister and the *Mabakhes* chief and contact me in a few days.

Several weeks passed without any sign from the minister. I was compelled to take the initiative and ask to meet him urgently. As usual, he received me warmly, informed me that the matter was still under study and kept me for more than an hour exchanging niceties. In the same period, the Israeli foreign minister, David Levy, was on an official visit to Egypt and raised with President Mubarak the perennial issue of the missing soldiers. I took advantage of this opportunity to tell the president of my contacts with the interior minister and requested his personal intervention. He reacted that, as a soldier himself, he was very sensitive to the issue and would immediately give adequate instructions. A few days later, the president received Levy a second time and I asked him directly if his instructions had been conveyed to the interior minister and if I could now fix a meeting with him. Mubarak answered that the minister himself would contact me in a few days. Levy urged the president to give the matter the highest priority and Mubarak reiterated his promise to see to it personally that things moved rapidly. And indeed, a few days later, the interior minister summoned me. He informed me officially that all necessary authorizations had been received and that, from then on, the issue of the missing soldiers was entrusted to the *Mabakhes*. He added that it had already formed a special police team to tackle the matter. I urged the minister to let me know the name of the commanding officer and to instruct him to remain in close contact with me so that I would not have to bother the minister himself more than necessary on this matter. I also requested him to allow a team of Israeli experts to brief the special team on all the material it had assembled over the years and co-ordinate with it the broad lines of investigations and searches. In reply, I received a nice smile from the minister and many *ahlan wa sahlan* (welcome) for the coming of the team but no date was set for the visit and no name was mentioned. It took me several phone calls and two more meetings with the minister to receive finally the name of the senior officer who had been appointed to centralize the special *Mabakhes* team. I was not surprised when I was informed that the matter had been entrusted to Police General Hany, the head of the Jewish and Israeli bureau in the civilian security service.

I met with him immediately and, after several more days of nagging, the Israeli team of experts arrived and met with Hani and two of his immediate subordinates. The experts briefed them extensively on each case and presented a series of proposals for co-ordinating and intensifying the searches. Hani rejected all the proposals *en bloc* and stressed that the Egyptian police did not need foreign help. He also refused to set a monthly meeting for briefing our team on the progress of the searches and instead promised to convene a meeting only when there would be something to report. We waited and waited but Hani did not call another meeting. Again, I had to run around and urge the Egyptians to let the Israeli team come again and receive the *Mabakhes* report. They finally agreed. Again, after a few postponements, the team arrived and met with General Hani and his immediate collaborators. The verbal report of the special team was detailed but added up to the words: *nada, niente*, nothing … ! We requested to meet personally the officers who had carried out the various investigations to make sure all possible angles had been covered. General Hani categorically refused, claiming that such meetings were in breach of Egyptian police regulations.

A few weeks before I left Cairo for India, I succeeded in arranging one more meeting and even in persuading General Hani to allow our team to visit the various locations where the missing soldiers had last been seen. We thought that it was a breakthrough but, after a short while, the Egyptians informed us that the police investigations had reached a dead-end and would be discontinued because they were a waste of time and money. To our great dismay, we were also told that the police had not been able to locate, for interrogation purposes, the addresses of retired army officers who had been involved in previous searches and that it was better if we applied directly to the army liaison office. After months of strenuous efforts, we were back to square one and the missing soldiers' issue became again a perennial topic on the agenda of the military committee. I must confess that I resent, to this very day, this cruel maneuver, which demonstrates more than anything else Egypt's *modus operandi*. The sudden discovery of Aran Cohen's body, almost a year after I left Cairo, is in flagrant contradiction to the Egyptians' categorical assurance that the searches had been exhaustive and that nothing more could be done. Clearly, stubbornness and perseverance bring results! A little goodwill on the Egyptians' part would literally do miracles and bring to an end this gloomy affair but, to our great sorrow, this goodwill does not exist. On the contrary, there is manifest bad faith and the obvious intention to stall the searches and turn the issue into a source of political gains. Incidentally, the remains of the submarine Dakar were located in mid-1999 far from the Egyptian coast, and so this issue has been erased from the military committee's agenda; but the issue of the missing soldiers is still ritually debated. Towards the end of 1999, two more bodies were found in the Egyptian desert exactly where our experts had been pointing for many years. It took repeated personal pleas by President Weizman to President Mubarak to find those bodies.

Let me now turn to an altogether different topic. According to the military annex, the second phase of withdrawal was conditional on the prior stationing of a substantial UN force in zone A (the belt along the Israeli border) and Zone B (most of Sinai) to supervise the faithful implementation of the annex provisions and prevent infractions. The UN, however, rejected the Camp David accords in all their components and refused to provide UN forces, which would have meant an indirect legitimization of the agreement. Up to the last moment Egypt hoped that after things had calmed down, it would succeed with US help in changing the negative UN stand despite the Arab consensus against Camp David. However, this proved to be wishful thinking – there was no chance whatsoever of getting the UN Security Council to agree to the stationing of a UN force in Sinai. Clearly, this *impasse* could have been a major impediment to the implementation of the withdrawal provision in the agreement but, happily, the annex had an escape provision that allowed an alternative solution.

Israel, for its part, was not enthusiastic from the outset to have the UN play a leading role in the implementation of the Camp David accords. It bore in mind the sad precedent of 1967 when the then secretary-general, U 'thant, refused to heed Israeli pleas and decided to vacate UN forces from the Gaza Strip and the Sharm el Sheikh region upon Nasser's unilateral demand. Israel was also conscious of the tremendous influence that the Arabs and their automatic supporters carried in the UN, which precluded genuine neutrality in cases of possible conflict of interpretation and implementation of the military annex. Nevertheless, it yielded to Egyptian pressure and agreed to the stationing of UN forces but it was careful to include in the military annex an escape provision that allowed, if need be, the creation of an alternative international force that would assume the UN's role. After it became clear that the UN would not change its stand, Egypt had no alternative but to agree to enforce the escape provision.

As I have said, the Egyptians were convinced that Israel was looking for a pretext to postpone, or cancel altogether, the second phase of withdrawal and feared that this issue might provide such a pretext. Their apprehension increased in the light of Prime Minister Begin's public statement that, without the stationing of a supervising military force in Sinai, Israel would postpone the withdrawal. They protested at Begin's statement but soon after they gave their agreement to the creation of an alternative international force. With time running short, the negotiations between the two parties on the composition, tasks and powers of the force (as well as the contacts with countries that might contribute to it) were carried out at a feverish pace, with the active mediation of the USA. Despite the military nature of the negotiations, they were not entrusted to the military committee but to a mostly joint civilian committee.

On the Israeli side, the director-general of the foreign ministry, Dave Kimche, headed the negotiating team in which participated: the legal adviser to the government, Yitshak Zamir, the legal adviser to the foreign ministry, Ruth Lapidot, a member of the Israeli embassy (myself) and representatives of various ministries and institutions. As usual, Egypt was represented by the same team of diplomats who dealt with Israeli affairs with the addition of Admiral Hamdy, the chairman of the joint military committee. In contrast with their *modus operandi* in other fields, the Egyptians did not pile up obstacles and did not drag their feet; on the contrary, they strove to make up for lost time. One should not infer from this that the negotiations were easy and that Egypt automatically agreed to all Israeli wishes as if they were *sine-qua-non* conditions – the Egyptian delegation engaged in very tough bargaining. It insisted on each comma and full stop in the agreement, strove to limit as far as possible the responsibilities and powers of the international force as well as its composition and strength, and efficiently prevented the slightest infringement – implicit or explicit – of Egypt's sovereignty over the whole of Sinai. Nevertheless, it had finally to accept the creation of a substantial and well-armed force, agree to have it stationed in most of Sinai and grant it free movement and extra-territorial rights in conformity with the provisions of the military annex.

The Israeli delegation also stood firm on each and every point that was of real importance. We did not have the intention, declared or concealed, of infringing upon Egyptian sovereignty or humiliating Egypt in any way. Our only goal was to make sure that the international force would be strong enough to carry out its duties and that its deployment and powers allowed it to function efficaciously without undue intervention on the part of the Egyptian authorities. Prime Minister Begin attached the utmost importance to the negotiations and supervised them personally on a day-to-day basis. He considered the stationing in Sinai of an international force with teeth as the sole guarantee that Egypt would indefinitely abandon military confrontation and thus ensure the success of the whole Camp David process. Throughout the discussions, he received up-to-date reports from Dave Kimche, sent clear-cut instructions to the Israeli delegation and directed its steps down to the smallest detail. More than once, he instructed the delegation to retreat from from a given position that did not meet with his approval or on which he had second thoughts.

The negotiations were concluded successfully and the agreement reached between the parties was faithfully and rapidly implemented – in both letter and spirit. There were no delays, no procrastination and no haggling. The multinational force consisted of some 5,000 men from all army disciplines and was equipped with all the material necessary for fulfilling its tasks. It was deployed in strategic points in Sinai just in time to make possible Israel's withdrawal on 25 April 1982 as stipulated in the Camp David accords. In accordance with an Israeli demand, only countries that maintained full diplomatic relations with Israel were allowed to participate in the force. The USA provided the largest contingent and agreed to cover one-third of the forces' budget (the rest was to be borne by Egypt and Israel in equal shares). An American diplomat was appointed director-general of the force and was based in Rome. Two representations were established, one in Cairo and the other in Tel Aviv, to co-ordinate the forces' activities and ensure its smooth functioning. One of the most important provisions in the agreement specified that any changes pertaining to the multinational force – its composition, manpower, deployment, equipment, budget, tasks and removal from Sinai – necessitated the prior consent of both Egypt and Israel.

In the period when I was not directly involved with Egyptian affairs, I never came to hear of any problem with Egypt concerning the multinational force. When I returned to Cairo in 1990, the resident representative in Egypt was among the first foreign diplomats to pay me a courtesy call (previously, he had served as the American military attaché in Cairo). During my stay, he maintained a close relationship with me, responded willingly to my social invitations and did not hesitate to invite me to social events in his residence, attended by the Egyptian military top brass. In Cairo, where Israeli diplomats were practically ostracized, this was not a trivial matter, especially if we recall that army officers were under strict orders not to have any contact with Israelis. I also had excellent relations with the force commander, a Dutch general, who was quite sympathetic to Israel, but always made sure he showed absolute neutrality and treated each side equally as befitted his position. The director-general was stationed in Rome and would come to Cairo only from time to time. He always paid me working visits and responded to my social invitations.

The USA continued to furnish the main nucleus of the force (and still does). The force functioned like a well-oiled machine and did not encounter obstacles in its work placed by the local authorities, by contrast with other fields of interaction with Israel. The military personnel was not particularly overworked – officers and soldiers spent most of their time in observation points in the middle of the desert, carried out routine patrol duties and inspection tours, and lived in rather uncomfortable barracks. They kept an ever-watchful eye on what was happening and reported faithfully on the slightest infraction by either of the two parties. However, infractions were quite rare and boredom was the key word. As a rule, violations of the accords were tackled by the joint military committee (liaison office) and were solved in a spirit of co-operation and understanding. Only in very rare cases (as with the infringements of

Egyptian air space or the entrance of Egyptian officers into zone A) was the matter referred to the diplomatic and political levels with a view to emphasizing the gravity that one of the two sides attached to it.

In my second period, the Egyptian press began to criticize the force for the way in which it performed its duties and for the cost of its maintenance. There were also a few articles hinting that it was no longer needed. Knowing that the Egyptian press normally reflected their Master's Voice and that there could be no smoke without fire, I put out a few feelers and double-checked my information. My doubts were confirmed and I reported to Jerusalem that Egypt would soon try testing Israel's resolve in maintaining the multinational force in its original structure and tasks. Indeed, a few weeks later, the topic began popping up in my conversations in the foreign ministry, at first indirectly and then openly. My interlocutors casually drew my attention to the criticism in the press, then pointed to the total inactivity of the force and its great cost (at the time $150 million per year). Later, they stressed the excellent relations between our two countries that made the presence of the force unnecessary in the light of the almost total lack of infractions by either side. I would listen attentively and refrain, as much as possible, from direct answers or comments. Finally, the Egyptians hinted that they might officially request holding in-depth discussions on the future of the force and/or request a revision of its structure and tasks. I reported to Jerusalem and received instructions to kill the matter before it took on dangerous proportions.

I waited until the Egyptians raised the topic again and, for the first time, I reacted directly. I gave them my personal opinion that Israel strongly believed that the multinational force remained indispensable and that it would not agree to any changes in its structure, tasks, strength, budget, deployment or functioning. The Egyptians got the message (it was clear that I could not have been so assertive without instructions from Jerusalem) and refrained from raising the topic officially at the political level. They availed themselves of the annual discussions on the force's budget and called for a substantial reduction in expenses, in particular dispensing with costly units such as helicopters, light planes and gunboat units. Israel, wanting to preserve the good atmosphere prevailing in respect of the multinational force, agreed to slight cuts in the budget. However, (supported by the USA) it refused to dispense with any of the above-mentioned units or to reduce their strength, stressing that they were all necessary for efficacious supervision. In the wake of this meeting, the topic disappeared from our conversations with the Egyptians and at the same time miraculously vanished from both government and opposition press.

Let me add that, in addition to their regular tasks, the officers and soldiers of the multinational force were always ready to extend their help to Israeli tourists stranded in the desert or to accident victims. Several times, they flew injured Israelis back home in their helicopters and, to our sorrow, the bodies of people involved in accidents. In emergencies, we never hesitated to address ourselves to them and they, for their part, never refused to meet our requests despite the increasing number of cases and the heavy burden that this represented.

A secondary problem linked indirectly to military topics is that of Egyptian citizens arrested for terrorist activities against Israel during the occupation of Sinai and condemned to long periods of imprisonment by Israeli military courts. Already in early 1981, the Egyptians raised the issue several times – at first they put out feelers to test our reaction, but later they officially demanded the immediate release of Egyptian prisoners, arguing that they were prisoners-of-war like all other Egyptian soldiers captured by Israel. They insisted that the terrorist actions that they had perpetrated were at the time legitimate acts of war carried out on the instructions of the Egyptian military authorities and part of Egypt's legitimate struggle for the liberation of its occupied territory. Israel rejected the Egyptian claims and stressed the intrinsic differences between legitimate military actions and vile terrorist attacks against civilian populations. The Egyptians did not desist and, from time to time, they raised the issue again. However, they did gradually cease to present it as a request for the release of prisoners-of-war and dwelt instead on the humanitarian aspects of the problem, insisting that Israel make a goodwill gesture as a tangible expression of the peace existing between the two countries. Finally, they suggested that the prisoners be transferred to Egyptian jails for completion of their sentences and pledged not to release them before the end of their time. At this stage, the embassy in Cairo recommended that Israel make a gesture of goodwill and remove from the agenda an issue that was poisoning the atmosphere and had ceased to be relevant. The foreign ministry supported this recommendation and raised the matter before the relevant inter-ministerial committee. The security authorities flatly refused, arguing that there was no justification in granting preferential treatment to terrorists and murderers only because they held Egyptian citizenship and warned that Israeli public opinion (especially the victims' relatives) would vehemently oppose such a course of action. The Egyptian plea was rejected and our interlocutors were profoundly disappointed. They expressed in sharp words their resentment at Israeli stubbornness, lack of feelings and political wisdom, stressing that the issue was fanning internal unrest and that the opposition was accusing the government of abandoning to their bitter fate Egyptian citizens who had bravely fought for Egypt. The Egyptian stand made sense and the embassy appealed against the decision of the inter-ministerial committee, stressing among other arguments that conditions in Egyptian jails were much worse than those prevailing in Israeli prisons. Again the foreign ministry supported the embassy's stand and argumentation but again the decision was negative.

When I returned to Egypt in 1990, seven years later, I was surprised that many prisoners holding Egyptian citizenship were still in Israeli prisons. The Egyptians requested an up-to-date list and, after several weeks, it was handed to them. It apparently did not cover all the names that were on their own list (which they had compounded from the prisoners' relatives) and included names of prisoners who were not Egyptians. Lists came and went without bridging the discrepancies because of the difficulty of identifying Arab names (which are in general composed of three forenames and can easily be interchanged). In spite of the Egyptian insistence and repeated requests, only one prisoner was released during my second period in Egypt at the personal request of the Egyptian foreign minister, Amr Mussa. The prisoner in question was an elderly man sentenced to life whose health had seriously deteriorated. He was handed over to the Egyptians at the Raffiah terminal through the military liaison office. Since I left Cairo in 1992, I have not followed developments in this matter. However, I recently read in the Israeli press (February 1999) that the longest-serving Egyptian prisoner had been released as a gesture of goodwill. Incidentally, we are witnessing nowadays exactly the same *quid-pro-quo* with the Palestinian authority regarding the release of Palestinian prisoners serving sentences in Israeli jails for terrorist activities.

In the 1990s, as in the 1980s, the military committee was responsible for the day-to-day relations between the two armies. In addition to the perennial topics (such as the search for the missing soldiers) which were still on the agenda, most activity focused on marking the border between the two countries and preparing adequate maps and aerial photographs. The Egyptians had an ambiguous approach to this. On the one hand, they were interested in clearly demarcating their border with Israel and, on the other hand, they understood that Israel would take advantage of the occasion to create a *fait accompli* in the Gaza region and in the region of Taba (particularly in relation to the territorial waters). They began piling up obstacles and under various pretexts they postponed topographical surveys and measurements that had been decided in the military committee with their own approval. Finally, the embassy had to raise the matter to the political level and the Egyptians spelled out frankly their fears. It was decided therefore to start the demarcation of the borderline (and other related steps) from the center point and to proceed gradually on one side towards Gaza, and on the other side towards Taba, hoping that in the meantime a solution would be found. When I left Cairo, the works had just begun and I can only assume that by now a cosmetic solution has been found to the problems that worried the Egyptians and that the borders between the two countries have been clearly demarcated.

Another perennial topic, which the military committee still dealt with, was the co-ordination between the two countries for preventing infiltration of hostile elements (read: Palestinian terrorists) from Egypt to Israel through the barbed-wire fence along the border. In general, the border was quiet and each side respected its commitments. However it was far from being hermetically sealed and, from time to time, there were infiltrations that levied a heavy price in lives and property (not to mention the smuggling of arms and drugs). In general, these infiltrations were carried out through narrow tunnels dug in the sandy soil under the border fence (a means used to this very day by terrorist infiltrators and smugglers). It is difficult to determine to what extent individual Egyptian soldiers and officers were/are involved in facilitating these infiltrations, or whether they turned a blind eye. One of the deadliest infiltrations was indeed that of an Egyptian policeman in uniform who crossed the border in broad daylight, ambushed a bus on the main road to Eilat, killed and wounded several Israeli civilians and fled back to Egypt. He was arrested by the authorities, brought to trial and condemned to a heavy jail term. Throughout the trial, the Egyptian press depicted him as a national hero and the lawyers (who volunteered to defend him) as well as the judges supported his brave action against the Zionist enemy. The opposition, from left and right, insisted vociferously that he be immediately released and decorated for bravery. Worse, the authorities did not allow the embassy to delegate an observer to the trial and was not even given a copy of the judgement, despite its reiterated requests and protests. Added to previous similar incidents, especially the Ras Burka incident and the bus attack near Cairo, the toll on Israeli lives was dreadfully heavy. I did not hesitate to emphasize to my Egyptian interlocutors that 'the so-called border of peace is much bloodier in terms of civilian casualties than all the other Israeli borders put together'.

Let me turn now to an altogether different issue, which is still very much on the agenda and has far-reaching implications. It kept us busy throughout my stay in Cairo as ambassador and is one of the major areas of contention between the two countries. I am referring to what the Egyptians define as Israel's nuclear capability. Egypt strongly believes that Israel has not only achieved a nuclear option but also has in stock a substantial number of nuclear weapons, both strategic and tactical. No one and no argument can move Egyptians from this axiomatic credo. It is not a new development; it goes as far back as the independence war in 1948. I recall, in my youth in Cairo, that everyone in Egypt was convinced that 'the Jews' had received nuclear devices from their brethren in America and were on the verge of using them to overcome the tremendous superiority of the Arab armies. Every air raid on Cairo provoked not only panic but also aroused the acute fear that the end of the world was coming and that the Jews were going to drop an atom bomb on Cairo. No nuclear bombs and not even conventional bombs! – all Israel did (and could do at the time) was to drop from light aircraft a few hand grenades that did not damage the city in the slightest. Nevertheless, the Egyptians' certainty – people and government – that the Jews had nuclear weapons became stronger from year to year. Clearly, articles in the international press as well as reports to that effect by intelligence agencies and the annual ritualistic debates in various UN institutions on Israel's nuclear weapons (as if it were an established fact) contributed to a great extent to exacerbating this Egyptian conviction. Already in the mid-1970s, Egypt and other Arab states took the initiative in raising the issue on three fronts and continue to do so to this very day. In the First Committee of the General Assembly, Egypt tables every year a draft resolution calling for the nuclear disarmament of the Middle East, along the same lines as the regional arrangements in South and Central America. At first, the draft resolution pointed an accusing finger at Israel, but in order to have it passed by consensus (and thus magnify its political weight) Egypt refrained from citing Israel by name. Each year, Egypt tries to revive the original draft but has to back down in the light of Israeli and western threats to vote against the resolution. Egypt then has to agree to a more moderate version and the resolution (virtually identical to the resolution passed the previous year) is adopted by consensus with Israel's active support.

In parallel, a second front is opened in the same committee. Each year, an item entitled 'Israel's Nuclear Armament' is placed on the agenda and a fully-fledged debate takes place after the presentation of a report by a special commission appointed by the secretary-general (in accordance with the previous year's resolution). A new resolution, more severe and more explicit, sponsored by the Arab states and their supporters, is passed by a majority vote and instructs the secretary-general to continue investigating the matter and report to the next General Assembly. Indeed, the secretary-general has established a permanent body to supervise what goes on in Israel in the nuclear field, and to prepare an annual report for the General Assembly. Israel co-operates with that body and agrees year after year to receive a small group of experts to investigate the situation *in loco*. No evidence has ever been found and the annual report relies heavily on press speculation and unsubstantiated reports by various intelligence agencies. To this day, there is no UN document that specifies that Israel possesses nuclear weapons of any kind but this does not deter Egypt and other Arab states from raising the matter every year and passing a new one-sided resolution.

The third front is, paradoxically, linked to the struggle against the former apartheid system. The attack on Israel takes place in the Third Committee, which deals with human rights and decolonization. The Arabs, with Egypt at their forefront, have succeeded over the years in portraying Israel as an active partner of the former racist regime in South Africa and in equating the situation of the black community in that country with the situation of the Palestinians in the territories. Each year, and by overwhelming majority, they passed resolutions condemning the economic ties of the western powers with South Africa, singling out by name Israel and Israel alone. Moreover, they even succeeded in passing resolutions (that had no bearing whatsoever on human rights) condemning the nuclear co-operation between Israel and South Africa and calling for its immediate cessation though, at the time, there were no more than unsubstantiated rumors to that effect.

After the bombing by Israel of the Iraqi nuclear reactor in 1982, Egypt increased its attacks on Israel in the nuclear field. In private conversations, the Egyptians did not conceal their satisfaction at the removal of a potential danger for the region (and for themselves) and expressed their admiration for the manner in which the Israeli airforce had carried out such a complicated strike. Publicly, however, they led the Arab onslaught in the international arena demanding condemnation of Israel and the imposition on it of sanctions, including suspension from the relevant international organizations.

At first, in the 1970s–early 1980s, the Egyptian initiatives did not stem from apprehension for Egypt's security and were mainly indended to harass Israel in the international arena and contest its legitimacy. Gradually, with the increase of press and intelligence reports about Israel's nuclear capability, the topic became very real for Egypt. Amr Mussa, who was appointed foreign minister in 1990, made it a top-priority issue of Egypt's foreign policy with the declared goal of compelling Israel to join the Non-Proliferation Treaty (NPT) and abandon all nuclear weapons that it might possess. As a former permanent representative to the UN, he knew from personal experience that the topic found resonance in world public opinion. He appointed the former counselor of Egypt's representation to the UN and its chief delegate in the First Committee, Ismail Fahmi (currently Egyptian ambassaador to the USA and son of the former Egyptian foreign minister, who resigned in protest of the Camp David agreement), as chief of his cabinet, directly responsible for disarmament issues. Mussa entrusted to his experienced hands the nuclear-related campaign against Israel and, after the Madrid conference, appointed him concurrently head of the Egyptian delegation to the multilateral disarmament committee. The Egyptian press (as usual, upon instructions from above) periodically and pungently raised the matter and called on the USA to abandon its biased attitude towards Israel and pressure it into joining the NPT, as it was doing with other countries that had not yet adhered to the treaty. In parallel, Egyptian diplomacy initiated a worldwide campaign, approaching all countries repeatedly and raising the issue in each and every international institution.

As part of this campaign, President Mubarak put forward a well publicized proposal for a complete ban on all weapons of mass destruction in the middle east (and not only nuclear weapons) claiming that the chemical weapons in the Arab arsenals were intended to counter-balance Israel's non-conventional capability. He insisted that there was no moral justification in demanding that the Arabs renounce their chemical weapons as long as Israel did not abandon its nuclear arsenal. He also hinted that Egypt would not renew its adherence to the NPT if Israel did not first join the treaty. The Egyptian foreign minister, Amr Mussa, was much more incisive: he stated repeatedly that Egypt was determined not to sign the NPT's renewal if Israel did not do so beforehand. At the same time, he visited the Arab capitals to convince them to actively support the Egyptian stand and to present a united Arab front.

I reported to Jerusalem and forecasted that the nearer the date set for the NPT conference, the more Egypt would intensify its activity and become threatening. I suggested that we should not react to the Egyptian provocation beyond consistently reiterating our traditional stand that Israel would not be the first country to introduce nuclear weapons in the region. I also suggested that we reiterate Israel's readiness to discuss (in the framework of the multilateral disarmament committee in Madrid) general disarmament in the middle east – both conventional and non-conventional. I warned against being dragged into endless discussions with Egypt or trying to conciliate it by offering concessions that, in any case, would only increase their appetite. I expressed the opinion that as the renewal of the NPT was a major American interest, we should leave the matter entirely to the USA. It was bound to use all the leverage it had to prevent the creation of a united Arab front against the renewal of the NPT in 1993 and would find a way to twist Egypt's arm. From the developments that occurred after I left Cairo at the end of 1992, I deduce that my recommendations were not accepted and, on the contrary, Israel made great efforts to soothe the Egyptians by putting forward various conciliatory proposals. As I had forecasted, Egypt rejected proposal after proposal and made it clear that it would not accept anything less than Israel's immediate adherence to the NPT. Finally, as expected, Uncle Sam stepped in and Egypt not only did not succeed in organizing a united Arab front but also signed the NPT renewal without Israel adhering to it or even promising that it would do so in the foreseeable future.

To sum up this aspect of Egyptian–Israeli relations, let me say that beyond political and propaganda tactics and prestige considerations, there is no doubt that Egypt is genuinely concerned by the possibility (from its standpoint – the certainty) that Israel possesses nuclear weapons. It is not because Egypt fears that Israel might use those weapons in a future military confrontation between the two countries or against a sister Arab state – it knows for certain that this possibility is nil. Egypt realizes that possession of nuclear weapons would magnify Israel's intrinsic weight in the region well beyond its geographical and economic size making it into one of the leading powers and Egypt's rival. As is well known, Egypt's motto is that Israel should be cut down to its natural dimensions (I will later discuss this point in more detail). As I see it, Egypt will not rest until it reaches parity with Israel, either by attaining nuclear capability or by compelling Israel to renounce its nuclear option. This matter has become a major goal of its foreign policy and a top-priority issue for its diplomacy. I firmly believe that – after Egypt achieves secondary goals such as a comprehensive peace in the region and the creation of a Palestinian state – the nuclear issue will become its central target and it will not relent until a satisfactory solution is found. Amr Mussa has repeatedly stated that Israel's full integration in the region is inconceivable as long as it continues to possess arms of mass destruction that endanger its neighbors.

After the Rabin government came to power in mid-1992, I expressed my assessment to Dr Yossi Beilin during his first visit to Egypt as deputy foreign minister and urged him not to raise the nuclear topic in his meeting with Amr Mussa. Nevertheless he tried, in the most persuasive manner, to convince Mussa to moderate Egypt's attacks on Israel in the multilateral disarmament committee and in the Egyptian press. He stressed that widening the scope of diplomatic confrontation at this stage, when the new Israeli government was preparing public opinion for fundamental changes of policy and major concessions, would only complicate matters. Amr Mussa promised to study Beilin's request but, clearly, the Israeli plea fell on deaf ears (how could it be otherwise?). The Egyptians continued their attacks and even intensified them. The topic was too important for them to engage in diplomatic niceties with Israel or try to achieve tactical co-ordination with it. They had their own agenda and pursued it persistently (and still do).

Incidentally, in my last year in Cairo, on the occasion of UN day, the American College invited me to participate in a panel on disarmament. It was the first and only time I had been invited to speak before an audience of youngsters in Cairo (maybe because most of them were foreigners and the organizers were Americans). My colleagues in the panel were (to my great surprise) the foreign minister, Amr Mussa, and the adviser to the president, Osama Elbaz. Their children were studying at the College and it seems that they could not refuse to appear together with the Israeli ambassador on such an occasion. The debate was meant to be of a general character and cover disarmament issues worldwide but both men devoted their intervention exclusively to Israel and depicted its nuclear capability as a cardinal danger to world peace. They called for a radical and immediate solution and stressed that, without it, no genuine and lasting peace in the middle east was possible. Mussa also voiced Egypt's position that the international community, with the USA at its forefront, should compel Israel to sign the NPT and to desist from any present or future nuclear option. Elbaz was more pragmatic. He expressed the opinion that, as long as the USA supported Israel, it was impossible to compel it to do anything against its will. He added that the nuclear issue would have to find its solution in the framework of a comprehensive regional negotiation to which also Iran, Iraq and Pakistan would be a party. He stressed that these negotiations would have to lead not only to an absolute ban on all weapons of mass destruction but also to a substantial reduction in conventional weaponry and military strength, which were no less a danger to peace and stability in the region. It was the first time that I had heard a top Egyptian personality make a link between the two issues and indeed adopt the longstanding Israeli thesis that conventional and non-conventional weapons were intimately linked and would have to be tackled together, like two sides of the same coin. Elbaz's position was in contrast to the official Egyptian policy (and still is) and has never been voiced in any official forum or private conversation. I do believe that, in the last resort, Egypt will have to agree to linking conventional and non-conventional weapons. However, it will never turn a blind eye to the nuclear issue and, on the contrary, it will continue to put it forcefully at the center of the stage.

I will now proceed to the Taba issue – an issue that burdened relations between the two countries for seven long years (1982–89). Taba is an enchanting enclave of 1,020 square meters on the Red Sea. The background to the differences between Israel and Egypt is widely known. At first, the joint military committee dealt with the issue but it was later entrusted to an ad hoc civilian committee. The topic arose a few months before the implementation of the second phase of withdrawal from Sinai. The Egyptians contested the ongoing construction of the Sonesta Hotel (today the Taba Hilton) in Taba by an Israeli promoter, Eli Papushado (incidentally, an immigrant from Egypt). Egypt formally pointed out that Taba was within Egypt's recognized international boundaries and was due to be returned to Egypt in the framework of the Camp David agreement. Israel insisted that, in accordance with its maps, Taba was an Israeli territory – construction of the hotel continued uninterrupted and was even speeded up. The Egyptians raised the matter at every opportunity and demanded an immediate stop to construction works. Every meeting and conversation began with Taba and finished with Taba. On one occasion, in the middle of an inflamed explanation that Taba was within Israel's boundaries and that Egyptian maps must be mistaken, my interlocutors interrupted me, brandishing a small map of Israel that had been distributed worldwide by the Israeli ministry of tourism. The map showed clearly that Taba was inside Egypt – well beyond the Israeli boundary! I was confused for a moment but I very quickly recovered my spirits and claimed brazenly that the map was too small to reach a conclusion. I added that objective surveyors would define the border in the field and Taba would prove to be on the Israeli side of the border. I returned to the embassy and sent an urgent cable to the ministry reporting the unpleasant incident and drawing attention to the fact that our right hand seemed not to know what our left hand was doing. In response, the ministry instructed all our embassies to cease distributing the map and destroy all their stock. It was too late; the Egyptians already had several copies and taunted us by pulling out the map each time we assured them that Taba was within Israel's boundaries.

An even more embarrassing incident happened to Ambassador Sasson. He was on an inspection tour to the Taba region together with the then

Egyptian foreign minister, Kamal Hassan Ali, and the head of the joint military committee, Brigadier-General Dov Sion as well as several other Egyptian and Israeli personalities. Suddenly, as the group approached a small hill, Kamal Hassan Ali, who had been posted as a young captain in the region, claimed that to the best of his recollection there was at the top of the hill a border-stone marking the border between the two countries. The Israelis maintained that there was no such stone but, after a little digging, remains of the stone were found. They had to concede that the stone marked the border but they claimed that old maps of the region showed that from the top of the hill the border slanted up to the sea, leaving the Taba enclave inside Israel.

As always, the Egyptian press was mobilized in support of the Egyptian stand and viciously attacked Israel, claiming that the Egyptian people would never abandon a single grain of sand of its national territory and that the Taba issue was jeopardizing the entire peace process. The press demanded that the enclave be returned immediately to Egypt and for months an orchestrated campaign raged, blowing the issue out of any reasonable proportion. Taba was depicted as a formidable strategic and economic asset and one of the most important locations in the world: whoever controlled it, it was claimed, controlled the whole Red Sea. According to the Egyptian press, if Israel succeeded in perpetuating its hold on Taba, it would represent a major danger not only for Egypt but also for all the riparian Arab countries and would deal a death-blow to the prospects of tourism in Sinai.

In Israel, all those who dealt with the Taba problem knew that if the only criteria were the location of the borderline between the former Egyptian Kingdom and Mandatory Palestine, there was no doubt that Taba was within Egypt's boundaries. Israel's case was justified only if the scope of the dispute were widened to encompass the situation that prevailed in Palestine before the British mandate. This assumption was at the basis of the Israeli stand and dictated the tactics of negotiation with the Egyptians. Moshe Sasson and I did not see eye to eye as to the best way to tackle the matter. Moshe feared that the Taba issue might impair the peace process and leave negative after effects, especially if Israel delayed finding a solution acceptable to Egypt or imposed an outcome in its own favor. From the first moment, he considered the issue a thorn in the flesh of peace and advocated its prompt solution. I, on the other hand, considered the issue as of marginal importance and believed that Egypt was blowing it out of all proportion with a view to using it as a bargaining chip in wider and more important issues. I did not agree with the opinion that procrastinating or imposing on Egypt a solution in Israel's favor would endanger peace or seriously damage relations with Egypt. Equally, I did not believe that a prompt solution along the lines advocated by Egypt would bring the two countries closer or bring about a significant change in the normalization process beyond the parameters defined by Egypt from the outset. To Moshe's credit, he did not prevent me from expounding my views, verbally and in writing, to the decision-makers in Jerusalem. In any case, the outcome did not depend on the embassy's assessments. The policy line was decided upon at the highest level and was closer to my views than to Moshe's. As a matter of course, both of us complied faithfully with the instructions from Jerusalem and implemented them in letter and spirit. The difference between Moshe and me did not create any tension between us and we continued to work hand in hand in understanding and friendship.

The Taba issue reached its climax on the last day before the date set for the final withdrawal from Sinai. Weeks of intensive discussions had not brought any closer the parties' divergent positions and they could not agree, even in broad outline, on how to proceed with the issue and certainly not on how to solve it. The Egyptians feared that Israel might postpone the withdrawal or impose a solution to its liking; they invited to Cairo a delegation headed by the then director-general of the foreign ministry, Dave Kimche, with a view to making a last-minute effort to find a solution. It was a marathon of non-stop discussions that lasted in to the small hours of the morning. The Egyptian team was headed by Boutros Ghali himself but, as usual, was composed of the same diplomats who always dealt with Israeli affairs. In our internal consultations, I advocated that we tell the Egyptians bluntly that they would have to renounce the Taba enclave and that it was a relatively small price for receiving back the whole of Sinai. I warned our decision-makers that sticking to the argumentation that the issue was a purely technical one, which would be solved by an accurate survey of the borderline, was tantamount to losing Taba. I stressed that the Egyptians were not looking for a face-saving device, as some of us believed, and that, in the absence of a political decision at the highest level to the contrary, they would persevere until they attained their target. I added that, after our withdrawal, their hands would be free to do so without fearing any backlash. After a short discussion, my proposal was rejected on the assumption (which proved unfounded!) that time and the *fait accompli* worked in our favor. It was decided to persevere with our original argumentation and refrain from creating a situation that might have an adverse effect on the normalization process with Egypt and the continuation of the peace process. We did not insist on an immediate decision in Israel's favor (which in the circumstances of the time could have been obtained) and did not condition the implementation of the second (and last phase) of withdrawal from Sinai on solving the Taba issue. The Egyptians sighed with relief and, at the last moment, agreed that the Taba enclave and 14 less important locations under discussion would remain temporarily in Israeli hands until the experts of the two countries carried out a thorough study of the existing maps and defined the exact borderline. It was also decided that the joint military committee should deal at a stepped-up pace with the arrangements related to the transitional period. The crisis had been avoided and the next day the last Israeli soldier pulled out from Sinai.

Only a few days went by before the Egyptians again raised the Taba issue and formally requested, in accordance with the Camp David agreement, to bring the matter to arbitration. Israel did not reject the Egyptian request but insisted that we first exhaust the other two possibilities mentioned in the agreement for settling differences between the parties: direct negotiations and mediation. The relevant provision did not specifically state the order of the three possible procedures and did not determine how the parties would decide which procedure to adopt and when. Nevertheless, since the three procedures (direct negotiations, mediation and arbitration) were cited in that order, Israel maintained that this was the order of precedence set by the agreement and should, therefore, be strictly adhered to. The Egyptians had no alternative and they agreed to start direct negotiations in the framework of the military committee, as decided by Boutros Ghali and Dave Kimche on the eve of the Israeli withdrawal. They also understood that the matter would not be settled in a matter of days as they had first thought and that, in the meantime, it was in their best interests to calm spirits in Egypt. Overnight, the Taba issue vanished from the press, the attacks on Israel ceased and the enclave was depicted as a God-forsaken location, which had no strategic or economic value. One of the most eminent Egyptian military correspondents, Mohamed Abd El Moneim (a few years later he was appointed spokesman of the presidency and was very close to President Mubarak) was specially dispatched to Taba. He published a long feature article in the weekly *Al Mussaouar*, accompanied by a score of pictures in which he depicted Taba as no more than a few hillocks of sand that had no military or economic value. Again – if there was still any need – this proved that the Egyptian press was and still is orchestrated from above.

One should not conclude that Egypt abandoned the cause. On the contrary, it increased its pressure in the framework of the military committee and raised a series of demands related to the transitional period that were rejected outright by Israel. The Egyptians demanded, among other things:

- Joint administration with Israel of the Taba enclave with equal powers and rights;
- Posting Egyptian police alongside Israeli police;
- Free access for Egyptian citizens to the enclave without the need to present identity documents as was the case with Israeli citizens entering the region;
- Bringing to trial criminal offenders in the enclave before Egyptian and not Israeli courts;
- Application of Egyptian laws and regulations to the enclave;
- Closure of the Sonesta Hotel and the Raphi Nelson holiday village;

271

- Discontinuation of all tourism activities;
- Transfer of the enclave's administration and control to the multinational force.

Finally, after lengthy and bitter discussions with the active mediation of the USA, complicated arrangements were put in place that for all practical purposes left the enclave in Israeli hands but guaranteed that the issue would remain alive. Among other steps, Israel agreed to the stationing in the enclave of a small unit of the multinational force without defining either its legal status or the scope of its tasks and powers.

With the conclusion of this interim agreement, Egypt claimed that the phase of direct negotiations had reached stalemate and was therefore concluded. They demanded that the matter be brought before arbitration. Israel insisted on continuing the search for a settlement through direct negotiations but, after several more fruitless meetings, it agreed that it was time to move to the second phase: mediation and not arbitration as the Egyptians wanted. The reason was self-evident: in an arbitration process, contrary to a mediation process, the rules of procedure are not flexible and the arbitrators are bound to take into consideration only written documents and contractual commitments. They do not strive to conciliate between the positions of the parties and make a ruling exclusively on the legal merits of each party's arguments. In this case, agreeing to go to arbitration would automatically have entailed the upholding of the Egyptian position since Israel had specifically agreed in the Camp David accords to withdraw to the mandatory boundaries. There was no doubt whatsoever that, during the British mandate, Taba was administered from Cairo and not Jerusalem. In mediation, parties can raise arguments that go beyond the narrow framework of written undertakings. If the mediators find them *prima-facie* reasonable and substantiated, they can (and will) attempt to reach a compromise that will safeguard, as much as possible, the interests of both sides. Israel had very strong arguments to support its historic rights over Taba. It had been, beyond any doubt, for hundreds of years, an integral part of the Palestine province within the Ottoman Empire and was transferred to Egypt at the beginning of the century for administrative convenience. The Egyptians, again because they had no alternative, agreed to mediation but on condition that Israel undertook to refer the matter to arbitration if mediation also reached a dead-end within a limited period of time.

At this stage, towards the end of 1983, I left Cairo for Geneva. My direct involvement in the Taba issue ceased but I continued to keep myself in the picture through the ministry's periodic reports and the Israeli and international press. I followed the ups and downs of the negotiations and, when Israel finally agreed in 1985 to go to arbitration, it was clear to me that the inevitable outcome would be the restitution of Taba to Egypt. It was also clear that Egypt would make a gesture of goodwill and facilitate

Israeli tourists' access to Taba – this was more in Egypt's than Israel's interest. I did not buy the description of the ideal relations that would prevail between Egypt and Israel after the solution of the Taba issue; nor was I impressed by the promise to cancel the yellow card, increase Egyptian tourism to Israel and lift restrictions on commercial, cultural and social relations. I knew better! An Egyptian popular proverb says 'Do not ask a physician, better ask a man of experience'. I had ample experience and I knew for certain that, once again, Egypt would not live up to its commitments and that there would be no idyll between the two countries as wishful thinkers in Israel believed. I refrained from sending any comment to the foreign ministry and kept my assessment to myself. I did not think it fit to intervene in a matter that was beyond my jurisdiction. In any case, it would have had no effect on the course of events.

Nevertheless, during the visit of the then prime minister, Shimon Peres, to Geneva for a meeting with the president of the Ivory Coast, Hophouet-Boigny, I took the liberty to raise the matter with him. I had known him for many years and I felt that I could speak to him frankly. I told him in a private conversation that, on the Taba issue, Yitshak Shamir's (then foreign minister) position was right and that going to arbitration meant the automatic return of Taba to Egypt. I expressed my understanding for his desire to foster relations with Egypt and revitalize the peace process, even at that price. I warned him, however, not to take the Egyptian promises at face value and not to commit himself publicly to the view that, this time, they would live up to their commitments – it would take only a few weeks for the people in Israel to realize that this was not so. I concluded:

> The Egyptians have sold you merchandise which they have sold us numerous times in the past and they did not even bother to change the wrapping paper for you. They will not fulfill the promises they have given you, as they did not fulfill the promises that they gave to your predecessors. The most you can expect in return for Taba is that they will agree to a summit meeting between you and Mubarak and promote Mohamed Bassiuni from chargé d'affaires a.i. to ambassador. [This is exactly what happened.]

Peres listened carefully to my remarks and answered that he wanted to move ahead rapidly with the peace process in the region and needed Egypt's goodwill and active support.

A few months later, I concluded my mission in Geneva and returned home. The then director-general, Dave Kimche, informed me that I had been appointed deputy director-general for Middle Eastern affairs (which included the Egypt department) and requested that, until the post became vacant, I go to New York to help our delegation during the General Assembly. In the meantime, the rotation at the head of the government between Peres and Shamir took place (Shamir became prime minister and Peres replaced him as foreign minister). A few weeks later, I received a cable in New York informing me that I had been appointed head of the international co-operation department (*Mashav*), which is responsible for Israeli aid to developing countries. I was happy with my new posting, which was tremendously challenging and gratifying, but I could not refrain from feeling that I had been pushed out of Middle Eastern affairs because of the frank comments that I had voiced in my conversation with Peres. I wrote him a personal letter in which I expressed my disappointment and emphasized that, as a professional diplomat, I was trained to uphold, to the best of my ability, the policies of the government in place notwithstanding my own personal opinion. I received an answer that there were no grounds for my disappointment and that he had not been informed that I had been appointed to head Middle Eastern affairs by the previous foreign minister.

When I returned to Cairo in 1990 the Taba issue was behind us. The topic arose only in respect of the difficulties encountered by Israeli tourists in northern Sinai and the restrictions put on Israeli navigation in the Red Sea near the Egyptian coast, as dealt with in chapter 12.

17 · *Presidents and Prime Ministers*

It is not my intention to engage here in a comprehensive study of the personalities who stood at the helm of Egypt and Israel during the period covered by this book and who initiated and led the various moves that made peace into a tangible reality. I will limit myself to those events with which I have been closely associated and which complement the picture that I have tried to present to the reader.

I had the opportunity to meet the late Menahem Begin for the first time in 1976, when I was consul general in Rio de Janeiro. He was at the time leader of the opposition and he had come on a mission for the United Jewish Appeal. I received him with all due honors as befitted one of the founders of the State of Israel and I organized personally all his meetings and social events and took the initiative of calling in his honor a mass rally of the Jewish community. Our security officers objected to publishing an open invitation in the press and I had to send thousands of hand-delivered letters to all community members. Begin, not knowing of the steps I had taken, insisted on having ads published and reacted angrily when I refused because of the security constraints. We exchanged sharp words but the success of the event, which was attended by several thousand people, removed all misunderstandings and for the rest of the program he relied on me totally.

Our next meeting took place four years later, when I was appointed minister plenipotentiary to Cairo and came to receive his instructions (he was then prime minister) before I took-up my posting. I was surprised when he recognized me immediately and recalled the Rio incident in a friendly manner. In our conversation, he stressed the importance of peace with Egypt and the heavy burden that lay on the shoulders of the diplomatic staff in Cairo. He praised Eliahu Ben-Elissar (the first ambassador to Egypt and previously director-general of the prime minister's office) and expressed his conviction that he would steer relations with Egypt onto the right course. He also stressed the very warm relationship that had developed between President Sadat and himself, saying that it was characterized by mutual trust and a genuine effort to accommodate their mutual needs. He also recalled, with manifest yearning, the warmth with which he had been received by the Egyptian masses during his official visit to Egypt and how thousands of people had crowded around him, wanting to touch him or shake his hand.

As early as in February 1981, I had the opportunity to test the validity of Begin's impressions. I was then chargé d'affaires a.i. and I had to organize a summit meeting between the two statesmen. Such meetings always entail a score of small details to be co-ordinated with the local security and protocol authorities (not to mention the political groundwork at the level of both the presidency and the foreign ministry). I held several working meetings with the Egyptians and we planned the event down to the last detail. Contrary to what occurred in other fields, my interlocutors were efficient and manifestly interested in the success of the summit. They did not haggle for haggling's sake, did not erect artificial obstacles and did not try to downgrade the visit or conceal it from the general public. All our requests were promptly agreed to and, more surprisingly, implemented down to the last detail.

The summit was to take place in Alexandria. The Egyptians suggested lodging the prime minister and his retinue at the Hotel Palestine but, knowing Begin's sensitivity, I stressed that the name had a negative connotation and was like waving a red cloth in front of a bull. The Egyptians insisted that it was the only suitable accommodation in Alexandria but I remembered, from recollections of my youth, a beautiful summer resort on the seashore – the San Stephano Hotel – and I suggested lodging the entire Israeli delegation there. My interlocutors were not happy with the suggestion but they graciously acceded to my request. A few days before the summit, I came to Alexandria to finalize the preparations and I took the opportunity to have a look at the San Stephano. I was stunned: it was literally crumbling and had no elementary facilities. I immediately requested a change of venue though I still opposed the Hotel Palestine. Finally, it was decided that Begin and his close collaborators would reside in one of the palaces in the center of the city (which was used as the governor's offices); the rest of the official delegation would be lodged at the Sheraton Hotel (which was still under construction) and the many accompanying journalists and security personnel would, nevertheless, reside at the San Stephano.

As always, the Egyptians hosted the delegation in the most lavish manner and spared no effort to make their stay enjoyable. Mrs Sadat and her daughters came from Cairo especially to keep Begin's daughter company (she had accompanied him because his wife, Aliza, was prevented from doing so in view of her illness). My wife, Sarah, joined them. The atmosphere was familial and almost devoid of ceremonial constraints and etiquette. The chemistry between Begin and Sadat worked perfectly and both personalities showed manifest sympathy and appreciation for each other (which to the best of my judgement were absolutely genuine). The discussions took place in a relaxed and friendly atmosphere and were characterized by frankness and goodwill. The two leaders spoke straight to the point and, in a few hours, reached agreement on a series of issues which the respective delegations had not been able to solve in long months of negotiations. The main decisions had a bearing on concrete steps for intensifying normalization and stepping up the autonomy talks. The embassy staff, and I among them, were elated and believed that the summit had brought about a significant breakthrough and that at last we would be able to fulfil our duties normally and develop meaningful and in-depth relations both at the official and personal levels.

We were still naïve and believed that the difficulties we were encountering were incidental – after more than six months in Egypt, we should have known better! Very quickly, even before the summit's hubbub had quietened down, we realized once again that nice words and promises had nothing in common with the actual enforcement of undertakings. The great majority of the agreements reached between Begin and Sadat evaporated at the lower levels of the Egyptian bureaucracy and never became a reality. No revolutionary changes were felt and Egypt's basic policy towards normalization, as had been determined from the outset, continued to be implemented rigidly.

As for Begin's recollection of the enthusiasm with which he had been received in his previous visit by the Egyptian people, it could not be put to a direct test but, nevertheless, it proved to be unfounded. This time no crowds lined the streets, no cheers were heard and no one tried to touch him or shake his hand. Indeed, there had been no sudden change in the attitude of the Egyptian masses either towards Begin or towards the peace process: the reason was much more prosaic! Contrary to what had happened on his first visit, the authorities did not bother to bring out people to cheer him. In one of the co-ordination meetings, prior to the summit, I raised the need to intensify security measures in order to forestall unnecessary risks in case the crowd surrounded Begin as had happened in his previous visit. My Egyptian interlocutors chuckled and replied that there was no need for additional security arrangements, since this time the visit was not official and there would be no similar outbursts of popular enthusiasm. When I insisted, they disclosed that on the previous visit some 2,000 people had been especially hired and transported from place to place to cheer Begin and create the impression of a popular welcome, as is commonly done for top Egyptian personalities and important official guests. I never revealed to Begin what the Egyptians had told me – I did not want to shatter unnecessarily the warm memories he had from his first contact with the Egyptian masses and the supposed spontaneous expressions of affection they had bestowed on him.

To add a personal note, let me say that the Alexandria summit taught me a most important lesson, which has since been for me a guiding principle in organizing such events. I learned the hard way that, to ensure the success of such visits, it was imperative to dedicate the utmost attention to the journalists and make hospitality and entertainment arrangements similar for them to those made for the official retinue. In Alexandria, this was not the case: the journalists had been accommodated at the San Stephano and suffered from intense cold, bad service and awful food, not to mention bugs, mosquitoes, mice and other small plagues of the kind. Furthermore, they were located far from the official delegation and found it difficult to cover the various events and follow up what was occurring at the summit (especially since they had to make their own transport arrangements). They complained all the time, felt tense and neglected and, understandably, this reflected negatively on their coverage of the summit.

During my first period in Egypt, the day-to-day contacts with the Israeli prime minister were, as a matter of course, assumed by the ambassador – first Eliahu Ben-Elissar and then Moshe Sasson. The ambassador met frequently with the prime minister to brief him on the current situation, exchange opinions and receive instructions (a similar procedure continued with Yitshak Shamir and when I became ambassador to Egypt in the early 1990s). After each meeting, the ambassador called a staff meeting and reported the main features of the conversation with the prime minister. Later, he also brought to my knowledge the more confidential aspects that had been discussed. I thus learned, from first hand, the immense importance that Begin attached to relations with Egypt and the close attention with which he followed the ups and downs in these relations.

Begin's next, and last, meeting with Sadat took place in June 1981 in Sharm el Sheikh (still in Israeli hands), just a few days before the bombing of the Iraqi nuclear reactor near Baghdad. Moshe Sasson participated in the summit and I remained in Cairo to replace him as chargé d'affaires (I have already elaborated on this meeting). The last time I met Begin was a few months later at Sadat's funeral. Let me make a small digression here – the Egyptians leaders, through an intensive campaign of misinformation and deceit, have succeeded in making the masses believe that the Yom Kippur war was a major Egyptian victory. The historical fact that the Israeli defense forces reached 101 kilometers from Cairo is totally irrelevant. A museum has been built to immortalize this alleged victory and popular celebrations are held every year to commemorate it (although, the upper layer of the population knows the bitter truth!). Until Sadat's assassination a military parade was also held and was attended by all the Egyptian top brass and all foreign representatives. In the first year (1980), Ben-Elissar attended the parade without consulting Jerusalem on the premise that 'if the Egyptians want to celebrate a defeat as a victory, it is their privilege to do so!' His attendance was strongly criticized in the press and he was called to order by the ministry. The next year (the assassination year) Moshe Sasson (who, in the meantime, had replaced him) asked for permission to attend the parade, but the ministry refused. After a series of phone calls and cables to Jerusalem and back, permission was finally given to attend the parade but not at ambassadorial level. Being the next in line, I was instructed to represent Israel but fate decided differently: the circumcision ceremony of my newly-born grandson was scheduled for the same day (Yom Kippur) and I was compelled to drive back home to take part in the religious ritual. Israel could not decently send a junior diplomat to represent it and the ministry had either to boycott the parade or allow Moshe Sasson to attend. Finally, the green light was given and Moshe had the dubious privilege to be present during the assault that cost Sadat his life and levied the lives of several guests, including the Belgian ambassador, who was seated near him. Moshe was sneaked out by his Israeli and Egyptian security guards and rushed to a nearby private residence where he remained until the situation became clearer. I did not attend my grandson's circumcision; I heard the news about Sadat's assassination on the radio and took the next plane back to Cairo to be with my colleagues in these fateful hours. The situation was as hazy as it was tense; no one knew what the next day might bring and where Egypt was heading. All eventualities were open – a popular revolution, an army take-over or an armed confrontation with the Muslim extremists. Peace could collapse overnight and the personal security of our diplomatic staff was in jeopardy. None of these ominous eventualities materialized and the orderly transfer of powers to Vice-President Hosni Mubarak took place without any difficulty. Incidentally, since then the military parades have been discontinued and now Israeli ambassadors participate, as a matter of routine, in the many celebrations marking the October Victory. The explanation we give is simply that 'these celebrations mark the victory of peace, which is an Israeli victory as much as an Egyptian one!'

Let us return to Begin. After my hasty return to Cairo, I plunged into intense activity. First and foremost, we had to assess what was going on under our noses, scrutinize closely each and every development in the delicate situation, and collect and double-check whatever bit of information that might give the slightest indication on where the wind was blowing from. In addition, I had to co-ordinate with the Egyptians the coming to Sadat's funeral of a large Israeli delegation headed by Begin himself. Normally, organizing an Israeli delegation's visit was not an easy task and, in the special circumstances of the time, it entailed particularly sensitive diplomatic considerations and many complicated technical and security arrangements. My Egyptians interlocutors did not jump for joy – to say the least – when I informed them that Begin intended to attend the funeral with a large Israeli delegation. They expected, or more exactly hoped, that many Arab leaders would come and obviously were not interested in Begin's presence. At first, they tried to discourage us, expressing apprehension that his presence might provoke spontaneous popular demonstrations, which might endanger him and make ensuring the safety of the other VIP guests more difficult. To avoid any misunderstanding, I made it clear immediately that Begin was determined to come, whatever the difficulties and dangers, in order to pay his last respects to Sadat who, together with him, had brought peace to our region and had become his close personal friend. The Egyptians then raised difficulties around the location where Begin and his delegation would be hosted. They wanted them to stay (for alleged or genuine security concerns) in one of the big hotels in the center of Cairo, at a distance of some 15 kilometers from where the funeral was to take place. Since the funeral was scheduled for a Saturday and the Israelis could not, decently, drive to the funeral (Saturday being the Jewish Sabbath), it meant either walking some 30 kilometers or not attending the funeral at all. I turned down the Egyptians' suggestion outright and insisted on finding a suitable residence within walking distance. After bitter haggling, they suggested a small hotel at a distance of five–six kilometers, presenting this as a take-it-or-leave-it situation. I myself, without consulting anyone, rejected the Egyptian ultimatum outright. It was clear that Begin, whose health was already very low, could not walk such a distance. Abandoning diplomatic language, I accused the Egyptians of trying to manipulate us into canceling Begin's coming and later to put the blame on him. I pointed out that it was inconceivable that in a neighborhood where there were so many military camps, government offices, clubs, schools and private houses, proper accommodation for one or two nights could not be found for the prime minister of Israel and his delegation. I made it clear that, if Begin were prevented from coming because of the manifest bad will of the Egyptian government, we would not hesitate in publicly putting the blame on Egypt and drawing the underlying conclusions.

The last thing the Egyptians wanted, at that fateful moment, was to clash frontally with Israel and provide it with a pretext to postpone, or even cancel, the second phase of withdrawal from Sinai. After a few hours of a total breakdown of communication, I was urgently summoned to the director of the security department in the ministry of foreign affairs. He informed me officially that Egypt was 'very keen that Prime Minister Begin should attend Sadat's funeral and will do its utmost to make his coming possible'. He offered to put at my disposal one of his senior officers to look, together with me, for suitable accommodation in a location near the funeral site that would be at a reasonable walking distance. I willingly accepted and, the next day, I went out with the Egyptian official combing the neighborhood thoroughly. I was allowed to enter military installations (which normally were hermetically closed to Israelis), government buildings and even private houses. To be frank, the choice was rather limited, and we only found two suitable possibilities: a magnificent villa built on a small artificial hill, just in front of the funeral site, and an abandoned school at a distance of one kilometer. My escort requested (not to say begged) that we strike off the villa because it belonged to a former vice-president of the Nasser regime, who was living there practically under house arrest. The school remained the only alternative and he promised to have it repaired, painted and equipped thoroughly within the next

48 hours. I had no choice but to agree. I requested, however, that on the second evening after the Sabbath, Begin and his entire retinue be transferred to more comfortable accommodation in the small hotel that had previously been suggested by the Egyptians.

Begin's delegation was composed mostly of security guards, well armed and well prepared to meet any danger. A few ministers accompanied him (among them Foreign Minister Yitshak Shamir and Defense Minister Ariel Sharon) as well as several political personalities and top government officials. Moshe Sasson and I joined them and we all settled down in the school that had been renovated, just in time. Even so, living conditions were rudimentary. Only Begin had a separate room and a decent bed; everyone else was put in several large dormitories and passed a nightmarish night attacked by scores of enormous mosquitoes. The next day, apparently for security reasons and without informing the general public, the Egyptians transferred the religious ceremony to a location closer to the school where the Israeli delegation was staying. Nevertheless, Begin, and with him the entire Israeli delegation, had to walk several kilometers and he did so at a firm pace without the slightest complaint (though he arrived sick and exhausted). The funeral was attended by several heads of state and numerous world leaders (to the disappointment of the Egyptians, very few Arab leaders came). Begin's presence aroused much interest. On this occasion, he met for the first time with Hosni Mubarak. The two men embraced and exchanged promises to persevere with the peace process and speed up normalization between the two countries. They decided to meet as soon as possible for more in-depth talks. (In chapter 11, I related the misunderstanding that emerged from this hasty conversation and I will refrain here from elaborating further.)

To complete this almost surrealistic picture, tension among those who attended the funeral was at its peak. There were persistent rumors of a plot to assassinate the new president during the funeral and orchestrate a fundamentalist coup with the aid of a number of dissident army units. Suddenly, it seemed that these rumors were becoming reality. The paratroopers' company which was marching immediately after the coffin and in front of the VIP guests performed an unexpected about-turn and began running in the direction of the VIPs, brandishing their machine guns. At the same instant, the paratroopers' company which was marching behind the VIPs and separated them from the mass of other mourners, began running towards the VIPs also brandishing their weapons. For a moment, everyone froze, certain that the soldiers were launching an attack on the president and top Egyptian leaders as well as on the foreign personalities attending the funeral. Bodyguards pulled out their guns and prepared to defend with their lives the personalities entrusted to their care (I personally saw Henry Kissinger's bodyguards drawing their guns) – a futile fight obviously lost in advance. The paratroopers, on both sides, got as far as the rows of VIPs but then stopped running as suddenly as they had begun; then the front company again made an about-turn and resumed its forward march at a reduced pace. Everyone sighed in relief (one could actually hear the sighs), the bodyguards returned their guns to their holsters and the cortege continued to move towards the burial site – the monument to the unknown soldier – a few meters from the spot were Sadat had been murdered. Later, we learned that the reason for the turmoil was that the commanding officer, worried by the increasing distance between his paratroopers and the VIPs, had decided to close the gap to avoid security loopholes. The gap was indeed closed quickly but at the cost of a panic that could have been tragic.

Sadat's assassination was a heavy blow to the peace process, and to a lesser extent to the normalization of relations between Egypt and Israel (he was the father of Egypt's strategy and tactics in both realms). There is no doubt whatsoever that Sadat was the main architect of peace. Without his far-reaching vision, his daring, his readiness to take personal and national risks, his ability to assess short- and long-run historical processes, it is almost inconceivable that peace with Egypt would have become a reality in our generation. True, Egypt's objective situation called for desperate steps to overcome the military, political and economic mess which it was in, but only an outstanding leader of Sadat's stature could have taken the risk to sign a separate peace with Israel despite unanimous Arab condemnation. We have to admit – even at the cost of shocking Egyptian sensitivity – that, at the time, it was no more than a separate peace in the fullest meaning of the term. Only many years later did the other Arab states, and the Palestinians, come to the conclusion that Sadat's vision was right – strategically and tactically – and follow in his footsteps, taking as a springboard the principles laid down in the Camp David accords which they had so categorically condemned.

Notwithstanding the above-mentioned situation, it is misleading to simplistically present Sadat as the victim of peace and as having paid with his life for his betrayal of the Arab cause (read: the Palestinian cause). The motives for his horrendous assassination were much more complex and peace with Israel played only a marginal role in them. This is clear from the minutes of the public trials held at the time and the widely published discussions between the murderers (and hundreds of other arrested Muslim extremists) and leading Egyptian journalists, intellectuals and religious leaders. Beyond doubt Sadat was murdered because the essence and style of his regime were in flagrant opposition, according to the Muslim fundamentalists, to 'the edicts and precepts of the Holy Koran'. They despised him for all that he represented and criticized him bitterly for allowing his wife, Jihan, to play a political role, wear western clothes, and appear conspicuously on television screens. In this matter, as in everything else, there is also a Jewish aspect. Menahem Begin, upon his arrival to the Alexandria summit, not only shook Jihan's hand but also kissed her on both cheeks as is common in the west, forgetting that Egypt was a Muslim country undergoing an accelerated process of religious radicalization. The next day, pictures of the 'obscene' kiss were on the front page of all newspapers. The entire press, including the government organs, launched a vicious attack on Begin, accusing him of having purposely demeaned the president's wife, dishonored the president publicly and trampled under foot Islamic tradition and the pride of the Egyptian people. The opposition press went even further and directed open criticism at the president himself for having allowed his wife 'to adopt decadent western behavior' and called on her to remain in the sanctity of her husband's home as all honorable Muslim women did.

Notwithstanding what the fundamentalists thought of Sadat, he was a profoundly religious man and a practicing Muslim. Five times a day, he prayed with fervor in conformity with the Koran's basic tenets. One could easily distinguish on his forehead a small black mark provoked by frequent contact during prayer with the soil (this mark is common among very religious Egyptians). Furthermore, at the beginning of his political activity in the early 1930s, he was quite close to the Muslim Brotherhood and, when he assumed the presidency after Nasser, he allowed the movement to resume openly (though not legally) its activities, which had been outlawed by his predecessor. He hoped that he would thus win their support but he was not ready to desist from leading Egypt headlong into the twentieth century or bring to a stop the process of modernization and westernization that he had initiated. On the contrary, he stepped up the pace of his policy of *Infitakh* (opening of Egypt to foreign investment and culture). He tightened links with the western powers, called on them to invest in Egypt, liberalized commercial and financial transactions and encouraged joint industrial ventures, fostered the import of advanced technologies and agreed to the settling of thousands of foreign experts in Egypt. He pinned his hopes especially on the USA, which he considered the only real superpower and which, he repeatedly stated, 'holds in its hands all the cards of the economic and political game in the international arena'. Muslim fundamentalists increased their public criticism of the regime and of Sadat himself while the underground societies launched a series of bloody attacks throughout Egypt. Sadat had no choice but to retaliate forcefully and arrest hundreds of Muslim activists, among them many religious leaders. The extremist organizations reacted by declaring him a renegade to the main tenets of the faith and an enemy of Islam.

Though many, both in the West and in Egypt itself, exonerate the Muslim Brotherhood of extremist tendencies and terrorist activities, in my humble opinion the movement not only condones them but also stands behind them – directly or indirectly (not to say instigates and orchestrates them). Its overt goal is to topple the secular regime and it does not exclude the use of force and subversion. However, it is careful to hide behind obscure extremist groupings (of which it probably pulls the strings) to avoid a confrontation with the regime that might endanger its very existence. In two previous such confrontations, the backlash was awesome for the brotherhood: the movement was outlawed for many years and its leaders thrown into jail. Furthermore as a result of the first confrontation (under King Faruk) the movement's founder, Sheik Hassan El Bana, was hanged for his role in the murder of the then prime minister, Mohamed Al-Nokrashi. In the second confrontation (during Nasser's regime) the brotherhood's supreme leader, Sheik Said Al-Kutub, and two of his close associates were hanged in one of Cairo's central squares. (I will deal in more detail with Islamic fundamentalism and its underlying causes in the next chapter.)

After the *fatwa* (religious edict) pronounced by the extremist Muslim leadership, the assassination of Sadat became a religious duty that was to be carried out at any cost. Sadat did not take lightly the seriousness of the threat to his life. He clearly understood that not only his personal safety was at stake but also Egypt's very future. He instructed the security services to act swiftly with an iron fist. On the eve of his assassination, the number of detainees had reached several thousand – mostly Muslim organization activists but also many left-wing pro-Nasserist supporters. At the time, I sent a long report to the ministry on the confrontation between the secular authorities and the religious establishment expressing the opinion that it had reached the point of no return. It was bound to culminate in a sweeping victory for one of the two opponents: either the regime would succeed in breaking the backbone of the Islamic fundamentalist movement or Sadat would be assassinated. I concluded that the second alternative – the assassination of Sadat – was more likely since it was easier to kill one man than eradicate a movement that had deep roots in the country, whose leadership was not clearly defined and which mostly operated in the underground. A few weeks later, to my deep sorrow, I was proven right: Sadat was assassinated in a sophisticated and daring terrorist operation during the military parade held to celebrate his alleged October victory. Anwar Al-Sadat was violently brought down from the stage of history but his imprint, his vision and his achievements continue, and will continue for many years, to shape the history of the Middle East.

Sadat could not make peace alone. He found in Menahem Begin a partner and an ally of the first magnitude. Begin also, in his greatness and clear grasp of historical long-range processes, had the courage – like Sadat – to slaughter holy cows and abandon patterns of thought and action that had been deeply-rooted in the Israeli national consciousness for more than a century. He did not hesitate to take great risks and gamble on Israel's future. Were it not for his charismatic leadership at the right moment in history, it is probable that the peace process in the region would not have taken off and Israel would have been at war with

Egypt to this very day. Beyond the enormous differences in background, education and temperament between the two statesmen, it seems that Sadat and Begin shared qualities that brought them together. They rapidly developed a mutual trust and a warm relationship that helped them overcome the abyss separating them. True, they had divergent, even conflicting, interests and their long-range goals and aspirations were in open contradiction, but they were wise enough to put them aside and move forward to what their two countries needed most: peace.

They did not hide their views and expectations and stated them publicly and repeatedly (though Begin was less outspoken than Sadat). Anyone who has dealt with the peace process between Egypt and Israel knows that for Begin, the major accomplishment of peace was, first and foremost, the dropping out of Egypt from military confrontation and permanent conflict. Strategically speaking, peace with Egypt was without a doubt an outstanding breakthrough and a tremendous contribution to Israel's security, reducing the danger of a future war with the Arabs and allowing Israel – so it seemed at the time – a free hand in the occupied territories. In return, Begin was ready to pay the necessary price in terms of territory and abandon the whole of Sinai to the last grain of sand, thus removing a potential cause of conflict with Egypt. Although he insisted on normalizing relations between the two peoples and countries, and even made it a *sine-qua-non* of peace, he considered normalization an important bonus on top of his priority targets. He realized that Egypt was reluctant to proceed swiftly in this realm and would drag its feet as much as it could but he hoped that the dynamics of life would gradually remove artificial obstacles and bad will.

Sadat, on the other hand, did not conceal from the outset that he did not see the peace agreement with Israel as a separate peace between the two countries and that Egypt's dropping out from military confrontation did not mean that it ceased to support the Palestinian cause. Sadat made it crystal-clear that he was making only a first step towards a comprehensive peace in the region and that he was taking the struggle for Palestinian rights from the battlefield to the negotiating table. In his historic speech to the Knesset, in interviews with the written and electronic media, in each and every political conversation with Israeli and foreign personalities, he stated clearly and strongly Egypt's unchanging support for the Palestinians. He emphasized Egypt's determination to help them – through political means – to achieve their national aspirations and establish an independent state in all the territories occupied by Israel in the 1967 war. Notwithstanding his dislike for the PLO in general and for Yasser Arafat in particular, he insisted that Israel should recognize the PLO and conduct direct negotiations with it that would lead to that outcome. There were ups and downs in his relations with the Palestinians depending upon the political situation of the moment but, to his last day, his active support for them was unwavering. True, Sadat exerted in this respect only moderate pressure; he was in no hurry – the Palestinians had waited 30 years and could wait until Egypt recuperated its land and strengthened its international and inter-Arab position. For him Egypt's interests came first but he made it clear that, when the time was ripe, he would do his utmost to help solve the Palestinian issue in a manner that would meet their aspirations. Many in Israel preferred to turn a blind eye to Sadat's repeated statements and considered them empty lip service for internal Egyptian and Arab consumption. This was not so! It is difficult to substantiate this contention empirically since Sadat disappeared at a very early stage. However if we accept the assumption that Mubarak is continuing in Sadat's footsteps and implementing his policies (I personally have no doubt whatsoever that this is the case), then Egypt's behavior in these last 15 years is the best evidence of its validity.

As for normalization, Sadat saw in it a necessary evil that could not be avoided and could not be left to future generations as he had previously wished. To achieve his immediate goal – the recuperation of Sinai – and other vital interests of Egypt, he had to agree at Camp David to a clearcut framework for normalizing relations with Israel. Nevertheless, from the first moment he strove to reduce the interaction between the two countries to no more than the minimum necessary to ensure that peace would not collapse. Egypt's strategy to take upon itself binding commitments in this realm and simultaneously forestall their implementation by erecting artificial difficulties and administrative barriers was conceived during Sadat's time. The administrative and security apparatus necessary for achieving this aim was also put in place during his period – with his full knowledge and blessing. However, by nature, Sadat was not a doctrinaire and did not stand on the strict implementation of this policy to the last detail. More than once he intervened personally, prompted by Israeli personalities or the embassy in Cairo, to ease tension and remove obstacles. Our contact person with him was his personal friend, Anis Mansur, the chief editor of the weekly *October* and the court journalist of the time.

In early 1981, a major confrontation developed when the Egyptian foreign ministry forbade delegations to Israel to attend meetings in Jerusalem. I was chargé d'affaires at the time, and took advantage of an audience with Sadat on agricultural co-operation to raise the matter with him. From his reaction, it was clear that he was aware of what was going on and had probably approved the foreign ministry's stand. He listened to me carefully and pointed out that he himself had gone to Jerusalem but that his visit did not imply in any way that Egypt recognized Israeli sovereignty over the city. He said there was no objective reason to prevent Egyptian officials from going to Jerusalem but that a creative solution had to be worked out in order not to crudely overrule the foreign ministry's decision. I suggested that, as a compromise, Egyptian officials should reside in Tel Aviv but attend working meetings scheduled in

Jerusalem. The president liked the idea and, towards the end of our meeting, he presented it as his own and promised to instruct the foreign ministry accordingly. He kept his promise and the compromise worked smoothly for many years and was known as the Sadat formula. On another occasion, he gave strict instructions to the culture ministry to immediately cancel its decision not to allow Israel to take part in the annual book fair. It is difficult to evaluate what would have been the state of normalization between the two countries today if President Sadat had continued to rule Egypt. In my view however, the only difference would have been in the manner of implementing the basic Egyptian policies rather than in their scope and goals. As the French say, *le ton fait la musique*.

Towards the end of Sadat's presidency, one could clearly sense that he was becoming increasingly estranged from the masses of the Egyptian people and from the realities of their lives. His speeches, like those of Fidel Castro, were becoming longer and more frequent from week to week. He painted the future in the brightest colors, and spoke of ideals and world peace while the people's economic situation worsened and corruption spread. People listened to him with impatience and his grandiloquent words were received with frustration and disinterest, not only by the intelligentsia but also by the common man. After people recovered from the shock of his assassination and the anxiety caused by uncertainty as to what the future held in store for Egypt, one could clearly feel a sense of relief at Sadat's disappearance. In my intensive search for suitable accommodation for the Israeli delegation to Sadat's funeral, only a few days after his assassination, I spoke to scores of Egyptians from all strata of society. To my amazement, I seldom heard the words *Allah Yierhamou* (May God have mercy on his soul!) when Sadat's name was mentioned, as is the common practice among Egyptians when referring to a recently deceased person. That was the case during the rest of my stay in Egypt (two more years) and on my occasional visits subsequently. On the contrary, a witchhunt developed against his family, especially his wife, though President Mubarak had taken them under his protection and tried to diminish the slander. Some say that he could have done more had he really wanted to and that he condoned controlled persecution to allow Sadat's opponents (who were numerous) to release steam and thus divert attacks on him during the delicate transitional phase. In 1990, when I returned to Egypt, things had changed: people spoke with longing about the Sadat period, praised him and his achievements and never failed to add *Allah Yierhamou* whenever they mentioned his name.

Despite the dwindling of Sadat's popularity towards the end of his presidency and the sharp criticism of his style of government, his peace policy was backed almost unanimously by the Egyptian masses and the military establishment (which was, and still is, the regime's backbone). Without this active support, Sadat could not have gone as far as he did and, in any case, peace would probably have collapsed after his death. This did not occur and, on the contrary, his successor, Hosni Mubarak, continued to faithfully implement Sadat's policies. Paradoxically, one can say that Mubarak is carrying out Sadat's policies better than Sadat himself. True, the messianic fervor and the urbanity which characterized Sadat have faded away but the main tenets of his policies – in almost all fields – are practically the same to the exclusion of slight incremental changes to adapt them to the ever-evolving situation.

At the beginning of Mubarak's presidency, there was a brief period during which, on the advice of his close collaborators, he sought to disavow Sadat's legacy and present himself as Nasser's heir. He even appointed a few Nasserist ministers (especially in the economic field). However, he very soon came to realize that, if he persisted in this pretence, he would have to abandon Sadat's policies – which he had helped design and which he believed served the best interests of the nation. Mubarak was not ready to do this and, within a few weeks, he reverted to his old self and changed drastically the style and nature of his public statements.

The transfer of power to Mubarak took place smoothly but it took him several years before he became the uncontested leader and guide of the nation in the eyes of the masses. For some inexplicable reason, his first steps as president were accompanied by a despicable campaign of jokes and anecdotes aimed at belittling him and blemishing his intellectual and leadership abilities. Egyptians like jokes (it is an inherent feature of their national character) and frequently joke about themselves and their leaders, but this campaign of disparagement was far from being substantiated by logic or reality. Mubarak was well prepared for the challenges of power – he was a fully-fledged general, had commanded the Egyptian airforce during the October War and, for several years, had been one of Sadat's closest collaborators. In any case, time has proven that his detractors were absolutely wrong: he has now been in office for 21 years and is the longest-serving Egyptian president (at the age of 73, he has been re-elected to a fifth consecutive mandate of five years). Despite all the difficulties and the continuing demographic explosion, he has dramatically improved Egypt's socio-political situation, and brought her to the threshold of genuine democracy and to a privileged standing in the international arena. He has also restored Egypt's position in the Arab world without abandoning peace with Israel and has brought the Arab states and the Palestinians to toe the Egyptian line, accept the existence of Israel and seek a comprehensive peace – from an Israeli standpoint, this is certainly Mubarak's main achievement.

Incidentally, Mubarak's regime is characterized by a remarkable stability and very few changes in the country's leadership. Over the years, there have been several reshuffles of government but changes have been gradual, not to say marginal, and several key ministers remain since Sadat's time (including the previous prime minister, Kamal

Al-Ganzouri). His faithful and able political adviser (who is not too friendly towards Israeli ambassadors), Osama Elbaz, remains as influential and active as he has been since the days of Mubarak's vice-presidency. Gradually, Mubarak has also succeeded in forging for himself a privileged position with the international media. At first, he did not fully master the English language, had little experience of international press conferences and made a number of blunders. His advisers convinced him to be less outspoken and to address the press in Arabic. The government press office announced that the president would speak only Arabic 'out of national considerations' and his words would be translated into English (and improved if need be). Very quickly Mubarak realized that he was losing personal contact with the international press and damaging his prestige in the eyes of his own people. He reverted to English, studied the language assiduously and is now one of the world leaders most interviewed.

Mubarak does not normally receive foreign ambassadors for courtesy calls or routine *tours d'horizon*; he leaves that task to his foreign minister. I maintained regular contact with the president through his adviser for intelligence affairs, Dr Mustapha Al-Fiki, with whom I could meet at very short notice whenever I wanted to. To be frank, I did not find it necessary to meet the president beyond the frequent meetings in which I took part when he received visiting Israeli personalities. I always took advantage of these opportunities to raise topics that I wanted him to hear first hand from me. I always found him well informed and he reacted immediately without needing to refer to his advisers. From this point of view, not only was I not discriminated against but I was certainly in a better position than most ambassadors in Cairo with the exception of the American ambassador, Frank Wiesner, who met practically every other day with the president or his close advisers. To the best of my knowledge, all matters pertaining to Israel are (or at least were) centralized in the president's office and all decisions – large or small – are taken only after consulting him personally or bringing them to his knowledge. As a person, Mubarak is charming and straightforward. Sometimes he can be quite blunt and crude and, at times, he gives the impression of belittling his interlocutors' intellectual ability and knowledge of facts and realities. Paradoxically, the warmth that radiates from him and his sense of humor add a special flavor to meetings with him and contribute to his interlocutors' positive feelings, even when the meeting's results are poor or non-existent.

I have often been asked to draw a comparison between Sadat and Mubarak and I have always answered by quoting what the Egyptians themselves told us in the early 1980s. At the time, we had very little information about Mubarak's personality and political views and, after Sadat's assassination, we were apprehensive as to the future of the fragile peace that had just been established. Our Egyptian interlocutors would calm us down, saying more or less:

There is no reason for you to be worried. On the contrary, you have now been given an excellent opportunity to test Egypt's seriousness. You have always asked yourself what would happen after Sadat and wondered whether peace will survive him. Now, you have been given the opportunity to get a decisive answer to these questions even before you have completed your withdrawal from Sinai and see by yourselves, much earlier than you thought, what happens after Sadat. You will certainly reach the conclusion that Egypt's policies are stable and longstanding and that peace was not one man's decision. It was a strategic option – not a tactical one – fully supported by the entire Egyptian people and Mubarak himself, who took an active part in the decision-making process leading to peace. He will continue in Sadat's footsteps and implement Sadat's policies better than Sadat himself would have done. Sadat was a visionary, a man of great perspicacity and daring and, without his leadership, Egypt would not have made peace with Israel. But when it comes to the daily running of the country, his head was in the clouds; he defined the broad lines of policy but disregarded details; he gave instructions of a general nature and never took the pain to verify if and how they were implemented. The lower levels of government felt free to interpret Sadat's instructions as they thought best and took operative decisions without referring to him. They did not fear being caught or reprimanded and, for all practical purposes, they were running the country. With Mubarak things are different. He is first and foremost an army officer, not a statesman or a policy-maker; he has neither worldwide vision nor a sense of historical processes. He does not gamble or take risks, personal or national, but for him an order is an order – it has to be carried out to the last detail and he will make sure that it is. By nature, he is suspicious and meticulous; the smallest details are important to him and he will constantly check, along the whole line of command, if and how his instructions are being carried out. If Mubarak had ruled Egypt instead of Sadat in the late 1970s, he would not have had the daring to sign a peace treaty with Israel against the consensus of the Arab world. However, now that peace is a reality – a fact of life which cannot be reversed without major risks – he will continue to toe the line defined by Sadat, which has the support of the Egyptian people, the military establishment and Mubarak himself.

I believe that, by now, the reader has enough evidence to judge whether or not this comparison is substantiated by the events of the last 20 years.

Mubarak did not like Yitshak Shamir, Israel's prime minister. He considered him intransigent and doctrinaire and saw in him an enemy of peace as well as an obstacle to Egypt's purposes in the region (he later transferred these feelings of animosity to Benjamin Netanyahu). It is possible that he disliked Shamir because of his abstention on the Camp David accords or because he had been, in the remote past, the commander of the Stern group (a clandestine splinter organization) and was perceived as unyielding on the concept of a Greater Israel. In any case, still at a very early stage, Mubarak severed personal contacts with Shamir, behaved towards him in the crudest possible manner and stubbornly refused to meet him, in Egypt or elsewhere (incidentally, he also refused to meet Menahem Begin). Mubarak simply waited for a change of government in Israel and for Shamir to leave the stage. He repeatedly interfered in Israel's internal politics, and continues to do so, by inviting Israeli politicians to Egypt, addressing himself directly to the Israeli public and hinting that he was yearning for a change of leadership in Israel. Shamir was well aware of Mubarak's feelings towards him and of his efforts to topple him. Understandably, it reduced almost to zero his confidence in Mubarak's dedication to peace and vindicated his determination not to allow Egypt a leading role in the peace process.

During my tenure as ambassador, I would meet Shamir at least once a month. He gave me all the time I needed, even when he had more pressing business. Once, he received me for almost two hours between two meetings with the then American secretary of state, George Schultz. Shamir gave Egypt high priority and dedicated his utmost attention to reports and cables from Cairo. He wanted to hear, first hand, each and every detail and assess the situation personally. He listened to my briefings tensely, asked numerous questions and requested clarifications. There was one thing that he could not understand, or condone, and he repeatedly asked me: 'Why is Mubarak so unfriendly to Israel? Why does he exacerbate confrontation instead of trying to seek a compromise? Why does he allow the Egyptian press to fan anti-Semitism? How does he envisage fostering peace in the region without maintaining a dialogue with the Israeli government?' I never heard him say one harsh word about Mubarak and he never asked me to try to persuade the Egyptian president to meet him, though it was clear that the lack of direct communication with the Egyptian leader disturbed him enormously. I often raised this matter with him on my own initiative. As ambassador to Egypt, I considered it my duty to promote such a meeting and I tried to create propitious conditions by suggesting a few soothing gestures. Shamir stressed, however, that he was not ready to pay the smallest price for the mere pleasure of shaking Mubarak's hand and even less ready to agree in advance to parameters dictated by him as a precondition for holding a meeting. I insisted repeatedly but with no success (to be quite frank, I was far from being convinced that Israel should pay a price). For example, I suggested that Israel agree to hold the international peace conference (which became known as the Madrid conference) in Cairo. Later, I suggested that at least the continuation meetings should take place in Egypt. Shamir refused claiming, rightly, that in Cairo Israel would find itself under constant and vicious attacks by the Egyptian press. He was also adamant that Egypt could not lead the Arab diplomatic onslaught on Israel and, at the same time, be an honest broker working objectively for a settlement in the region. On another occasion, I suggested that Israel should express public support for Boutros Ghali's candidature as United Nations secretary-general, stressing that he would in any case be elected. Again, Shamir refused. Paradoxically, he warmly praised Ghali's qualities but felt it would be wiser to adopt a position of neutrality since Israel's support would automatically ensure his election. As he saw it, the UN was sufficiently anti-Israeli without having an Egyptian secretary-general at its helm and it would be self-defeating for Israel to help elect Boutros Ghali.

Shamir was an ideal target for the Egyptian press. The journalists poured on him a torrent of insults that not even the most democratic of government and supporters of free press would ever have tolerated. I mentioned in a previous chapter the case of the senior journalist who, instead of apologizing to the prime minister of Israel as he had been instructed to do, 'apologized to the monkeys, tigers and butchers for having compared them to Yitshak Shamir'. This is not an isolated case: I could fill an entire chapter with similar examples. Shamir was also a favorite target for vexatious lawsuits lodged before the Egyptian courts by private citizens. He and the Israeli embassy were never summoned to appear in court or answer the pleas but the courts did not reject outright such lawsuits, which were clearly beyond their competence. The Egyptian foreign ministry also refrained from calling the courts' attention to the immunities due to a foreign head of government. The courts dragged out the lawsuits for months on end and held session after session, permitting, and using, the vilest language against Shamir, Israel and the Jews. As a matter of course, the Egyptian press always joined the chorus promptly and launched a tirade of abuse on each occasion.

On the other hand, Egypt was quite capable of protesting vigorously at the slightest sign of disrespect or infringement of the immunity of *its* government and representatives in Israel. I remember that when the families of the victims of the Ras Burka incident (the killing and wounding of Israeli tourists by an Egyptian soldier) introduced a lawsuit in Israel against the Egyptian government, I was urgently summoned to the legal adviser in the Egyptian foreign ministry. He pointed out that, in accordance with international law and practice, the government of Egypt was protected by diplomatic immunity and could not be sued in a foreign court for whatever reason. He demanded that the Israeli foreign ministry inform the court accordingly and requested it to reject the plea on the basis of its incompetence in the matter. I knew that he was right from a juridical standpoint but, for nuisance value, I made a positive answer conditional on a similar step on his side in a lawsuit pending against Prime Minister Shamir and the government of Israel. He agreed immediately and pledged he would appear personally in court, stressing that he would do so independently of Israel's reply to his own request. A few days later, one of his junior colleagues informed me that the legal adviser would not be able to appear before the Egyptian court and he was consequently withdrawing his request. The reader will certainly have guessed by now that the legal adviser had not been given the green light by Big Brother – but that the Israeli foreign ministry did appear in the Israeli court, in conformity with diplomatic practice, to sustain the Egyptian claim to immunity. Many in Israel were angered by such one-sided behavior, but the law is the law and the Israeli government could not evade its obligations because its Egyptian counterpart refused to act in conformity with its own obligations.

With the change of government in Israel in July 1992 and the election of the late Yitshak Rabin as prime minister, the atmosphere in Cairo eased overnight – at least, on the face of it. A period of grace in Israeli–Egyptian relations, and in the attitude of the Egyptian press towards Israel and the new government, began. Rabin decided that his first visit abroad – a few days after assuming office and before a scheduled meeting with the president of the USA – would be for a meeting with President Mubarak. He wanted to show, beyond all possible doubt, that there had been a dramatic turnabout in Israel's policy and that Israel was now looking forward to a greater role on Egypt's part in the peace process. In the embassy, we were not too happy with this decision. We saw in Rabin's step a *post-factum* legitimization of Egypt's offensive behavior as well as an unjustifiable contribution to the strengthening of its international and inter-Arab positions before it had proven its sincerity. For us, the sudden thaw in relations was one more period of 'smiles' similar to many that we had witnessed in the past. We were convinced that it would be shortlived and that, at the first clash between the two countries, the situation would revert to what it had always been – an unceasing seesaw of ups and downs in conformity with Egypt's changing needs. We knew for certain that such a clash was bound sooner or later to occur since it was obviously impossible for Israel to abandon its fundamental interests and accede time and again to Egyptian wishes. It was also evident that, despite the renewed honeymoon, the elaborate apparatus Egypt had set up for regulating normalization would not be dismantled and, at most, it would be instructed to show greater flexibility for a while. We were also convinced that Egypt would not be satisfied only with the 180° turnabout that was already taking shape in Israel's attitude towards the Palestinians and that its goals were much wider.

The embassy did not deny the need for such a visit. It believed, however, that it should take place only after thorough diplomatic preparations, several weeks after Rabin's meeting with President Bush, and on the understanding that Mubarak would reciprocate by finally paying a visit to Israel. This was not to be and Rabin's visit took place as scheduled (and, to our great sorrow, Mubarak's return visit – his one and only visit to Israel – took place four years later on the occasion of Rabin's funeral). I did not send my comments as to the timing of Rabin's visit in writing. Indeed, I was not given the time to do so; the visit and date had been decided upon even before the elections. A few days after Rabin took office, I received a phone call from chief of cabinet Eitan Haber who had just assumed the position. He informed me that the prime minister had decided to meet as soon as possible with President Mubarak and he requested me to co-ordinate the technical details with the Egyptian authorities and fly to Israel to brief Rabin on the current state of relations with Egypt. Haber apologized for bypassing the foreign ministry because of the short time available and promised that the ministry would send me formal instructions in a day or two. He also informed me that Ambassador Bassiuni had already been contacted and was co-ordinating the visit's exact date. I went into action immediately and, within a few hours, I co-ordinated with the Egyptian authorities all the details involved. The visit was to be very short and it did not necessitate complex arrangements. On the program were a private meeting between Rabin and Mubarak, a joint press conference and an official lunch offered by the president.

In parallel, I sent foreign minister Shimon Peres a long cable (with a copy to Rabin) in which I summed up the parameters that could be expected from Egypt in the wake of the change of government in Israel. I especially stressed what should *not* be expected if we did not want to engage in wishful thinking. I stressed the permanent factors which, in my opinion, molded Egypt's policies with regard to bilateral relations and the peace process. I specified that, despite the increase of fundamentalist terrorism and the stepped-up Islamization of the country (with the tacit blessing of the government), the regime was in control of the situation and no upheavals were to be expected in the foreseeable future. I added that there had been no major changes in Egypt's political options and pragmatic approach and that the restoration of its economy remained a priority target of its foreign policy. I also pointed out that Mubarak would undoubtedly be re-elected though his re-election for a third term entailed amending the constitution (since then Mubarak has been re-elected not only to a fourth but also to a fifth term in office). I stated frankly that Egypt was delighted with the change of government in Israel and had, *a priori*, a sympathetic attitude towards a Labor government in view of the personal ties that had been forged in the past. Furthermore, Egypt believed that it would be easier to do business with the new government and that the coalition's composition indicated that Israel would adopt a less ideological and more pragmatic approach. I pointed out that Egypt was giving us only a conditional credit and that it intended to put our reliability through unceasing tests while continuing to mobilize international pressure on Israel on the assumption that in matters of vital interest there was no great difference between the right and left in Israel. As a matter of course, the cable was intended to prepare an adequate platform for my meeting with the prime minister. I will try to recapture here, from memory, the main points of that cable because I earnestly believe that they are as relevant in 2001 as they were ten years ago and sum up Egypt's philosophy and *modus operandi*:

a. Egypt's policies towards Israel are shaped in the light of two major and conflicting factors; on the one hand, absolute adherence to peace and constant efforts to bring to the negotiating table more Arab states and, on the other hand, a strong determination to regain its former position of leadership in the Arab world. Paradoxically, this dichotomy leads Egypt to identify automatically with the narrowest Arab interests and to strive for maximal Israeli concessions in line with Arab aspirations.

b. Egypt adopts cautious and pragmatic stands with regard to the solution of the Palestinian issue and its policies are based on a step-by-step approach. In principle, Egypt has prefered to leave difficult problems to the final settlement phase and is ready, for tactical considerations, to agree to interim phases and temporary partial solutions. However, it has and will always make sure that each and every one of these phases is the best it can possibly be at that time for the Arab side, and serves to lay down the foundations of an overall settlement that fulfils Arab aspirations. It will vehemently oppose any interim agreement that does not fit these criteria (even if the Palestinians themselves, for their own reasons, might tend to accept it). (This is true even now in the final settlement phase of negotiations. Recent disagreements have caused an outburst of violence and sharp Arab and Egyptian criticism.)

c. In the wake of the Gulf War, maintaining close relations with Syria, Libya and Saudi Arabia is crucial to Egypt for strengthening its inter-Arab position. Though it is careful not to be tricked into formally joining the bloc of confrontation states, it refrains from any step or statement that might displease them and strives to appear more Catholic than the Pope in all that concerns the Palestinians and other Arab interests. More than anything else, Egypt does not wish to be perceived by Arab public opinion as an American stooge in the region, despite its obvious dependence on the USA and the well-known fact that it co-ordinates most of its steps with Washington.

d. The final settlement which Egypt desires is based unequivocally on the principle of peace in return for land – and by land it means all the territories that Israel occupied in 1967 including East Jerusalem. It is ready to support a two-phase solution as defined in the Camp David accords (and reformulated by the Madrid conference) provided that the first phase clearly states that the second phase will be the establishment of an independent Palestinian state under the leadership of the PLO. Nevertheless, Egypt might not oppose – at least on the face of it – some kind of loose confederation between the Palestinian state and Jordan. It will however never agree to a Jordanian solution.

e. One should take at face value Egyptian public declarations even if, in closed meetings, Egyptian leaders voice statements more pleasant to Israeli ears. Egypt means exactly what its leaders say publicly and it will strive to attain the goals it has defined by all possible means, excluding military confrontation.

f. Egypt is a most important asset for Israel on the strategic level since it is committed to peace and is genuinely working towards broadening its scope. It also rules out military confrontation and is striving to reach a settlement around the negotiating table and not on the battlefield. However, on the tactical level it is piling up obstacles and making things more difficult for Israel. It is Egypt that has conceived the present Arab policy of depicting Israel as the intransigent side while radiating alleged Arab moderation, goodwill and readiness to live in peace with Israel with a view to gaining western support for a settlement in line with Arab aspirations. Egypt has not only put its international influence and its wide experience of negotiating with Israel at the disposal of its Arab partners but also co-ordinates their steps, conciliates their conflicting standpoints and leads the Arab diplomatic offensive on the international arena.

The above-mentioned points lead to the following prognosis and conclusions:

1. On the bilateral level, the longstanding Egyptian carrot-and-stick policy will continue to be enforced in spite of the apparent warming of relations in the wake of the change of government in Israel. It will continue to be used as a tool for obtaining political gains and cooing Egyptian and Arab public opinion. The complex apparatus put in place by Egypt to prevent the normal flow of relations between the two countries will be expanded. Egypt, for considerations that go well beyond the ups and downs of the peace process, opposes Israeli cultural and economic penetration and the steps it has taken are meant to forestall, in both the short and long run, that danger. In the next few months, there will certainly be a series of small gestures of goodwill intended to create an atmosphere conducive to more Israeli concessions, but the parameters of normalization as established from the outset will not be widened. At the first crisis – and a crisis is bound to occur sooner or later – the situation will revert to what it was before the warming-up of relations.

2. Egypt has allegedly agreed to a Palestinian representation in the peace process along the lines established by the Madrid conference (a joint Palestinian–Jordanian delegation). In reality, it is striving to legitimize the PLO and to make it officially the sole negotiator for the Palestinians. Egypt will also continue to help the PLO economically and diplomatically with the aim of forestalling the creation of a Syrian–Palestinian axis that might jeopardize its own leadership.

3. Egypt is publicly paying lip service to the multilateral track of the Madrid process. In reality, it considers that track as having no independent life of its own. It will prevent any significant progress on the multilateral

track as long as there is no progress on the bilateral one in accordance with its own views.

4. On the face of it, Egypt will try to reach an understanding with Israel for co-ordinating positions and moves in the peace process, and it may even agree to the setting up of a special mechanism of consultation and co-ordination. In reality, as long as Israel does not adopt in broad outline Egyptian views, Egypt has no interest in genuine co-ordination with Israel. In any case, it will continue to co-ordinate its own positions and moves with its Arab partners, especially the Palestinians and the Syrians. It will bring to their knowledge any information it might gather in the framework of its contacts with Israel and advise them on the negotiating tactics they should adopt to forestall Israel's moves and increase pressure on it. Whatever the moves allegedly co-ordinated with Israel, in the last resort Egypt will always toe the Arab line.

5. Egypt will in no circumstances join hands with Israel to isolate Syria as it did in the late 1980s when Rabin, then defense minister in the government of national unity, convinced Mubarak to do. It will insist on immediate progress simultaneously on both the Syrian and Palestinian tracks and oppose moving ahead exclusively on the Palestinian track. It will also put pressure on the Palestinians not to agree to such a move. Egypt is adamant that the only acceptable solution on the Syrian front is the total withdrawal of Israel from the Golan Heights, the dismantling of the settlements and an unconditional pullout from the security belt in Lebanon.

6. As for the Israeli settlements in the West Bank and the Gaza Strip, the Egyptian position is that their fate should be identical to the fate of the settlements in Sinai – the dismantling and unconditional pullout of all Israeli settlers. Egypt deems totally unacceptable the distinction between political and security settlements put forward by Rabin. In this respect, Egypt will increase its attempts to mobilize European and American pressure on Israel and will insist on immediately bringing the settlement process to a complete standstill.

7. Egypt considers the autonomy phase a corridor leading, within a short time, to an independent Palestinian state. It will never agree to any transitional arrangement that does not ensure the achievement of this goal. It will certainly reject any attempt to limit the powers of the Palestinian authorities in the transitional period.

8. Egypt realizes that the problem of Jerusalem is a very sensitive and complex one. It prefers, therefore, to tackle it in the last stage of negotiations on condition that Israel refrains from taking demonstrative measures which would exacerbate the situation. In the long term, it might agree to some face-saving solution if it meets with the approval of the Palestinians, the Arab states and the Muslim world. As long as such a solution is not found, Egypt will present itself as the standard-bearer of Islam in the struggle over Jerusalem and adopt increasingly radical and vociferous stands.

9. Dismantling Israel's nuclear arsenal (alleged or real) is no longer a diplomatic gimmick to embarrass Israel in the international arena – it has turned into a genuine preoccupation for Egypt and a priority goal of its foreign and security policies. There is no doubt that in the coming months it will increase its diplomatic offensive in every possible forum with the aim of bringing Israel to sign the Non-Proliferation Treaty and any other international instrument that would place restrictions on Israel's nuclear capability. Egypt will repeatedly call for a total ban on all weapons of mass destruction in the middle east. It will also try to create an Arab and third world united front for this purpose and will use the disarmament committee of the multilateral track to increase pressure on Israel. In my opinion, there is no possibility of co-ordinating positions with Egypt on the nuclear issue or reaching an understanding with it to lower its profile and postpone the confrontation to a later stage. All such efforts are bound to remain fruitless and, on the contrary, will only encourage the Egyptians to step up their initiatives, make their positions more intransigent and increase their attacks on Israel.

10. Egypt, like all other Arab states, looks on the continuation of Jewish immigration to Israel as a potential danger for the region and strives to bring it to a complete stop. At this stage, it is focusing on preventing the settling of new immigrants in the territories and on putting pressure on the USA not to grant Israel loans or financial guarantees for the absorption of immigrants from the former Soviet Union. It is leading Arab efforts in this field and using all the leverage it has in the USA and Europe. It is also putting direct pressure on Russia to close its gates and stop the stream of Jewish emigration.

11. To this very day, Egypt does not recognize Israel's legitimacy or its right to be an integral part of the region. It is ready to live with the *fait accompli* and maintain peaceful – but limited – relations with Israel and will do its utmost to prevent (or delay) Israel's regional integration for fear of potential economic and political competition. Reading these lines, readers must certainly ask themselves if history does not indeed remain the same. Regardless of the efforts of the past twenty years, little has changed. The premises of Egyptian tactics and goals remain the guidelines of Egypt's policies toward Israel with regard to the resolution of the Arab-Israeli conflict.

At the time, I also received a request from the new director-general of the foreign ministry, Uri Savir, to send my suggestions for the bilateral topics that we should raise in the Rabin–Mubarak summit. In reply, I strongly recommended not raising bilateral issues on our initiative – to the exclusion of the perennial missing soldiers' issue. I stressed that, from our past experience, it was clear that the Egyptians had no intention of making significant changes in their longstanding normalization policies and would again use our evident eagerness as a lever to serve their goals of the moment. I expressed the opinion that Rabin would be playing into their hands and that all that could be expected was a new set of the same worn-out promises that would not be fulfilled, just like the previous ones. My contention was (and still is) that the importance that Israel attached to normalization and its readiness to humble itself time and again was a counterproductive policy. Repeatedly raising the same requests with no tangible results was sending a message that Israel would suffice with crumbs from the normalization table and that all Egypt had to do to satisfy us was to make occasional limited gestures of goodwill. These gestures, which had no weight whatsoever in the over-all context of normalizing relations, were (and still are) a fig-leaf that allowed Egypt to evade its contractual commitments and present to the world an image of goodwill, moderation and compliance with the normalization agreements that it had signed. In conclusion, I suggested that we focus in the summit on regional issues and the peace process, and leave bilateral topics to the embassy in Cairo in the framework of its routine give-and-take with the Egyptians. The only exception I made, as I have already mentioned, concerned the missing soldiers' issue. I hoped that, in the atmosphere that prevailed of a renewed honeymoon, Rabin would succeed in squeezing out of Mubarak a promise to put an end, once and for all, to this dreadful matter that they had been dragging out for 20 years.

I flew to Jerusalem to meet Rabin, hoping that my two cables had pre-pared the ground for me. I feared, in the light of his public statements, that he might not like what I had to tell him, but it was my duty to speak with the utmost frankness and bring to his knowledge my assessment of the situation and the margin of maneuver that he had. I had met Rabin as long ago as 1964, when he received, as chief of staff of the Israeli defense forces, the then president of Chad, François Tombalbaye (whom I was accompanying in my capacity as ambassador to his country). Over the years, our paths had crossed several times and, before leaving for Cairo in 1990, I met with Rabin (he was then leader of the opposition) for a lengthy background talk. He shared with me his views about the peace process, the role of Egypt and the best way to move ahead. He thought at the time that Yitshak Shamir had made a major mistake in agreeing to initiate a negotiation process with Syria so as to alleviate American pressure to step up negotiations on the Palestinian track. He concluded forcefully: 'We have nothing to give the Syrians. Shamir has opened a second front that will lead us to a dead-end which is bound to increase tension. We must move ahead quickly with the Palestinians and do our utmost to drop the Syrians from the equation.'

On my way to meet Rabin in the prime minister's office, I went over that conversation in my mind and came to the conclusion that my first task would be to convince him that, from Egypt's standpoint, the situa-tion had changed dramatically since 1988. This time, Egypt would not support a move aimed at neutralizing Syria even temporarily and allow the peace process to move ahead only on the Palestinian track. At that juncture, in the wake of the Gulf War, Egypt needed Syria more than Syria needed Egypt – and Egypt was once again seen by the Arab and Egyptian intelligentsia (who regarded Sadam Hussein as a hero of the Arab nation) as no more than a US mercenary.

To my great surprise, my two cables had not been brought before the prime minister. It seems that they had fallen victim to the disorder that characterized the first days of the transition of power. Instead of focusing on the technical and operative aspects of the summit, I was compelled to summarize verbally all that I had written in my cables. The meeting lasted for an hour and I do believe that my message got through. I also told Rabin about my misgivings as to the timing of the summit, but the train was already running full speed ahead and no one could stop it. I left in the hands of Haber (the chief of cabinet) a copy of the two cables and requested him to make sure that Rabin read them before the summit. Two days later, I flew back to Cairo with the Israeli delegation.

The summit run smoothly and met, as expected, with great success. The Egyptian prime minister, Atef Sidky, and the entire Egyptian government received Rabin at the airport and he was immediately taken to the presidential palace for a private meeting with Mubarak. From the short report that Rabin presented to the Israeli delegation and the subsequent press conference, it appeared that the two statesmen had found common ground and that Mubarak did succeed in moving Rabin from his stand on Syria. In his statement to the press, he stressed that Israel 'will strive to move ahead quickly and simultaneously on both the Palestinian and Syrian tracks and will not give priority to either of the two tracks'. As I had recommended, bilateral topics were not raised at all, to the exclusion of the missing soldiers' issue. Mubarak again promised to speed up the investigation and this time the promise had a tangible result: after a short while, a single body – that of the navigator Aran Cohen – was located (precisely where our experts had anticipated from the outset). To our great sorrow, the overall problem remained, and remains, unsolved, though two more bodies were 'found' in one of the 'smiling' periods during the Barak government.

I met Rabin for the last time a few months after my transfer to India when I accompanied the chief minister of Gujarat, Chimandai Patel, to a meeting with him. He asked me: 'Ephraim, how is it in India after Egypt?' I answered without hesitation: 'Like going from an icy shower to a hot bath!' He laughed loudly and it was clear that he had grasped what I meant (and I am sure that the reader has too). I returned to Israel on 1 November 1995, a few weeks before retiring from the ministry. Three days later, together with the entire Israeli nation and the entire world, I was filled with revulsion at Rabin's horrendous assassination. I watched on television Mubarak's first and only visit to Israel and listened to his disappointing speech at the grave of his partner in peace – Yitshak Rabin, God rest his soul!

I will not go again into the historic visit of President Yitshak Navon to Egypt in early 1981; its main features have been amply covered in previous chapters. I will also not touch on events that took place after I left Egypt or in which I was not personally involved. Furthermore, I will not describe the many meetings I had with the Egyptian prime ministers nor go into events related to them. I had the honor to know most of them personally: Mustapha Khalil, Fuad Mohie-El-Din, Kamal Hassan Ali, Atef Sidki and Kamal El-Ganzouri. Some of them I met during their tenure, others when they were occupying other positions or after they had retired from political life. All of them always received me kindly and promptly in my capacity as minister or ambassador and listened sympathetically to my requests and complaints. Some even genuinely tried to help. However, I quickly learned that all that pertained to Israel was not within the competence of the prime minister and it was pointless bothering them with our problems. Israeli issues were dealt with exclusively (and still are) by the president, the foreign and interior ministers, the chief of the security services and a few officials whose specialization was Israeli affairs. I also learned that in Egypt former prime ministers and former senior ministers carried little weight and could not influence the course of events. However, for us Israelis, who met difficulties in being received by the decision-makers, they proved to be a valuable channel of communication and we had to use their good services more than once.

18 · Egypt, Israel and the World

At a very early stage of his presidency, Anwar al Sadat realized that the longer Israel remained in Sinai and along the banks of the Suez Canal, the more the world became accustomed to this situation. He came to the conclusion that Egypt's only chance of compelling Israel to soften its position on its territorial gains in the 1967 war was to take the struggle to the diplomatic arena where Israel was in a position of inferiority. He realized, however, that an all-out military confrontation was essential to prepare the background for his diplomatic offensive and that any diplomatic move would, necessarily, have to pass through the battlefield. Indeed, Sadat went to war in order to make peace! He initiated the 1973 war not because he believed that Egypt could prevail militarily over Israel, but because he wanted to provoke a major upheaval that would defrost the status quo and bring about the active involvement of the great powers. No one in Israel (or elsewhere) took seriously Sadat's repeated threats and indeed he caught Israel with its pants down when his armies crossed the Suez Canal on 10 October 1973 on Yom Kippur. The war, which as expected ended militarily in Israel's favor, broke the ice and focused world attention on the need to work out a compromise solution to the protracted Arab–Israeli conflict. The end result of the war – which had started with all the advantages of surprise on the Arab side – convinced Sadat (if he still needed convincing) that the Arabs could not vanquish Israel on the battlefield – at least, not in the foreseeable future. The diplomatic arena became more crucial than ever and, now that the October War had set the stage, he stepped up the political struggle.

Indeed, this was a continuation of the relentless diplomatic war waged by the Arabs against Israel over the years and long before its inception. However, Sadat's target was altogether different: not obliteration of the Jewish state but minimization of Arab losses. At the core of the renewed Arab offensive, spearheaded by Egypt and closely co-ordinated with the communist bloc and the non-aligned movement, were two major goals; to radiate an image of Arab willingness to reach a historical compromise with Israel, and to strip Zionism of international legitimacy and isolate Israel as a leprous state on a par with apartheid South Africa. The principal arena, as a matter of course, remained the United Nations and its specialized agencies where the Arabs and their allies enjoyed an overwhelming and automatic majority. (Abba Eban used to say that the Arabs 'could easily pass a resolution affirming that the Earth was flat. Only a very few countries would dare openly oppose this preposterous contention; some would abstain but the great majority would vote in favor.' From my personal experience in the UN, I can vouch that Abba Eban did not exaggerate ...)

The renewed Arab diplomatic campaign, after the Yom Kippur War, was a great success. Practically all the African states, the communist bloc and most of the non-aligned movement cut diplomatic relations with Israel and branded it the aggressor notwithstanding the fact that Egypt had attacked Israel. A score of extreme resolutions against Israel was passed in all international fora (the annual average exceeded 100). But altogether, this was no more than a flood of verbosity that had no practical effect on the situation in the field – these resolutions piled up in the UN archives and accumulated a heavy layer of dust. In the Security Council – the only international body with teeth – all attempts to impose military or economic sanctions on Israel were foiled by American vetoes. On the terrain, Israel constantly strengthened its grasp on the occupied territories while its economic situation improved, its population increased substantially and its military might became more overwhelming. On the other hand, Israel was no longer perceived by world opinion as a small and weak David courageously withstanding the mighty Arab Goliath – it had lost much of the sympathy associated with the underdog, a role which the Palestinians now assumed.

Resolutions and sympathy were far from sufficient for the Arabs, who realized that relying exclusively on the UN would lead them nowhere. Israel's bilateral relations prospered while the support of the USA and world Jewry (and to a lesser extent the Western countries) remained as strong as ever. The Arabs – especially Sadat's Egypt – reached the conclusion that only a shift of sympathy in the West that would lead it to exert pressure on Israel, combined with threats to impose sanctions if Israel did not heed the voice of reason, would bring tangible results. They focused their efforts, therefore, on undermining traditional western support for Israel and convincing world public opinion (including world Jewry) of the Arabs' readiness to make peace as contrasted with Israel's intransigence. As a matter of course, such a peace was to be based on two principles: peace in return for land and fulfillment of the Palestinians' inalienable right to self-determination (read: their right to establish an independent state on all the territories occupied in 1967).

Here too the unceasing Arab efforts brought significant results. Already at the end of the 1970s, the European Union adopted these two principles and made them their official policy in the Venice declaration (though not all the individual states supported them with the same enthusiasm). Tacitly, the USA also adopted this stand, especially after the

Madrid conference. Indeed, to the best of my understanding, the American interpretation of the Camp David accords was from the outset very close to that formulation. Sadat, more than anyone else, grasped the golden opportunity to reverse the course of history with the active support of the west. His historic visit to Jerusalem and his speech to the Knesset, where he coined the motto 'No more wars', won the heart of Western governments and peoples. It convinced even the most skeptical observers of Egypt's determination to renounce the use of force to regain its territories and secure Palestinian rights. The door to improving Egypt's relations with the West and bringing it to adopt Egypt's concept of peace was opened wide. For Sadat, the USA was particularly important – because of its special links with Israel and the unwavering support it extended to Israel economically, militarily and diplomatically. I heard him say time and again: 'All the cards are in the hands of the USA. It is the only power in the world that can bend Israel's stubbornness and compel it to withdraw from Arab land and accept a political compromise.' His dream (and today Mubarak's) was to undermine the unwritten alliance between the USA and Israel and gradually reach a situation where Egypt would replace Israel as the USA's main strategic partner in the middle east or, at least, become as important to the USA as Israel. He decided, in a very bold and dangerous step for him at the time, to free Egypt of the anti-American rhetoric that had become, during Nasser's regime, part of the inner being of most Egyptian and Arab intellectuals (and still is). He severed Egypt's close ties with the Soviet Union and openly cast his lot in with the USA relying on it almost exclusively for rebuilding his army, restoring his economy and orchestrating the peace process.

Sadat spared no efforts in winning over American public opinion which, he knew, was decisive. He devoted special attention to the American Jewish community, which he perceived as a leading factor not only in the USA but also in the entire western world. In one of my conversations with Boutros Ghali (himself a Copt, married to a Jewish woman), he told me that Sadat had entrusted him with the task of maintaining close contacts with the Jewish communities around the world with a view to convincing them of Egypt's sincerity and mobilizing their support. According to him, during a ten-year period, he met with more than 2,000 (!) Jewish delegations of all kinds and levels. Boutros refrained from telling me that his main task was to drive a wedge between Israel and the Jewish communities and induce them to exert pressure on their brethren in Israel and on the Israeli government. At the same time, on several occasions Egypt did not hesitate to appeal directly to the Israeli public to put pressure on its government. I have to admit, somewhat shamefully, that on both tracks Egypt met with relative success. Let me add that the reverse situation was absolutely out of the question and Israel was strictly denied access to the Egyptian media, public organizations and associations (and, in most cases, even private individuals).

This short presentation of the Egyptian strategy is, no doubt, schematic but it does reflect the course of events and the main ideas that prevailed at the time – and still do – in Egypt and among the other main players. In this respect too Mubarak is following in Sadat's steps and is relying almost exclusively on the USA, though he has developed the conviction that the European Union is more supportive of Arab stands and should, therefore, play a more active role in the peace process. He calls periodically on Europe to exert pressure not only on Israel but also on the USA (each time it shows reluctance to support Arab moves or refrains from putting overt pressure on Israel). Until now, he has met with little success, not because the Europeans are not eager to increase their role in the middle east but because they are reluctant to clash with the USA and realize that they have limited influence on the march of events. Still, Mubarak does not let go and demands, time and again, increased European intervention. He also guides the Palestinians and the Arab states to adopt the same line, provoking much anger in Israel and more so in the United States. Like Sadat, Mubarak knows that all the cards remain in the hands of the USA and that Egypt will be totally dependent on American assistance for many years to come. He persists in advocating (or rather threatening) an increased European role, more for nuisance's sake than because he believes it is a feasible option in the light of Israeli and American opposition. Twice a year, year after year, Mubarak embarks on a semi-official visit to the USA with the aim of strengthening Egypt's international position (and his own position at home) and of co-ordinating, as much as possible, stands with the USA and obtaining further assistance and support. He meets with the president, ministers, senators and congressmen, the press and the entire Who's Who including leaders of the American Jewish community. On his way to the USA and back, he generally pops in on two or three European countries (mostly France and Germany) for short visits. He exchanges views with their leaders, strives to convince them to take independent initiatives in the peace process and obtains more or less explicit declarations of support. Before and after these voyages, the Egyptian media orchestrates a fully-fledged publicity campaign, depicting them as historic events of unprecedented magnitude and praising their results profusely (though, most times, the results are very poor or non-existent). Egyptian intellectuals are not fooled by the lavish compliments poured on the president in the press and do not refrain in private conversations from expressing their scorn.

On the American front, though Egypt has very much improved its intrinsic weight, it is still very far from replacing Israel as the USA's strategic partner in the middle east. Each time it seems to Egypt that the special relationship between Israel and the USA is on the verge of collapse and that the USA will finally use the big stick against it, comes a sudden reversal of the situation, leading to disappointment and disillusionment. At the peak of the crisis, against all odds the tension fades away leaving unimpaired the intimate relations between the two countries. To Egypt's amazement and frustration, Israel emerges unscathed from each confrontation, public sympathy becomes stronger and economic, military and diplomatic support increases. Again and again, Egypt witnesses American vetoes in the Security Council, pro-Israeli resolutions in Congress, the allocation of supplementary funds, the supply of sophisticated weaponry, sympathetic political statements, reconciliation with Israel's longstanding refusal to adhere to the NPT, and reluctance to impose sanctions on Israel or even to threaten the imposition of sanctions ... Each time, the Egyptian government bites its lip and reacts with a thundering silence. The press (which in Egypt reflects its Master's Voice) gives expression to Egypt's collective disappointment, resorts to the anti-American lexicon of the Nasserist period, blames the Jewish lobby and viciously attacks Israel. I tried my best to explain to my Egyptian friends that the relationship between the USA and Israel is not based on considerations of the moment and that it has very deep roots which stem from common values. My explanations fell on deaf ears – no Egyptian, and indeed no Arab, can accept such an abstract motivation and most of them (not to say all of them) remain convinced that American Jewry controls the US government and public opinion by dint of its financial power. As disappointment follows disappointment, frustration and anger grow in Egypt. However, the sweet hope of succeeding in driving a wedge between the USA and Israel (and between the American Jewish community and Israel) remains, now more than ever, one of the main tenets of Egyptian foreign policy.

In this context, the best opportunity for Egypt arose during the Gulf crisis (1990–93). Egypt took sides, though somewhat hesitantly, with the USA and the western coalition and even dispatched a small contingent of troops to the front. Its military contribution was less than marginal but it played an essential role in giving Arab legitimization to the western campaign against Iraq. Egypt helped crystallize an Arab anti-Iraqi coalition and seemingly convinced Syria to join it (in fact, Egypt's brokerage was marginal and Syria acted out of economic and military considerations of its own). I was in Egypt at the time and I could follow closely the ups and downs of the Egyptian moves and witness Mubarak's wriggling between his pro-Iraqi public opinion and his own pro-western pragmatic considerations. Up to the last moment, he made pathetic efforts, almost to the point of ridicule, to convince Saddam Hussein to bend until the storm passed. He even hinted that, at a later stage, he might support holding a referendum in Kuwait that would solve the issue in favor of Iraq (the Kuwaitis still do not forgive Mubarak).

Nevertheless, in the west in general and in the USA in particular, Egypt's contribution was perceived as primordial. Sympathy for Egypt increased tremendously and massive economic and military assistance was lavishly poured on it – well beyond Mubarak's expectations. The USA cancelled altogether Egypt's military debt, which amounted to many billions of dollars, and allocated to Egypt substantial supplementary financial support and sophisticated military equipment. The Paris Club (the European Union and other western countries) yielded to American pressures and erased half of the Egyptian debt – both military and commercial. It also agreed to reschedule reimbursement of the remaining half over a long period of time. In the wake of this agreement, Egypt applied unilaterally the same arrangement to the settlement of its commercial debts to other countries (including small sums that it owed to a few Israeli firms). In addition, all members of the European Union – collectively and separately – granted Egypt substantial supplementary financial assistance. To the best of my knowledge, the overall amount bestowed on Egypt, as tangible expression of western appreciation of its role in the Gulf crisis, added up to more than $20 billion! An eminent Egyptian journalist, abashed by the momentous amount, told me in one of our conversations: 'Mubarak ought to erect a full-sized statue of pure gold to Saddam Hussein in the middle of Liberation Square [the main square in Cairo] in recognition of his outstanding contribution to Egypt's economy.' Seeing my surprise, he explained that 'owing to Saddam's stupidity, Egypt had received $20 billion without taking the slightest risk ...'

No one finds $20 billion in the street and indeed it was a major success of Egyptian foreign policy. However, even in the circumstances of the time, American gratitude for Egypt's role did not go so far as to impair Israel's popularity in the USA or erode its special status in the administration's eyes. On the contrary, support for Israel in the USA (and in the world) grew substantially thanks to the restraint it showed regarding the shower of Iraqi missiles that fell on its urban civilian population (though it was not a party to the Gulf War). These indiscriminate attacks on the civilian population reminded international public opinion of the deadly dangers confronting Israel and the sea of blind hatred that surrounded it. In spite of Egypt's tremendous gains from the Gulf War, one could feel in conversations with Egyptian officials and intellectuals (or simply by reading the press) profound disappointment and frustration that Egypt had not received dividends in terms of a decline of American support for Israel. The fact that Israel also had derived economic, diplomatic and military benefits from a war against a sister Arab state made them particularly bitter. My friend the eminent journalist recycled his joke about Saddam's statue and wrote in his daily column:

> Yitshak Shamir ought to erect a golden statue of Saddam Hussein in the main square of Tel Aviv. Thanks to his folly, Israel has gained immense sympathy, received massive economic aid, secured the most sophisticated weaponry in the world and succeeded in bringing about the destruction of the Iraqi arsenal without taking part in the war and without even firing a single bullet.

From the beginning of the Gulf crisis, Egypt feared that Israel might take military action in the wake of Saddam's threats to destroy it and, later, it was afraid that such a move on Israel's part would jeopardize the Arab coalition against Iraq. It thus requested the USA and other western countries to put pressure on Israel not to interfere militarily in the war. It exerted direct pressure too and I was summoned several times to the Egyptian foreign ministry. Initially, Israel was requested to turn a blind eye (or better a deaf ear) to Iraqi provocation and not to take any military action unless it was physically attacked. Later, when Iraqi missiles began to fall on Israel, the Egyptians requested Israel not to react in order not to jeopardize the integrity of the anti-Iraqi coalition. I was instructed by our government to communicate officially to the foreign minister, Amr Mussa, that Israel did not and could not abandon its legitimate right to self-defense and that it would respond to the Iraqi attacks at a time and in a way it found proper. I was also instructed to tell the Egyptians in vague terms – without spelling it out explicitly – that Israel would resort to such action only in a worse-case scenario (Iraqi attacks with chemical missiles). I was also instructed to explain that Israel could not state publicly that it would not retaliate because this would be an open invitation to Iraq to continue its attacks. The message was relayed and well understood.

The Gulf states too rewarded Egypt for its part in the Iraqi crisis though they were much less generous than the west and indeed had less reason to be generous. Saudi Arabia, Qatar and Kuwait donated in cash some $2–3 billion and increased substantially their foreign currency deposits in Egyptian banks – thus improving Egypt's financial balance and allowing it to raise loans on the international market. In reality, the Gulf states were far from enthusiastic about Egypt's performance in the crisis or during the war and were outraged at Mubarak's repeated attempts to help Iraq out of the mire. The Egyptian press reacted with wrath to the Arabs' ingratitude and called on the government to make Egypt's future participation in the defense of the Gulf states conditional on an annual payment of several billion dollars (in advance!) not as a charity but as a right. The press pointed out that the Gulf states had flooded Iraq with billions of dollars during its war with Iran while they had thrown miserable crumbs to Egypt in the several wars it had waged, on behalf of the Arab nation, in defense of Palestinian rights and Arab honor. As always, the press reflected the thinking of the Egyptian leadership, who felt that the Gulf War had created an opportunity for Egypt to dictate its conditions to the rich oil emirates and extort protection fees that would compensate for the stinginess of the past. But the Gulf states were not interested in having Egypt protect them. They did not believe that Egypt had the capability – political or military – to do so and they did not feel they needed Egypt's good offices to obtain US intervention on their behalf. They rightly thought that they had more leverage with the USA than Egypt and saw no reason to pay protection fees for empty words and irrelevant political maneuvers.

With the conclusion of the war, I followed closely, together with my colleagues in Cairo, Egypt's pathetic efforts to squeeze itself into a leadership position and to present itself as the main factor in the defense of the Gulf. It called a conference in Damascus of the confrontation countries (the Arab countries that had participated in the war) and pressured them to pass bombastic resolutions recognizing Egypt's predominant role and barring the participation of any external factor (read: the USA, Europe, Pakistan, Turkey, Iran). These resolutions remained a dead letter in spite of Egypt's repeated efforts to breathe life into them. The Gulf states (and probably also Syria) were not ready to implement them, preferring to rely on the USA for their external defense and on Pakistan and Bangladesh for their internal security. They were also very careful not to ostracize their awesome neighbor Iran and drop it from the regional equation. I believe that I am not exaggerating if I say that the Gulf states considered Egypt a troublesome, and ultimately useless, element.

Understandably, these developments disappointed Egypt. The press went wild, accusing the Gulf states of ingratitude, shortsightedness and betrayal of Arab solidarity. Egypt, however, had limited leverage with the Gulf states and finally had to accept a face-saving compromise that gave it a minor role in regional defense arrangements (and indeed was never implemented).

The texture of relations between Egypt and the other Arab states has always been complex. Only a skilled psychologist could analyze in depth the tangled web of the conflicting factors which shape their relation at a given time or in the long run. I have no such skills and all I can say is that beyond the kisses and embraces, the alliances and reconciliations, the treaties of co-operation and pledges of Arab solidarity, there have always been acute rivalries, noisy exchanges of insults, reciprocal subversion and even armed confrontation.

There is no doubt that Egypt, as the biggest and most populous Arab state, has played, and still plays, a leading role in the Arab world and has always been at the core of the Arab being – cultural and political. However, although they recognize its specific weight, the sister countries have never accepted its leadership as self-evident – to the exclusion, perhaps, of a very short period at the peak of Nasser's popularity in the mid-1950s. With the signing of the Camp David accords, Egypt was branded a traitor and expelled from the Arab League. President Sadat hurled insults at his Arab brethren (who reciprocated in no less virulent terms) and, for a short while, pretended to sever Egypt from the Arab world and return it to its pharaonic roots. In reality, he was very cautious not to burn his bridges for a future reconciliation, taking various steps to prevent aggravating the rift and to minimize the damage caused by the Arab economic and political boycott against Egypt. The policy of slowing up the normalization process and keeping Israel at bay was used to signal to the Arab countries that Egypt did not intend to get into bed with

Israel or forsake the Palestinian cause and pan-Arab interests. Millions of Egyptian citizens continued to work in the Arab countries, trade and economic relations remained unhampered despite the official boycott, and air and land transportation did not cease ... After a few months, Arab tourism returned to its usual size (when I arrived in mid-1980, Cairo was already crowded with Arab tourists). Paradoxically, the Arab diplomatic missions in Egypt also continued to function normally at chargé d'affaires level and the PLO maintained its ambassador in Cairo. Furthermore, Egypt stood behind Iraq unequivocally throughout the war with Iran. It not only gave its tacit agreement to the drafting into the Iraqi army of thousands of Egyptian citizens residing in Iraq but also supplied Iraq with arms and essential spare parts and, at a later stage, dispatched pilots to man Iraqi planes and technicians to maintain sophisticated weaponry. It even concealed from the general public the heavy casualties suffered in the war by the Egyptian draftees.

With his accession to the presidency towards the end of 1981, Mubarak set, as the second most important goal of his foreign policy, Egypt's reintegration into the Arab world and the restoration of its leadership role. The first goal was (and remains) the preservation and strengthening of the peace in the region along the lines defined by Egypt. He entrusted both tasks to his faithful and able adviser Osama Elbaz, who also dealt with the peace process and relations with Israel and could thus strike the right balance between these conflicting goals. Let me point out that, at the time, if Mubarak had been prepared to recognize publicly that Sadat had been mistaken (or gone crazy) when he signed the Camp David accords, he would have been hailed as a hero by the Arabs. Egypt would have been reintegrated into the Arab world ten years earlier – without even having to rescind the peace treaty or sever diplomatic relations with Israel. But Mubarak persevered with Sadat's peace policy out of the conviction that it not only served Egypt's vital interests but also global Arab and Palestinian interests. He also believed that the Arabs could achieve far more around the negotiating table than on the battlefield, as had been the case with Egypt itself.

Like Sadat, Mubarak also had to cope with many attacks and insults from his Arab brethren but, unlike Sadat, he did not allow himself be dragged into a sterile exchange of words. He showed maximum restraint and put the leash on the Egyptian press in order not to poison the atmosphere and jeopardize his diplomatic moves to rejoin the Arab world. A short time after Mubarak had assumed the presidency, King Saoud of Saudi Arabia passed away and he decided to attend the funeral notwithstanding the fact that he had not been invited and that the king had not come to Sadat's funeral. Mubarak was received with manifest coolness by his hosts and the other attending Arab leaders. At each opportunity, he rushed to embrace everyone present despite their evident reluctance. (I witnessed such scenes myself on Egyptian television, and journalists in his retinue told me that the president, who did know who was who, also hugged the Arab personalities' bodyguards.) Under Mubarak's strict instructions, attacks on Arab leaders in the Egyptian press were discontinued and the press refrained from reacting to Arab attacks on Egypt and its leaders. In a drastic about-turn, Egypt threw its full support behind extreme Arab stands and made every effort to establish a close relationship with the radical countries (such as Syria and Libya). Clearly, by paving its way back to the Arab world Egypt also had to pay a toll in Israeli currency: anti-Israeli and anti-Jewish statements, as well as vicious attacks in the press, increased substantially and Egypt openly supported Arab moves against Israel in the international arena and even took the initiative with many of them. At the same time, it refined the mechanisms it had set in place to forestall normalization with Israel and almost brought relations between the two countries to a standstill. Happily, it did not involve itself militarily in the war in Lebanon (1982–83) but it led the diplomatic onslaught on Israel, recalled its ambassador for consultation, and granted unhampered passage to Yasser Arafat and his men during their flight from Beirut and helped them find a save haven.

Mubarak's policy of restraint bore its first significant fruit when Egypt was invited in 1990 to participate, though still as an observer, in the Casablanca conference and played an important role in the drafting of what is known as the Casablanca resolutions. These resolutions were interpreted worldwide as a first step in the adoption by the Arab states and the Palestinians of the Egyptian peace approach. Paradoxically, it was the PLO that forestalled Egypt's reintegration as a fully-fledged member of the Arab League during that conference. But this was only a slight mishap – the way was paved for Egypt's return to the Arab fold! Less than two years later, Egypt was not only readmitted with all due honors in the Arab League and Arab diplomatic representation restored to ambassadorial level, but also the League's seat was moved back to Cairo (to its former offices, which Egypt had kept unoccupied for the entire period). Egypt's success was complete a few months later when Ismat Abd El Meguid, its foreign minister, was elected secretary-general of the League. The cheers of victory in Egypt (and I was in Cairo at the time) were resounding. At last the stigma of betrayal had been erased, Egypt's policies had been proven right and the Arabs had reinstated Egypt in a leading position, notwithstanding the Star of David flying over the Israeli embassy in the center of Cairo.

Cairo was again officially the heart of the Arab world and of Arab diplomatic activity. For us, the Israeli diplomats, it was a heart-warming experience – we could follow Arab interaction from the front row and we were literally rubbing shoulders with Arab diplomats (though they were very careful not to have any relations with us or even shake hands in accidental meetings). The embassy continued to function normally apart, of course, from the usual harassment by the Egyptian authorities and the restrictions imposed on us from the outset (these had in effect become part of normality for us). The only outward changes were the cutting off of our contacts with Ismat Abd El Meguid and the discontinuation of invitations to attend inaugural sessions of parliament. In respect of the invitations, I have to admit that the Egyptians did it with elegance – they claimed a lack of space in the guests' galleries and ceased to invite any non-Arab ambassador (not just the Israeli ambassador). All my colleagues knew what the real reason was behind this unusual step and some of them protested officially but to no avail.

Ismat Abd El Meguid severed all contacts with us. He was considered one of the pioneers of the peace process and one of its staunchest supporters. As ambassador to the UN, he had taken an active part in the Camp David negotiations and had maintained behind-the-scenes relations with various Israeli personalities. Furthermore, as Egypt's foreign minister, he had been at the forefront of the daily interaction with Israel and his door was always open to Israeli diplomats and visitors. Understandably, he had many friends in Israel and all hurried to congratulate him on his election as secretary-general of the Arab League. Among others, President Haim Herzog and foreign minister David Levy sent him letters of warm congratulations and channeled them through the embassy in Cairo. I knew this was a non-starter and that Abd El Meguid could not reasonably continue maintaining open contacts with Israeli personalities. In order to avoid a diplomatic incident and an unnecessary slap in the face, I tried to persuade them not to forward the letters but they insisted on pointing to their excellent personal relations with Abd El Meguid. The foreign ministry, for its part, believed that it was an excellent opportunity to establish contact with the Arab League and instructed me to deliver the letters. I had to abide by my instructions but, instead of requesting a meeting with Abd El Meguid to hand the letters over personally (which obviously would have been refused), I decided to send them by special messenger to his office in the Arab League, together with a *Note Verbale*. Several days later, the letters were returned unopened (at least apparently) through the mail. The underlying message was clear but I was instructed to try again. This time, the security guards at the League's gate refused to receive the letters and warned the messenger not to come again. The next day, I was called to the ministry of foreign affairs and requested to discontinue my efforts to contact Abd El Meguid on the basis that:

> In his new functions as secretary-general of the Arab League, Abd El Meguid now belongs to the Arab Nation and represents the entire Arab world. As such, he is bound by Arab collective decisions and prevented from maintaining contacts with Israel or Israelis as he used to do in his functions as foreign minister or Egypt's ambassador to the UN.

To sum up, after years of strenuous efforts and much patience, Egypt has managed to return to the center of the Arab stage and, from the first moment, it has positioned itself – to the dissatisfaction of most Arab states – as the uncontested leader of the Arab world. It intervenes in every Arab conflict, claims it is the shield of the Arab nation, convenes conferences and consultations, sends emissaries, claims to act as a broker with the west and demonstrates intense activity – necessary or not – on each and every Arab issue. On the Israeli front, it spearheads the diplomatic moves against Israel, uses its leverage to induce the USA and Europe to pressure Israel into concessions, raises extreme demands (often more vociferously than the parties directly involved) and is at the forefront of each and every anti-Israeli initiative. Furthermore, Egypt presents its wide experience in negotiating with Israel and its deep insight into the Israeli soul as a formidable asset for the Arabs: it is keen to teach them how to foster Arab interests around the negotiating table by taking advantage of Israel's eagerness for recognition and peace. It also strives to show them how they can make peace with Israel and, at the same time, prevent it from securing gains in terms of bilateral normalization and regional integration by establishing, like Egypt, a well-oiled machinery to forestall such gains.

Egypt never desists! Its hyper-activity is constantly increasing – even when the results add up to nil and its Arab brethren show manifest displeasure. For many years to come, one may assume that this phenomenon, and the related seesaw in the interaction with Israel, will accompany us. There is no doubt that Egypt has succeeded in placing itself in a leading position in the peace process (to a certain extent with Israel's blessing) but it is far from having achieved Arab recognition for its overall leadership in the region. The Arab states do not want or need Egypt's good offices in their relations with the USA and the west in general or its mediation in their bilateral and regional relationships. They neither trust the sincerity of its intentions and the honesty of its policies nor believe that it is strong enough to defend them – militarily or politically. Their attitude towards Egypt is ambivalent: on the one hand, they appreciate that it is the largest Arab country and that without it they are less effective in the international arena; on the other hand, they mock its pretentiousness and empty activity. They stress that everything and everyone in Egypt can be bought for a price. They openly describe the Egyptians as *Shahatim* (the Arabic word for beggars) who have an insatiable appetite for money and gifts and are ready to debase themselves and their country for the sake of personal gain. Let me add that, on the Egyptians' side too, there is very little empathy towards their Arab brethren. They consider them illiterates who squander Arab wealth on the pleasures of life in the most irrational and criminal manner. At the same time, they envy their wealth and harbor deep feelings of inferiority and frustration towards them. They resent the fact that Mother Nature has been so stingy with Egypt while it has endowed the Gulf states with infinite reserves of oil and they resent, even more, being compelled to resort to the Gulf states for financial assistance and lucrative employment. As is well-known, millions of Egyptians, who would otherwise have been unemployed, find their livelihood in the rich Arab states, where they receive salaries that are many times higher than the average income in Egypt. Agricultural hands, specialist workers, teachers, journalists, physicians, nurses, engineers, household employees, academicians – the list is limitless – flock to the Arab states for work. They accept the harshest treatment provided they can extract themselves from the unemployment and abject poverty that are their lot in their own country. Clearly, these gloomy facts of life have an adverse effect on the national mood in Egypt and on the masses' self-esteem, which stands in sharp contrast with the pretentiousness, vociferousness and hyper-activity of their rulers.

One of the opposition leaders in parliament (albeit a well controlled opposition) illustrated these sentiments, in one of our many conversations. He provided as an example the case of a close woman-relative of his, a senior pediatrician. In Egypt, she had reached the top of her field and the position of deputy dean of the school of medicine. She earned an annual salary of some 7,000 Egyptian pounds (around $2,000), including fringe benefits. However, she could hardly support her family and, in the end, she jumped at the opportunity to work in a Saudi hospital as director of the pediatric division. Her monthly salary was 15,000 Egyptian pounds ($4,500) plus free lodging, a service car and household personnel. After a few months, she clashed on a trivial matter with a Saudi nurse and brought the matter before the hospital director (also a Saudi) threatening she would resign if he did not reprimand the nurse. Her resignation was accepted on the spot and, less than two weeks later, she found herself back in Cairo back at her old job and on her old miserable salary. Now, concluded my interlocutor:

> Her professional honor is safe but she cannot provide a decent livelihood for her family. I am compelled to help her financially though I am not myself a rich man. I have no alternative but to ask influential friends in Saudi Arabia to intervene on her behalf and have her taken back. If need be, she will have to apologize to the hospital director and to the nurse notwithstanding the frustration and the personal affront it involves. It is not easy for destitute people to safeguard their honor, professional or personal. One does not eat honor and does not feed one's children by putting honor on their plates! This is the gloomy truth at the personal level and this is the gloomy truth at the national level!

Paradoxically, though Egypt is at the forefront of the struggle for Palestinian rights, there is no excessive love (to use a mild formulation) between Egyptians and Palestinians. Mutual mistrust and contempt are deeply rooted in their relationship, which has experienced over the years an unceasing seesaw of ups and downs. The Palestinians – despite the many wars that Egypt has fought against Israel on their behalf, the blood it has spilled and the enormous damage it has suffered – perceive Egyptians as treacherous, venal and despotic. They do not forget, or forgive, the difficult years of Egyptian control in the Gaza Strip and the heavy hand of the Egyptian administration. They recall with bitterness the stubborn refusal to allow Palestinians to reside permanently in Egypt (contrary to the case in Lebanon, Syria and Jordan) and the quotas imposed on Palestinian students in Egyptian universities. They also deeply resent Egypt's patronizing attitude and its unceasing attempts to interfere in Palestinian affairs and dictate – as a function of its own selfish interests – courses of action and policies and even the composition of their leadership. For the Palestinians, the signing of the Camp David accords and the establishing of diplomatic relations with Israel represented the ultimate betrayal on Egypt's part. They considered Sadat's peace initiative an abandonment of the territories and their inhabitants into Israeli hands and a cynical move to regain Sinai and obtain massive American aid at the expense of the Palestinians' vital interests. For years, they saw Egypt's total dependence on the USA, Israel's stronghold and main supporter, the 'mother of all sins' (nowadays, they themselves rely almost exclusively on the USA). The Galilee operation and the five years of *Intifada* strengthened them in the conviction that, apart from verbosity and empty measures, Palestinians could not expect substantial assistance from Egypt, and certainly not a reversal in their military confrontation with Israel.

For the Egyptians, the Palestinians are a people of exploiters who suck the bone marrow of the Arab nation and are ready to fight Israel up to the last Egyptian soldier. They consider the Palestinian leaders as corrupt and totally disconnected from the Palestinian masses, whom they let rot in refugee camps while they themselves live in luxurious apartments and five-star hotels and greedily enjoy life's pleasures at the Arab nation's expenses. They accuse them of extorting hundreds of millions of dollars from the Arab countries using terror, blackmail and subversion while at the same time shamelessly undermining their regimes. Egyptians despise, more than any other Arab leader, Yasser Arafat, the founder of the PLO and the Palestinian supreme leader. They consider him a pathological liar, an indefatigable manipulator and a chronic traitor who, time and again, has stuck a knife into Egypt's back. Over the years there have been several serious incidents that have exacerbated the Egyptians' revulsion for Arafat but it reached an unprecedented peak during the Gulf War in the wake of his public support for Iraq. Let us recall that in 1990 Arafat also prevented Egypt's readmission to the Arab League at the Casablanca conference. In December 1993, during the signing ceremony of the Cairo agreement between Israel and the PLO (brokered by Egypt and the USA), Arafat tried at the last moment to extort more concessions and refused to sign. One could see Mubarak clearly on the television screen, his face distorted by anger and disdain, threatening Arafat. Readers might think that I am exaggerating in my description of the Egyptian–Palestinian relationship or that I am quoting selected paragraphs of Israeli propaganda pamphlets (especially in the light of the present honeymoon between them). This is far from the case! I am faithfully depicting only a small part of the opinions that I have repeatedly heard, in private and in official conversations, from Egyptian interlocutors – political leaders, intellectuals, officials, diplomats, journalists, students and the man-in-the-street. These opinions are amply reflected in the Egyptian press, especially in periods of crisis, with various degrees of intensity. I will provide here only two characteristic examples (out of hundreds) that speak for themselves.

An eminent Egyptian leader once told me in an outburst of contained wrath:

> They [the Palestinian leaders] are full of money and they are throwing it out of the window with no account. They have extorted it from the rich Arabs – easy come, easy go! Let me take you to the parking lot at the Palestinian embassy in Cairo and you will find there no less than 17 Mercedes cars – the most luxurious models – which we Egyptians cannot afford, even for the presidency.

At the peak of the Peace for Galilee operation, a leading Egyptian journalist, Ibrahim Al Waradani, wrote in his column in *El Akhbar* and I summarize from memory:

> An over-righteous and compassionate lady from high society requested me to help her arouse public opinion to the Palestinians' sufferings. She wanted me to use my column to incite well-off Egyptians to donate money and equipment to assist them. I asked her to give me a few days to think the matter over and promised to phone her as soon as possible. Indeed, I tried several times to contact her but I always missed her; she was never at home – she was probably running around on behalf of the poor Palestinians. Since I was not able to speak with her, I will use my column to give her my answer. I want to tell her that the Palestinians are far from being destitute – in the Arab countries and Egypt alone (not to speak of far-away countries), there are several thousand Palestinian millionaires. They have enriched themselves at the expense of the Arab nation and do not lift a finger on behalf of their brethren who are rotting and starving to death in refugee camps. I would advise my over-righteous and graceful friend to address herself to these Palestinian millionaires and cease harassing the Egyptian people, whose financial possibilities are quite meager. Egypt has already sacrificed hundreds of thousands of its best sons for the Palestinians and has become impoverished in a score of wars waged for their sake while they themselves dwelt in safety and hoarded wealth ...

Notwithstanding the mutual dislike and mistrust between the Palestinians and Egyptians, Egypt – even after the peace treaty with Israel – has never forsaken the Palestinians or ceased working for the restoration of their rights and securing for them the best possible compromise (the key word being compromise). Naturally, one of Egypt's considerations is that active support for the Palestinians is an efficacious tool to enhance its inter-Arab and international role but that is, by no means, its sole consideration or the most important one. First and foremost, Egypt is driven by a genuine concern for the plight of the Palestinians and by a sense of duty as the major Arab country. It has also the conviction that, as long as the Palestinians' aspirations are not met to their entire satisfaction, the region will continue to be plagued with violence and instability leading to the spread of Muslim fundamentalism thus endangering the Egyptian regime as well as other moderate Arab regimes. Egypt is ready to go to great lengths to help the Palestinian cause and it spares no efforts to create conditions conducive to the most favorable solution from their viewpoint; however it adamantly refuses to be maneuvered back into military confrontation with Israel. It is convinced that, on the diplomatic front, the Arabs have the advantage over Israel and – if they play their cards well – they can squeeze far-reaching concessions from Israel around the negotiating table with the active support of both the USA and Europe. Since the Madrid conference, which marked the definitive adoption of the Egyptian line by most Arab countries, Egypt's relations with the Palestinians have improved. With the Oslo agreement (in which Egypt played no part), mutual criticism and verbal attacks have come to a complete stop and a very close co-operation has developed. The sides co-ordinate their steps and work hand in hand. However, diverging views and conflicting interests may re-emerge in the more or less remote future, and reverse the situation from embraces to abuses (in my opinion, this is bound to happen sooner or later).

Inter-Arab relations have been, and will remain, an interminable see-saw of ups and downs, short-lived alliances and inherent conflict. Abba Eban used to say that it was a mistake to speak about the Arab world as if it were a single entity with a single common purpose and outlook. There are 22 separate Arab states – each with its distinct identity, its own regime and political system, its specific interests and aspirations and its unique cultural background. Several decades of independence have deepened these inherent differences and fostered local nationalism. True, in the early 1950s, the pan-Arab movement had a period of revival, thanks mainly to Nasser, but it was a short-lived phenomenon. Behind the bombastic declarations on Arab unity and fraternity, there are undercurrents of division and competition. Alliances fold and unfold, blocs rise and disintegrate, conflicts and confrontations grow and fade away, regimes consolidate and others crumble and the inter-Arab game continues interminably … Egypt participates in the game actively and pretends to lead it – for better or worse.

317

The main feature of Arab interaction in the last decade has been not unity and stability, as they would like us to believe. It has been, to our great sorrow and theirs, the rapid growth and spread of extreme Islamic fundamentalism and its readiness to use all means (including the bloodiest terrorism) to overthrow the regimes in place and establish the rule of *Sharia* (Koranic law). Assuming that this were to take place in the remote future (and I doubt it), it would not mean that the differences in the Arab world would automatically vanish. On the contrary, the acute disputes prevailing among the various Muslim currents will combine with the national conflicts and aggravate them. Instead of unifying the Arab world, fundamentalist Islamic regimes might exacerbate inter-Arab competition, add to it a religious dimension and bring about confrontations more violent and uncompromising than the ones presently prompted by political, economic and national rivalries.

In any case, the growing strength of Islamic fundamentalism in Egypt and its increasing resort to terror is seriously worrying the regime and it seems that it is perplexed about the ways and means of tackling this phenomenon. For the time being, the policies adopted by the authorities are basically contradictory. On the one hand, they strive to curb with an iron fist militant underground Islamic fraternities and they take the sternest security measure to attain this goal. On the other hand, in order to conciliate the Islamic establishment and the semi-legal Muslim Brotherhood, they consciously encourage the fast Islamization of the country through a series of steps initiated by the regime with the assumption that if you can't beat them, join them! These policies – two sides of the same coin – were established under Sadat. Being himself a practicing Muslim, he was willing to allow a mild Islamization of the country but he was determined not to retreat from the process of modernization and westernization he had initiated. In the first stage, he allowed the Muslim Brotherhood to resume openly and semi-legally its social activities and to publish a daily newspaper named *Al Daoua* (The Call). At the same time, he encouraged Islamic indoctrination in the media and various outward expressions of Islamic behavior that spread rapidly and became characteristic of daily life in Egypt. In spite of his gestures of goodwill, Sadat found himself in confrontation with radical Islam and could not avoid the inevitable clash between the two worlds that he thought he could conciliate. It cost him his life! (I have dwelt on this tragic event in a previous chapter.) The lesson was not learnt and the policy of trying to find a *modus vivendi* between radical Islam and modernization continues under Mubarak – even more energetically. A few months after he assumed power, before the trauma of Sadat's assassination even abated, thousands of Islamic activists were released and the Muslim Brotherhood was allowed to resume its activities (again semi-legally) including the publication of its newspaper *Al Daoua*. At the same time, the external signs of Islamization were stepped up and a huge annual budget was dedicated to maintaining (read: bribing) the official and semi-official religious establishment and paying the salaries of thousands of religious cadres.

When I returned to Egypt in 1990, only seven years after I had left, I was overwhelmed by the tremendous changes that had taken place in this respect. The wearing of traditional clothes by women and the covering of their hair had become a common feature in the street, even among the westernized upper class. Drinking alcoholic beverages (including beer) in public establishments had been prohibited for all Egyptian citizens and several attempts to pass local bylaws outlawing the manufacture of these beverages had been made (and foiled at the last minute because of the heavy financial losses that would be involved). The number of mosques had increased substantially and, from the small hours of the morning, the muezzins' traditional calls resounded from every side, amplified by deafening loudspeakers. Five times a day (especially on Fridays), thousands of worshippers said the ritual prayers in the middle of the streets, paralyzing traffic for long periods and creating total chaos. Censorship of public performances and television programs had become more stringent and more puritan: no nudity (even minimal), no kisses, no belly dances (so popular in Egypt) ... The censors' scissors worked non-stop, disregarding common sense. The number and length of the religious sermons broadcast daily by the three television channels and the various radio stations had substantially increased. All newspapers published religious supplements every day and the number of Muslim dailies had tripled. All official events opened with prayers and the reading of verses from the Koran. Pro-Islamic groups had become predominant in most professional associations and, in many cases, control had actually passed into the hands of personalities identified with the Muslim Brotherhood. Let me add that, in the wake of the turmoil in Algeria, the possibility of allowing the Muslim Brotherhood to create a political party and participate in the general elections was seriously considered and finally ruled out.

This carrot-and-stick policy towards Islamic activism did not lead, as planned by the regime, to national reconciliation or peaceful coexistence. On the contrary, it exacerbated the confrontation between the extremist fundamentalist groups and the regime. These circles – and their so-called moderate mentors – refused to be satisfied with the crumbs thrown at them by the regime. They simply wanted to overthrow the regime. The more they received gestures of conciliation on the part of the regime, the more they became convinced that their target was attainable and that, sooner or later, the regime would collapse as a result of the combination of political, religious and social action, and terrorist attacks. It is difficult to understand why the regime, despite its gloomy experience in this regard – more than 70 years – persevered in its wishful thinking and its fruitless attempts to gain the support of the Muslim establishment. It is even more difficult to comprehend how, in the light of its experience, the regime did not come to the obvious conclusion that conciliation and

319

religious extremism do not, and cannot by definition, go hand in hand. Clearly, it is impossible to compromise with fanatics who are convinced that the sole truth has been deposited in their hands by the almighty himself. It is perhaps only possible to postpone the inevitable final confrontation by making continuous gestures of goodwill and concessions that erode the very foundations of the regime.

In recent years, terrorist activities have substantially increased and terrorist attacks have become more daring. It is clear that behind these actions is a co-ordinating hand and an overall scheme. They deal the regime blows where it hurts most, targeting foreign tourists and the political and police leadership. The number of youngsters joining the underground militant groups (*Gamaat*) is increasing by the day. The mosques, the Muslim Brotherhood and the various social and charitable organizations (which function legally) are hotbeds of indoctrination and a fertile source of new recruits. The more the regime encourages outward Islamization and legal Islamic activities, the more fish there is for the extremists to catch in their nets! The mosques have come to resemble social clubs where the mass of believers can find not only spiritual comfort but also social and material assistance. Under their roofs one finds health dispensaries, legal counseling offices, charitable organizations, small-loan facilities, kindergartens, women's clubs, cultural activities, religious and political indoctrination and so on. All activities are carried out by volunteers and are dispensed free of charge – with a smile and a good word for everyone. As compared with the authorities' inefficiency, the almost-total neglect of the popular districts and remote villages, the arrogance and rampant corruption of government employees and policemen, this is a refreshing phenomenon for the common Egyptian and one that gains his sympathy and loyalty.

Let me give only one example: during the Gulf crisis, thousands of Egyptians fled or were expelled from Kuwait and Iraq and returned to Egypt, crossing the Red Sea on overcrowded ferries. They reached their homeland after long days of wandering in the desert and on the sea in the most difficult conditions and torrid heat. No official personality came to welcome them and the authorities did not lift a finger to assist the distressed refugees (refugees in their own country!). On the contrary: port and customs officials treated them cruelly, and policemen made them stand for long hours in interminable queues under the burning sun. The only relief came from the Muslim Brotherhood: it sent hundreds of volunteers – women and men – to receive and comfort them, erected large tents to provide shade, distributed cold water and food and even volunteered to assist them in finding temporary lodging and work. No wonder that many of the refugees joined the Muslim Brotherhood and a few found their way to the underground terrorist groups.

Incidentally, Israel also expressed its readiness to help Egypt cope with the flood of refugees. I was instructed to convey to the foreign ministry that, in view of the shortage of ferries, Israel was willing to help transport by land (through the Eilat and Taba terminals) tens of thousands of Egyptian refugees. They were stranded in the Jordanian desert and awaited for sea transportation in tent-camps hastily erected by humanitarian organizations. I was flabbergasted when my interlocutors rejected outright our offer, alleging that everything was under control and that they did not need any help. It was self-evidently untrue but the Egyptian authorities preferred to let the refugees rot for several weeks in inhuman conditions rather than accept help from Israel, even for such a marginal matter as a short passage through Israeli territory. It caused unnecessary suffering to tens of thousands of human beings and, probably, also cost many hundreds of innocent lives. It seems that this was a reasonable price to pay for preventing the Egyptian people from getting a favorable impression of Israel.

Let me return now to the Muslim establishment and its subversive role. The Muslim clergy and the so-called moderate religious leaders receive government salaries and operate openly and legally and are apparently not directly involved in illegal activities. However, they have a very important role in the Islamic overall scheme – their task is not only to indoctrinate the mass of believers but also to identify from among the ever-increasing crowds coming to the mosques, youngsters who are potential recruits for the *Gamaat*. They pointed them out to the secret societies' recruiters and act as liaison officers until the youngsters are actually recruited and go underground. The new recruits are given jobs, lodging, financial support and sometimes dowry money (*mohar*) for acquiring a bride. Their whole world centers round their organization and they devote all their time to religious studies, political indoctrination and training in the use of weapons and explosives. They see themselves as *Mojahedin* (Fighters of Allah), are totally dedicated to their cause, and are willing to sacrifice their lives in the service of Allah. A new and disturbing phenomenon, especially in the southern provinces, is the flocking of university graduates to the *Gamaat*. Most of them have been unemployed for long periods and see no prospect of any change for the better. Frustration, envy, a feeling of helplessness and religious and political indoctrination make them easy prey for the extremists. Their recruitment by the terrorist organizations is a great contribution (quality-wise) for these organizations, which previously relied mainly on the uneducated classes for their recruitment. In contrast to the *fellahs* (peasants), these new Soldiers of Allah do not run away at the first exchange of shots with the security forces. On the contrary, they carefully plan their actions, choose the most vulnerable targets, fight with bravery and tenacity, and withdraw in an orderly manner to pre-planned hiding places.

According to the authorities, the terrorist groups receive substantial quantities of arms from Iraq, Iran, Libya and especially Sudan. They are smuggled into Egypt through the very long desert borderlines, which are practically uncontrollable, with the active help of members of religious sects and hundreds of thousands of Sudanese citizens residing permanently in the country. The Egyptian authorities do their utmost to block the breaches but it is an almost impossible task and weapons and explosives continue to flow into the country. The confrontation becomes increasingly violent on both sides. For the time being the regime has the upper hand. It does not hesitate to curb with ruthless force (especially in the south and the Fayum Oasis – the strongholds of the *Gamaat*) demonstrations and subversive activities and tries, with relatively limited success, to infiltrate agents into the underground terrorist cells and the legal Islamic organizations. The regime tries to project to the general public and to world opinion an image of stability and pastoral calm and, to a great extent, it succeeds in concealing the extent of the problem. In my humble opinion, notwithstanding the aggravation of the confrontation and the increase in violence, there is no existential danger for the regime in the foreseeable future. The armed forces, the police and the many security services are still a reliable and strong support for the regime. They can cope easily with any internal uprising and foil any attempt to overthrow the regime by force. In the recent past, in both Sadat's and Mubarak's period, there have been a number of cases of local rebellions in the security forces such as a mutiny of conscripts that had been drafted into the anti-uprising police units. It was triggered by a baseless rumor that their already very low salary was to be cut by one-third. They looted shops in the center of Cairo, burned down three luxury hotels and finally were subdued peacefully by regular army units only after receiving a solemn pledge that their salaries would not be reduced. There have been no such mutinies in the army but, at least twice, the army high command refused to send troops to curb violent popular demonstrations until the government agreed not to increase the price of bread and curtail subsidies on basic products. However, all these were exceptional incidents that did not jeopardize the regime's stability. In my opinion, only an uprising from within the armed forces can topple the regime, but this seems a very remote possibility – indeed the regime is an emanation of the armed forces and enjoys their unrestricted backing. As long as they continue to support it there is no fear of its sudden collapse under the blows of fundamentalist terrorist attacks or in the wake of a popular uprising. The extent of Islamic infiltration in the armed and security forces is not known but informed sources estimate that it is still quite marginal. The fact that pro-Islamic army officers assassinated Sadat during a military parade should not lead us to hasty conclusions – these were only a handful of men who acted on their own and did not gain the army's support even after they succeeded in slaying Sadat.

Paradoxically, Egypt uses Islamic fundamentalism and the danger that it entails for the moderate Arab regimes to mobilize the sympathy and support of the west and induce it to put pressure on Israel. Egypt claims that Israel's rigidity and arrogance increase frustration among the Arab and Muslim masses, exacerbate anti-western feelings and provide fertile soil for the spread of fundamentalism. Clearly, as is indicated by the cases of Turkey, Algeria, Tunisia, Iran, Iraq and Sudan, there is no direct correlation between the spread of fundamentalism and increasing Islamic militancy with the solving or non-solving of the Palestinian–Israeli conflict. It is a phenomenon that stems exclusively from the local reality in each of the Muslim countries and differs from country to country. This is true not only for the Arab countries but also for the Muslim countries in general as well as for the Muslim communities scattered in the western countries. Islamic fundamentalism is not limited to the middle east; it is a worldwide phenomenon and it is preposterous to blame Israel for it. It may be a convenient way of avoiding the problem but it is certainly not the best way to solve it – either in the short term or in the long term. The west, which at first tended to adopt the Egyptian thesis, is beginning to realize that the real reasons for the spread of Islamic militancy are much less simplistic. It clearly grasps that this worldwide phenomenon is the direct result of the gradual decay of the local regimes and the growing despair of the masses. It is also beginning to grasp the fact that Islamic militancy is part and parcel of the cultural war that is developing between western and Islamic values (as defined by the fundamentalists) and that it would not fade away even if Israel were brought to make maximal concessions to the Arabs. I could distinguish this gradual change in western perceptions in a score of discussions that I had on the issue with my western colleagues in Cairo and the UN.

To complete the picture, it is also important to visualize how Egypt perceives Israel after 20 years of peace, and analyze the implications of its perceptions on relations between the two countries. As I have done in previous cases, I will again rely on statements that I have personally heard from top-ranking Egyptian personalities. I must confess that, at first, I could not believe my own ears and accept the fact that these statements portrayed Egypt's real beliefs. Since my first steps in Cairo, I have had, over the years, hundreds of private and official conversations with Egyptian personalities in Egypt and outside Egypt. Little by little, I have reached the inevitable conclusion that it is indeed the gloomy truth. It is sufficient to point out that the Egyptian press voices similar views almost every day in the crudest language. Whoever has had the opportunity to discuss the matter with Egyptian personalities will confirm – to my great sorrow – that the statements I am making here truthfully reflect the reality of Egyptian thinking and perceptions. Egyptians themselves do not try to conceal their views or camouflage them behind nice wording. They do not hesitate to repeat them, loud and clear, every time the topic arises and there is no doubt that they reflect their deepest beliefs. Only someone who buries his head in the sand can disregard what his eyes see and his ears hear. As usual, I will rely on my memory and summarize to the best of my ability what I have heard from my Egyptian interlocutors. Even if I do not quote the exact wording, the reader may rest assured that I am faithful to the spirit of the views they expressed.

On an early morning in mid-1981, I hurried to Cairo airport to receive Ezer Weizman. Boutros Ghali was already waiting for him in the VIP reception hall. The arrival of the plane had been delayed for two hours and, in the traffic conditions of the time, there was no point in returning to our offices. We stayed in the airport and killed time by discussing topical problems. I was happy with the opportunity given to me to exchange views with Boutros Ghali, one of the Fathers of Peace and the Wailing Wall of Israeli diplomats in Cairo. In our conversation, I stressed the importance that Israel attached to Egypt and to its relationship with it. Among other things, I expressed the opinion that, over the years, there would gradually develop between the two countries common interests that would lead to the establishment of an Egypt–Israel axis for the greater benefit of the region in terms of stability, co-operation and economic development. Boutros looked at me with a mix of anger and scorn and embarked on a lengthy monologue, which I summarize as follows:

> My young friend, you are totally wrong! There is no basis whatsoever to what you are saying. Clearly, Egypt is important for Israel – it is the largest country in the region and its natural leader. This is a fact of life and Israel must adapt itself to that fact and live with it. The reverse is not true – for Egypt, relations with Israel are totally unimportant. It is a small state, virtually a dot on the map of the region – it has no weight and no significance in a global perspective. We – the Arabs – in our stupidity and short sight have blown Israel out of all proportion and made it into a giant. It is high time for us to bring it back to its real size – and it is no more than a dwarf in terms of population, area and economy. It exists by virtue of the massive assistance it receives from the USA and world Jewry and it will stumble on insurmountable difficulties when this assistance ceases and, sooner or later, it will come to a stop! The sources of immigration to Israel will also dry up when the messianic spirit which animated hundreds of thousands of Jews from the four corners of the world fades away. The inter-communal conflicts will exacerbate and bring about violent clashes. The Sephardi [Jews of Spanish origin], who have emigrated from Arab countries, are bound to rebel against the Ashkenazi [Jews of European origin] minority, who despise them and prevent their economic and cultural advancement. Add to that the inevitable exacerbation of the confrontation between the religious and secular sectors of the population and you have a pretty gloomy picture of Israel's prospects in the not-too-distant future... For years, we have put Israel at the center of Arab preoccupations and activities; we have relentlessly

fought it militarily, diplomatically and economically and have neglected our real interests. We looked at the whole world through Israeli glasses. Destroying Israel became for us an obsessive goal – practically our only goal! We dedicated all our strength, all our resources and all our genius to attaining that goal and we over-looked the need to invest, first and foremost, in the promotion of our peoples – economically and educationally ... Now, with the establishment of peace, Egypt can finally free itself of Israel and look at the world map with more objectivity and cleverness. It can turn again to its real mission and its in-born vocation to reach out to the entire world. We must first dedicate ourselves to restoring Arab unity and lead the Arab nation into occupying its rightful place in the international arena. But this is not the only sphere of interest that Egypt has; it also has vital interests in Africa, global responsibility in the Muslim world and a predominant position in the non-aligned movement – these are our natural spheres of influence, our markets and our political support. We have to unite them under Egypt's leadership, harmonize their actions and guide them. Israel has no place in our future plans ...

Boutros could read surprise and concern on my face – I was hearing an updated version of the Nasserist theory of the Three Circles – the Arab, Muslim and African circles of Egypt's vital spheres of interests (Boutros had added a fourth one: the non-aligned movement). He was speaking in great detail and elaborating on each of the circles as if he were standing before a class of university students. He continued:

You look worried, but this is the plain reality. We will maintain correct relations with Israel and live up to our commitment not to resort again to military confrontation. We will not, however, allow Israel to take once again a predominant or preferential place in our considerations and we will not let it cloud Egypt's true interests or distract us from our determination to achieve them ...

At this stage, I tried to appease him by expressing my awareness of Egypt's 'greatness and leadership vocation' and stressed that Israel wished 'to work hand in hand with Egypt and has no intention of jeopardizing its interests or of competing with it'. I mentioned our common commitment to peace and stability in the region as a good starting point and expressed the conviction that the web of common interests, which were bound to form with time, would bring us closer. All my diplomatic skills did not move Boutros an inch from his unequivocal assessment that Egypt had finally ridden itself of 'its Israeli obsession' and that it was 'high time to bring Israel back to its true size' (in Arabic, *khagmaha altabii*).

I changed the subject – there was no point in continuing a one-sided discussion and the last thing I wanted to do was to offend Boutros Ghali.

We moved to other topics until Ezer Weizman finally arrived. The next day, I sent off a detailed report of my conversation with Boutros Ghali, pointing out its importance for the future of our relations with Egypt, and went back to my day-to-day tasks. I believed and hoped that time would have a healing effect and that Boutros's thesis (or should I say strategy) would prove wrong in the light of the common interests that would form naturally between the two countries. It is I who was proven wrong! The many years that have passed and the facts of life have brought me to the conclusion that my hopes were totally unfounded. Egypt, consciously and consistently, is implementing the strategic lines that Boutros Ghali expounded before me in Cairo airport in 1981 – only one year after the establishment of diplomatic relations. I have also learned since then that, from the Egyptian standpoint, this policy line is logical. It stems from Egypt's apprehension that Israel is infiltrating its economic and social setups and competing with it for political influence and markets in the Four Circles that are – as Egypt sees it – its natural and traditional territory.

For Egypt, the old middle east is ideal. It is the middle east where it has had the leading role for several decades in the political, cultural and economic game. It has no intention or desire to introduce a new player as dynamic as Israel that would necessarily compete with it for political influence and markets and with which it would have, in the best case, to share what it considers its birthright. At most, Egypt is willing to allow Israel a limited foothold in the region and a narrow margin of maneuver. It certainly does not envisage fair competition or an equal partnership but rather a benevolent patronage similar to the one granted by the Muslim rulers to the Jews in Muslim land – the *Dhimmis* – who bought safety and protection by paying a heavy tax (the *Djisia*). It might be a legitimate stand on Egypt's part but it is certainly not what Israel aspires to.

During the visit of President Yitshak Navon in early 1982, I received a second lesson on Egypt's long-range strategic concepts, this time from Mustapha Khalil, Egypt's prime minister at the time of the signing of the Camp David accords and the then acting vice-president for external affairs of the ruling party. Let me add that Khalil is widely recognized as one of the staunchest supporters of peace and there is no doubt that he has played an essential role in fostering the peace. As I have previously related, Navon's program did not include a visit to the Egyptian parliament and, at our insistence, the Egyptians had invited him to address a special meeting of top party activists (several hundred, including most parliament members and ministers). The welcome was particularly warm and Navon was swept away. He spoke at length and mentioned repeatedly the Jewish people's deep roots in the middle east and its historical rights to the land of its forefathers. Clearly, the Egyptians were not pleased and, at the end of Navon's address, Khalil took the floor again and delivered a short and most enlightening impromptu speech. I will summarize it here in my own words:

Mr President, you are a beloved and most welcome guest in our country. I have no desire whatsoever to insult you or hurt your feelings but I cannot fail to react to some of the comments that you have just made. It is better – even at this early stage – that you in Israel know exactly how we in Egypt look upon the events of these last few decades ... We do not accept the assumption that you have historical rights or deep roots in this region. We see you as invaders that have come from the Four Corners of the world and despoiled by force the rightful owners of Palestine, taking advantage of international collusion and temporary Arab weakness. You have conquered a land that belongs to another people and you have neither rights nor roots in that land. We opposed you with all our strength and we tried to push you back to your countries of origin. We did not wish to destroy you but we could not turn a blind eye to the despoliation of the Palestinians and accept the presence of a foreign entity in the heart of the Arab Nation. We have waged against you war after war, we have ostracized you and boycotted you, we have launched diplomatic struggles against you in each and every international instance and we have invested enormous resources and energy in uprooting you from the land you have forcefully conquered. It has been to no avail – we have failed to achieve our goal because we were weaker than you were. We realized that, in the process of wanting to repel you, we were harming ourselves more than harming you and were mortgaging our children's future ... We came to the conclusion that we had no choice but accept the *fait accompli* that you forced upon us and agree to let you stay among us permanently. Our only condition is that, for your part, you let go of the territories you conquered in 1967 and do not oppose the creation of an independent Palestinian state. In itself, this compromise is a blatant injustice – after all, you are sitting on a land that belongs to the Palestinians and has been theirs for many centuries. You cannot brandish the Holy Bible and claim that you have a *Koushan* (property deed) on that land and that God himself has given it to you. Even if it were true, thousands of years have passed since then, and your *Koushan* has no legal or moral validity. If the international community accepted the norms you are trying to impose and go 2,000 years back instead of only 100 years, the entire world system would be totally disrupted. From each side territorial claims would arise, nations would disintegrate, states would collapse, wars would rage – it would be a return to the law of the jungle in which the strongest prevail ... No, Mr President, justice not strength must and shall prevail! You are strangers in this region, which is totally Arab region, and you have no historical rights here whatsoever. We have no choice but to accept you, live in peace with you and even maintain good neighborly relations with you – but we will certainly not go beyond that!

Navon did not react but one could feel that he was very upset by this outburst. We all refrained from commenting on the incident – it would have been 'pouring salt on the wound'. The visit was running smoothly and successfully: there was no point in clouding it with ideological confrontation with the Egyptians. We in the embassy were aware of their views and had engaged more than once in lively but vain discussions with them. We preferred to make the most of Navon's visit for fostering normalization issues in the hope that time and interaction would soften the ideological differences. It did not happen and, in the light of my Egyptian experience, I can say for certain that there has been no change whatsoever either in Egypt's perception and beliefs or in its long-range strategy. Pragmatism dictates Egypt's day-to-day policies but ideology has not been pushed into a corner – it is still very vivid and has a great impact on its decision-making process. It is also the oil that kindles the fire of hatred for Israel and the Jews in the Egyptian press, the mosques and the hearts of the Egyptian intelligentsia.

I received a third lesson of this kind after my return to Egypt as ambassador in 1990. I used to hold, at least once a fortnight, a long *tour d'horizon* with the director of the Israel department in the foreign ministry, senior ambassador (*Safir Mumtaz*) Mustapha Hanafi. Though he was strictly prohibited from accepting my invitations to social events or working meals, relations between us were correct and gradually developed into mutual respect and appreciation. Our conversations lasted for hours and covered every possible topic. I knew that he had no real authority and could not solve any problem on his own but I could not go every second day to the foreign minister and other top-brass officials and I needed a connecting rod with the decision-makers. He was a good channel for conveying messages and keeping a finger on the pulse of events. Before tackling the day-to-day issues, Hanafi would embark on a long lecture in which he expounded time and again his views and perceptions, which no doubt faithfully reflected the official Egyptian stands. I will summarize, again from memory, a few of the pearls he repeatedly gratified me with:

> Peace serves, first and foremost, Israeli interests – in the long run, only Israel derives advantages from peace. Egypt has opened for you the gates of the region and this creates for you great opportunities and prospects. You are a people of merchants and you will be able to trade freely with 200 million Arabs and one billion Muslims and make great profits. Jews all over the world have proven their commercial ability and indeed they control the whole financial and commercial setup in the western countries and in the world in general. They identify with Israel and compel the western powers to support you financially, militarily and diplomatically but this situation will not last forever. It is bound to come to an end – interests change and influences dwindle ... Why are you so stubborn and so

arrogant? You cause everyone, even your closest friends, to hate you. There must be a good reason for the persecution you have suffered in so many different places throughout history – they must stem from your own behavior and national character. Why don't you change? You know that you cannot oppose the whole world ... You are a small country and Arabs surround you on every side – you will not be able to withstand indefinitely the will of 200 million Arabs and one billion Muslims. They will never renounce Jerusalem and will not desist from establishing a Palestinian state. Clearly, you are the weaker side – in the October War of 1973 you were saved *in extremis* by the USA and, had it not been for the American nuclear umbrella and the threat to use atomic weapons against Egypt, we would have wiped you off the map ...

Hanafi would elaborate at length on each point, obviously pleased with the intellectual depth of his analysis, and not let me interrupt the flow of his ideas. He went on and on:

Egypt can be a bridge to the Arab world for you. It can help you open a dialogue with Syria, Lebanon, Jordan and the Palestinians. However, it is essential that you first make tangible gestures of goodwill, which will demonstrate your readiness to negotiate in good faith and reach a true and lasting peace, based on justice and the implementation of all the decisions of the international community. You cannot continue to swim against the tide. You must realize that the world will not let you despoil another people ... In the end, we are cousins; we should be able to live together. It is a golden opportunity for you to trade with countries in the region, sell technology and goods and obtain enormous economic gains. As a matter of course, there are preconditions that you must meet to be accepted among us and be able to trade freely. You would have not only to withdraw from the territories occupied in 1967 and allow the establishment of a Palestinian state but also to stop Jewish immigration to Israel completely. The constant growth of your population compels you to look for *Lebensraum* and expand territorially at the expense of your neighbors. Put simply, you have to realize that you have no more physical space to absorb more immigrants. You will also have to renounce your nuclear weapons and cease to increase your military strength – conventional and non-conventional. If you continue, it will bring about a hectic arms race in the region that will impoverish you without yielding any result. Nowadays, military strength is, in any case, worthless – we have already proven that you cannot impose by force your will on the Arab nation. A middle east where peace prevails is a middle east of trade and commerce. You the Jews are a shrewd and hard-working people and you will, more than any other people, be the ones to pluck the fruit of peace with the active help and support of your brethren around the world.

It is difficult to sum up in a few lines numerous conversations each of which lasted several hours. However, I think I have succeeded in giving the gist of Hanafi's thinking, which to my great sorrow reflects the over-all approach of many eminent Egyptians – not to say of Egypt's official-dom and intelligentsia. Hanafi's reasoning speaks for itself and there is no need for me to elaborate. I would wait patiently for him to conclude his diatribe and respond bluntly to each of the points he had made. Like him, I never tired and meeting after meeting, lecture after lecture, I would explain that *The Protocols of the Elders of Zion* was a tsarist forgery. I stressed that commerce and money were not the purpose of everything for the Jewish people and that profits and financial gains did not dazzle Jews, as he believed. I emphasized that they were animated by a genuine devotion to peace, peaceful coexistence and human fraternity and equal-ity. I reminded him that Islam and Christianity stemmed from Judaism and that the Holy Koran was explicit on this matter. I also did not refrain from shattering his pretence of Egypt's victory in the October War and reminded him that the war ended 101 kilometers from Cairo. I also made it clear that Israel would never put a stop to Jewish immigration because it was its *raison d'être* and that all Jews were welcome to come if they so desired or they needed to. I explained in detail Israel's positions on Jerusalem, regional disarmament, regional integration, the Palestinian and Syrian issues and bilateral relations and commented on any other topic raised by Hanafi.

Understandably, we never came to see eye to eye. Each of us stuck to his own views but we always discussed and parted amicably and met for a new round two weeks later (and often, even before). It was a futile exercise but it was part of the diplomatic game of give-and-take which, in the conditions prevailing in Egypt, was limited and unrewarding for Israeli diplomats. Naturally, after each conversation with Hanafi I would report faithfully to the ministry in Jerusalem exactly as he must have reported to his superiors. Some of my telegrams were leaked to the Israeli press and aroused a public uproar. On one occasion, when Hanafi had been particularly abusive, I was instructed to protest officially on the anti-Semitic opinions voiced by the director of the Israel department. I had to explain to my ministry that Hanafi was not a congenital anti-Semite but was speaking in good faith and repeating stereotypes which he had been taught. I added that I had heard (and reported) similar ideas, and much worse, from the top brass of the Egyptian leadership and that every day the Egyptian press was full of such abusive language and reasoning. Finally, I convinced the ministry to formulate our protest in general terms without specifically referring to Ambassador Hanafi in order not to cloud my periodic meetings with him. As expected, our protest did not impress the Egyptian authorities and indeed they did not have any impact.

Over the years, I have received many more lessons on Egyptian think-ing and strategy but I believe that the three lessons I have brought here are more than enough to give an insight to the reader. They are charac-teristic and encompass theory and practice. We Israelis should always keep them in mind and not be lured by wishful thinking especially when we bear in mind that Egypt is heading the Arab diplomatic anti-Israeli struggle in the international arena. Egypt has also done its utmost to pre-vent the resumption of Israel's diplomatic relations with the African states and the countries of the ex-communist bloc and it is presently dis-couraging other Arab states from establishing even limited relations with Israel. During my stay in Cairo, I raised the matter several times in the foreign ministry and with Egyptian personalities at all levels of power. They usually voiced, with a sarcastic smile, polite denials and assured me that there was no truth whatsoever in the reports that I had received. Some of them added non-official comments: 'It is Egypt's duty to prevent Israel from normalizing its relations with the international community as long as it refuses to implement UN decisions and continues to trample Palestinian rights under foot. Do you expect us to fold our arms and remain passive?'

If I needed (and I did not) more tangible proof that Egyptian denials were baseless, I found it in India, where I was transferred to from Cairo. I could there, from the front row, witness the pressures exerted by Egypt – at first, to prevent the establishing of diplomatic relations and exchange of ambassadors and, later, to contain the rapid growth of interaction between India and Israel. My colleagues in the Indian foreign ministry told me many times about Egypt's angry protests at the bilateral level and their vicious initiatives against Israel in various international organi-zations and in the framework of the non-aligned movement. They would tease me gently, saying: 'We know that you come from Cairo but are you really sure that you have a peace treaty with Egypt and maintain a peaceful relationship?'

19 · *Peace Nevertheless ...*

I have dealt in this book with numerous aspects of the complex relationship between Israel and Egypt throughout almost 20 years. I have tackled an ocean of details basing my findings on my personal experience. Using the scalpel of diplomatic analysis, I have tried to point out the general trends, interests and considerations which chart Egypt's course and mold its outlook on its leadership vocation in the region and its role in the peace process. I have also stressed the *modus operandi* that it has consciously adopted in its interaction with Israel and its approach to Israel's integration in the region. The picture that emerges from my analysis is, to my great sorrow, far from being heart-warming. It evokes wonder about the past and anxiety for the future and casts doubt on the cleverness of some of Israel's reactions to Egypt's behavior. Some readers may reach the conclusion that Israel struck a bad bargain when it restituted to Egypt tangible assets (the whole of Sinai – a territory four times the size of Israel) in return for what is commonly defined as a cold peace. This conclusion seems to be justified in the light of the fact that Egypt continues to spearhead the anti-Israeli diplomatic offensive, wantonly and openly violates most of the agreements it has signed, systematically prevents the normal flow of relations, fans hatred and anti-Semitism and feeds Israel with numerous affronts.

It is not so. In my opinion, those who adhere to this view – and are depressed by it – overlook the positive side of what has been achieved. They are like someone who looks separately at each tree in an orchard and fails to see the orchard itself. The Orchard of Peace is indeed quite dense though there are still plenty of bare patches: some saplings did not grow, some were not irrigated on purpose, others did not develop at the desired pace, and many were wantonly uprooted ... But the orchard, as a whole, has prospered and its beauty and vitality are impressive. The price it has cost us and all the efforts we have invested were worthwhile and we already have much ripe fruit – though not all the fruit we had expected and were entitled to expect. In less picturesque wording, peace is here to stay and that is the most important thing – all other elements are dwarfed in face of the disruption of the vicious circle of military confrontation. As I have previously said, peace *per se* has no temperature; it is neither cold nor warm – it is an absolute value and not a relative one. It either exists or it does not! On the other hand, the relations between two countries may be cold or warm, close or distant, intimate or shaky, but peace is an essential prerequisite for any kind of relationship to develop. Israel and Egypt have been at peace for the last 20 years. Peace has withstood major difficulties, surmounted numerous obstacles and proven its solidity and today, despite the ups and downs it has experienced, one can definitely say that peace with Egypt stands on its own merits and independently of the overall context of the Arab–Israeli conflict. It seems that, in the foreseeable future, no major upheaval is to be expected. The possibility that the wheels of history might return to the military confrontations of the past is remote. Peace is a strategic choice made consciously by both Egypt and Israel. It serves the supreme interests of both countries and, as long as it continues to serve these interests, it will withstand all difficulties of the moment.

I remember the days after Sadat's assassination and the great anxiety that arose in Israel for the fate of the newly planted sapling of peace, which had not yet struck root and could dry up at any moment. Since then, almost 20 years have gone by and demonstrated that, after Sadat, came another Sadat (Mubarak) who continued to tread the line of peace and coexistence. I believe, with all my heart, that when Mubarak steps down from the stage of history, another Mubarak will come under another name and peace will not collapse because the supreme interest of both countries is to preserve and nurture it. There is no stronger peace than a peace built on mutual interests and that is the situation in the case of Egypt and Israel. Neither the war in Lebanon, which has been going on for the past 18 years, nor five years of civil uprising in the territories (*Intifada*) have succeeded in opening breaches in the stockade of peace. Neither the verbal and diplomatic clashes nor the violent incidents (which have regrettably occurred over the years including the ongoing Al Aksa Intifada which begun late in September 2000) have weakened the determination of both countries not to be dragged again into military confrontation. Peace, like war, has its own dynamics – the more the years go by, the stronger it becomes and, by virtue of the force of inertia, relations also develop and deepen even when there are instructions from above to forestall their normal flow. Gradually, the vested interest in peace increases for both countries and they become more careful not to cut off communications between them or resort to extreme steps that might imperil their mutual gains in terms of political, financial and economic returns.

True, relations between the two countries have not developed at the desired pace and are ice-cold most of the time. True, cold winds are constantly blowing from Cairo and the Egyptian authorities are hampering normalization, following a deliberate policy. Nevertheless, one should not ignore the 'ground level of relations' that they have been allowing for the last 20 years: embassies, open channels of communication, oil supplies, free passage in the Suez Canal, open borders, tourism (at least in one direction), regular connections by land, sea and air, a tenuous flow of commercial and cultural exchanges, religious enforcement of all military commitments, and much more ... It is a great asset for the present and a good springboard for the future. Nevertheless, we should not take wishful thinking for reality. Egypt is, first and foremost, an Arab country and it strives, understandably and legitimately, to foster Arab interests – as long as they do not clash with its own interests. Egypt is not, and cannot be, an honest intermediary. It was and remains a party to the conflict and, no doubt, it will always strive to obtain the best deal for the Arabs (and for itself) around the negotiating table in the same way as it has tried in the past to impose Arab views by resorting to military force. Clearly, Egypt wants to widen and strengthen peace in the region and it is working towards achieving this goal but it does not view through Israeli eyes the foundations on which it will be established. It has its own outlook and its own agenda. It does not wish to share with Israel its hegemony in the region and it is not ready to allow Israel's regional integration as an equal partner. On the contrary, Egypt does not hide its wish to reduce Israel to its natural size and is implementing a concerted policy of forestalling Israel's economic, cultural and political infiltration into Egypt and other Arab countries. It has set in place a sophisticated machinery – a Defense System – to prevent this from occurring and, presently, Egypt is volunteering to teach its brethren how to 'put a brake on Israel's appetite' and limit relations with it to a bare minimum. Normalization has been from the first moment, and will be for many years to come (even after the conflict is settled and the Palestinian problem solved to their satisfaction), a tool in Egypt's hands to regulate the interaction with Israel and foster its interests and goals of the moment. As long as smiles have a price and Israel is willing to pay that price again and again, normalization will continue to go from cold to warm and from warm to cold in an ever-continuing merry-go-round.

In spite of the frustration and the pain, this situation should not deter us from persevering in the path of peace. Peace with Egypt is the cornerstone for building a middle east where Israel will be able to coexist with its neighbors and will not fear being attacked suddenly and thrown into the sea – a middle east where the Arab countries accept the *fait accompli* of Israel's existence. I am not naïve enough to believe that it will be a new middle east in which Israel will be fully integrated and will co-operate with its neighbors in all fields – economic, political and cultural. But the limited achievements I have described are, by no means, to be belittled. I do not rule out that, with time, the dynamics of peace will bring about a more open relationship between Israel and its neighbors, based upon reciprocal dignity and mutual interests. At the present stage, and for many years to come, this possibility will remain within the boundaries of a beautiful dream and a worthy (but remote) target. If ever it becomes a reality (and I pray with all my heart that it will), it will be the end result of a very slow process. It is preposterous to believe that Egypt will – against its own interests – go out of its way to make Israel's dreams come true more rapidly. The contrary is the painful truth – Egypt will do its utmost to prevent Israel's full integration in the region as an equal partner. We must abandon sweet illusions that have no hold in reality and plan our future steps accordingly.

Egypt has never concealed its aspirations. It is enough to listen again to Sadat's interview on Israeli television in early 1980 or go quickly through the Israeli embassy's reports of the time to grasp Egypt's credo as it has been defined by Sadat and still remains the official policy of Mubarak's Egypt. Let me recapitulate the main tenets of this policy:

- Camp David is not a separate peace with Israel. It is a first step that must lead to a comprehensive peace in the region based on justice and the implementation of all relevant UN resolutions;
- The abandonment of military confrontation and the settlement of all issues around the negotiating table;
- Israel must withdraw from all the territories occupied in 1967 including East Jerusalem, the Golan Heights and Lebanon;
- The establishment of an independent and sovereign Palestinian state as the sole possible solution to the Palestinian issue;
- Direct negotiations with the Palestinians (read: with the PLO) and Syria on this basis and the active involvement of Egypt in the negotiating process;
- 'Bringing Israel back to its natural size' with all that this entails in terms of regional integration and disarmament issues including the nuclear one;
- Restriction of relations with Israel to a bare minimum essential for preserving peace on the bilateral level and keeping the peace process in the region alive;
- The return of Egypt to the Arab world and to its leadership position in that framework;
- Disrupting the continuation of Israel's special relationship with the west, and especially with the USA, and the aspiration to replace Israel as the main strategic ally of the USA in the region.

At this stage of history, going through this list of goals of Egyptian foreign policy does not arouse shock or indignation. They seem normal and logical – most of them have become a common platform for all the parties concerned including Israel itself, the Arab consensus and world opinion. But we should keep in mind that, at the beginning of the road, Egypt was completely isolated. It bore on its forehead the stigma of betrayal, had been kicked out of the Arab League, was on the verge of being expelled from the non-aligned movement and from the organization of Islamic states and was repeatedly condemned by the international community.

The west in general, and the USA in particular, looked upon it with mistrust and were not sure where it was leading. The Soviet Union (still very much alive at the time) had cut all arms supplies to Egypt and was plotting to overthrow Sadat and regain its influence. Israel was lured into believing that by renouncing Sinai it would neutralize Egypt and gain a free hand in the territories. No one believed that Egypt genuinely meant what it was saying and repeating to everyone who was ready to listen; and no one could imagine that, only two decades later, the policies it was advocating at that time would be adopted in broad outline by all the parties involved. The slight differences that still remain are becoming increasingly blurred with time. From a position of abysmal weakness and inferiority, Egypt has succeeded in maneuvering itself into the position of 'leader of the game' and gradually it has persuaded all the players to accept the rules it defined at the outset.

As previously mentioned, Egypt – already in Sadat's days – came to the conclusion that the USA was the only international factor that could move the process in the direction it wanted. It also realized that it was the only power that had sufficient leverage to put pressure on the parties (and especially on Israel) and compel them to accept a compromise that limited Arab losses to a bearable minimum. Egypt gave the highest priority to developing an intimate relationship with the USA and convincing it that it could be a solid bridge to the other Arab states and help increase American influence in the region. The disintegration of the Soviet Union towards the end of the 1980s and its disappearance from the international and middle eastern scenery facilitated this task. At the same time, Egypt made intensive efforts to persuade the USA that the only way to bring about a lasting settlement to the Arab–Israeli conflict was to induce the parties to adopt the solution advocated by Egypt in its broad outline. It also convinced the USA and the western powers (and to a certain extent Israel itself) that it had to limit normalization of relations with Israel to a bare minimum so that it did not forsake its Arab legitimacy and remain a useful partner in the peace process.

Let me add that, to Eygpt's credit, it was no less consistent and outspoken with its Arab brethren. It withstood with resolve all the pressures they exerted and refused all the lavish offers they made to bring it to abandon the Camp David accords or dissociate itself from Sadat's policies. It made it crystal-clear that it would not deviate from the path of peace and that it was in the Arab interest to follow the Egyptian strategic line, abandon warmongering, and negotiate with Israel a pragmatic compromise that would be, as much as possible, in their favor. The return of the Arab League to Cairo and the election of Ismat Abd El Meguid as its secretary-general (1991) marked not only Egypt's rehabilitation from the stigma of betrayal but also the vindication of its long-term strategy and tactical moves. The Gulf War drove the last nail into the coffin of the Arab obsession with obliterating Israel and opened the door wide open for Egypt to lead the Arab world into a pragmatic settlement, along the parameters that it had defined from the outset.

As for the issue of Israel, again to its credit, Egypt never concealed its credo and, from the very first, it repeatedly stated in the clearest terms where it was leading. It tried to persuade Israel by all possible means – legitimate and less legitimate – to make its positions more flexible and listen to the 'voice of reason'. It has never relented and has put constant pressure on Israel. It plucked the first fruit of its persistence in 1991 when the Shamir government agreed to hold the Madrid conference and in its wake entered into direct negotiations with the Palestinians (read: the PLO) and with the Arab states on both bilateral and multilateral tracks. The change of government in Israel and the return of a Labor coalition to power in 1992 brought about a more intimate dialogue with Egypt but not a stepping up of the normalization process. For all practical purposes, Israel adopted the main principles of the line advocated by Egypt – it recognized the PLO and made it into a legitimate interlocutor at the negotiating table. The Oslo 1 and 2 accords and the Cairo agreement signed with the PLO were a vindication of Egypt's policy.

The return to power of the right in Israel in 1996 and the rigid stands adopted by the Netanyahu government brought about an increase in tension between the two countries and a further aggravation of Egypt's carrot-and-stick policy. To speak frankly, the situation was not basically different even when the peace process moved rapidly on all fronts under the Rabin and Peres governments. There were some limited gestures of goodwill on Egypt's part and the atmosphere in general was more relaxed, but the underlying policy in respect of normalization remained unchanged and the apparatus established to prevent it from developing freely continued to function full steam ahead. Even then, attacks on the Israeli leadership continued, the anti-Semitic and anti-Israeli campaigns in the press did not stop, and Egypt persisted in spearheading anti-Israeli moves. It also tried its best to prevent the rapid thaw of Israel's relations with third-world countries and the former communist bloc and pressured other Arab states not to move too quickly. Furthermore, Egypt opened new fronts of contention with Israel and continued to depict it as Enemy No. 1 – the pendulum of relations between the two countries continued to move from cold to warm and vice versa, as if nothing had happened. Concessions by Israel and progress in the peace process along the lines advocated by Egypt brought in their wake a limited ration of 'smiles' and so-called gestures of goodwill. Divergences even on minor points or a stalemate in the process as a whole brought about a recrudescence of attacks and a large ration of peevishness. It was so for all Israeli governments from Begin to Netanyahu including for Rabin, Peres and Barak though it is true that under Shamir and Netanyahu, bilateral relations reached their nadir.

Ehud Barak, immediately after becoming prime minister, made his first official visit abroad to Egypt as Rabin had done. Seeing history is repeating itself I could not refrain from sending to Ehud Barak on 27 June 1999 – together with Yitshak Oron, the former head of the research department and my colleague in Cairo in the first days – the following letter (and for once I quote the exact wording):

Dear Prime Minister,

We realize that you know the topic of Egypt–Israel relations in all its details and better than anyone else. However, we have read in the press that circles close to you are suggesting that you meet with Mubarak before your expected visit to the USA, as the late Yitshak Rabin did in 1992. Apparently, the purpose of this step is to bring a turnabout in relations with Egypt and enlist its good services in the advancement of the peace process. We would like to put before you another opinion (based on our experience in the field) and we hope that you will devote a few minutes of your precious time to considering the approach that we are presenting here.

It is precisely the late Rabin's visit – which contributed to enhancing Egypt's strategic–political position (especially in the USA) – that demonstrates that no positive Israeli step or goodwill gesture can bring about a change in Egypt's basically hostile stance or yield any advantage for Israel on the regional level.

Egypt considers it a vital interest to preserve, strengthen and widen the peace in the region but it strives for a peace that will bring Israel back to its natural dimensions, weaken it and lead to a balance of forces in line with its own vision. It views Israel as a competitor, an adversary, not to say 'the main enemy'. Accordingly – despite the fact that Israel under Rabin reached positive agreements with Jordan and the Palestinians – Egypt aggravated its anti-Israeli policies (among other topics, in relation to the nuclear field and Israel's regional integration) and significantly increased its hostile activity on the international arena. The anti-Israeli/anti-Semitic incitement in Egypt was not discontinued for a single moment and Mubarak persisted in his stubborn refusal to pay a return visit to Israel. It thus makes the many visits to Cairo by Israeli presidents and prime ministers look as if they were similar in weight to their visits to Washington.

The relations between Egypt and Israel have crystallized in a very unique pattern: a one-sided rivalry reaching a zero-sum situation on the part of Egypt – a kind of one-sided cold war. Egypt has been able to conduct such a policy for an indefinite period of time because, in most cases, Israel has played into its hands and accepted the rules of the game it dictated. In its policy towards Egypt, Israel has tended to ignore two important factors. First, Egypt's influence on its Arab partners is marginal because it has nothing tangible to offer them. The Oslo accords and the peace agreement with Jordan were reached without any involvement on the part of Egypt (on the contrary) and Assad, for his part, is relying completely on the USA. Second, Egypt took sides – and will always take sides – with the Arab stands because of its own inter-Arab interests and its enmity towards Israel. The assumption that Israel can establish close co-operation with Egypt in the political process and co-ordinate positions with it has not been – and will not be in the future – sustained by the test of reality.

In the field of normalization, the view that the present deadlock is due to the inflexibility of the former government is widespread, as it was when the late Rabin assumed power. It is not the case now, exactly as it was not the case then: the very narrow confines of normalization were defined in the Sadat period and the machinery to regulate it was put into place then. Egypt has adopted a very sophisticated policy based on a very simple principle: the more it aggravates its approach to Israel, the more the slightest relaxation is perceived as a major improvement that entails an Israeli response serving the Egyptian interest. Even when Egypt makes gestures of goodwill in the field of normalization, they are worthless as compared with what Israel has a right to expect – the strengthening of peace at the popular level. These gestures are dwarfed in the face of the sea of hatred spread by the Egyptian media and the various professional associations – on the authorities' instructions or with their tacit approval. It would be wiser if Israel dispensed with that kind of normalization and refrained from lending itself to the Egyptian game.

We suggest that Israel's policy towards Egypt be re-assessed with a view to basing it on a balanced and true give-and-take process without going so far as to take the initiative of a confrontation or striving to punish it, as some suggested in the past. An important topic that has to be decided at this stage is the prime minister's prospective visit to Mubarak before going to Washington. Israel has no interest whatsoever in according Egypt the prestige that such a visit implies – a prestige that will, no doubt, be exploited by Cairo to enhance its position in the USA (including in the domain of military assistance) as well as in the Arab countries and among the Palestinians. Postponement of the visit to Cairo will not impair the peace process on the Syrian and Palestinian tracks, exactly as its implementation at this stage will not contribute to its progress and will not change Egypt's basic attitudes and positions.

Writing this letter to the prime minister was swimming against the tide. No Israeli leader would miss the opportunity – especially in his first steps at the helm of the nation – to meet with President Mubarak and thus initiate a new area with the Arab world. Two days after he was sworn in, and even before convening the first meeting of his government, Ehud Barak flew to Alexandria for a short summit meeting with Mubarak. The visit ran on the same pattern as Rabin's first visit after he had assumed office: reception at the airport by the Egyptian prime minister, a private meeting between the two leaders, an informal business meal with the participation of both delegations, and a joint press conference. From the public statements by Mubarak, Amr Mussa and other top Egyptian leaders one can deduce that the game we have witnessed year in year out is resuming with the same rules, tactics and moves that Egypt set from the outset. On one hand, they expressed satisfaction at the change of government in Israel and their hopes that the peace process would now move rapidly forward on both the Palestinian and Syrian tracks. On the other hand, they warned of too great an optimism, and made it clear that they were not content with words and promises and wanted to see 'concrete steps in the field'. They stressed that 'until Israel lives up to its obligations, there will be no gestures of goodwill on the part of Egypt' – hinting that normalization would again be used as leverage to lure Israel into meeting Arab and Egyptian expectations. Again, we witnessed the pendulum of relations between the two countries going from 'smiles' and reversible gestures of goodwill at each Israeli concession to anger and cold showers at each confrontation and Israeli refusal to bow to Arab demands. I do hope that, this time, Israel will not be ready to pay again for empty promises and for the same parcel of normalization that has been bought so many times and has never been delivered by Egypt. As for me, for the reasons that I have explained earlier, I doubt if there will ever be a genuine breakthrough in normalization with Egypt even after a comprehensive peace has been established in the region. As I have said, Egypt's normalization policy is meant as a means of self-defense against Israeli competition in the region and its possible infiltration into its own economic and cultural systems.

However, in spite of everything and above everything, Egypt is a valid partner in leading the region towards a comprehensive peace – which is the common interest of both countries. Israel can and should seek Egypt's help but it should not rely on its goodwill as if the two countries were on the same side of the fence. As I have pointed out, Egypt cannot be an honest broker but it certainly can contribute to help clarify Arab stands, foster mutual flexibility and promote reciprocal understanding. It would be a mistake to neutralize Egypt in the peace process but, in the same way, it would be a mistake to put it at its center and let Egypt become the ultimate arbitrator. Israel should understand Egypt's limitations and accept them as a fact of life. Above all, it is essential for Israel to detach the normalization of relations with Egypt from the peace process *per se*. Israel's tendency to link the two casts a heavy shadow on the peace with Egypt and arouses tension and strife without contributing in the slightest manner to fostering normalization. On the contrary, Israel plays into

Egypt's hands, and indirectly into the Arabs' hands, by making it possible for Egypt to use normalization as a lever to achieve gains in the realm of the peace process and other domains. The more Israel shows eagerness to foster normalization, the more the weight of normalization increases and the more efficacious it becomes as a means of pressure. Inviting a minister, convening a joint committee, the allocation of an import or export license, a visit of a group of Egyptian tourists, the liberation of an Israeli detainee, and a thousand other insignificant small gestures become, time and again, a formidable political instrument in Egypt's hands.

It is not logical that Israel should lend itself to Egypt's carrot-and-stick policy. It is not logical that Israeli ministers, whom the Egyptians perceive as moderate, should accept invitations to visit Egypt while their colleagues, perceived as less moderate, are ostracized. It is not logical that Israel should raise, at each and every opportunity, day-to-day incidents related to normalization and beg for tiny gestures of goodwill. It is not logical that Israel never raises the overall problem of Egypt's systematic violation of the normalization agreements and never demands the dismantling of the apparatus it has put in place to forestall the normal flow of relations. I do not comprehend why Israel should be cautious so as not to rock the boat; in any case its restraint does not bring any positive results – not even incremental ones. I do not comprehend why Egypt's arbitrary steps and bombastic anti-Israeli declarations surprise Israel on each occasion, and why Israel reacts as if it were the first time and chooses to ignore what is a crystal-clear pattern of behavior on the part of Egypt from day one. We should realise by now, after 20 years, that the Egyptian *modus operandi* is not about to change and that it is the result of a strategic decision that has been adopted by Egypt after careful evaluation of the benefits and risks. I comprehend even less why each time that a crisis – artificial or real – emerges in our relations with Egypt, we ourselves present it as a major catastrophe that might lead to the collapse of peace and to a return to military confrontation. This assumption, and the underlying consequences that it implies, is totally baseless – peace is solid and stable. Normalization, on the other hand, is sick with the same ailment that has been impairing it from the first day: it is not a God-sent disease but a Man-inflicted one – designed and carefully regulated by the Egyptian authorities to serve their purpose.

What has made it a well-oiled instrument of pressure that efficiently serves Egypt's policies is Israel's obvious and constant eagerness to seek crumbs from the normalization table and its readiness to pay repeatedly for them. Indeed, Israel has no leverage to compel Egypt to live up to its commitments in the field of normalization: it cannot go to war or sever diplomatic relations over secondary issues that do not endanger its existence. Egypt is aware of Israel's limitation and makes the most of it, cynically using normalization as a weapon in the diplomatic war it is waging against Israel. The only power that has the means to change the

341

situation in a significant manner is the USA (which, no doubt, holds all the cards as Sadat used to stress), if only it would have been ready to use its leverage and put pressure on Egypt. Unfortunately, at a very early stage (1980–81), it became clear to both Egypt and Israel that the USA was not prepared to use the big stick to enforce what it views as an unimportant byproduct of peace in the overall context of the peace process. On the contrary, the USA tends to exert pressure on Israel to turn a blind eye to the freezing of normalization and to the systematic breaches of binding agreements by Egypt and to incite it to agree to more concessions, even when they are not met with reciprocity.

True, Israel does not have many alternatives – above all, it wants to preserve peace with Egypt and reach a comprehensive peace in the region. It is compelled to play the game according to the rules which have been set by Egypt and are condoned by the USA. However, Egypt too does not have too many alternatives and, as long as it is in its vital interest to preserve and widen peace, it has to take into account Israel's reactions and wishes and amend these rules to meet Israel's needs. There is no reason for us to allow the Egyptians to define unilaterally the rules of the game – if we insisted that they live up to their commitments and take adequate steps, our input would be as decisive as theirs. As it is commonly said: 'It takes two to tango'. Clearly, we cannot sever relations with Egypt because it does not send us belly dancers or refuses to have cultural exchanges with us. We also cannot unleash tanks on Cairo because the professional associations in Egypt continue to boycott Israel and the press continues to slander it. The conclusion is self-evident: we have to accept the parameters of normalization that Egypt has laid down and discontinue our unceasing, but fruitless, efforts to widen its scope. We would thus deprive Egypt of a formidable political tool and neutralize normalization as a factor in the peace process. Only then can Egypt become for Israel a useful catalyst in the peace process without Israel having to yield constantly to its demands from fear that normalization will be impaired if we do not meet its wishes, at least partially. Extracting normalization from the middle eastern equation would enable Israel to take decisions free of other considerations on the fundamental issues related to the wider aspects of the peace process. We would also cease paying, time and again, for the same merchandise and the dialogue with Egypt would continue unhampered by bilateral problems which, in any case, are not about to find their happy solution. We should also take into account that, though Egypt has entered into a peace agreement with Israel and has maintained with it an open interaction for the last 20 years, it is basically on the other side of the fence and caters exclusively to Arab and its own interests.

Israel has a reasonable margin of maneuver since Egypt is totally committed to peace and will not retreat from it because of secondary differences. Peace serves its supreme interests and, like Israel, it is striving to foster a comprehensive peace in the region. We have already passed the point of no return and we can continue to proceed confidently towards peace, security and coexistence without being deterred by momentary difficulties that await us along the road. Whatever the tensions and the clashes, the gloomy situation of our day-to-day relations and the difficulties of our interaction with Egypt, it is peace nevertheless and it is here to stay ...

20 · Epilogue

As this book goes to press, crucial events are taking place in the region and are unfolding at a dramatical and hectic pace. Only time will tell where we are heading and what will be the short and long-range impact of current occurrences. These events, and subsequent developments, are impacting on the day-to-day relations between Egypt and Israel. It is important to complete the overall picture presented in this book and put, once again, the assumptions and premises that I have lain before the reader to the test of reality. I shall, therefore, sum up very briefly and schematically what has happened since the joint letter of 27 June 1999 sent by Yitshak Oron and myself to Prime Minister Ehud Barak (see pp. 338–9). Being retired, I have no first hand information but I have followed with a professional eye the events and commentary in the press, and I think that I am presenting a fairly accurate and objective account.

Not only did Prime Minister Barak go to Egypt immediately after assuming the premiership, he also went, time and again, to consult with President Mubarak and request his intervention in solving difficulties encountered in different aspects of the peace process. He especially hoped to enlist Egypt's help in softening the increasingly rigid Palestinian positions and in dissuading them from resorting again to violence and terror. Like Rabin, he gave Egypt a key role in the process and considered it a reliable and trustworthy partner.

Determined to reach a comprehensive peace swiftly, Barak stepped up the pace of negotiations on all fronts and stated publicly and repeatedly that Israel was ready to make major concessions that had been previously unthinkable in terms of the Israeli national consensus. Exactly one year after he assumed power, Israel unilaterally withdrew from Southern Lebanon to the international border in accordance with Security Council resolution 425. With regard to Syria, he accepted total withdrawal from the Golan Hights up to the international border and reduced Israel's security demands to a bare minimum. On the Palestinian issue, he agreed to withdraw from 95 per cent of the territories occupied in the 1967 war, compensate the Palestinians for the remaining 5% with alternative territory and dismantle all isolated settlements (some 40 settlements with a population of 60,000). He also agreed to the establishment of a Palestinian sovereign state, the partition of Jerusalem and even to renouncing Israeli sovereignty on the Temple Mount (the *Haram al Sharif*). He believed that his straightforwardness, his dedication to genuine peace and his generous proposals (which he believed responded to all Arab expectations and objective claims) would bring about a major breakthrough and lead to the final settlement of the Israeli–Arab conflict.

He courageously bet all his chips and lost! The Lebanese border remained as ever a ticking bomb, and Hezbullah continued not only to threaten Israel with terrorist actions but also carried out armed operations inside Israel and abducted three Israeli soldiers. Syria turned down Barak's proposals and insisted, as a pre-condition for continuing negotiations, that Israel agree to an unconditional withdrawal to the 1948 cease-fire lines, giving it thus partial control of the Sea of Galilee (*Yam Kinereth*) – negotiations broke down and have been in deep freeze for many months. The Palestinians, for their part, rejected the Camp David package brokered by President Clinton and began a new intifada, which they called the 'El Aksa Intifada' alleging that it had been triggered by Ariel Sharon's visit to the Mount. This time, the intifada was not limited to throwing stones at Israeli soldiers. Very quickly it became a fully-fledged war of attrition: unceasing armed attacks on Israeli settlements, shooting at Jewish quarters in Jerusalem, bombing buses inside Israel and in the territories, killing and lynching stranded Israeli citizens, ambushing civilians driving in the territories, etc. Most of these acts of terror were organized, and often perpetrated by the Palestinian police and security services – with the benediction of the highest Palestinian leadership. Naturally, Israel responded to violence with violence and the vicious circle of attacks and retaliation flared up.

Even then Barak did not recoil and continued negotiating under fire, trying to reach an agreement at all cost. President Clinton increased his personal involvement, hoping that an agreement could be reached during the final weeks of his administration. He summoned the parties to Washington and presented a comprehensive framework for a final settlement. The Palestinians allegedly accepted this framework but raised a series of reservations that were tantamount to its complete rejection. Direct negotiations between the Israelis and the Palestinians continued and the Taba talks were convened in a last minute attempt to work out a compromise agreement. That was not to be – the Palestinians insisted (among other demands) that Israel take the responsibility for the creation of the 1948 Palestinian refugee problem and agrees to the right of return for exiled Palestinians. Barak, despite his goodwill and eagerness to reach a peace agreement, refused to give in to these demands – accepting such an ultimatum would have been national suicide for Israel. At the same time, the Palestinians stepped up the uprising and renamed it 'Intifada of the right of return'.

On the internal political front, Barak's coalition collapsed very quickly and, for several months, he ruled the country with a minority government. Finally, he decided to resign and seek a new mandate from the Israeli people. Prime ministerial elections were held on 6 February 2001. Barak was the candidate of the united left front and Ariel Sharon was the candidate of the united right front. Barak presented his concept of peace with the Palestinians based on painful concessions and a physical separation between the two peoples. Sharon ran on a peace and security platform, pledging that he would form a government of national unity, restore internal security and lead the country to peace with the Palestinians and its Arab neighbors. The people of Israel voted massively for Sharon (62.4% against 37.6%) – a page in history was turned over.

In the light of the above account of events, let us return to the subject of relations between Egypt and Israel, and scrutinize the Egyptian role in the negotiations and behavior. With Barak's election, after the tense relations that prevailed during the Nethanyahu government, came a few weeks of 'smiles' during which Egypt condescendingly threw some crumbs from the normalization table into Israel's lap (as occurred during the beginning of Rabin's administration after the tense relations with the Shamir government). At the same time, the Egyptian government made it clear, in repeated public statements, that it was granting the new Israeli government 'conditional credit' for a limited time. It stressed that it wanted first to see confidence building measures on the part of Israel and a real breakthrough in the negotiations with Syria and the Palestinians. It left no doubt as to its absolute support for the Palestinian's and Syrian's demands and positions. Some in Israel chose to believe, once again, that these statements were 'lips service' for internal and wider Arab consumption and did not reflect Egypt's actual stance. They were also convinced that, behind closed doors, Egypt was genuinely helping Israel and spoke the language of moderation and restraint.

Egypt, for its part, pretended to play a positive role in reducing tension and bridging gaps between Israel and the Palestinians and Syrians. It encouraged Israel and the USA to use their good offices, called meeting after meeting to solve this or that specific difficulty and assumed the role of an honest broker that strives to bring closer the parties' positions and is eager to prevent the collapse of the peace process. It soon became evident that Egypt was doing exactly the opposite and was indeed inciting the Palestinians to take extreme and uncompromising positions on cardinal issues and raise new demands each time Israel yielded to previous demands or softened its positions. In many cases Egypt interfered at the last moment and prevented the reaching of agreement, claiming publicly that the Palestinians had no authority and no mandate to desist from legitimate Arab rights. Needless to say the 'smiles' also ceased very quickly.

This Egyptian deception became evident to all, especially in Egypt's role in the failure of the Camp David discussions, in spite of the very substantial concessions (I would say 'revolutionary') made by Israel. Egypt also did very little to influence the Palestinians to curb the outburst of violence. On the contrary, it condoned their assumption that the aggravation of violence would erode Israel's positions and force it to make more concessions. Egypt blamed the upsurge of violence on Israel, called for international intervention and recalled Ambassador Bassiuni 'for consultations' as it had done with Ambassador Mortada in the early 1980s during the Peace for Galilee Campaign. This is not only an unjustified step in the circumstances but also a flagrant infraction of the provisions of the peace treaty. By recalling its ambassador at such a crucial stage, Egypt lost a very important strategic asset and a lever for influencing the decision-making process in Israel. Bassiuni is more than Egypt's ears and eyes in Israel, he also wields tremendous influence on Israeli politics and is very close to the decision makers. Who knows when, or even if, he will return or when another Egyptian ambassador will resume the posting in Tel Aviv. It will, no doubt, take a long time and Israel will certainly have to pay a price as it did in the past. Let me add that throughout the Barak period the Egyptian press never stopped, even for a single day, its slanderous and vicious attacks on Israel and the Jews and Egypt continued to spearhead the Arab onslaught on Israel in the international arena.

By now the reader will not be surprised by the Egyptian *modus operandi*. It is consistent with what has been described in great detail throughout this book and is identical to Egypt's behavior towards Israel from day one of peace. Clearly, it substantiates the ten year old prognosis brought in chapter 17 (see pp. 296–8) as well as the analysis of the situation in the letter to Ehud Barak of 27 June 1999 (see pp. 338–9).

Indeed, Egypt was and is, no doubt, genuinely interested in fostering peace in the region and finally settling the Palestinian issue. However, as I have many times stressed in this book, this does not mean that Egypt saw or sees eye to eye with Israel what the tenets of peace should be. Egypt is even less willing to coordinate with Israel on the strategic and tactical moves of the peace process or take upon itself the task of convincing its Arab brethren to follow suit and accept what it has agreed upon with Israel. That was not, is not and will not be the case! Egypt has never and will not renounce its Arab vocation – it is after all the biggest Arab country and claims, rightly or wrongly, to be the leader of the Arab world. It is more than logical (and I would add also legitimate) that it would want, first and foremost, to use its leverage and influence to foster the interests of its Arab brethren. This is exactly what happened during the Barak Government, as well as during the Rabin Government and all other Likud led administrations since the signature of the Camp David Accords.

But not everything is dark and foreboding, there is a bright light that balances the picture – Egypt has stood firm in its dedication to peace and its determination not to be maneuvered by the Palestinians and other hyper-militant Arab brethren into military confrontation and armed conflict. President Mubarak and other top Egyptian leaders have repeatedly stated in various forums, including the Arab League and the Egyptian Parliament, that Egypt did not see war as an option for solving the Palestinian issue or other issues and that it would not participate in any war provoked by others. It also emphasized that the only way to solve all of the outstanding issues was around the negotiating table. More indicative than anything else for affirming Egypt's continuing commitment to peace, is the fact that these statements have been well publicized in the Egyptian press for everyone – in Egypt and in the Arab world – to know. Furthermore, Egypt has not shown any sign of increasing its military alertness and has continued to respect scrupulously its commitments under the military annex of the Camp David Accords.

Now after the landslide election of Ariel Sharon to Prime Minister of Israel, a new situation is evolving, though I do not believe that it will bring about major changes either in Egypt's *modus operandi* or in the fundamental tenets of its policies and its commitment to peace. Sharon has been well known to the Egyptians since the early 1980s and is seen as a great military and political leader though, at the same time, they see him as a living symbol of what they allege to be Israel's arrogance and power policies. They consider him to be unpredictable, somewhat fear him and have misgivings as to what he might do next but they respect his integrity and know that he is a man of his word who will live up to any commitment he makes.

There is a possibility that we might be returning to the situation that prevailed during the tenure of Yitshak Shamir – a total collapse of communications between the leaders of the two countries, accompanied by profound mistrust, personal enmity and strong mutual dislike. Even at this early stage, regrettably, the first signs of this are beginning to show. In an interview aired on the second channel of the Israeli television, on the eve of the elections in Israel, President Mubarak referred to Sharon in a patronizing (not to say rude) manner saying: 'If he has something positive to tell me, he can phone me. I have no time to lose on courtesy visits and small talk'. On the very same day, Sharon reacted: 'Mubarak should not worry, I had no intention of phoning him' though later, he spoke in a very positive manner about Mubarak and even sent emissaries to Egypt to find ways to establish a dialogue. President Mubarak, however, did not congratulate Sharon upon his election in conformance with international protocol as most world leaders and even Yasser Arafat did (although he may do so at a later stage).

On the contrary, Mubarak publicly warned Sharon not to fan tension in the region by refusing to pick up negotiations with Syria and the Palestinians where the previous Israeli government had left off. The Egyptian Defense Minister, Marshall Hussein Tantaoui, declared that 'Egypt should prepare itself thoroughly for the next war' (he did not mention Israel by name but, in the context, the reference was clear). For the reader's guidance: from the outset of the election campaign, Sharon had warned Barak that he had no mandate to continue negotiations with the Palestinians in the pre-election period. He also stated forcefully that he would not be bound by any agreement or declaration of principles that might be reached. In any case, in spite of the fact that negotiations continued until five days before the election, no document was signed or officially agreed upon. After his defeat Barak stated in an official declaration and in a letter to President Bush that the new Israeli government was bound neither by President Clinton's framework nor by the Taba understandings. He stressed that they never became an international instrument and had not been brought before the Knesset for ratification.

It is my hope that the two leaders will find a common platform, in addition to the dedication of both to peace, and will develop a relationship based on mutual respect and understanding. This is essential for cementing the twenty year old peace between Egypt and Israel and hopefully, 'warm' somewhat the relations between the two countries. This is also essential for fostering a comprehensive peace in the region and working out a pragmatic and feasible settlement of the Palestinian issue, which puts aside the extreme aspirations and dreams of the parties and meets their bare vital interests.

In conclusion, it seems that we have now completed a full circle and are back to the starting-point. Perhaps it would have been more accurate to title this concluding chapter 'Prologue' and not 'Epilogue'. In my modest opinion the rules of the game remain practically the same and peace is there to stay.

Index